This book is dedicated to my beautiful and patient wife Carla,
and to my wonderful children Jacob and Callie.

Contents at a Glance

Contents

About the Author

David Birmingham has built large-scale solutions on a variety of platforms from embedded micro-controllers, real-time robotics, machine intelligence engines for military fighter aircraft, solutions in massively parallel environments and host mainframes. He's worked in a variety of flavors of assembler, C, C++, and then commercially used C, Visual Basic, Java, and a host of proprietary languages.

David's been on short-strike projects, "never-ending" projects, and engaged in efforts with good, bad, and ugly management. Experiencing the issues across the spectrum of technology, people, pitfalls, and successes, some developers follow his lead, some are passive observers, and some he drags kicking and screaming. In the end, most embrace a common perspective, which defines a good part of this book.

In August 1998, David wrote an article entitled "The Ultra Thin Client" through Pinnacle Publishing's *Visual Basic Developer*. It contained a working example of some concepts in this book, and through the article's high visibility on the Internet, David received feedback from all over the world from developers and technologists of all kinds, asking for more. He certainly hopes this effort meets their (and your) expectations.

David and family live in Dallas, Texas. He is the President and CEO of Virtual Machine Intelligence, Inc., promoting the *vMach* metamorphic framework for Visual Basic. David and Virtual Machine Intelligence have five patents and attendant trademarks pending on the technologies and concepts presented in these pages.

For more information on the Software On A Leash (SOAL) approach, contact him at info@virtualmach.com.

About the Development Editor

Valerie Haynes Perry has worked as a development editor based in the Bay Area since 1992. Beginning that same year, she enjoyed a five-year stint on the staff of Ziff-Davis Press, which was located in Emeryville, California, until the summer of 1997. Since then, she has freelanced as an editor and indexer for a variety of national publishers in the computer book industry. In tandem with this work, she writes novels and waits for future opportunities to see her name on the front covers of fiction. In the meantime, it has been her pleasure to collaborate with David and Apress on this project. Valerie and her husband, Fred, are grateful to start this year by moving into a new house.

About the Technical Editor

Tom Schraer is a Technical Systems Engineer for The Reynolds & Reynolds Company and holds an MCDBA and MCSE certification. He's an "equal opportunity" programmer/DBA and works with SQL Server, Oracle, Informix, Visual Studio, and especially Visual Studio .NET. Tom has been programming and doing database work for the past 13 years and has never lost his passion to be on the cutting edge. He's also president of the Cincinnati SQL Server Users group (http://communities.msn.com/CincinnatiSQLServerUserGroup), is technical editor for Apress on other books, and has been published in Pinnacles SQL Server Professional. Tom found it a pleasure to work with David and Valerie, who are both very talented and innovative individuals. You can reach Tom at tom_schraer@cinci.rr.com.

Acknowledgments

Many thanks to Karen Watterson for her experience and insight, Valerie Haynes Perry for many months of her hard work and talent, Tom Schraer for his sharp technical insight, and Dorothy Carmichael, high school essay teacher extraordinaire.

Many thanks also to my teachers, mentors, and colleagues, including Dr. Richard Reese, Bryan Hunter, Dr. Kim Hall, Denton Cormany, Phil Qualls, Ben Gonzales, David Duncan, Tony Brown, Bill Herman, Paul Lake, Chuck Conrad, Tony Uster, and J. D. Sullivan, who make the dreams happen.

Foreword

From the perspective of building large-scale solutions, a number of critical drivers always arise. These include determining if we can leverage prior work, if we have knowledgeable people who can make it happen, and if we can capture our successes (and mistakes) for giving us a competitive edge. All of these drive our ability to characterize the scope, risk, and ultimately the cost and profitability of a technical solution.

The SOAL approach, (and the building block approach in particular), gives a team the ability to snap together solutions quickly, with lower risk, and provides a generally more resilient product. Since early 1999, I've seen SOAL in action, with very large scale and complex data environments and highly demanding users. There seems to be no upper limit for the complexity that SOAL can handle. Our teams could deploy new screens, implement data model changes, and deliver the desktop application much faster than any general development practice. The exploitation of structural and behavioral metadata to express an application—rather than letting the programmed software do it—was more than innovative. It actually gave us the rapid delivery edge we were looking for.

I can see a number of other non-technical positives of using this approach. We can catalog elemental capabilities, providing an inventory of plug-and-play resources. Thus, when scoping a new effort we can better characterize what we need to add or enhance. Also, we can organize people for architectural strength in the center, mentoring the intermediate technologists or novices toward a common knowledge base. This can boost troubleshooting, maintenance, and production operation because each elemental component has an expected behavior. It creates a great platform for synergy between the developers and end users, because they can work together closely, even by the hour to close off feature requests. In reality, we get more than just a strong development turnaround—we get a fast, reliable delivery.

It's been called a "metamorphic" model for good reason—one software program can express an unlimited number and types of applications. The program doesn't know what the application will be until run time, and just blossoms into existence based on what it discovers—or is fed.

As the approach was originally explained to me, and as the author explains it in this book, a common response is often, "Well of course—why wouldn't we do it this way?"

I would only encourage application and software developers to approach SOAL as a different way to solve problems, rather than something to merge into their own application-based practices. It can revolutionize a team's success and a company's competitive edge, and I think the author has only scratched the surface of what we could realize once we take this path.

Ben Gonzales is a Senior Manager with KPMG Consulting in the Dallas, Texas, offices. He is Chief Architect of KPMG's Customer Relationship Management Practice. The views expressed by Mr. Gonzales are not necessarily those of KPMG Consulting.

Introduction

Welcome to the starting gates of learning and applying high reusability, true rapid application delivery, and engaging in an exciting way to build software products. Many things you'll see in these pages are not found elsewhere, and some of them might challenge your understanding of software development.

While so many books and white papers speak about technology in *unleashed* terms—unlocking the power from the box and all that stuff—we as developers still must get the technology under control so we can deliver something valuable. Let's remember that the development process is a blast, and what makes it ugly is the feeling that it's out of our control. When we put it on a leash, it's a walk in the park, so to speak.

Who This Book Is For

This book is largely for intermediate or advanced developers with several years of professional experience, who have witnessed some development pitfalls and successes, but want a consistently successful approach toward developing applications. Technical leads and architects will find more insights here than a hardened code warrior, but often such trench-running developers are looking for ways to get more out of what they do, and the ability to leverage prior work.

I'm about to take you in a direction that is very different from what you're used to. Don't worry—I'll use standard terms to avoid confusion, but I'll organize them differently from what you may be accustomed to and ask you to think about their roles and natures in a (perhaps) unfamiliar form. I won't take any leaps without fair warning, but some of them may require a deep mental breath on your part.

How This Book Is Organized

We'll start with foundations and concepts and then lead into how they apply and what to watch for. I'll point out pitfalls, goals, and tourist attractions in the form of margin notes. At the end of each chapter, I'll give you a short project with some startup code to tie together the concepts you've learned. Here's a summary of what each chapter will cover:

- **Chapter 1: The Starting Point** is an introduction to a different way to build our products to get high reuse of software and rapid delivery of software products.

- **Chapter 2: Building Blocks** covers how to separate application-specific structures from the software, replacing them with consistent, more dynamic structures.

- **Chapter 3: Best Behavior** shows how to leverage dynamic structures as a foundation to manufacture reusable behaviors. Doing so allows an application's features to emerge from the software rather than being embedded in it.

- **Chapter 4: Power Tools** describes a set of multi-dimensional tools for manipulating data and shows how to build and activate complex, dynamic frameworks.

- **Chapter 5: Virtual Frameworks—Error Control** takes us through a simple, powerful way to get concise and meaningful error management.

- **Chapter 6: Virtual Frameworks—Modeling Data Dynamically** takes us into the maelstrom of mapping a chaotic data model into a framework that can wrap itself around data model changes on-the-fly without changing software.

- **Chapter 7: Virtual Frameworks—Screen Prototyping** takes us through a high-speed way to capture and render Visual Basic screen design dynamically, making screen changes (in VB) without recompiling software.

The last three chapters take us through some powerful ways to leverage tools and concepts, allowing advanced metadata to drive application features and behavior. We'll have a way to deliver features at high speed without touching program code.

Coding Examples and Chapter Projects

In an effort to reach as many developers as possible with the coding examples, the language of choice is Microsoft Visual Basic. However, I cannot emphasize enough that this book contains portable architectural concepts that are viable in any development setting. As such, if you are coding in another language, the book's concepts and ideas are easily portable, and you'll get a feel for this in the first chapters.

The primary examples are in Visual Basic .NET and leverage the .NET Framework where applicable. To developers who perhaps have not yet upgraded, you're still in the zone with Visual Basic 6.0 or later.

You can download the chapter projects from the Apress web site at http://www.apress.com. Go to the Downloads section, find the download for this book, and follow the prompts.

The self-extracting download will automatically unzip into the C:\SOAL location, and the projects are configured to launch with this as the default. If you are comfortable with how .NET configures projects, feel free to change this destination. All of my discussions will assume you are navigating from the extracted directory level.

All original directories will be unzipped and created for you, starting in two top-level directories: VB6 and VBNET. Under each of these you'll find *Project1* thru *Project7* directories containing the chapter projects. The *vUIMDemo* directory contains a binary executable as a working example.

CHAPTER 1

The Starting Point

In This Chapter:

- Finding the right starting point

- Contrasting the application-centric and architecture-centric views

- Practicalities and pitfalls of high reuse

- Patterns to enable reuse

- The metamorphic superpattern

- Using semantics to activate knowledge

The first and most critical decision we (or an enterprise) will make is in defining and embracing a starting point for our approach to product development. At the software project level, when organizing the user's requests, examining the available technology and converging on an approach, at some point the leader(s) must commit and begin the effort.

Many of us have broken open the technology boxes, jotted down a short list of user requests and *burst* the features from our desktops. If we did a great job, the user wanted even more. If we did an inadequate job, the user wanted rework to get their original requests fulfilled. Either way, we found ourselves sitting before the computer, thinking about a rework or rewrite, and consequently considering a new starting point.

The real question is: Where do we start? What is the *true* starting point, to eliminate or minimize the need for wholesale rewrite? Starting off on a deterministic, application-centric path makes us feel like we are in control. This might be the case until the user expands or changes the feature requirements and unravels our carefully crafted architecture.

Knowing Your Product—Software Defined

Our most appropriate starting point involves defining our understanding of "software." Everyone has a presupposition of what software is and what's required to develop it, and it's highly likely that we have different perspectives. Consider the following definitions:

- *Software* is simply textual script used to define structure and behavior to a computing machine. It is beholden to a published language definition (such as Visual Basic, C++, Perl, etc.) and requires interpretation within its language domain.

- *Program* is the compiled form of software. A language compiler will interpret the software, build machine-ready instructions, bundle it together with any required components, and write the results to a disk drive as an execution-ready program file. Just-in-Time (JIT) compilers may write directly to CPU memory and execute.

- *Application,* for the majority of developers, refers to a customized program. Software embedded in the program addresses specific user-defined entities and behaviors.

Application = Program?

For most software developers, the preceding definition of program encompasses a very broad domain. In typical developer's terms, application means "how we apply the software," or the physical code inside the program. They are one and the same. If the application is a custom program, then the database requirements, third-party components, and other supporting programs are part of a *solution.* A custom program pulls together and integrates other programs or components, rarely stands alone, and is highly and often directly dependent on deep details in other parts of the solution. A single change in a database definition, or a web page, or even an upgrade to an operating system parameter can initiate rebuild of the custom programs on the desktop or elsewhere.

Custom programs are often beholden to the tiniest user whim or system constraint.

Ideally, we want to service user requests without changing software or rebuilding the program. This is only possible if we redefine application to refer to user-required features, not program code. This definition serves to separate programs *physically* and *logically* from applications.

We'll want a program to address architecture and technical capabilities, while an application will address user-requested features. Our goal is to use the program as a multiple-application highway, but this requires us to place the entire realm of technology within the program on a leash. The next section explains how to embark on this journey.

Application <> Program!

Overcoming the Application-Centric View

We must separate our software from the volatile realm of user-driven application logic.

The *application-centric view* is what most of us understand and practice. It is *requirements driven*, meaning that nothing goes into the software that is not specifically requested by an end user. Anything else inside the software is viewed as necessary for support, administration or debugging, but not "part of the program" as defined by the end user. Therefore, these components could be expendable at a moment's notice. What I'll loosely call the *Common Development Product* depicted in Figure 1-1 is the natural outcome of the application-centric view.

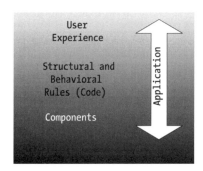

Figure 1-1. The Common Development Product weaves the application into the program so the two are hopelessly entangled.

The Common Development Model shown in Figure 1-2 is the standard methodology to deliver application-centric products. It includes deriving business justifications, specification and formulation of feature descriptions, followed by hard-coded feature representations and structures to deliver the requested behavior. As such, software is the universal constant in feature construction and deployment. Any flaw in a design requires software change and product rebuild. Any flaw or change in requirements is even more dramatic, often initiating redesign. To accommodate change, the end result is always a program rebuild and redelivery.

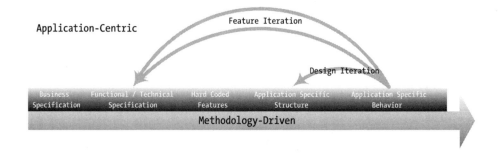

Figure 1-2. The Common Development Model for delivering application-centric programs is great for solution deployment but flawed for software development.

User requirements must justify every line of code.

Software developers at every level of expertise invoke and embrace the application-centric view. It's where we are most comfortable and sometimes most productive. However, application programs require constant care and feeding, and the more clever we get within this model, the more likely we will stay hooked into the application well into its maintenance cycle. The model is ideal for building applications, but not *software*. It is a highly flawed software development model and suffers from the following problems:

- Inability to deliver the smallest feature without a program rebuild.

- Necessity to maintain separate versions of similar software, one for quick maintenance of the deployed product, and one for ongoing enhancement.

- The laws of chaos impose a cruel reality: that an innocuous, irrelevant change in an obscure corner of the program will often have highly visible, even shocking affects on critical behaviors. We must regression-test *everything* prior to delivery.

- There is little opportunity for quick turnaround; the time-to-market for fixes, enhancements, and upgrades is methodology driven (e.g. analysis, design, implementation, etc.) and has fixed timeframes.

- Inability to share large portions of software "as is" across multiple projects/applications.

- We keep large portions of application functionality in our heads. It changes too often to successfully document it.

- Rapid application delivery is almost mythological. The faster we go, it seems, the more bugs we introduce.

The list could go on for many pages, but these practical issues often transform software development into arduous tedium. The primary reason we cannot gain the traction we need to eliminate the repeating problems in software development is because, in the application-centric approach, we cannot get true control over reusability. If we can reuse prior work, the story goes, we can solve hard problems once and reuse their solutions forever.

And these are only a few of my "favorite" things.

Desperately Seeking Reusability

After completing one or more projects, we earnestly scour our recent efforts for reusable code. If object-oriented software is about anything, it's about solving a problem once and reusing it. *Reusability* is the practice of leveraging prior work for future success. We don't want to cut and paste software code (snippets or large blocks) from one project to the next, but use the *same* software, with no changes, for multiple projects. Thus, a bug fix or functional enhancement in a master code archive can automatically propagate to all projects.

If we can deliver applications without modifying core software, we will have fast, reliable deployment and happy users.

The (Im)practicality of High Reuse

High reuse can be an elusive animal. We can often pull snippets or ideas from prior efforts, but rarely migrate whole classes or even subsystems without significant rework. Thus, we mostly experience reuse only within the context of our own applications or their spinoffs.

Here's the real dilemma: every software company boasts reuse as a differentiator for faster time to market, and every customer wants and expects it. However, while customers are happy (even demanding) to use work from our prior customers, they don't want *their* stuff reused for our future customers.

Software development efforts are very expensive, and no customer will let us give away their hard-won secrets for free. This creates a significant ethical dilemma, where we can't tell customers we'll start from scratch or we'll likely not get the contract. But if we use their business logic on the next round, probably with a competitor, we open ourselves up to ethical questions, perhaps even litigation.

Successful reuse requires a way to build software that leverages vast amounts of prior work without reusing application logic. In the application-centric model, this is impossible.

Many of us sincerely believe that high reuse is attainable, and some of us look for it under every rock, almost like hidden treasure. Amazingly, high reuse is right in front of us, if we *don't* look in the application-centric model as our initial starting point.

The term reusability always elicits notions of high reuse of vast percentages of prior work rather than snippets or widgets.

High reuse is technically and ethically impossible in the application-centric model.

Harsh Realities of Application-Centric Reuse

Many development teams take a quick assessment of the language, third-party widgets, and interfaces and then take off in a sprint for the finish line. We create hard-wired, application-specific modules with no deliberate plan for reuse. Looking back, we realize our mistake and rightly conclude that we picked the wrong starting point. We reset, believing that an application-centric *methodology* is needed, such as the one shown in Figure 1-2. More discipline creates a better outcome, right?

 NOTE *End users believe that undisciplined developers create havoc, but the native development environment breeds mavericks. Methodology and lockstep adherence may give users comfort, but it's an illusion.*

Methodologies abound, where companies codify their development practices into handy acronyms to help developers understand one thing: methodology is policy. Industry phenomena such as eXtreme Programming (XP) work to further gel a team into lockstep procedural compliance. Online collaboration in the form of Peer-To-Peer (P2P), Groove, and so on helps a team maintain consistency. However, if the team does not approach the problem from the correct starting point, the wheels still spin without traction.

Methodology Mania

Many companies expend enormous effort codifying and cataloguing their software and technology construction/deployment cycles, primarily to reduce the risk of project failure or stagnation. The objective is to congeal the human experiences of many project successes and failures so new projects can race toward success without fear of repeating the mistakes of the past.

Such companies expect every technologist to understand fully the methodology and the risks of deviating from it. Common prototypes include the basic stages of requirements gathering, design, development, deployment, and maintenance.

As for execution, two primary models exist: the *Waterfall*, where each stage of development must close before the next one commences, and the *Iterative*, where each stage can swing backwards into a prior stage. Waterfall methods have fallen out of favor as being unrealistic. Iterative methods require more architectural structure to avoid unraveling the software and the project effort.

NOTE *Perot Systems Corporation has codified their development methodology into an innovative acronym: **Requirements, Analysis, Design, Development, Implementation, Operation** (RADDIO).*

If we tap the application-centric view as the only realm of understanding for project ideas and answers, we'll always pick another starting point within this realm. We may try giving more attention to *application detail* in the beginning of the project to yield better results at the end of the project. We may standardize our approach with detailed methodologies, still to no avail. We find ourselves changing software every time the end user speaks, and only see redesign and rewrite in our headlights. Our vision is often blurred by fatigue, fire-fighting, and support and maintenance concerns. We lack the time, funding, and support (perhaps experience) to think the problem through. We're simply victims of the following misconceptions:

Process alone is not enough. If the methodology is flawed, or the approach is wrong, the outcome is still unacceptable.

Misconception #1: High reuse is generally attainable.
Reality: In an application-centric model, *high reuse is impossible.* Try and try again, only snippets remain.

Misconception #2: Application code should be reusable. All that software we built for *Client XYZ* and we can't use it somewhere else?
Reality: *Application-centric code is never reusable.* And, even if we could reuse it technically, would we risk the ethical questions?

Misconception #3: We can cut and paste software "as is" from project A to project B and keep up with changes in both places.
Reality: Don't kid yourself.

Misconception #4: Leaders, users, clients, and decision-makers share your enthusiasm about reuse.
Reality: They might share the enthusiasm, but doubt its reality so cannot actively fund it or support it.

Misconception #5: We can find answers for reusability questions within the application-centric model.
Reality: The only answer is that we're looking in the wrong place!

Application-centric development is a dream world, and envelops us like a security blanket, creating the illusion that nothing else exists. If we remain a prisoner to the computer's rules, protocols, and mathematical constants, and assume that our chosen software language is *enough,* we'll never achieve high reuse.

We must overcome these artificial constraints with higher abstractions under our control. If we use software to enable the abstractions, we will forever separate our software from the maelstrom of user requirements, and every line of code we write will be automatically reusable. Read on to discover how to achieve this goal.

Revealing the Illusion of Rapid Application Development

We think in terms of rapid development, but what the user wants is rapid delivery.

The terms *rapid* and *application* cannot coexist in the application-centric delivery context. Once we deliver an application, we'll have significant procedural walls before us, including regression testing and quality assurance, all of which can sink the redelivery into a quagmire. These processes protect us from disrupting the end user with a faulty delivery, but impede us from doing anything "rapid" in their eyes.

The application-centric model is tempting because we can use it to produce 80 percent of application functionality in 20 percent of the project cycle time (see Figure 1-3). This effect leads end users to expect quick delivery of the remainder. Unfortunately, we spend the remaining 80 percent of the cycle time on testing and integrating against problems created from moving too quickly. While this model apparently delivers faster, it's really just an illusion.

....

Rapid Application Development

Developers want ways to burst features from their desktops. All the user cares about is turnaround time—how long between the posting of a request and the arrival of the feature on *their* desktops?

The difference in these two concepts creates a disparity, sometimes animosity, in the expectations of the two groups. Developers might receive the request and turn it around rapidly, but the quality-assurance cycle protracts the actual delivery timeline. Of course, we could forego the quality assurance process altogether, and risk destabilizing the user with a buggy release (a.k.a. the "Kiss of Death").

....

TIP *The concept of Rapid Application Development is inadequate. We must think in terms of rapid* delivery, *encompassing the entire development and delivery lifecycle.*

Figure 1-3. The application-centric model automatically protracts testing.

A prolonged project cycle soon bores our sharpest developers, and they find a way to escape, sometimes by leaving the company. Once leading developers leave, the workload only increases for the remaining team members. They must complete the construction and testing of the lingering 20 percent of features, and work slows further.

Many such software projects finish up with less than half of their original core development staff. People leaving the project vow never to repeat their mistakes.

Some companies have a cultural joke, that the only way to leave a project is to quit the company or go feet first!

 NOTE *Developers don't like to compromise quality because we take pride in our work. Because users tend to make us ashamed of brittle implementations and prolonged project timelines, swift and accurate delivery is critical, and its absence is sometimes a personal issue.*

Because the application-centric model usually focuses on features/functionality and not delivery, the team saves the "final" integration and installation for the end. This too, can be quite painful and has many times been a solution's undoing. Teams who can recover from program installation gaffs breathe a sigh of relief on final delivery.

However, another trap is not considering the product's overall lifecycle. We may not realize our *final* delivery is actually the *first* production delivery, with many more to follow. We recoil in horror when we see the end user's first list of enhancements, upgrades, or critical fixes. This, too, can be a solution's undoing.

The application-centric view, and the Common Development Model illustrated in Figure 1-2, are fraught with the following major, merciless pitfalls, each threatening to destabilize the effort:

Software's so-called "final" delivery is actually the first in many redeliveries for the duration of the product's lifecycle.

Pitfall #1: Inability to meet changing user requirements without directly modifying (and risking the destabilization of) the software program(s)

Pitfall #2: Assuming that the "final" delivery is just that, when it is usually the first in many redeliveries (starting with the first change request).

Pitfall #3: Wiring user requirements into the software program, only to rework them when requirements change, morph, or even disappear.

Pitfall #4: Taking too long to finish, and risking change in user requirements before completing the originally defined functionality (a moving target).

Pitfall #5: Losing valuable team members because of boredom, increasing risk, and workload on the remaining team.

Pitfall #6: Encountering an upgrade, enhancement, or (gulp!) misunderstood feature that cannot be honored without significant rework, even redesign.

These pitfalls are visible and highly repeatable in development shops worldwide. Rather than ignoring them or attempting to eliminate them, let's embrace them, account for them, assume they will run alongside us, and never go away, *because they won't*.

The problem is not the developer, the methodology, the inability to deal with pitfalls, or even the technology. The problem is *systemic*; it is the application-centric view. The only way to escape this problem is to set aside the application-centric view *completely*, and forsake the common development model *outright*. We'll still use them to deploy features, *but not software*! However, we cannot toss them out without replacing them with another model—the architecture-centric view.

Embracing the Architecture-Centric View

The *architecture-centric view* depicted in Figure 1-4 addresses technical capabilities before application features. These include the following (to name a few):

- Database and network connectivity

- General information management

- Screen rendering and navigation

- Consistent error control and recovery

- Third-party product interfaces

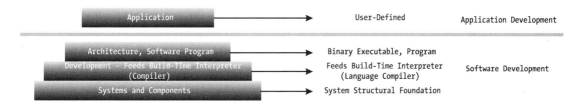

Figure 1-4. The architecture-centric model prescribes that the software program (the binary executable) is oblivious to the user's requirements (the application).

However, these are just a fraction of possible capabilities. This view is based almost solely in technical frameworks and abstractions. Where typical methodologies include the user from the very beginning, this approach starts long before the user enters the picture, building a solid foundation that can withstand the relentless onslaught of changing user requirements before ever applying them.

This model is a broker, providing connectivity and consistent behavioral control as a foundation to one or more applications. It separates software development from application development. It is the most robust, consistent, scalable, flexible, repeatable, and redeliverable model.

Apart from supporting the user's features, what about actually testing and delivering the product? We'll need infrastructure capabilities for dynamic debugging and troubleshooting, reliable regression testing, seamless and automatic feature delivery, and the ability to address enhancements, fixes, and upgrades without so much as a hiccup. While users want the benefit of infrastructure, they believe it comes for free (after all, we're professionals, aren't we?). We fool ourselves when we believe the infrastructure really is for free (doesn't the .NET Framework cover all that stuff after all?).

This approach requires us to define software in terms of elemental, programmable capabilities and features in terms of dynamic collections of those capabilities. For example, say a customer tells me they'll require a desktop application, integrated to a database server with peer-to-peer communication. I know that these requirements are common across a wide majority of desktop programs. The architecture-centric approach would address these problems once (as capabilities) and allow all subsequent efforts to leverage them interchangeably. Conversely, the application-centric approach would simply wire these features into the program software wherever they happened to intersect a specified user requirement and would exclude them if the user never asked. Which approach will lead to a stronger, more reusable foundation?

Architecture-centric software physically separates the application (user features) from the program (compiled software).

NOTE *Design and construction should be the hard part; rebuilding and redeploying the program should be effortless. Enhancing and supporting application features should be almost fluid.*

The first and most important steps in driving application-centric structures and behaviors out of the software program include the following:

- Form capabilities using design patterns (discussed next) to radically accelerate reuse.

- Strive for metamorphism (discussed shortly) rather than stopping at polymorphism. Rather than shooting for rapid application delivery, go for *shockwave* application delivery.

- Define a simple, text-based protocol for feeding instructions into the program, including reserved lexical rules and mnemonics (such as symbols and keywords). This practice is discussed later in this chapter under "How Semantics Activate Knowledge."

- Design and implement the program itself in terms of elemental capabilities, each with programmable structure and behavior (see Chapters 2 and 3).

- Formulate power tools to establish and enable reusable capabilities, providing structural and behavioral consistency (see Chapter 4).

- Formulate frameworks around key capability sets, such as database handling, screen management, or inter-process/inter-application communication (see Chapters 5, 6, and 7).

- Formulate frameworks to accept external instructions (advanced metadata) and weave them dynamically into an application "effect" (see Chapter 4).

- Invoke separate development environments, one for the core framework (software development) and one for advanced metadata (application development).

Following these steps ultimately produces highly reusable software programs, where software code is reusable across disparate, unrelated applications. Doing so allows us to separate completely the volatile application-centric structures and behaviors into advanced metadata, with the software itself acting as an architecture-centric metadata broker. This promotes radically accelerated reuse coupled with rapid application *delivery*. Our end users will experience whiplash. Our deliveries will have a surrealistic fluidity.

To achieve these goals, we *must* separate the application structure and behavior from the core software program. Software will be an assembly of programmable capabilities. The application itself will appear only in metadata form, driving the software to weave capabilities into a fabric of features.

We tend to hard wire many user requests just to meet delivery deadlines. When we approach the next problem, the same technical issues rear their heads, but we have no real foundation for leveraging more than snippets of prior work. This is because those snippets are so closely bound to a prior custom application.

Therefore, to gain high reuse, we won't focus on the user's whims *at all*. We focus on harnessing the software language and interfaces to other systems, the physics as they affect performance and system interaction, the connection protocols, and the mechanics of seamless migration and deployment. We then build abstractions to expose this power in a controlled, focused form, rather than a raw, unleashed one.

The primary path toward building such a resilient framework is in understanding and embracing software patterns.

The principal objective is to understand, embrace, and harness the technologies, and enable their dynamic assembly into features.

Exploring Pattern-Centric Development

Once we master the language environment, productivity increases tenfold. However, once we master the discovery and implementation of patterns, productivity increases in leaps and bounds. This is because patterns promote *accelerated* reuse, so our productivity is no longer measured by keyboard speed alone.

DEFINITION Accelerated reuse *is the ability to reposit and leverage all prior work as a starting point for our next project, ever-increasing the repository's strength and reducing our turnaround time.*

The bald eagle's wings are perfectly suited to provide effortless flight in the strongest winds. Eagles have been noted gliding ever higher in the face of hurricane-force resistance. Could our programs have the aerodynamics of an eagle's wings, providing lift and navigation in the strongest maelstrom of user-initiated change?

DEFINITION *A pattern is a theme of consistently repeatable structural, behavioral, or relational forms. Patterns often tie together capabilities, and become fabric for building frameworks and components.*

Structural patterns *converge all objects into an apparently common form, while* behavioral patterns *emerge as frameworks.*

While a newer developer is still under the language environment's harnesses, and an experienced developer has taken the reins with brute force and high output, the pattern-centric developer has harnessed both the development language and the machine as a means to an end. He or she leverages patterns first (and deliberately) rather than allowing them to emerge as latent artifacts of application-specific implementations.

CROSS-REFERENCE *Gamma, et al. have built an industry-accepted lexicon for defining patterns and their rules in Design Patterns.[1] Developers with no exposure to these terms or concepts will have difficulty pinpointing and addressing patterns in their own code.*

Applying patterns, such as wrapping a few components, yields immediate benefits. Each time we bring an object into the pattern-based fold, we get an acceleration effect. If we apply patterns universally, we get a shockwave effect, not unlike an aircraft breaking the sound barrier.

DEFINITION *The transition from application-centric, brute-force output into accelerated reuse is something I loosely term* virtual mach. *It has a shockwave acceleration effect on everyone involved.*

Objects using both structural and behavioral patterns are able to unleash framework-based power. For example, one development shop chose to wrap several critical third-party interfaces with an Adapter pattern (the most common and pervasive structural pattern in software development). The shop mandated that all developers must use the adapters to invoke the third-party logic rather than invoking it arbitrarily. This practice immediately stabilized every misbehavior in those interfaces. The implementation of the adapter pattern was a step into the light, not a calculated risk.

 CROSS-REFERENCE *Chapters 2 and 3 dive deeply into the patterns required to enable accelerated reuse.*

Every program has embedded creational, structural, and behavioral patterns in some form. Even without direct effort, patterns emerge on their own. Once we notice these *latent* patterns, it's usually too late to exploit them. However, even when we retrofit structural patterns, we catch wind in our sails, and see patterns popping up all over the place.

Another benefit emerges—structural patterns automatically enable interoperability because we expose their features to other components at a behavioral pattern level, not a special custom coding level. New and existing components that were once interoperable only through careful custom coding and painful integration, now become automatically interoperable because we've driven their integration toward structural similarities.

Any non-patterned structures will remain outside of the behavioral pattern model, requiring special code and maintenance, but bringing them into the fold will stabilize their implementation. We learn quickly that transforming an object into a structural pattern both stabilizes its implementation and enables it to be used in all behavioral patterns.

This model sets aside standard polymorphism (embracing and enforcing the uniqueness of every object). Rather, it promotes what I'll call *metamorphism*, which moves all objects toward manifesting their similarities. Polymorphism and metamorphism are discussed in the next section.

When we experience the power of applying patterns, our skill in bursting high volumes of software diminishes in value and we place greater emphasis on leveraging prior work. Because high output alone is a linear model, it requires lots of time. However, high reuse is not a linear model. It is a radically accelerated, hyperbolic model that pushes our productivity into the stratosphere with little additional effort.

With stable program-level capabilities in place, we can deploy features with radical speed. This foundation establishes a repeatable, predictable, and maintainable environment for optimizing software. Consider the process depicted in the sidebar, "Full Circle Emergence."

Over time, we will tire of banging out software, at whatever speed, for mere linear productivity.

We can produce end-user features well within scheduled time frames, giving us breathing room to increase quality or feature strength.

Full Circle Emergence

When we first produce application software, *latent patterns* emerge.

When we first acknowledge patterns, *understanding* emerges.

Upon first exploiting patterns, reusable *structure* emerges.

Upon first exploiting structural patterns, reusable *behavior* emerges.

When we combine structural and behavioral patterns, *frameworks* emerge.

When we combine frameworks, *applications* emerge.

Note the full circle, beginning with the patterns emerging from the application and ending with the application emerging from the patterns. In an architecture-centric model, *the application is along for the ride*, not embedded in the compiled software.

Using Metamorphism versus Polymorphism

If you've been in object-centric programming for any length of time, the term polymorphism has arisen, probably with subtly different definitions. Since polymorphism and inheritance are closely related, I'll provide a boiled-down working definition of each:

- *Inheritance* is the ability of a class to transparently acquire one or more characteristics of another class (subclass) such that the inheriting class can exploit (e.g., reuse) the structure and behavior of the subclass without re-coding it from scratch. Conversely, the inheriting class can extend the capabilities of the subclass.

- *Polymorphism* literally means multiple forms, where "poly" is *multiple* and "morph" is *form*. Polymorphism enables a class, primarily through inheritance, to transparently align its structure and behavior with its various subclasses. Thus, the class appears to have multiple forms because it can submit itself to services that were originally designed for the subclasses. The objective is to enable reuse through designing subclass-level services and converge them into a larger, polymorphic class.

Discussions on polymorphism follow a common template. Consider the objects cheese, milk, and soda. We identify each one through properties (weight, color, volume, taste, and so on) and examine their behaviors within this context. We can consume any of the three. However, we would measure cheese by weight and milk by volume. We would drink the milk or soda, but chew cheese. Milk and cheese carry all the properties of dairy products, while milk and soda carry all the properties of liquid refreshment.

These are all healthy and useful examples, but they have one flaw: they are all application-centric! Examine practically every use-case analysis book on the market, and all of them advocate, and charge us with one directive: Build application-centric objects into our software programs and allow them to inherit from each other. Before we're done, we'll have things like *DairyProduct.cls, Milk.cls, Cheese.cls, Soda.Cls, Refreshment.cls* and might bring them all to a *Picnic.cls*!

This practice will embed and directly enforce uniqueness into the software program. Practically every line of code touching these objects will be intimately tied to their structure and behavior. When we're done, we'll find lots of inheritance, probably stellar and creative polymorphism, and magnificent reuse *within the application*—but not a lot of reuse outside the application. Rather than standardize on common patterns, we've accommodated and even enforced application-centric uniqueness.

 NOTE *A primary objective of pattern-based architectures is to thoroughly eliminate dependence upon uniqueness among objects, allowing them to play in the same behavioral space because of their sameness.*

After diving deeply into patterns, *superpatterns* emerge. Superpatterns are assemblies of pattern-based structures and behaviors that define another level of useful abstraction. One of the more dramatic superpatterns is *metamorphism*. Metamorphism is the run-time ability of a programmable object to completely change its structure and behavior.

For example, a given object may initially instantiate as *Milk*. It may enhance its status into a *Refreshment*, or metamorph into a *HotDog*, or perhaps a *Hamburger*, a *Horse*, a *Screwdriver*, or a *Mack Truck*. In every case of metamorphosis, it is still technically the same internal object reference, it's just been reprogrammed—rebooted if you will—with an entirely different identity and instruction set. And all this happens magically without changing a single line of program code! Metamorphism is a dramatic, even quantum leap in programmatic machine control. Its primary fuel is advanced *metadata*.

Metamorphism allows an object to morph into a class definition that was unknown at design time.

Metadata

Meta denotes both change and abstraction. We use symbols to abstract ourselves from expected volatility and software to address rapid and chaotic change.

Sadly, industry and product literature often define metadata solely within the static realm of data warehousing or information management: "Information about information." But this is a limited definition.

Metadata itself is volatile information that exists outside of a program with the ability to influence the program's structure *and* behavior, effectively changing the way the program operates.

Programs that subscribe to metadata are run-time programmable. But programs that are dependent on metadata as a sole source of fuel are the most powerful products in the world. Objects using metadata to dynamically define their internal structure and behavior are *metamorphic*.

NOTE *Clearly, the volatility of user requirements is the perfect domain for advanced metadata. If we can meet all user requirements for application structure and behavior through metadata, we minimize and eventually eliminate the need to change and rebuild programs to meet user requests.*

Metadata appears in two forms: *structural*, to define information and entities as building blocks; and *behavioral*, to describe processes that apply to information or entities (e.g., instructions). These forms allow metadata to provide high-octane fuel to a run-time interpreter. A metadata interpreter then interfaces and organizes structural building blocks and core behaviors into application-level features, enabling run-time programmability.

Apress Download

If you have not already downloaded this book's supplemental projects, get a copy of them from the Apress web site at http://www.apress.com in the Downloads section. Unzip the file into the working directory of your choice. For consistency I will use the relative directory structure in the zip file's extraction.

One top-level directory is VBNET, containing the .NET software, while another top-level directory is VB6/, containing the Visual Basic 6.0 versions of everything discussed in the book.

Under the top-level directory set is another directory called vUIMDemo/. Underneath this directory you'll find a Visual Basic .NET Solution file called Proto.sln and a program named vUIMDemo.exe. Follow along in the version you are comfortable with.

Follow these steps to watch metamorphism in action:

1. Double-click the program file (vUIMDemo.exe) and it will pop up a screen similar to Figure 1-5.

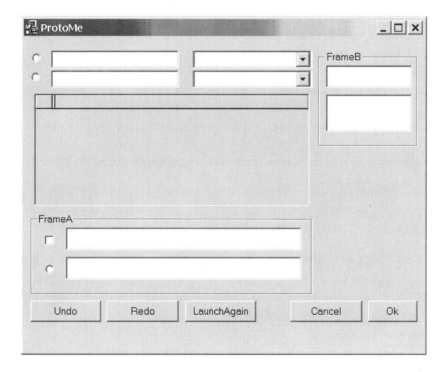

Figure 1-5. A display from the program file vUIMDemo.exe

2. Double-click the Proto.sln project to bring up Visual Basic, then open up the ProtoMe form inside it. You'll see the design-time rendering of the screen depicted in Figure 1-5.

3. Next, in the ProtoMe screen, delete the TreeView box above the Cancel/Ok buttons, and click/drag the Cancel button into the center of the open space, then save it (Ctrl+S).

4. Go back to the running vUIMDemo and click the LaunchAgain button at the bottom center of the screen. The vUIMDemo now renders your version of the screen.

5. Click the caption bar and drag it to the side, revealing both screens. The program, vUIMDemo, *is still running!* The screen changed without changing the program! We'll dive deeper into these capabilities in the Chapter 4 projects, with detailed discussion in Chapter 7.

You can repeat this exercise, adding to, reshaping, and changing the ProtoMe file. Each time you click Launch again, your work is instantly available. This is *metamorphism* at work, and we've just scratched the surface.

Pattern-based metamorphic architecture is devoid of any application-level knowledge. It does not recognize any internal distinction between applications for marketing, science, accounting, astrophysics, human resource management, and so on. The architecture simply executes, connects services, obeys external commands, and the application *happens*. This is a very different and abstract approach than the Common Development Product depicted in Figure 1-1, which embeds the application into software.

The metamorphic approach is an exciting and perhaps natural step for some developers, while a quantum leap for others.

If our software is to respond to advanced metadata, manufacturing the application "on-the-fly," we need a means to symbolically bridge the metadata to the underpinning technology.

Understanding the Language of Symbols

If we start with software code as textual script, we must understand what the script means. Special symbols understood by a compiler will ultimately bring our creation to life. It is what the compiler does with the symbols, not what we do with them, that determines their ultimate usefulness.

To grasp it all, we must commit to thinking in terms of symbolic representation rather than software code alone. Symbols can bundle and clarify enormous amounts of "noise" into useful knowledge. We understand symbols both automatically and relationally, but the machine only understands what we tell it. More importantly, the machine's symbols must always reduce to some form of mathematics.

Patterns in Mathematics

Galileo declared that mathematics is the only universal language, and this is an absolute in computer science. Math is pervasive in all computer systems and is the foundation for every activity, instruction, and event inside a programmable machine. Software is a *mnemonic,* or symbolic means to represent the details of the computer's math. Software represents instructions to the computer as to what mathematics to perform and in what sequence. These may be simple additions, complex multiplication, or just counting bytes as they move from one calculated memory address to another.

However, human thinking processes use math as a tool, not as a foundation. Humans have difficulty in programming machines to think because so much of thought is relational, not mathematical. In fact, mathematicians are persistent in finding and exploiting patterns in numbers and numeric relationships to better promote their understanding to peers and students.

Our goal is to abstract the software language's raw, elemental, structural definitions and instructions into higher and simpler symbols and semantics.

....

A Perfect 10?

Consider that the decimal (base 10) digits zero through nine (0-9), the familiar mental foundation for all decimal counting operations, is sometimes misused or misrepresented. A recent visit to a toy store revealed that most electronic counting games for small children teach them to count from 1 to 10. While this sounds simplistic, *ten is not a digit!* Ten is a combination of the digits 1 and 0.

However, a machine structure only understands the 0-9, and the position represented by *9* is the *tenth* element in the sequence. We may ignore this and get bitten when trying to access the element at position *10* of a zero-based array. We must understand *how the machine represents the structure*, not how humans understand it. This is the primary first step in mapping virtual structures into the human knowledge domain.

We must learn to think on the machine's terms. Avoiding this issue by twisting the structural and conceptual representations of objects and underpinning math will only increase our dependency on the language environment, the machine's rules, and the software code. Our goal is to master the machine and the programming language.

....

Our mistake is in resting on the software language alone, rather than using it to define and activate a higher, more dynamic but programmable, symbolic realm.

Every action, algorithm, and operation within a machine is a sequence of mathematical operations. If we can bundle sequences of actions at the appropriate elemental levels, we can treat these bundles as macro statements. When statements are strung together, they represent *methods*. If we can string them together at run time, we have a fully dynamic method. From this point, we can construct or reconstruct the method at will, and it becomes metamorphic. When we label it with a symbol, we can interchange it seamlessly across multiple metamorphic objects.

The mathematics inside a machine are too complex and dynamic to grasp without symbols, hence the need for software language.

Abstracting Knowledge

Albert Einstein proposed that a great chasm exists between the concrete and the abstract. He defined *concrete* as objects in the physical world such as wood, rocks, metal, and so on, and *abstract* as the *understanding* of wood, rocks, metal, and so on. This was Einstein's contention:

> *We have a habit of combining certain concepts and conceptual relations (propositions) so definitely with certain sense experiences that we do not become conscious of the gulf—logically unbridgeable—which separates the world of sensory experiences from the world of concepts and propositions.*[2]

Einstein asserted that the human mind creates the necessary bridges *automatically*, and we are unable to bridge them *logically*. This assertion has profound implications, because logical mechanisms are all we have inside the computing domain.

Einstein asserted that the key is symbolic verbal or written language as a common frame of reference. While human language effortlessly uses symbolic labels to represent tangible, concrete items, computer language must use symbols to represent abstract, virtual items. The difference between the human-understood symbols and their actual electronic representation creates yet another chasm, the *Cyber Gulf* (see Figure 1-6).

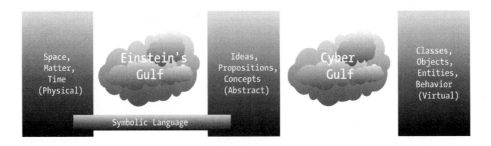

Figure 1-6. Understanding the Cyber Gulf

The machine has no means whatsoever to represent the physical world; it is completely and utterly removed from it. Nothing is concrete inside the machine's software processing domain. Computer representations of physical objects are virtual collections of mathematical abstractions, understood by humans only through similarly abstract symbols. This is a significant limitation for expressing highly complex human concepts such as humor, love, mercy, justice, and so on.

Another significant problem is in testing the computer's representation of these concepts, because at least two people must agree on the computer's conceptual representation. (We can't imagine two humans agreeing on an ultimate, mathematically accurate definition of a concept such as humor.) We rarely think of our work in such abstract terms, because programming is already so difficult and time-constrained that rising above it into abstract realms requires unavailable time and extraordinary effort.

 NOTE *Just as humans automatically use symbolic labels for simplifying the physical world, we must learn how to instruct a machine to use symbols rather than hard-coded application instructions, and we must automatically think of programming in these terms.*

The difference in the two approaches is profound. The hard-coded approach only leads to rework, where the technology has mastered us. The abstract approach leads to reuse and repeatability, where we master the technology. It is, in fact, the long-sought path to freedom. Overcoming the technology itself is the ultimate strategy to escape application-centric gravity.

How does this apply? We must negotiate objects from within virtual space and find a means to simulate their equivalents in a near-physical electronic forum; for example, an employee entity is not a physical employee. Bridging two gulfs simultaneously requires an enormous amount of thought labor and mental continuity not required in actual physical construction. While a builder and a homeowner can point to a house and agree that it's a house, a developer and an end user can observe programmatic functionality and completely disagree on the same thing.

Now step back and examine the vast domain under our control, and the many bridges, highways, and other delivery avenues required to fulfill the user's requests. None of it is easy, and it is absolutely imperative that we gain ultimate, sovereign control of this domain.

Software that is wired directly into the user's churning, subjective chaos is constantly subject to change and even redesign.

Okay, okay, I hear you—enough concept. The reality is that as feature requests become more sophisticated and complex, with shrunken time-to-market and rapid change of features over time, we no longer have the luxury of building an application-centric program. The knowledge domain is already too wide, even for the simplest technical objective. We must embrace a more productive, reusable, and resilient deployment model in order to survive and be successful in the boiling technical marketplace. Only the architecture-centric model, with patterns of reuse that allow a malleable, metamorphic, and symbolic approach to application deployment, will enjoy repeatable success.

Symbols can aggregate huge amounts of processing logic, or allow inter-change of complex details by reference rather than physical movement.

Dynamic versus Static Representation

Consider a class definition for *Rock* in application-centric mode. We must care-fully define the specific interfaces for *Weight()*, *Size()*, or *Density()*. This creates a "wired" object with specific purpose and limited reuse. However, while we may believe this static definition provides visibility and control, at run time the machine understands and represents it mathematically, through complex, embedded machine logic. It is not wired at all, but *already* a virtual abstraction beyond our control.

Now let's configure a more flexible object, with a properties "collection" symbolically representing otherwise hard-wired references. We'll use *Item("Weight")*, *Item("Size")*, *Item("Density")*. From the machine's perspective, this representation is identical to a carefully crafted static object, with one primary structural difference affecting reuse: the interface is infinitely extensible without changing its definition. If the machine cannot discern the difference, why create hard-coded, artificially propped constructs (static class definitions) to support something the machine will bypass or even ignore?

This is an important distinction, because of what many developers believe about how a machine represents objects. We'll declare a class as a specific, application-bound definition and manipulate it as such because it feels like greater control exists. This is an illusion propped up by the software language. Business-object or science-object development books and discussions strongly encourage us to build specific objects such as Employee, Account, Invoice, or Indicator, Thermometer, and Gauge. Development languages and design tools directly support these suggestions.

We can define objects specifi-cally or con-struct them in the abstract. The latter gives us freedom, and the machine doesn't know the difference.

In reality, these objects, their properties and methods are simply collections of smaller programmable parts and processes. They can be assembled with a hard-wired coding method, but should be assembled with a dynamic construc-tion method; the two are functionally equivalent. The dynamic method requires abstraction, but it is far more resilient, flexible, reusable, and metamorphic than its hard-wired functional equivalent.

Why should a complex action require a specific software anchor? When we consider that every method, regardless of complexity, reduces to a series of math-ematical functions, we simply aren't far from abstracting them already.

If each metamorphic object is influenced or managed by a run-time inter-preter for execution of methods, no further reason exists to directly hard-wire a method into an object. If a "custom method" is simply an assembly of smaller, reusable processes, every object can dynamically construct methods that are "apparently custom" but, in fact, never existed before run time.

Pervasive structural and behavioral metamorphism provides practically limitless reusability to a majority of methods and properties for building any application, in any context. It supports the concept of *metamorphic class*. Such a class exists only at run time and manages all properties, methods, and inheritance as a function of reuse, not hard-wired application logic.

By reducing our software-based classes to structural templates, the software can manufacture new, metamorphic classes with relative ease. The metamorphic class methods and properties are constructed from smaller, generalized, embedded structure classes. The best part is that we really need only one metamorphic framework, with all underpinning components focused on its support. We can then dynamically instantiate the framework into anything we want.

With dynamic properties, methods, and inheritance, all classes are defined at run time. Metamorphism (not just polymorphism) becomes the rule, not the exception.

Summary of the Metamorphic Superpattern

Here is a short list of the primary principles we must understand and embrace in order to fully exploit metamorphism:

- All machine quantities reduce to math.

- Symbols can represent all machine mathematics, including complex structures and relationships.

- Semantics can describe complex behaviors through assembling elemental behaviors.

- Humans can use high-level metadata to organize symbols and semantics for custom application effects.

- Metadata interpreters can accept symbols and semantics as run-time instructions, translating them into internal metamorphic structures, behaviors, and relationships.

For some, metamorphism may seem too complex and uncontrollable. It is, in fact, a perfect means to guarantee consistent behavior, structural integrity, and deterministic outcome for every application we deploy. It also represents a foundation for capturing our knowledge and re-deploying it to accelerate future efforts and upgrade prior efforts.

We must forsake the idea that software is the maker, keeper, and foundation of structural and behavioral rules. We must now begin to view software only as a tool for exposing technical capabilities into abstract, programmable form. We must then view application-centric features as virtual abstractions: dynamic, run-time definitions that don't exist, and never existed, before the program's execution.

Symbols allow us to anchor and assemble structure and behavior, but the order of their assembly, plus parameters and modifiers, are in the domain of semantics.

Realizing How Semantics Activate Knowledge

Unless we want to institutionalize chaos, we cannot start by directly embedding the user's wishes into the software code, so we must therefore pick another starting point. We must build code that enables the representation of the user's wishes rather than directly representing them. While software as textual script contains keyword symbols recognized by the compiler, the context of the symbols is highly significant in representing *application knowledge*, which entails the embedded intentions of the end user as applied by the developer.

We can tag objects, properties, and methods with high-level symbols, but we need *semantics* to shape the symbols into active knowledge. A *Rock* simply "is" and will "do" nothing unless we apply a semantic command to combine the object with an action. *Throw Rock* should give us a raw effect, but we may need to modify the action, such as *Throw Rock Hard,* or even more vectored detail, such as *Throw Rock Hard at the Window.*

Of course, if the Rock's Item("Density") *= "Low" or its* Item("Weight") *= "Light" we might have an action result of "Bounce"!*

Predefined keywords clarify semantics, especially when combining or copying information from one symbol to another. For example, *Set Rock.Item("Texture") = "Smooth"* is different language than *If Rock.Item("Texture") = "Smooth."* The first performs assignment and the second tests a conditional relationship.

NOTE Structured Query Language (SQL) *is a common semantic model used by most commercial database engines. In SQL, nouns (database tables, columns, or other entities) are instructed to behave according to verbs (insert, update, select, delete, and so on) with certain modifiers (search predicates, insertion, or update information, and so forth). The rules for syntactic construction are rigid enough to be accurate and efficient, but flexible enough to promote limitless reusability of the database engine for storage and retrieval logic.*

Think in terms of a development language compiler's syntax rules. Each rule is a semantic compiler cue to perform a certain task, build a particular construct, behave a certain way, etc. The compiler uses reserved keywords to affect its own programmable behavior. Nouns (objects) are the actors. Verbs (methods) are the actions, with modifiers (properties) to each action. Interpreted sentence structures can create dynamic objects, relationships, and activities that were unknown before program execution.

A language compiler provides the lexical and behavioral foundation for its own programmability. It is the ultimate programmable program, so examining its implementation provides insight to understanding how to put similar functionality into a dynamic application model.

Metadata instructions serve as pseudo-code, and cleanly separate the program's architecture from the application's structures and relationships. The software program containing the interpreter is compiled, deployed, and constantly reused thereafter. Run-time interpretation means the application logic can change at will, even by the minute, without affecting the program. We can build whole applications with textual metadata, then deploy them with a simple "file copy" to expose the metadata to the program. In fact, the application logic can change even while the executable is running. (See the vUIMDemo earlier in this chapter under "Metamorphism and Polymorphism" for an example of this.)

Our objective is to boil down the plethora of object and information types into their simplest abstract equivalents.

....

Shockwave Delivery

The vUIMDemo is a subsystem of a product (called *vMach*) that Virtual Machine Intelligence, Inc. regularly deploys on user desktops. Whenever we need to ship a new application upgrade to user screens, we bundle the metadata into a zip file and send it via email. The user unzips the attachment and it's installed. Can you imagine making changes to a Visual Basic screen in Visual Basic, then performing a simple file copy to deliver the goods? Or extending the database design without breaking existing code, with a model that "senses" and wraps itself around the changes rather than balking at them?

For users with a central file server, we send the changes to a central administrator, who in turn unzips them to the file server. The upgrade is instantly available to every desktop using the metadata. This transforms rapid application delivery into *shockwave delivery*.

....

We'll now use software code to build frameworks that manage actions between participating objects. The software will accept textual instructions as metadata, interpret them, and ultimately dispatch the activities between objects with no knowledge as to the nature of the activity itself. Whether system-specific or user-required, the software simply executes the action. The application *happens*.

The software program will interpret events, semantic commands or rules, and initiate activities. The program does not directly control the application behavior, only the semantic interpretation of metadata. It is therefore incumbent upon us to apply simplified interfacing capabilities to all embedded and dynamic entities, allowing the semantic interpreter to find and control objects quickly.

Now we'll use metadata— not software rebuild—to meet user requests. We can jot down notes at their desktop and deliver features "on location."

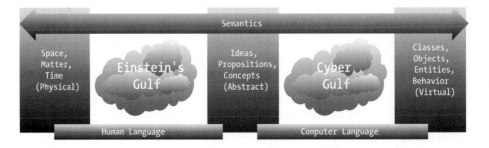

Figure 1-7. Virtual architecture symbolically spans the gulfs with semantics.

Like a symbolic skywalk (see Figure 1-7), a metamorphic architecture seamlessly spans the gulfs, from physical to virtual and all elements of understanding in between. It serves as an embedded language interpreter, actor, and observer, and puts a consistent and predictable leash on all behavior, regardless of processing domain or development language.

Developer in a Box

In an application-centric model, our "software development" activity consists of abstracting and arbitrating symbols across the gulfs as we communicate with the end users. This activity, when repeated a few times within and across projects, gets tedious and boring. What if we could embed enough intelligence into the software itself so this arbitration happens by proxy?

To contrast, we can define the symbols and build embedded software to enforce them, or we can build an arbitration mechanism that will act on our behalf just as we would. Once in place, we have effectively migrated our own development experience and expertise permanently into the software. Anyone else using it gains the immediate benefit of our accumulated experience, not just what a user asked for once upon a time.

We capture a developer's experience each time they touch reusable code. Like an Aladdin's Lamp, each time we rub it, the magic begins again.

This embeds our hard-won knowledge and skill into the architecture, rather than requiring us to repeat the same rote software development with each new application. This further accelerates reuse, so we can leverage our prior work, and others can too, and is rocket fuel for innovation because what we (and others) do is never lost again.

Development Projects

When executing projects using the architecture-centric approach depicted in Figure 1-8, all software is founded upon metamorphic, programmable capabilities. These form frameworks, driving the ability to dynamically generate complex features and thus, applications.

CROSS-REFERENCE *See Chapters 5, 6, and 7 for more detail on frameworks.*

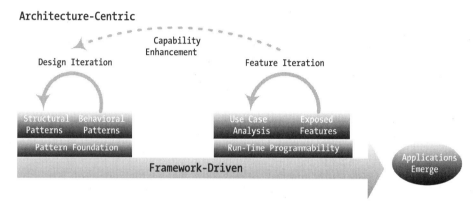

Figure 1-8. Architecture-centric project execution

Reviewing Figure 1-8, all feature changes occur within the metadata environment. When we cannot fulfill a feature with current capabilities, we identify the required capabilities and drive them back into the architecture as a capability enhancement. We are then able to fulfill the feature, but the capability remains for later reuse (by ourselves or others). This is the only true capability maturity model applicable for reusable software.

Capability (im)Maturity

Many companies build volumes of process engineering notes to track the development of "capabilities," mostly in an application-centric context. For example, a company might log that some of its developers rolled out a human resources application, a supply-chain solution, or a retail sales data mart. Invariably, the solutions are completely custom and not positioned for re-hosting to subsequent projects.

In each case, the company records the solution as part of a knowledge base, but it is in fact the accumulated experience of its employees. Many technologists balk at being pigeon-holed into repeating the same application endeavors, regardless of the potential success (and thus avoid re-assignment). Some employees are promoted out of direct implementation roles, while others leave the company.

The result is the same: the company isn't really gathering steam in developing or maturing capabilities. They are only creating a marginally viable portfolio that rapidly grows stale. The company, like many others, will only be as good as its last success.

Note that all capability enhancements are available to all features, not just the feature that initiated the change. We can deploy the same capability set, or binary program, for multiple applications. This is the only true high-reuse model, and as promised, enables reuse of every single line of compiled software.

As the architecture and capabilities stabilize over time, we drive fewer changes back into the program code. Architects have freedom to make the software program more powerful, faster, easier to install, or otherwise technically superior. Application developers using the program can depend on a reliable, reusable, and solid foundation for feature deployment. Additionally, because the software program is fueled with metadata, application-level deployment doesn't require a program rebuild, only a textual modification and file copy!

In the vUIMDemo, our change was instantly available to the end user without changing the software. As quickly as we can change the metadata, we can change the structure and behavior of the application-level features.

Architects can dive deep into technical issues, vicariously delivering their expertise and hard-won knowledge to the metadata interpreter.

Utilizing metamorphic objects, run-time programmability, and a stable, consistent application delivery, every known development methodology either stands itself on its head, or experiences stratospheric productivity.

Smooth Delivery Effect

Upon initial construction, the pattern-based and architecture-centric model doesn't deliver features right away. Developers and designers spend significant hours formulating and building structural and behavioral foundations for later feature deployment. When features appear, they arrive at a steady and sometimes dramatic pace from beginning to end. Because the end users experience a steady stream of smaller parts, the delivery highway for both features and binary software will be in solid order and smooth operation by the time of a "go-live" production delivery.

The initial time frame could be protracted because the team is trying to deliver features while also building capabilities, but the product will be consistently solid and the user won't see the brutal 80/20 effect of the application-centric deployment model.

In follow-on projects, users experience feature delivery in a relative fraction of the time required in the initial project. Capabilities are already present and stabilized, ready for reuse, enabling us to deliver features at *mach* speed compared to the application-centric model. Any new capabilities become automatically available to prior projects and applications.

The architecture-centric approach automatically supports incremental redelivery. Architects can focus on technical installation of the base program plus the mechanics of metadata transmission and make these processes rock-solid. This creates a repeatable delivery highway. Feature deployment, using metadata, becomes so rapid and regular it appears fluid.

Ideally, this approach supports later maintenance activities. In fact, the initial delivery happens so early in the cycle it's often forgotten. Some architecture-centric solutions deliver hundreds of preliminary feature versions during iterative development. If the so-called final feature delivery is actually iterative delivery #289, what of it? By the time the application enters the maintenance cycle, its delivery mechanism is well-oiled and humming.

When first developing a metamorphic model, it does not quickly deliver in the front of the project cycle, and many development teams feel under pressure to deliver *something*. Thus it often falls on the sword of expedience, otherwise known as trading off the important (reuse and maintenance) for the urgent (quickie delivery).

However, this is a sensible delivery model for the following reasons:

Business: We can schedule, deploy, manage, and close the feature requirements in a timely manner. Once a feature is in front of the user for an extended period, it erodes their ability to arbitrarily change it later. Maintenance costs are lower because fewer programmers are necessary for upgrades and changes. Because of high productivity, team leaders can quickly prototype *working* proof-of-concept models rather than empty demonstrations. Rapid iteration creates manageable client satisfaction, streaming functionality into their hands rather than experiencing start/stop delivery.

Technology: As new technology arrives in the marketplace, the core program can assimilate it without breaking existing applications. New applications can directly leverage it while prior applications can access it at leisure. In fact, even if forced to replace the underpinning technology, including the development language, operating system, and components, we can avoid impacting the application. Additionally, business managers can negotiate with current clients to provide upgrades for additional revenue.

Quality: Fewer programmers touch the core software, releasing it less often than the metadata for application features. The core software release cycle becomes much more stable and manageable, occurring on boundaries under the control of the master architects. We then use

If a project is like an airplane, iterative delivery is like scheduling multiple flights, with passengers (features) arriving regularly.

metadata to meet user requirements, on a separate and more volatile release cycle. The users can get what they want without the inherent destabilization of a program rebuild.

Human resources: Master developers can oversee initial application design and have a footprint in multiple projects. Novice developers get productivity boosts using the architectural safety net provided in the core software. We can divide technical resources along flexible lines: those that work in core architecture, those that work in application-level logic, those that manage technical teams of both, etc. The high productivity of an architecture-centric model provides schedule flexibility and personal time for developers. It's also a lot of fun to work with, consistently achieves the "Wow" effect on delivery, and generally boosts the morale of any team regardless of the delivery context.

Implications to Development Teams

The architecture-centric model provides a platform for creatively challenging our developers and keeping users happy.

Many experienced developers believe that business and functional requirements are the primary variables from project to project. *Feature-point analysis,* which involves breaking the project deliverables into irreducible minimums, should yield a fairly predictable delivery schedule. When setting such schedules, we often use past experiences in order to predict scope of effort and time lines for upcoming projects.

For stable teams with little attrition, this method is ideal, in fact, perfect. For the average development shop with relatively high attrition, feature-point analysis is less predictable. The required knowledge base is unstable because developers take knowledge with them when they leave a project or company.

In an application-centric model, the skills of the developers, their relationship as a gelled team, and the complexity of the product all form convergent *variables,* creating a higher project risk. In fact, a developer's skills (not the user's requirements) are the most variable and volatile quantities from team to team.

As application complexities and feature-richness increase for competitive advantage, enormous pressure builds to assemble and keep a skilled team. It is, therefore, incumbent upon project and company leadership to keep the team's skills sharp, their energy focused, and their minds challenged.

The architecture-centric model captures knowledge, stabilizes teams, and abates attrition (generally), allowing feature-point analysis to gain more foothold and predictability. The model can satisfy the most demanding team's professional and career needs, because senior developers get the opportunity to gravitate toward technical issues and new developers find themselves in a rich mentoring environment as they deploy applications using the technology. With a stable workforce, innovation also has a stronger foothold.

We've seen enough of success and failure to know what works and what doesn't. Because software development, and especially innovation, is high-intensity thought labor, mentoring is effective for handing down experience and transferring knowledge, but only if we can keep our teams together. The architecture-centric model is an ideal mentoring foundation.

Innovation leverages prior effort, but only if the knowledge workers (or their experience) is available for reuse.

Implications on Revenue

Managers know they can make tons of money with custom development projects billed to a client by the hour. If enabling accelerated reuse shrinks delivery time, it also changes revenue equations: shorter projects mean less overall revenue if billed by the hour. For an artificially extended project, the end user might not know the difference if deliverables are on time and of high quality. They might smile and cut a check.

However, if the clients, or end users, realize they paid high dollars for custom craftsmanship when they could have paid much less, they will feel cheated, and rightly so. If a young, agile upstart-startup company masters reuse, it will drive a wedge into market share that a non-reuse company cannot remove. Even if the reuse-masters take the same amount of project time, they'll still have a higher quality product.

The conclusion is that the architecture-centric model gives us more options to increase quality, feature-richness, and keep the project timeline under our control rather than racing breathlessly to the finish line with a marginally functional product.

Companies using the architecture-centric model can deliver in a fraction of the timeframe required by the application-centric model. Does a quick-turnaround diminish the value of the deliverables? Hardly! If anything, it gives the company an extreme competitive advantage. Companies that bill by the hour will have to rethink their billing practices. They will have to assign value to their speed of deployment, increased product quality, and overall value of the application to its end users. Faster time to market is highly valuable, and savvy leaders can and will exploit this to competitive advantage.

Charge more for delivering higher quality and richer features in a more manageable time frame. Once delivered, keep the momentum and deliver more.

The true software development starting point exists well before the user pens the first application requirement. It exists before the developer breaks open the language development tools. We find it when we invoke pattern-based abstractions to meet user features, rather than wiring them into the software. When we begin to automatically think of programming in these terms, we've crossed the *virtual mach* boundary with a shockwave in our wake. Those who begin there will emerge with a firm technical, structural, and behavioral foundation for building all sorts of applications.

If we begin in the application realm, we've already lost. The application realm must rest on the foundation we prepare in software, and must be the result of core reusable software acting on metadata, not with application logic embedded in the software.

If the software development cycle is a continuum, the application realm actually marks the 80 percent point and moves toward closure at 100 percent. Beginning there forsakes the foundation itself. We will have missed four-fifths of the architectural maturity required to build highly reusable code.

Keeping the Momentum

Now that I've proposed a different approach, touting the possibilities of the architecture-centric view; the propulsion of accelerated reuse; the power of metamorphism; the positive traction it creates on our careers, our lives, and professional satisfaction; it's time to show you some of its finer details. I will strongly implore you to examine and perform the project exercises that you'll find throughout this book because each one builds on the last.

Project 1—Groundwork

Let's close out this chapter with a light example of some symbolic-tagging concepts. They will provide a lead-in to the following chapter, which introduces structural patterns. These are the primary project elements:

- Structural tools

- Factories

- Object/property manipulation

- Supporting code

The project language examples will be in Visual Basic .NET, but I've also included the Visual Basic 6.0 versions, (a minimum of Service Pack 3, preferably Service Pack 5). You won't need any other third-party products to support the examples. I've tested them under Windows NT 4.0 and 2000 Professional. The .NET, Visual Basic projects use the *.vbproj extension, while VB 6.0 uses the *.vbp extension.

Additionally, in the interest of clarity all project examples in the book will use the shorthand version of class names (e.g., vTools.TurboCollection will appear as TurboCollection in the book content).

If you've not downloaded the book's project listings and examples from Apress, do so now and extract it into the working directory of your choice. Each project has its own subdirectory, and a separate directory called VB6/ contains the Visual Basic 6.0 equivalents.

ProjectOne includes a number of class modules and a *main* module used as a skeleton to browse and manipulate their activity. Enter the ProjectOne/ subdirectory and *double-click* the ProjectOne.sln file to load the project skeleton. Answers to inquiries are available at info@virtualmach.com.

TurboCollection

The first structure requiring attention is the TurboCollection. It appears as two separate class objects, the *TurboCollection.cls* and the *ParmNode.cls*. The Turbo-Collection is an *Iterator* pattern. It hides and manipulates a *list* of objects, in this case ParmNodes. The TurboCollection acts by containing and linking ParmNodes to each other, then browsing and manipulating the links. The ParmNode is a simple *Container* pattern. It provides a memory-based storage location for both simple and complex information. Together, these classes form structural glue to enable metamorphism, bind and automate all other structural and behavioral patterns.

The first exercise will add nodes (ParmNodes) to a TurboCollection to create a simple list. Note that each node is a self-contained, detachable/attachable container. The ParmNode is also an adapter of sorts, serving to wrap and anchor a structure of any kind. For the first example, we'll add and organize simple textual data and then move into objects.

Load ProjectOne and find the Public Sub Main() header (see Listing 1-1). You will see a number of data declarations at the top of the module. We'll enlist their aid as we move along. Supporting code also follows the Main() header.

From here, let's build a simple list of information points using a TurboCollection structure. Under *Public Sub Main()* find this code:

```
Dim tcTest as New TurboCollection()
Dim pWrk as ParmNode
```

This will instantiate one of the TurboCollection Iterators along with a ParmNode for workspace. Now, let's add a ParmNode container to the Iterator by invoking tcTest's Add:

```
tcTest.Add (New ParmNode())
```

Note that .NET will automatically wrap this statement with the appropriate parenthesis. This will allow the addition of a newly instantiated ParmNode to the Iterator's list. By default, the TurboCollection will add the node to the end, or *tail*. While this provides us with the power to add a pre-existing node, practically speaking, most lists are created on the fly, so this notation could get clunky and verbose. For agility, use the following shorthand:

```
tcTest.Add()
```

This assumes we want to add a ParmNode, so the TurboCollection will instantiate and add one for us. We can get access to the new ParmNode in one of two ways: on the TurboCollection or as a return value from the Add() method. Here's an example:

```
pWrk = tcTest.Add()
```

or

```
tcTest.Add()
pWrk = tcTest.Ref()    'Ref always contains the currently active node.
```

Next, let's add the following data to the ParmNode container. It has several generic properties, the *Item, Obj, ItemKey,* and *SortKey* among others. These properties are critical to node identification and manipulation.

Item: This property contains simple textual data associated with the node (text, numeric, etc).

Obj: This property contains a reference to an object (complex data) associated with the node.

ItemKey: This property contains a textual key to uniquely identify the node in the Iterator list.

SortKey: This property contains collating information associated with the node's other information, used to sort and order all the nodes in relation to each other.

Thus, the following property references are equivalent to set the Item, ItemKey, and SortKey properties, respectively. The first example shows how to set the values directly on the ParmNode:

```
pWrk.Item = "A1"
pWrk.ItemKey = "A10"
pWrk.SortKey = "A10"
```

While this second example shows how to set the values on the same ParmNode using the TurboCollection's current Ref:

```
tcTest.Ref.Item = "A1"
tcTest.Ref.ItemKey = "A10"
tcTest.Ref.SortKey = "A10"
```

Even this notation can get cumbersome when coding the construction of a list, so, since Item, ItemKey, and SortKey are the most-often used properties when building a list, another method on the TurboCollection facilitates this as a shortcut, the *AddItem*. Consider this example:

```
tcTest.AddItem ("A1", "A10", "A10")
```

This notation will perform the two following actions:

1. Create and add a ParmNode to the list.

2. Populate the Item, ItemKey, and SortKey values with the respective parameters shown.

Now if we want to add multiple nodes to the Iterator, we can invoke the following inline code:

```
tcTest.Clear() 'let's clear out the iterator first
tcTest.AddItem( "A1", "A10", "A10")
tcTest.AddItem ("A4", "A40", "A40")
tcTest.AddItem ("A2", "A20", "A20")
tcTest.AddItem ("A5", "A50", "A50")
tcTest.AddItem ("A6", "A60", "A60")
tcTest.AddItem ("A7", "A70", "A70")
tcTest.AddItem ("A3", "A30", "A30")
tcTest.AddItem ("A8", "A80", "A80")
```

Note that I have deliberately added them out of key sequence. To examine the TurboCollection list contents, let's perform this simple browse:

```
tcTest.MoveFirst()                  'move to the first
                                    ' Node in the list
Do
    Debug.WriteLine (tcTest.Ref.Item)    'display the Node's contents
tcTest.MoveNext()                   'move to the next node in the list
Loop While tcTest.More()            'repeat until all nodes
                                    ' have been displayed
```

This loop will print the list nodes in exactly the order they were added. If we want to retrieve any member of the list, perform a *Find* using the Itemkey value, as shown here:

```
pWrk = tcTest.Find("A30")
Debug.Writeline( pWrk.Item)  'should be "A3"
```

or

```
Debug.WriteLine(tcTest.Find("A30").Item)
```

To reorganize information, simply browse the list once and set the SortKey to a unique collating value prior to sorting. We've already done this upon creation of the list, so let's invoke it. I can also invoke a *Dump*, as follows, when it's done to review the contents:

```
tcTest.SortList (strParms:="Descending")
tcTest.Dump()
```

This notation will execute a *descending* sort on the nodes in the list, then dump the result to Visual Basic's "Immediate Window" for review.

By default, the SortList will perform an ascending sort. Let's try that now:

```
tcTest.SortList()
tcTest.Dump()
```

On a sort, the TurboCollection does not move data or ParmNodes around in memory. The TurboCollection organizes information using the ParmNode's next/previous pointers, thus, when reorganizing, it simply reshuffles forward and backward references without moving the actual information. This results in blinding speed in data movement and manipulation. More on this in Chapter 4: Power Tools.

The *Find()* function, while fast on smaller lists, has a diminishing return on larger lists. To optimize this, the TurboCollection uses *binary trees* to reorganize information. A binary tree takes a sorted list and creates a navigable tree-structure supporting a binary search. Recall that a binary search will split a sorted list into two, select a targeted half for continuing the search, then repeat the split-and-find operation until it finds the target key. Statistically, a list with 10,000 elements will require a maximum of 13 compares to find any key, with an average of 11 compares per search. Now that's some serious search power!

Let's use the current list and build a tree as follows:

```
tcTest.TreeBuild()
tcTest.Dump()
```

The *TreeBuild* function will automatically sort the list, then perform the build. The tree structure is best suited for large, stable lists of information, usually those pulled from a database source. However, anywhere we need significant speed, the tree will provide it—and once constructed we can still add nodes to it.

These simple exercises served to introduce lists, the Iterator pattern, the container pattern, and how each helps the other to create a more powerful whole. However, the ParmNode has a broader scope of capability: that of containing and describing a data point with embedded metadata.

Property Manipulation

Within any class, adding functionality for the storage and retrieval of properties often causes *interface-bloat,* which changes or updates the class interface to expose new properties. Each time a user requests new features, developers often race back to their software and UML drawings and start drafting the new interface. The ideal solution should require changes only to the internal software, not the interfaces. How is this accomplished?

For example, let's say a *RocketEngine* class goes through several releases and the end user (an intergalactic shipper) requests some brand-new functionality in the form of *warp speed.* This entails the ability to jump into hyperdrive, warp space, and reduce time-to-market. The Intergalactic Space Administration has cleared the way for your engine design, so now you need to modify the onboard computers to run them.

In any rocket-engine design, new features like this could require extensive rework. Your mission is to perform the engine and system upgrades and install them without significantly changing any of the core navigation and control software. But how?

Let's say you have these three new properties:

Drive: Possible values include Twin-Ion (normal) and Warp (high-speed point-to-point). Until now, Drive has always been Twin-Ion.

Navigation: Possible values include Visual Flying Rules (VFR) and Gravitational (keying on location and gravity cues of passing planets and stars). Until now, VFR was more than sufficient. High-speed travel will require automated cues.

Inertial Dampening: The jump to hyperdrive can leave the passengers queasy and disoriented. Dampening must be automatic.

The *normal* course of action is to directly attack the RocketEngine's software interface with the following notations:

```
Public Property Drive(enum TwinIon, Warp:Default TwinIon)
Public Property Navigation(enum VFR, Grav: Default VFR)
Public Property InternalDamp(True, False Default False)
```

Unfortunately, declaring these three properties changes the RocketEngine's software interface *and* requires the RocketEngine's software consumers to wire specific functionality into their own code to take advantage of it. In short, this track will initiate the reconstruction and deployment of most system software on board the spacecraft. So much for plug-and-play.

Now let's build our instance of *RocketEngine*:

```
Dim pEngine as New RocketEngine()
```

After the necessary background initialization of the class (including interfacing to the actual engine hardware), we now have the following interface exposed to the control and navigation systems. It's a very simple interface, mapping a single property, called *Item*, and allows it to map values into their appropriate locations *behind* the RocketEngine's interface. The *KeyValue* will be the actual property name, while the *ItemValue* will be the actual value of the property.

```
pEngine.Item("Drive") = "TwinIon"
pEngine.Item("Navigation") = "VFR"
pEngine.Item("Inertia") = "Dampening=False"
```

I've added one additional key value that will automatically set other key values behind the scenes. With such an interface, both the consumers and the developers have complete freedom to use it without fear of breakage or change. The developer can change literally anything within the RocketEngine core, exposing new features without breaking old ones. Here's an example:

```
pEngine.Item("Warp") = "True"
```

Now let's look at the internal implementations in Listing 1-1. The simple form of *Set Item* will accept a key and a value. It will attempt to change the key's associated value, if it exists, then call *ExamineItem* in order to determine if it should handle the "Warp" property key differently. For brevity, the action associated with "Warp" simply resets the Item values. In practice, it could kick off a whole host of background processing.

Listing 1-1. Item() and ExamineItem() Code

```
Public Property Item(Optional ByVal strK As String = "") As String
  Get
  On Error Resume Next
  Dim strVx As String
   strVx = Nothing                    'set to null in case Find() fails
   strVx = tcItem.Find(strK).Item     'do the find - if found will return value
   Item = strVx                       'return to calling proc
  End Get
  Set(ByVal Value As String)
    On Error Resume Next
    tcItem.Find(strK).Item = Value     'find and set the property
    If Err.Number <> 0 Then            'if not found, then need to add
        tcItem.AddItem(Value, strK, strK) 'else if ok to add then add it
    End If
  ExamineItem(strK, Value)             'and examine it further
   End Set
End Property
```

And now the definition of ExamineItem():

```vb
Private Sub ExamineItem(ByVal strK As String, ByVal strV As String)
    On Error Resume Next
    Select Case strK
        Case "Warp"                             'if "warp" is the key
            Item("Drive") = "Warp"              'automatically set the required
            Item("Navigation") = "Gravitational"    'default configuration
            Item("Inertia") = "Dampening=True"
    End Select
End Sub
```

This very simple strategy provides all consumers with a consistent property interface. In practice, the class initialization should internally build and expose the key-value pairs. The RocketEngine New()does this:

```vb
Public Sub New()
    Item("Drive") = "TwinIon"
    Item("Navigation") = "VFR"
    Item("Inertia") = "Dampening=False"
End Sub
```

While I've put some hard-wired values into the class definition, I've also cordoned them off into textual constants. Anything that can be reduced to text is a candidate to become structural, behavioral, or configuration metadata. Now that we have simple values under control, let's take a look at object manipulation.

Factories and Object Recycle

Within the scope of any software execution, especially object-modeled software, the need for memory and resource management is critical to maintaining control over the system and its performance. Memory leakage occurs in two primary ways: building instances of objects and not destroying them when appropriate, and destroying objects without the ability to fully reclaim all of the memory they acquired when first instantiated.

The first problem is fairly easy to rectify: simply exercise diligence and destroy objects after we're done with them. This usually requires discipline on the part of the individual developer, and sometimes presents a risk of runaway leakage.

The second problem is impossible to resolve completely. Each time our software instantiates an object, the system allocates memory for it along with additional memory to track the instance. When we destroy the object, the system does not necessarily throw away the tracking memory, only the original memory. Additionally, destroying the object automatically creates an object-sized hole in memory. The system will use this hole later to allocate an object of equal or lesser size. The result is memory fragmentation. Within high-speed systems, this effect can create a significant performance drag by literally throwing away useful memory and requiring its fresh reallocation.

These effects usually don't appear in slow-moving classes at the upper execution tier of a software program. They usually occur with the foundation classes, the ones that are the smallest, most used, and most often forgotten. The bad news is that a lack of attention on the part of our developers can create a runaway memory leak very quickly. The good news is we can track all of our memory and object allocations with a little forethought and the strategic use of the Factory pattern.

Within *main* the method *FactoryInit* calls *FactoryAdd* once for each of four classes already in ProjectOne. Each of these classes has a special interface to support factory generation. This interface allows any member of the class to be a "seed" object for multiple objects of its own kind. Thus FactoryAdd will simply add a single instance of the newly created object (Listing 1-2) and key it on the object's type name, also included in the call.

 NOTE *Many languages do not support the ability to convert an object's type into a string value for textual searching, or their typename() functions are too brittle for compiled executables. This is why FactoryInit and FactoryAdd include the class names explicitly as string constants.*

Listing 1-2. Factory Logic Described

```
Private Sub FactoryInit()
  On Error Resume Next
  FactoryAdd ("StringAdapter", New StringAdapter())
  FactoryAdd ("TurboCollection", New TurboCollection())
  FactoryAdd ("ParmNode", New ParmNode())
  FactoryAdd ("Observer", New Observer())
  End Sub
```

Note in Listing 1-2 that for extensive class lists, the FactoryInit could invoke a TreeBuild at the end. This would sort and slice the class list into a binary tree for blazing run time access. Practically speaking, don't try to push all objects into a single factory. Most framework-level functions (such as databases, screens, and so on) warrant their own factories and sometimes are never co-related with the other frameworks or software subsystems. Use multiple factories to increase plug-and-play freedom of subsystems so that none of them are directly dependent on a master factory. I'll show in the next chapter how an *Abstract factory* can provide brokerage to multiple factories without direct dependency. Listing 1-3 shows how to add objects to this factory.

Listing 1-3. FactoryAdd

```
Public Sub FactoryAdd(strK As String, iObj As Object)
   On Error Resume Next
   Dim pWrk As ParmNode
   pWrk = tcFactory.Find(strK)                'try to find it
   If pWrk Is Nothing Then                    'If not already there - then
      tcFactory.AddItem( "", strK, strK)      'add a new Item with the proper keys
      tcFactory.Ref.obj = iObj                'then set the ParmNode's Obj
reference
   Else
      pWrk.obj = iObj                         'otherwise, it's there,
                                              ' just add the reference

   End If
End Sub
```

Now that the tcFactory has "seed" objects with keys to each, let's build the following factory method to give us access to each type:

```
Public Function Factory(strK As String, iObj As Object) As Object
   On Error Resume Next
   Dim pWrk As ParmNode
   Factory = Nothing                            'prep in case not found
   Factory = tcFactory.Find(strK).obj.Create(iObj)   'find the seed, create new one
                                                ' from it, and return it.
End Function
```

Note how the first part of the function presets the Factory return value to Nothing. This is a best practice of proper error control (discussed later in Chapter 5). It will use *Find* on the tcFactory to retrieve the "seed," then call the seed's *Create*. Each member of the factory's list must support a Create function that returns an instance of its own kind.

What then, would be the most appropriate means to reclaim the object once it's no longer necessary? It seems a shame to build a factory function to manufacture them, but not use it to take them back. The *FactoryRelease* method allows a consumer to put the object back into the factory environment.

We will need to expand the roll of the tcFactory TurboCollection. Each node on tcFactory will now hold the seed object *and* another TurboCollection for storing the returns, now *available* objects. This will require the following simple change to the FactoryAdd method (highlighted):

```
Public Sub FactoryAdd(strK As String, iObj As Object)
  On Error Resume Next
  Dim pWrk As ParmNode
  pWrk = tcFactory.Find(strK)                'find it
  If pWrk Is Nothing Then                    'if not found then
    tcFactory.AddItem( "", strK, strK)       'add it
    tcFactory.Ref.obj = iObj                 'and populate the seed
    tcFactory.Ref.Ref = New TurboCollection() 'add the "available" list here
  Else
    pWrk.obj = iObj                          'otherwise populate the seed
  End If
End Sub
```

We will then need the following new function, *FactoryRelease,* to receive the reclaimed objects:

```
Public Sub FactoryRelease(strK As String, iObj As Object)
  On Error Resume Next
  Dim tcAv As TurboCollection                'allocate a TurboCollection
  Dim pWrk As ParmNode                       'and a placeholder
  pWrk = tcFactory.Find(strK)                'find the class type with the key
  tcAv = pWrk.Ref                            'and get the "available" list
  tcAv.AddItem "", strK, strK                'add the recycled object
  tcAv.Ref.obj = iObj                        'and set it to the list's obj
End Sub
```

Now we'll need to modify the Factory method, as follows, to take advantage of reusing the recycled objects before creating a new one (modification are in bold):

```
Public Function Factory(strK As String, iObj As Object) As Object
  On Error Resume Next
  Dim pWrk As ParmNode
  Dim tcAv As TurboCollection
  Set Factory = Nothing
  Set pWrk = tcFactory.Find(strK)
  Set tcAv = pWrk.Ref                       'get the available list
  If tcAv.DataPresent Then                   'If something Is on it?
    Set Factory = tcAv.Top.obj              'use the node on the top of the list
    tcAv.Remove tcAv.Top                    'then remove the top node
  Else                                       'otherwise it's empty
    Set Factory = tcFactory.Find(strK).obj.Create(iObj)
                                            'so create a new one
  End If
End Function
```

Now we'll just call to initialize the Factory (only once)

```
FactoryInit()
```

and invoke it to get a new instance of the Observer class.

```
Dim oWrk as Observer
oWrk = Factory("Observer")
```

Now put it back

```
FactoryRelease("Observer",oWrk)
```

and go get it again. It's the same object as before, only recycled.

```
oWrk = Factory("Observer")
```

The primary objective is to build a central clearinghouse for object creation and destruction rather than relying on the programmer's discipline alone. The alternative: having direct create/destroy functionality scattered throughout hundreds of thousands of lines of code, and encountering a pervasive memory leak we cannot pinpoint.

These constructs are more than strategies. They are patterns of plug-and-play capability that exist in every software program. By directly identifying and leveraging them, we enable them as building blocks for supporting all sorts of applications.

CHAPTER 2
Building Blocks

In This Chapter:

- Understanding the common application architecture

- The interface *rules*

- Examining object interaction

- Interpreting structural patterns

- Implementing stabilization rules with SOAL

- Managing resources

- Comparing application and metamorphic models

We can decompose complex systems into elemental, often disparate and dependent parts. An aircraft, for example, is an assembly of non-flying parts. Through design and organization, the parts work together to overcome gravity. If an application-centric model represents gravity, the architecture-centric model represents aerodynamics. (See Chapter 1 for a discussion of these two models.) Once we standardize our design for the parts, we will have a repository of building blocks ready for assembly into any structure we desire.

This chapter dives into the topic of software structural integrity. Technical managers may derive more from the general concepts in the first section, but in the end we'll be doing a hands-on exercise. In some sections I'll use conceptual abstractions of real software code (pseudocode) to encourage the reader's insight toward various languages. In the following chapters, I'll show how structure directly affects behavior, and our goal of putting behavior on a leash.

Understanding the Common Application Architecture

The most common application architectural approach includes linking together binary components (e.g., third party products or custom structures) with software source code and using this construction to manage the end user's experience (see Figure 2-1). The application and its various spinoff products still reach a common outcome: the application-level logic is embedded at every level of the architecture. This remains the first and most consistently used approach for application development.

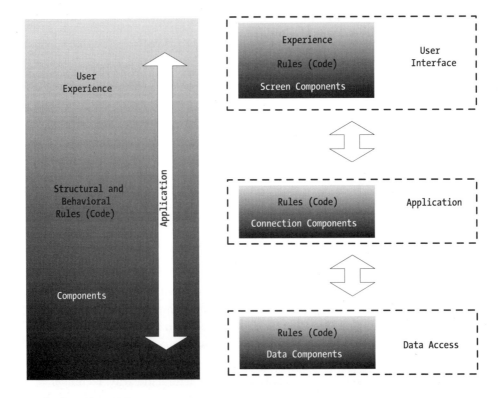

Figure 2-1. The most common application architectures are monolithic (left) and distributed/multiple-tier (right).

Generally, the architecture emerges in the two following primary forms:

- *Monolithic* in which all code and components are compiled into one executable

- *Distributed* or *multiple-tier* which layers the application into several parts

This architecture comingles the behavioral experience, application-level rules, and the supporting components at every level. In fact, within practically every software module, we'll find a firm and indelible user-centric footprint. At the technology level, this architecture uses compiled instructions to drive components directly through intimately connected application programming interface (API) calls. If the technology or the application's behavior must change, we must change the software code, rebuild the program, and re-deliver it.

The architecture's change-rebuild-redeploy cycle presents significant risk with each new release. Once-solid functionality can gradually exhibit brittleness and breakage because, during a rebuild, we inadvertently overlook some subtle nuance of the internal plumbing. Regression testing durations increase as feature strength increases, delaying re-delivery. As our senior developers migrate off the solution's focus and join other projects, the application's embedded complexity is placed at risk because maintenance developers are typically less familiar with it. Maintenance developers invariably find it easier to build peripheral functionality to support new requests rather than dig into the core application code. Complexity increases. Risk rises. Rework and even rewrite are inevitable.

If we rebuild the binary product for every change great and small, we create risk for the entire product, not just the part we changed.

We can say the architecture is one-dimensional because it appears as a flat, single-threaded, single-owner program, regarding events only where forced to do so. One-dimensional object models usually appear as *class hierarchies*—tree-like structures with wired locations, roles, and names for every class (see Figure 2-2).

Application change-rebuild-redeliver always reaches a dead end.

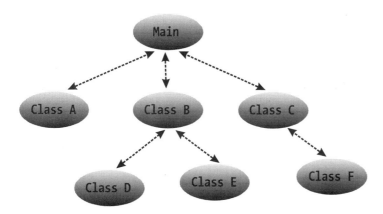

Figure 2-2. The class hierarchy of one-dimensional object models

The inherent weakness of the model is inflexibility. In Figure 2-2, *ClassF* is only available to *ClassE* through *ClassC*. A typical code example follows:

```
lngFind = Main.ClassB.ClassE.Find()                    'FIND
lngLoad = Main.ClassC.ClassF.Load()                    'LOAD
lngStat = ClassE.Parent.Parent.ClassC.ClassF.Status()  'STATUS
```

Because software code directly wires application-level behavior, all object model changes impact the software. What would happen to the preceding coding example if a user request or technology constraint forced a change to move *ClassE* underneath *ClassF*? Compare the prior notations to the following:

```
lngFind = Main.ClassC.ClassF.ClassE.Find()    'FIND
lngLoad = Main.ClassC.ClassF.Load()           'LOAD
lngStat = ClassE.Parent.Status()              'STATUS
```

If the user requirements drive the class hierarchy structure (a common condition) then the software code is always subject to rework with each change in the model. Both *Find()* and *Status()* in the preceding example underwent significant rework. Imagine the impact across the entire scope of the software! Such a model can only withstand minor structural change, because major change often requires extensive rework and even redesign. We can resolve this later in this chapter; see "Understanding Interface Dynamics" for the details.

 NOTE *A senior developer on a project decided to move a Student object's Address information into its own class, requiring former references like* Student.City *and* Student.State *to become* Student.Address.City *and* Student.Address.State. *He made this change one evening and went on vacation for a week, leaving the team to deal with the damage* all over the architecture.

The hard-coded approach delivers the application well, but only once, because repeatable delivery is already an Achilles Heel. It also assumes a self-contained, closed object model, where the individual structures, algorithms, reports, and behaviors will never be used elsewhere. Unfortunately, simple class inheritance only digs a deeper hole (because the application-centric classes and relationships are still embedded). We're painting ourselves into a corner with it, so let's stop now.

Many of us work within the common architecture and over time understand its flaws. Usually some priority for *openness* arises (usually driven by desktop or web availability, or performance demands). Applications built under this architecture are closed systems and cannot easily include these capabilities. We must break them apart and rewrite them.

As a developer, you may be reading this and thinking, "Well, it won't happen by magic!" Clearly, if the end user requests a new feature, then *something* must change. Is there a method of responding to user requests without changing and rebuilding the software? If so, would we pursue it? We can indeed give users what they want without a program rebuild, but we have to plan for it.

We must approach capabilities as building blocks, presenting them to an application developer in abstracted form. A building block approach requires some forethought and might delay initial delivery. We must generalize object interfaces and make them externally programmable. The result is more resilient and stable software that requires fewer secondary releases of the binary executable. We then handle user changes and requests largely through the externally programmable capabilities, not changes to the software.

If we construct programmable building blocks, we automatically promote flexibility.

The Interface *Rules*

When multi-threaded computing became readily available through microprocessor design and language support, developers exchanged a flurry of ideas on how to control information in context. It wouldn't do to have one process clipping along, become suspended by an interrupt handler, and have its workspace ravaged.

Developers demanded encapsulation (and interface-driven modules), requiring deep attention to the object-oriented approach for both elegance and behavioral integrity. Frequently used capabilities migrated into the systems and language environment. Once upon a time we carefully handcrafted designs that are now automatically supported at the language level. Objects also helped eliminate exposed global variables, batch-style input-process-output models, and moved toward interrupt-driven, highly interactive, and volatile designs. While the potential for misbehavior was extreme, the tradeoff became highly efficient and responsive software. Unfortunately, many developers relied too much on language-level power, resting on it as the solution rather than a foundation to something much stronger.

It's Not Easy

Do you think Visual Basic, JavaScript, HTML, or other more recent waves of object language environments will make design and architecture easy? If so, you're in for a bumpy ride. Excellence in design and architecture do not pop out of a box onto a desktop. The compiler vendors build no assumptions into their products about their final implementations. They are infinitely flexible and typically uncontrolled—rather *unleashed*—at the moment of purchase. A flippant approach ultimately fails or leads to redesign/rewrite.

Encapsulation required us to standardize approach and terminology, as evidenced in rise to the *class Property*. Information hiding (and thus operation/ algorithm hiding), requiring the *class Method*. With each event-driven process completing its mission quickly, we received an interesting and powerful artifact: *an inventory of elemental methods*.

We're accustomed to building objects to represent entities, but rarely do we build objects to represent process. We've been taught that we must encapsulate and hide processes.

The entities represent "nouns" and the processes represent "verbs," so we cannot have process without entity, the story goes.

However, the only way to properly interface entities and reusable behaviors is to balance the migration of common pattern-based processes out of their encapsulation, and expose them as process objects for use by the entity objects (more on this in the next chapter, where we'll examine building dynamic methods from elemental processes).

This requires an architectural approach that assumes the symbolic interchangeability of entity and process. We abstract the entities and processes as resources, then weave their behavior through simplified interfaces.

We automatically and effortlessly understand the same words as either nouns or verbs (light, move, run, phone). Why can't a machine interchange them, too?

The path to high reuse doesn't start with the entity or the process itself, nor does it start with the software language; *it starts with standardizing our class interfaces*. We don't care what happens beyond the interface, as long as the exposed side of the interface conforms to a few basic structural and behavioral rules.

A vast proliferation of articles and books have recently arisen to address the misunderstandings associated with interface-driven design. It seems that the Common Object Model (COM and its derivatives) and Common Object Request Broker Architecture (CORBA), and now the Microsoft .NET Framework, expose a wide array of features to manage interfaces. We have largely abused their capabilities by building brittle application-specific bridges *through* these protocols rather than use them as intended, as a highway to support robust application-*independent* interfaces.

Building Application-Independent Reusable Objects

We can churn out designs and software all we want, but when it comes time to publish our work, some implicit agreements exist that we cannot override or ignore. The agreements are enforced by industry interface standards and exist to protect our consumers.

Contracts versus Covenants

Let's not confuse our terms. Some industry leaders define an *interface* as a *contract* (see sidebar). I'll reshape this definition in another way. Conceptually, entities (of any kind) can enter one of two kinds of agreements: one is a *contract,* the other is a *covenant.*

A contract is based on mutual liability. It allows an entity to back out of an agreement based on the non-compliance of another participating entity. A covenant is based on mutual responsibility. It differs from a contract in that each entity is beholden to support its own end of the agreement regardless of the compliance of the other participating entities. Contracts are *enforced,* while covenants are *embraced.* Contracts represent the *letter* of agreements while covenants represent the letter and the *spirit* of them.

While my definition of covenant is practically identical to the industry's definition of contract, it's amazing that developers and designers truly treat their interfaces like contracts (inconsiderate of their users) rather than a covenant (high consideration of their users).

I also present this definition *to make us stop and think.* How do we view our interface specifications? As a contract (something we recklessly control) or as a covenant (something we treat with extraordinary care and preservation)?

....

Microsoft on Interface Specification

An interface represents a contract, in that a class that implements an interface must implement every aspect of that interface exactly as it is defined.

Although interface implementations can evolve, interfaces themselves cannot be changed once published. Changes to a published interface may break existing code. If you think of an interface as a contract, it is clear that both sides of the contract have a role to play. The publisher of an interface agrees never to change that interface, and the implementer agrees to implement the interface exactly as it was designed.

Visual Basic .NET Online Help, Interfaces Overview, Copyright © 2001 Microsoft All Rights Reserved.

TIP *Not to split fine meanings, but an interface is not a contract. It's a covenant. We must align with it and support it regardless of the cooperation or participation level of others.*

A *structural component interface* is a covenant using defined structures and behaviors. Interface publishers don't have the luxury of breaking their covenant; they are responsible for supporting it regardless of the use or abuse of the interface's consumers. For example, what would happen to our Windows desktop applications if Microsoft arbitrarily changed the Windows API (all or in part), breaking our carefully crafted software? What if Oracle threw away parts (major or minor) that our applications depended on? You see, once they publish features, removing them without warning is unacceptable.

Our software *must follow the same rules.* We cannot arbitrarily change our published APIs or features without expecting our calling consumers to incur penalties, because interface specifications always affect API calls and expected behaviors. Backward compatibility is absolutely essential, yet few custom applications give it a second thought. Each application-level revision usually stands on its own.

DEFINITION Backward compatability *supports former capabilities while exposing new ones.*

Dynamics of Interface Specifications

When developing solutions to the enterprise and beyond, business-to-business interface specification receives extraordinary sensitivity and attention. Businesses want their internal systems to exchange information with other business systems (both internally and externally), and know to focus on the rules for the exchange: *the interface.*

Typically, interface specification is one-sided. For example, a business may want to gain access to stock information, vehicle tracking data, weather statistics, and so on. Publishers of such services have predefined outbound data formats and will not change them for just one subscriber. Publishers expect subscribers to build a simple data transformer (for converting published information into their internal formats) rather than keep up with the many disparate formats of their subscribers.

With a stable interface, subscribers can create a transformer, deploy it, and enjoy seamless data interchange forever. Subscribers often access various publishers, and often serve as publishers themselves.

A universal rule exists in this maelstrom: Subscribers don't control interface specification, *publishers* do. As information exchange drives business, a pattern emerges: the interface is the ruler, it is not a passive participant.

Misuse of Encapsulation

Once we understand encapsulation, we typically set about coding an object's internal implementation and then introduce its features through specific, unique interface calls. For example, we might create a sine-wave algorithm for drafting plots and then expose function calls such as *SineBinary()*, *SineImage()*, *SineFor-Plotter()*, etc. We might build an accounting function for determining net worth, then expose a reference like *NetWorth()*. As publishers, we reserve ultimate authority over augmenting and extending these interfaces. We believe that as long as we don't touch the existing references, we can build as many new ones as we desire.

In most software designs, initially defining and freezing an individual class interface specification is anathema.

This practice causes our interface specifications to follow the development cycle *passively*, stabilizing original features but expanding to new features over time as the object increases in functionality. Furthermore, this practice gives us the de facto freedom and permission to modify the interface with each component release (a moving target). Consequently, our interfaces in general remain volatile, are often addressed last (or *in situ*), almost as an afterthought (a contract), rather than *first*, and *deliberately* (a covenant).

The practice of extending and augmenting class interfaces throughout their lifecycle is so common, in fact, that describing it as a flawed approach might seem very odd. In fact, many industry-strength products revise their interfaces (even incrementally) with every release, so shouldn't we follow their lead? After exposing a component's features, many developers then hope that, over time, the interface will stabilize.

Most software designs allow class interfaces to change, sometimes dramatically, as quickly as we can add new features.

However, the interface usually never stabilizes. It changes with every new feature deployment and is assumed *in flux* for the duration of the component's lifetime. Interface extension is a flawed approach because it continues to gravitate toward exposing unique component features rather than building an *interface pattern* to support all features now and forever. An interface pattern supports all of the primary features and options most pervasive among all interfaces. If we examine a small sample of interfaces in our current software project, we'll find repeating themes. The themes, not the interfaces themselves, are the pattern.

Our priority is to address, stabilize, and freeze an object's interface as early as possible. Only applying a pattern will achieve this.

Early Stabilization

Software development is the only technical discipline where on-the-fly interface specification is allowed, and even encouraged. So, it's a challenge for us to adopt an approach that promises to help us stabilize the interfaces as quickly as possible. Because this means *no interface changes* for the remainder of the class lifecycle, it creates anxiety for those of us who want to reserve freedom to change, or to experiment. If the interfaces stabilize early, all component interoperation stabilizes with them. We're then free to modify the internal parts of components at will. Subscribers *must* experience interface consistency with the freedom to exploit new features. Such a condition requires a highly flexible interface specification.

Stable Interfaces Enable Plug-and-Play

Some sharp hardware engineers influenced my early career. Among those, one was also a software guru, and his philosophy was that all software should exhibit the same behavioral control as hardware chips, surviving on the compliance of their interfaces. He wanted software he could install on any hardware system that would instantly conform and wrap itself around the hardware device. He wanted plug-and-play capability, *for the software*. Considering that plug-and-play (even for hardware) was ten years from being a marketplace reality, and that our team was using assembly language, we were in a lonely camp indeed.

This forced me into another mode of thinking: to view the computing environment from the machine's perspective rather than my own. A singular truth again arose from that experience, that the component *interface* (hardware or software), and its accurate, consistent definition, *rules everything*.

 TIP Stabilize interfaces toward *patterns, not specific references.* Component consumers care about the outward appearance, never the internal details.

Plug-and-play is a structural characteristic giving a system independence from components, and allowing components to have an "optional" presence.

We sometimes believe that defining uniqueness in class interfaces will provide built-in protection from interface violations and promote cool polymorphic effects. While this is a correct assertion, it also sacrifices interoperability and metamorphism—a poor tradeoff. *Metamorphism* enables a component's seamless and consistent integration and conformity to a variety of run-time domains. It also enables the quick introduction of new objects to the calling consumers, and gives existing objects access to new capabilities anywhere in the framework.

From a software perspective, consistent interface behavior is like a universal passport. It allows seamless and consistent interaction with all other objects and their connecting processes. Objects folded into the framework begin to behave as one interoperable whole.

By requiring conformity in each object's interface, calling consumers cannot superficially discern their differences at run time.

Understanding Interface Dynamics

When systems electronically and automatically connect and exchange information, we say they are *interoperable*, or that they have *connectivity*, or perhaps they are *integrated*. The real trick is in quick, even automatic integration, the ability to introduce new functions without breaking existing ones or changing their operating framework. With all the systems, components, and modules out there talking to one another, can we find a common pattern of operation among them? Our charge is to cherry-pick the standard that gives us the greatest freedom, flexibility, and power.

The following standards enable object connectivity:

- Common Object Model (COM) or Distributed Common Object Model (DCOM) protocol is in the Microsoft Windows environment.

- Simple Object Access Protocol (SOAP) is also in the Windows environment. SOAP is Microsoft's answer (in part) to our abuse of COM, helping software decouple itself from deep COM dependency.

- Common Object Request Broker Architecture (CORBA) is a dominant player in Unix environments.

- Sockets (e.g., WinSock and other TCP/IP exchange enablers) can play anywhere Ethernet is supported.

All of these options provide powerful connectivity capabilities for systems and processes. These protocols directly address our tactic of releasing components with new interfaces (as such, they don't artificially constrain us to a single interface specification). Subscribers to original versions of our interfaces can maintain connection integrity, and our development tools can be reinforced to keep us honest.

Interface protocol standards now provide industry-wide underpinning. So, software development languages, their supporting modeling tools, and information management systems in general will now enforce the standards. We can declare software as "well behaved" if it adheres, even minimally, to industry interface rules. In addition, we can buy software products off the shelf and (more) reliably deploy them because the rules provide its creators with signposts for their delivery pathways.

COM, CORBA, and DCOM

The COM/CORBA connectivity environment protects against inadvertently disconnecting dependent applications. Upgrades must always consider prior releases because of potential dependencies. These laws are enforced through stamping each component with a unique identifier such as a Windows CLSID.

CLSID dependency does not change in .NET, but we do have more options as to when it imposes itself, such as avoiding an automatic re-stamp of the Windows registry each time we perform a simple re-build.

Because the component is potentially visible at the Internet level, it cannot arbitrarily select its own identifier. It is assigned when the component is built, and is associated with the component's public interface, not its implementation. If the internals of the component experience radical change, but the interface remains intact, the protocol will not require a new unique ID to be re-stamped. The dependence on specific IDs creates a significant intrusion, even invasive structural presence, of the interface specification within our architecture. The dependency (between a consumer and the component) is real and presents a risk.

Apart from the various means to stamp the ID, the weakness in COM and CORBA is the human factor. They cannot guard against abuse or misapplication by those of us who might view them as fenceposts to be challenged rather than signposts to be heeded. The inflexibility of interface publication is a strength to keep us from destroying our work and relationships with end users.

In the COM model, the consumer receives a logical instance of a *RocketEngine* object that is part of an external physical *RocketEngine* service. As the consumer interacts with the local logical instance, it is affecting the external physical instance. COM will manage the relationship, such that the consumer will never know the difference. In the case of DCOM, the remote instance is on a different machine entirely, relying on the network as an exchange highway. The additional network overhead (and the network's integrity) ultimately affect the object's integrity and performance. A noisy network can create a brittle run-time instance (and a marginal software design leads to failure). Such an implementation often works great in development, but scaling it upward is problematic.

Our chosen object-level information exchange or connectivity standard must have the least possible structural footprint within the architecture.

Would those who complain about COM's inflexibility also decry the necessity of a home's breaker box to guard against electrical overload?

SOAP

Rather than continue to educate our errant ranks on the pitfalls of interface abuse, Microsoft developed SOAP alongside the .NET Framework to allow object interface references to stabilize while they exchange deep detail using textual XML. This migrates the interface-level volatility into a dynamic forum (XML) and thus permits interface extension without directly modifying binary interface references. It also addresses interface stabilization and gets us on a better path. However, we still have the ongoing freedom to make our object interfaces moving targets.

Microsoft actually enabled us to do the right thing with COM/DCOM, but the application-centric approach was our undoing. We started extending our interfaces and used them (abused them) as the first defense for satisfying a user request. We can do the same thing with SOAP and dig ourselves back into the same hole, so let's avoid it this time around.

Sockets, COM, and DCOM

In the virtual Socket Object Connectivity approach (vSOC) the object itself logically and physically exists in both the consumer and the remote service location (whether on the same machine or on the network). Within local context, the consumer has direct and speedy access to the object's services. If the consumer requests something requiring remote information, the two *RocketEngine* objects will communicate at the socket level.

NOTE *The local and remote* RocketEngine *objects are separate structural instances maintaining logical synchronization.*

The COM model, by contrast, directly manages the objects as the same logical and structural instance. In COM, if a service object breaks, the consumer crashes. In the socket-based model, if the service object breaks or even crashes, any other service on the network can take over. The communication services are recoverable without crashing the consumer, making the consumer (and ultimately the user's experience) more durable. One vendor (Synergy Software) calls this capability *HyperActiveX*. See Figure 2-3 for a comparison between COM and sockets.

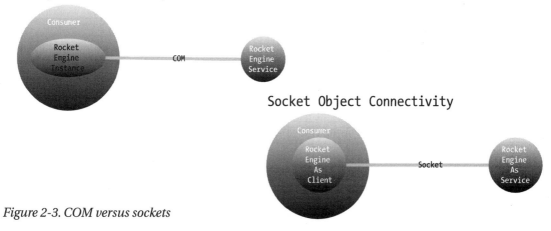

Figure 2-3. COM versus sockets

Compared to COM, socket-based distributed objects create a more flexible and responsive object implementation for both consumers and services. Only raw information (not binary COM object overhead) is transferred across the network. Socket technology is more stable than COM for transmitting data within a machine, across enterprises, and beyond.

When components exchange information across a network, all they really want is the raw data. Let's think about information exchange across a TCP/IP connection without the overhead of other protocols. On multiple machines, socket exchange is quick, lightweight, robust, and highly responsive compared to its more complex brethren. This is an obvious truth to many who have tried to deploy DCOM-based objects on an enterprise scale. Broadcasting and exchanging information in a connectionless, socket-based mode is more flexible than the specifically connected, binary-wired world of DCOM/CORBA.

Another benefit of socket-based distributed communication is the flexibility of run-time discovery and identification. Sockets identify themselves dynamically while COM-based objects identify themselves with the CLSID. COM does not allow a program to perform run-time discovery of (and dynamic linkage to) various run-time versions of the same component. Nor does it allow an object to dynamically change its own identity (metamorph). In short, with vSOC, *RocketEngine* Revision A running in production can peacefully coexist with its upgrade (*RocketEngine* Revision B) and we can dynamically and seamlessly redirect existing consumers to it for acceptance testing, training, or a host of other purposes. Why is this important? We absolutely require the ability to instantiate multiple versions of a service for testing, debugging, and troubleshooting. Invariably, I've been in release cycles where the customer wanted all these options and more.

Even when using COM's *CreateObject()*, we can only have access to the currently registered version of the class. By using sockets, we can redirect any consumer to any service (old versions or new) interchangeably and dynamically, with high flexibility. (See Figure 2-4.) Additionally, with sockets we can use current computing environments, while with COM we must have separate environments for each version. In reality, replicating computing environments to support versions, or configuration management, is impractical and expensive.

Sockets also provide us with a broader communication scope. If we have network objects running on a Microsoft server or a Unix server, we can always connect over a socket port. If we implement the networked object in DCOM and exchange information only through DCOM, we will not have extensibility into Unix.

Additionally, sockets enable us to unlink dependencies between objects and programs. This capability provides practical benefits, because when some consumers have dependent consumers, rebuilding one can initiate rebuilding another, and another. A simple change in one component's interface can necessi-

Socket Flexibility

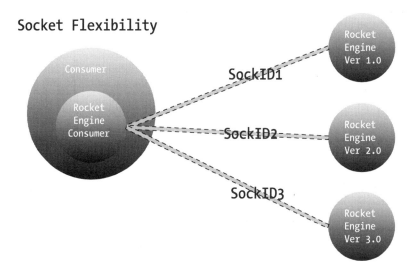

Figure 2-4. Socket flexibility

consumers. Sockets unlink dependencies so we, not the language environment, control when and how we target a binary product for reconstruction.

....

Cascading Reconstruction

We can change a component's public interface to extend its functionality, but consumers must include additional software to access it, and then submit to a rebuild and redeployment. This is the bane of a component-dependent architecture.

If a component is also a consumer, or component-consumers are chained into several levels, a change in the lower levels can initiate a cascading rebuild to all dependent consumers. For example, if our user interface (UI) depends on Application Object A, which in turn depends on Persistence Object C, in turn depending on Microsoft ActiveX Data Objects (ADO), a simple upgrade to ADO could initiate cascading rebuild all the way to the user interface.

A time will come when we'll want to make a single, surgical change in a lower-level component and deploy it for mass consumption. If we inadvertently change the public interface, we'll initiate a cascading change to all dependents and force their reconstruction and redeployment. Our objective is to avoid the cascading reconstruction, but this is not always possible.

We need a way to avoid cascading reconstruction forever, and it must be installed and burned into the interface specification deliberately, and early.

....

An original feature of Unix was make, a program that accepted a script describing the assembly requirements for an application. A developer could describe every dependency such that a change in a lower, even obscure, file would initiate the recompilation of all components depending on it. This virtually guaranteed that changes would not be accidentally ignored. It's an amazingly powerful utility, as evidenced by its popularity and functional inclusion into practically every development environment, including .NET. However, it institutionalized cascading reconstruction.

Automatic, cascading reconstruction (as part of change management) is a weak deployment strategy. It might serve well in the startup stages of development and testing cycle, but its integrity will diminish in the maintenance cycle. Our public component interfaces must stabilize very early in development. When we begin to experience cascading reconstruction, we're already on a slippery slope. Ideally, the rebuild or "touch" of a lower component should not *require* the reconstruction of its dependents.

....

Pinball Sniffer

One company built an elaborate sniffing algorithm called Pinball. When changes occurred, it would find and rebuild every dependent executable. It derived its name, Pinball, from the processing effect it created. A simple database column change could initiate dozens of cross-system cascading reconstructions, the system equivalent of a pinball machine.

....

Interface patterns can practically eliminate cascading reconstruction.

Examining Object Interaction

Let's move up a level, into the software language, to see how it typically manages object interactions and information exchange. The run-time environment addresses objects in two primary ways: sometimes called the *strong reference* and the *weak reference,* or respectively, early binding and late binding. The standard disclaimer is that late binding diminishes performance, but desktop and server CPU power double every few months, so what does it matter?

Early Binding

Early binding, or strong referencing, consists of using typed object variables. It encourages hard-coding to the object's interface, because it's visible at design-time/compile time. We tend to gravitate toward the interface's visibility as a de facto implementation standard. A Visual Basic .NET example follows:

```
Dim oEmp as Employee                    'defining a variable
                                        ' of a defined, custom data type

oEmp = New Employee()
oEmp.Name = "David Birmingham"          'directly referencing the Interface
oEmp.UserID = "dbirmingham"
```

Both Name and UserID are specifically defined and implemented on the object's interface, limiting the venues within which the Employee object can operate. In fact, the only areas of the program that welcome the Employee object are those that implement Employee's explicit interface. Unfortunately, "Employee" is a *user* concept driven from the application level. It requires us to wire the Employee object's implementation directly into the software because it's the only way to access Employee functionality.

Late Binding

In contrast to early binding, *late binding* (or weak referencing) is supported by *untyped* object variables (such as a "void pointer" or *As Object*). The variable itself behaves as a container for any type of object. At run time, software will set its value with a reference to an object of any type. As such, no interface actually exists until run-time.

While the same object variable could support multiple objects, we defeat the power of late binding if we continue to pass around user-centric objects. In the preceding example, we could change the code as follows to use late binding:

```
Dim oEmp as Object                      'defining a variable of a
                                        ' generic data type

oEmp = New Employee
oEmp.Name = "David Birmingham"          'directly referencing the Interface
oEmp.UserID = "dbirmingham"
```

If we go this route, we haven't really bought ourselves anything. We only gain power from late binding if we make the interfaces of the participating objects conform to a pattern. Only then will all objects appear the same to the software.

Thus, if multiple objects support a property such as *Item()*, the software may successfully reference *Item()* on the container's interface. Then, the interface will behave just as though the software had referenced the contained object directly. Many industry gurus decry the weak reference. Many others swear by them; the following example shows why:

```
Dim mObj as Object                          'defining a variable
                                            ' of a generic data type

mObj = New Employee()
mobj.Item("Name") = "David Birmingham"      'indirectly referencing
                                            ' the Interface

mObj.Item("UserID") = "dbirmingham"
```

The interface-level visibility of *Name()* and *UserID()* has vanished. As developers, we like to browse our various property name options on an object interface. However, if we add uniqueness to the interface, we erode interoperability. Consider the following loop to replicate Employee information to a similarly defined User object. We'll define tcProp as the list of properties to copy. I have bolded the object references for clarity.

```
Private Sub Replicate(oTgt as Object, oSrc as Object, tcProp as TurboCollection)
  Dim strItem as String
  tcProp.MoveFirst()                        'go to the top of the list
' execute loop
  Do
    strItem = tcProp.Ref.Item               'get the current node's Item
                                            ' (the property Tag to copy)

    oTgt.Item(strItem) = oSrc.Item(strItem)
    tcProp.MoveNext()
  Loop While tcProp.More()                  'repeat until done
End Sub
  '***********************

Replicate (oUser, oEmp, tcProperty)
```

COM/DCOM/-CORBA typically encourage early binding scenarios while socket-based connectivity encourages late binding (or for that matter, no binding).

Do you see how late binding can enable *Replicate*'s reusability for *any* two objects? What if we were to expose *Replicate()* as a building block process, able to perform a replicate with any two building block entities? Can you see the behavioral pattern developing?

At every opportunity, our objective is to remove dependencies on the environment, consumers, components, and other entities. Each time we remove a dependency we move closer to metamorphism. Judicious use of late binding will achieve this goal.

Weak Reference Yields Weak Performance?

Some architects protest the weak reference (late binding) because of its "slower" performance. This is only partially true and can be overcome with otherwise efficient software design. However, even with poorly constructed software, remember that CPU power doubles every few months, so don't sweat it. By the time you read this, CPU power will have quadrupled since the time I wrote it, and even today I would use late binding in a heartbeat.

Table 2-1 shows a comparison of both types of binding based on particular programming issues.

Table 2-1. Contrasting Early and Late Binding

PROGRAMMING ISSUE	EARLY BINDING (STRONG)	LATE BINDING (WEAK)
Class Type	Known at run time, source code will accept only one object type without deviation	Unknown at run time, source code can accept any object type
Methods / Properties	Directly referenced on known interface	Indirectly referenced on generic interface
"Raw" Performance	Negligible difference, and bad design is a greater enemy to performance.	Negligible difference, and good design can always outdo early binding.
Benefit	Interface visibility	Interface conformity
Disadvantage	Interface changes can initiate rework elsewhere	Limitations on run-time debug visibility
Testing	Interface-bound test code	Interface-independent test data injectors
Interface availability	Design time and run time	Run time

*Late binding
enables
run time
metamorphism,
the foundation
of accelerated
reuse.*

Reuse versus Accelerated Reuse

We find simple reuse within an application when we share application rules, database access rules, algorithms, and the like (a good practice). Accelerated reuse occurs at the architectural level, because multiple applications share the same run-time coding constructs and components (a best practice). All new application designs can use it to jump-start, immediately leveraging predefined and pre-built components, Adapters, and other mechanisms.

Which is better? To break land speed records one time in a well-defined vehicle we can see and touch, or sit breathless in a metamorphic vehicle flying through cyberspace with increasing and repeatable success? The metamorphic vehicle's performance will only increase in speed on top of the technology. Its integrity and viability will gather strength with every use. The wired solution will also increase in speed, but its viability will gradually diminish. Trading off incremental speed for unlimited reuse is a poor bargain.

Now let's take a look at how structural patterns[1] provide the pathway to defining interface consistency.

Interpreting Structural Patterns

Structural patterns directly implement encapsulation, and enable metamorphism by building conformity and removing interface uniqueness. The three following patterns carry the most interface standardization power for immediate use by a development team:

- *Singletons* include Visual Basic 6.0's *App* object; the .NET Framework's *System* object; the API of a single run-time instance of a service, such as Microsoft Outlook; and serialized queues such as posting mechanisms to IBM MQSeries or MSMQ.

- *Adapters or wrappers* include a database engine driver such as Oracle or MS SQLServer; agents or published API brokers such as Crystal Reports or Microstrategy; Winsock for managing TCP/IP message exchange; and background services such as TCP/IP clients, network services, or network accelerators.

- *Flyweights* include aggregation of multiple objects to form a dynamic relationship, such as the Microsoft Word/Excel *Document* and supporting objects, the Microsoft ActiveX Data Objects (MSADO) suite, and now the MSADO.NET suite wrapped with the *DataSet* flyweight.

CROSS-REFERENCE *See* Design Patterns[1] *for more detail on the Façade, Bridge, Composite, Decorator, and Proxy patterns.*

The Singleton Pattern

A *Singleton pattern* can provide a central object interface to common utility functions (see Figure 2-5). Rather than force software code to specifically wire utility functions, we can access and treat such features like properties or methods on a utility object. Examples of these features would be calls to system functions, posting user status or messaging, common dialog boxes on the screen, and so on.

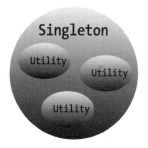

Figure 2-5. The Singleton pattern

A widely used purpose for the Singleton pattern is a *System* object, which we'll call *glb*. The *glb* class provides portability and stability to wrap the operating system API (e.g., Windows, Solaris, HP-UX, Linux, etc.) and remove operating system dependencies. For example, we could wrap Microsoft's common language runtime (CLR) into higher, portable abstractions rather than intimately tying our implementation to the CLR calls and extensions. Thus, if a given CLR feature is not completely supported on Unix, we can mimic it. Likewise, if a given Unix feature is not in CLR, we can mimic it as well.

No matter what the underlying language, operating system, or hardware, the *glb* object serves as a broker. If we find a great API implementation from a reference book or other source, we can include it in the *glb* object and expose the behavior in one manageable place. For example, standard DateTime formatting on Windows does not include the current Time Zone. We can derive this value from the operating system separately, but we can only merge it automatically into a single DateTime format in a utility environment like *glb*.

NOTE *Visual Basic provides the* App *run-time object as a Singleton for many run-time application values, such as the binary program's physical disk location* App.Path. *The .NET Framework actually calls it a* System *object.*

The *glb* object enables portability. This allows our software to remain stable on multiple operating systems because all system access must take place through a common interface. Software products with this capability exhibit enormous stability at the operating system level.

For example, the Visual Basic 6 environment has *App.Path* containing a textual string of the run-time directory path of a binary executable. VB6 also includes *DoEvents*, a global system call to fire all pending events.

By contrast, the .NET Framework provides a rather wordy version of the *App.Path*: `System.Reflection.Assembly.GetExecutingAssembly.Location` (which unfortunately includes the program name). Likewise, the VB .NET *DoEvents()* *equivalent is also verbose:* `System.Windows.Forms.Application.DoEvents()`.

However, a *glb* class can encapsulate these from direct access with simple calls to:

```
strPath = glb.Item("AppPath")
glb.Action("DoEvents")
```

We really don't care what happens under the covers, *no matter what the operating system.*

The stronger we make the *glb* object, the more it will exhibit the characteristics of an Adapter pattern, which is discussed next. While many of us have built Adapters for component interfaces, we might not consider creating one to address an entire operating system. However, this is one of many possible uses of a Singleton.

The Adapter pattern (a.k.a. Wrapper)

Faithful pattern adherence will free software from dependency on third party components, software language extensions, even the operating system.

The *Adapter pattern* puts a new face on an Application Programming Interface (see Figure 2-6). It controls the exposure of API features within the framework.

While Adapters quickly leash the behavior of highly complex APIs, the trick is in conforming all Adapter interfaces so they automatically plug-and-play elsewhere. We have no hope of achieving plug-and-play with a raw API.

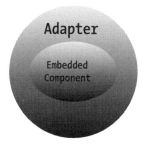

Figure 2-6. The Adapter pattern

Additionally, when the API rules without an Adapter, we tend to dig deeper and directly access its subtle nuances all over the framework. The more creative among us will provide "neat stuff" in one application area but neglect others. Going "API-direct" makes the API's presence latent, uncontrolled, and entangled throughout the software. The only way to consistently expose the most capability to the greatest number of consumers with the least risk is to wrap the API.

We should not stop with the large, complex APIs, the ones with big books to describe their features. Any component presenting itself as an external third party object (third party meaning one we did not create ourselves) invites an Adapter.

Adapters provide a repository to radically enhance an API's behavior, then package our API knowledge for reuse.

Adaptation

One developer was shocked when I suggested that the Microsoft Toolbox, full of unique APIs like the TextBox, CheckBox, and CommandButton, should have an Adapter for each control. He walked away shaking his head. I went back to my desk and shortly the vUIM was born. Take a look at the vUIMDemo in Chapter 1 and Project 4. Read more about it in Chapter 7.

This demo shows how we can conform all available technology into a metamorphic, reusable model by building similarities rather than accommodating uniqueness.

Every enterprise invariably encounters a need to upgrade, swap out, or transform large-scale systems to exploit greater performance and feature sets. Our consistency in applying Adapters provides protection when technology becomes obsolete, no longer meets application or performance requirements, or has a hot competitor with a stronger feature list.

The consistent use of Adapters protects our future freedom to change technologies without signifi- cant, even sweeping, impact.

Cottage Industries, Inc.?

On my desktop is an advertisement for a product claiming to scrub code. It veri- fies that all developers have implemented an API according to a team standard, and issues warnings if they haven't. The advertiser's statement tells the reader two things:

- It's okay to allow developers direct access to the various complexities of component API's anywhere in the software domain (a worst practice).

- The only way to control developer deviations is to sniff for and scrub them (automating a worst practice).

The Adapter washes away the need for such a product. By wrapping and exposing the component API through the Adapter's interface, all developers by default will use it correctly. The Adapter implementation will standardize the API's behavior, and will address extensions, enhancements, and bug fixes in one place.

Some vendors expose their API as several subclass interfaces. Whether each subclass requires an Adapter, or we can use only one, is a matter of best judgment. It will depend on how much functionality actually requires exposure. For a simple example, both Excel and Word have multiple public classes, but are easily managed with a single Adapter. ActiveX Data Objects, on the other hand, have enough complexity to justify multiple Adapters.

As a simple example, let's consider the Microsoft Toolbox's ComboBox control. This component allows us to load it with display values and associate them with indexed values. Thus we can drop-down, scroll, and otherwise manipu- late an on-screen list. How many different ways can a developer implement this interface, even with strong coding guidelines? In one project I counted over ten different ways to implement the interface, each one perfectly viable, but not consistent. Invariably, a developer would forget a simple facet of the ComboBox (introducing a bug), requiring revisit and recompiling. If another similarly imple- mented ComboBox elsewhere in the application had the same bug, it's now a ticking time bomb. An Adapter allows us to fix everything in one place *and* build a repository for the best practice in loading and managing the ComboBox.

Important Safety Tip: Custom ActiveX Controls Are *Not* Adapters

A custom ActiveX control may wrap an existing control's interface and enhance functionality, but it is still a component with the attendant overhead (CLSID, publication, registry, and versioning).

Adapters are embedded, compiled software used to wrap and control a component interface. They limit the interface's exposure to the remainder of the software, providing a single place to control its information and behavior. Custom controls are not embedded software, but another component interface entirely. They are external, disconnected and a poor choice to exploit the Adapter pattern.

 TIP *The Adapter's primary responsibility is to wrap interfaces inside the program, and requires* infinite *and sovereign control* over them. *The custom control does not fit this model.*

To provide initial, controlled exposure of key features, you can wrap a component's implementation. Then, internally automate or standardize other features. Ultimately, the Adapter will have complete control over the component's structural appearance and behavior. We then have the freedom to conform all Adapter interfaces to common interface rules. Typically, the software outside the Adapter will expect late binding, while the Adapter's internal implementation can use early binding. (See the discussions about early and late binding, earlier in this chapter.) We expect an Adapter to have intimate internal wiring to an API (early binding). We just don't want this wiring to escape the Adapter's walls.

We see Adapters everywhere. They're present in the capability of Visual Basic Runtime to wrap the complexity of Windows; in a device driver for a piece of hardware; and even in the ODBC driver for our favorite database engine. Each one provides a new face and a more accessible, rarified version of the underlying API. Our objective is to abstract these APIs to one more common level—*ours*.

Controlling interfaces with Adapters of our design is far easier (and more flexible) than directly accommodating the disparate designs of individual components.

The Flyweight Pattern

The *Flyweight pattern* wraps a group of disparate objects and recasts their interfaces into a single, common one (see Figure 2-7). Thus, a single Flyweight class can control a wide variety of components, each in turn controlling a particular system feature.

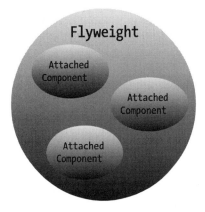

Figure 2-7. The Flyweight pattern

The Flyweight allows a single class to address many classes as one object, or to allow all of them to exhibit common behaviors without embedding behavior (or needing a separate Adapter for each).

Another subtle but powerful use of the Flyweight includes wrapping multiple, disparate objects for parameter-passing as a single object, rather than multiple objects of possibly unlimited count and type. Thus, if the return result of a function call could be several objects at once, the Flyweight can wrap all of them to return a single object. This increases the freedom of the function call to return one or more objects of varying types without ever changing the interface definition.

An additional usage is to wrap a number of components, each having disparate interfaces, but sharing common functionality as it relates to a higher level.

NOTE *The TurboCollection introduced in Chapter 1 can mimic the Flyweight pattern. We can snap together objects of various types using ParmNodes, contained by a TurboCollection instance to serve as the single Flyweight reference.*

Flyweights wrap many components with similar functionalities. For example, a reporting component suite might expose half a dozen subclasses for report generation, printing, document management, and other related features. A Flyweight serves to bundle and expose them as one.

We see Flyweights when APIs expose interface classes, such as the Visual Basic *err* object, the *RecordSet* class for ActiveX Data Objects, or the *Document* class for Word or Excel. Even though these objects can represent numerous supporting subclasses, their interface presence is lightweight. If we want to pass these around interchangeably, and independently, we'll need a way to wrap these with one more level of Flyweight abstraction.

CROSS-REFERENCE *See "The ParmNode Flyweight Container" example in Chapter 4.*

The objective is to wrap, control, and expose functionality—whatever the source. The Adapter and Flyweight are the leash for every external component interface, and the foundation for both encapsulation and metamorphism for their internal structures. This approach quickly stabilizes the wrapped component's structure and behavior.

Implementing Stabilization Rules with SOAL

We define object structure solely by its interface. Constantly changing interfaces destabilize structure and lead to uncontrolled behavior (the equivalent of building a highway on sand). Moving toward interface stability requires us to embrace the following firm structural rules, which we'll call SOAL (software on a leash):

1. *No global variables.* Wrap all data points minimally with a function call, but ideally with a Singleton pattern. This applies to all objects and simple, scalar variables. None should be "out in the open" or visible in scope to all other objects.

2. *Reduce the count of function calls per class.* The more classes, properties, and methods exposed on an interface, the more failure points multiply into the architecture. For example, two objects with two properties each have *four* possible failure points between them. Two objects with five

properties each have *25* possible failure points. Add another similar object for *125* possible failure points. The risk is multiplicative, not additive. *Simplify.*

3. *Reduce the total count of public classes.* Each public class requires its own CLSID. Reduce the total count (and registry clutter) of public classes, effectively reducing the count of CLSIDs associated with the component. *Simplify.*

4. *Reduce the parameter count and type.* Adding parameter references (optional or required) to expose new capabilities eventually erodes stability. Sometimes we like to enforce this rule by defining many little function definitions (contrary to Rule #2). *Simplify.*

5. *Ensure that no class interface directly exposes or implements application-level references.* Remove references to properties or methods like Employee(), AccountNum(), PressureValve(), CarPartNumber(), Seat(), FirstName(), LastName(), Address(), Country(), etc. These serve to hard-wire the unique and volatile application implementation into the object interfaces.

6. *Ensure that no class has a predetermined place in an application-specific class hierarchy.* We should never require Application Class A to always be a child or sibling to Application Class B. The application object "model" should be dynamic, malleable, and determined at run time.

7. *Identify each run-time object instance with a unique textual tag.* This is *not* the CLSID used to identify a class. It identifies an *instance* of a class, and will be globally unique across the framework so we can quickly pinpoint it.

At first glance, the first four rules seem virtually impossible to address. In the application-centric lifecycle of defining classes, hierarchies, and object models, these rules have no place. In the heated frenzy of development crunch, we would set them aside rather quickly. The last three rules are even more controversial because they are in general opposition to industry-accepted practices for application-object modeling.

XP Not a Likely Candidate

XP (eXtreme Programming) methodology promotes rapid rebuild and release of binary components, and focuses all team member workloads toward application-centric approaches. The product of an XP-based effort will be a viable solution, but doesn't guarantee high reuse across disparate solutions.

Application-centric software cannot comply with SOAL's rules, but interface patterns create nearly automatic adherence. Building class interfaces with a pattern rather than by specific definition moves the architecture toward a common structural goal: classes appear as building blocks.

Understanding the Interface Pattern

A pattern emerges if we carefully evaluate a sample of the interfaces in our current development environment. Start with the least functional utility component up to the highest-functioning multidimensional package interface. A common pattern, a thread of similarity, runs through all of them. Consider this sample:

```
Example 1: RetV = myFunc(myParm)
Example 2: oRef.MyMethod (objOne, objTwo, objThree, intParm)
Example 3: MyProperty(myParm) = myPropVal
```

The common patterns visible in these examples include the following:

- Property and Method roles

- Return values

- Parameters that are both complex and simple parameters

- Parameter passing

If we can support all of these aspects with a single interface pattern, we can use the pattern everywhere and instantly achieve structural stabilization.

Property and Method Roles

The two most common mechanisms, or roles, on any class interface are the *Method* (or function call) and the *Property* (or data encapsulator). With these functional windows into a class implementation, a consumer can drive any behavior. Rather than define a unique interface for each class, we discover the "common denominator" definitions and standardize on them.

If Properties and Methods are the most pervasive mechanisms, how can we represent them in abstract, common form? Essentially each class will require two public interface mechanisms, abstracting the Method role and the Property role. Once we create the object, consumers will use the Method role to initiate parameter-driven action. Consumers will use the Property role to modify/retrieve the object's state or internal information content. This strategy assumes the use of an Adapter to transform external directives into specific internal actions. The abstract Property/Method mechanisms will simply exchange information with an external consumer and see that it propagates internally to the appropriate internalized API behavior.

Properties

Regardless of what physical names appear on the class interface, the *role* is critical to the interface specification. Many components use *Item()* to abstract the *Property()* role. However, just as many will use names like *Value()*, *Text()*, *Key()*, *ListItem()*, and so on. The marketplace forever receives new tools and components with unique names for their proprietary *master property*.

If *Item()* is an unacceptable naming standard, use another alternative such as *Val()*. Whatever the final form, address the Property as a role or pattern. Just remember, this name will appear on all object interfaces so it should be intuitive. *Item()* is the most common implementation in third-party components, so will be the most transparent choice. A strong reason exists for the prevalence of *Item()* in the marketplace: a generalized public interface is a best practice!

For every API within our development domain (whether third party DLL/OCX, or canned screen controls), build an Adapter class and wrap it up.

Standardize legacy public classes interfaces with an Adapter to wrap them from view, then expose the Property role name as the interface. Doing so decouples components from the architecture and provides freedom to mix, match, remove, add, or otherwise manage objects in a generalized, pattern-based form rather than by explicit, bound reference. For rapidly moving or otherwise unstable interfaces, wrapping them *instantly* stabilizes the interface to all consumers.

Figure 2-8 depicts the *Item Interface*, with a number of *Test Objects (TO)* labeled A through F, wrapped by their respective Adapters. Two Adapters (wrapping objects TO-D and TO-F) directly exchange information through their *Item* interfaces. Adapters *TO-A* and *TO-E* receive information from an external source while B and C passively await data.

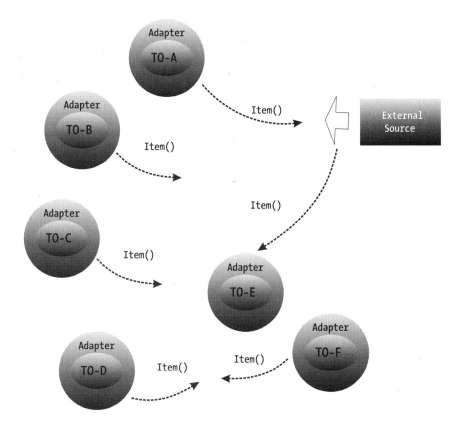

Figure 2-8. The Item interface

The *Item()* interface also enables a common information representation. Standardizing outbound information builds greater interface consistency. The objective is to drive Adapter behavior to what a consumer commonly expects, building conformity instead of accommodating uniqueness.

Some language environments implement the equivalent to Visual Basic's *Variant,* allowing all types (simple and object) of references to pass through them. This is impractical and not portable, so for simple data exchange, standardize on the *Item()* with *String/Text* for data. For complex (object) exchange, create another property called *Ref()*. This dynamic duo, *Item()* and *Ref()* will provide high flexibility for every consumer and still maintain our freedom to change their implementations beneath the interface.

Build conformity. Don't accommodate uniqueness.

Cascading Recursion

Interface patterns allow objects to perform transparent pass-through to downstream subscribers, presenting some interesting problems. What if one Adapter broadcasts inbound messages to all other Adapters, and another Adapter reflects each incoming message back to its source? If the first Adapter receives a message, it will forward it to the second, which in turn reflects it back. The first Adapter will then receive this message as an inbound message, and re-broadcast it, creating a deadlock-loop. This is *indirect recursion*. Some applications cascade a message through many layers of objects, inadvertently encountering an object already in the chain, creating a deadlock.

To avoid this recursion, include an internal switch in each *Item()* implementation. An example follows:

```
Dim blnLocked as Boolean                        'default value is False
Public Writeonly Property Item(sKey as String)
    Set ( sValue as String)
        If blnLocked then Exit Property         'if locked already then exit
          blnLocked = True                      'else lock it
          'Perform the usual Item stuff here, if it makes another call, it will be
          ' locked out of recursion
          blnLocked = False                     'now unlock it
    End Set
End Property
```

The blnLocked switch will keep the processing thread from indirectly returning into the object from another source. Rather than getting lost in an inter-object loop, this guarantees a processing thread's natural conclusion by denying accidental recursive re-entry. We could also implement a counter or other incremental limit (providing for more flexible but controlled re-entry).

Methods

Oftentimes, third-party component class interfaces have a host of method calls, each with a unique functionality and behavior. If software directly implements their unique definitions, it will forever bind the physical code to the object's implementation. If the object interface changes, or exposes new features, we must craft consumer code to either exploit or conform to the new interface. Conversely, if we can abstract the interface, consumer code will not have access to (or dependence on) specific capability references.

The Method role is an abstract initiator. It assumes certain common parameters as inputs and outputs. We can use a name similar to *Action()*, or *iCall()* as the Method role definition. Many patterns use *Action()*, so we'll reference it for discussion.

The *Action()* parameters tell which internal method to initiate and provide driving data, allowing consumers to control *Action()* with soft parameters in text form. By supporting textual commands and parameters, we enable text-based programmability. For example, with a textual semantic syntax using a noun/verb combination, we can translate it to an object/action combination. A semantic processor can select the object by name (noun) and drive the Action() (verb).

Figure 2-9 illustrates the *Action Interface*, which repeats the *Item* template for Figure 2-8. The figure shows the *Test Objects (TO)* labeled A through F, again wrapped by their respective Adapters. The *TO-D* object receives *Item* information from the return code of the *Action* call on the *TO-F* object. An external source also initiates an activity on Adapters *TO-A* and *TO-E* while Adapters B and C passively await instructions.

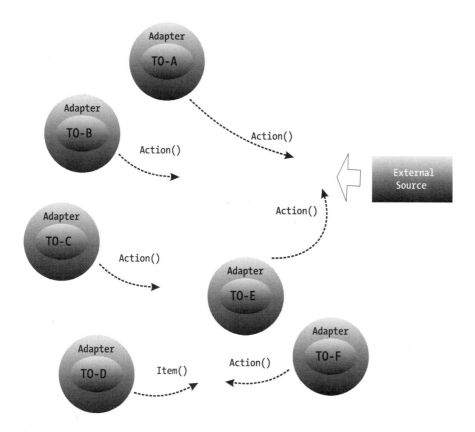

Figure 2-9. The Action Interface

Like the *Item* interface, *Action* standardizes the Adapters *to what the consumer commonly expects,* building conformity instead of accommodating uniqueness. The *Action* is also subject to indirect recursion problems, so it will need a locking mechanism, like *Item*. Wrapping components with an Adapter, exposing the *Item()* and *Ref()* properties and the *Action()* method, effectively creates an interchangeable, metamorphic interface pattern.

NOTE *Here is a frequent misunderstanding of this pattern: Developers like to use the automatic Property/Method "intellisense" of the Visual Studio environment. They like to hit the "dot" and have all available properties pop up for their selection. If we only expose Action and Item, developers will get confused, have to learn more, and it will slow them down.*

Fear of the unknown? I can only say this: Each time we apply this pattern, we experience flexibility and power that is totally unavailable with direct Method/Property references. After we apply it, we'll never go back. To get a taste of the advantages of this pattern, just complete the project exercises at the end of each chapter in this book.

We can still extend interfaces to benefit us where uniqueness has a localized purpose. However, if the framework must wire itself into the uniqueness, the interface presents no benefit, even if it's available at the touch of a "dot."

Nomenclature Faux Pas

The ultimate objective is universal meta-morphism. Conformity, not uniqueness, will achieve this goal.

In a large corporate client, a consulting team deploying the *Item()* and *Action()* naming conventions met significant, almost show-stopping resistance from the Information Systems department. It seemed that the corporation's business personnel used the term "*Action Item*" in reference to project management tasks, to a nearly nauseating level. The IS department felt, and rightly so, that implementing *Action()* and *Item()* would effectively institutionalize this persistent source of irritation. So, the consulting team settled on the names *iCall()* for the Method role and *iData()* for the Property role.

TIP *Use whatever works, but the selection must be consistent within a project and ultimately the enterprise.*

Parameters

After abstracting the Method and Property roles, we should also abstract their parameters. We might believe that methods and properties should have an unlimited potential for count and combination of parameters. However, this practice actually increases the potential for confusion, breakage, and eventual rework. Parameter proliferation and extension is a significant cause of behavioral destabilization. Simplification is the key to parameter definition control.

Consider the following interface:

```
Public Function ShowData(Optional ShowOff as Boolean=Nothing,
        Optional ShowDown as String=Nothing,
        Optional ShowMustGoOn as Object=Nothing,
        Optional ShowBiz as String=Nothing,
        Optional ShowTime as DateTime=Nothing,
        Optional ShowMe as enum=Nothing,
        Optional ShowBoat as MotionPicture=Nothing) as Object
```

We've now loaded this interface with lots of optional parameters. Consumers can invoke the function with any, all, or none of the parameters, so a consumer using *ShowMe* will never break. Consumers using *ShowBoat* might enjoy new functionality. If we need to add *ShowPreview* to the interface, we just include it right alongside the others. We have apparently reserved the freedom to infinitely extend it. Compare the requirements for invoking this function

```
    mRef = ShowData(ShowOff:=True)              'wired reference
```

versus invoking a pattern-based equivalent:

```
    strParm = "ShowOff=True"
    mRef = ShowData(strParm)                    'patterned reference
```

The first version in the preceding example enumerates all the parameters, and requires the calling software to know that a parameter called "ShowOff" actually exists, and must understand its data type. The second version will accept any textual string, so we can add any number of new parameters under the covers and the calling consumer can leverage any of them without changing existing code. This is because strParm's value could arrive from anywhere.

NOTE *We can sometimes use overloaded parameter lists for private base utilities and power tools, because these often stabilize quickly. We should avoid them for structural building blocks like Adapters, and always carefully consider our options before extending them.*

If we add or change a parameter (by name or type), we redefine the entire interface, not just the part that changed (and is no different structurally than adding a completely new Property or Method call). Its compilation will produce a new CLSID. With an overloaded interface, all consumers needing *ShowData's* services must undergo rebuild to take advantage of them.

Parameter variables fall into two broad categories: s*imple* and c*omplex*. A simple variable is just a scalar type (integers, character, byte, string, floating point, and so on). Complex variables are objects. When passing information directly into an interface, these functional separations work nicely. If simple information must persist in memory outside of the parameter context, an object may act as a container.

CROSS-REFERENCE *We'll use* simple *and* complex *as metadata-level keywords in Chapter 4.*

Compound Parameters

Interface patterns can also exploit *compound* parameters, using *Key/Value* pairs such as the following to inject varied parameter lists into an interface:

```
"ID=14|Employee=David|City=Dallas|State=Texas"
```

Here's the XML equivalent:

```
"<ID>14</ID><Employee>David</Employee><City>Dallas</City><State>Texas</State>"
```

We can inject a virtually limitless variety and count of simple parameter information with a single Property call. Each pair is a key and a value, separated by the equal (=) sign. We can separate each pair with the vertical bar (|) or with XML tagging. The calling consumer can include or exclude any parameter or place them in any order without affecting interface-level behavior. The underpinnings of the *Item()* call will parse the pairs and dispatch their values.

CROSS-REFERENCE *Project 7 in Chapter 7 will dive directly into activating XML.*

The XML equivalent includes common tagging syntax, also handy for pass-through from external sources (such as .NET Web Services). The XML version requires sandwiching the parameter value between two begin/end pairs as key values. The first tag will appear "as is" (e.g., <Tag>) and the second tag to appear as the first, preceded by a slash "/" (e.g., </Tag>). This is the simplest XML form, for "Message Oriented Middleware" (MOM).

The XML notation is more verbose than key/value pairs, but is a portable exchange standard, especially for complex structures. The "production" version of the TurboCollection supports XML automatically. This capability allows us to build highly complex structures, decompose them into XML, transmit them as strings (or even compressed text) over a socket port, and reconstruct them automatically. We can build an XML-ready hierarchical TurboCollection, with collections of collections hanging from each ParmNode. Furthermore, we can compress them into a single XML string with this:

```
strXML = tcTest.Item(strDelim:="<*>")
```

Then, we can reconstruct the original structure with the following:

```
tcTest = UnStringXML(strXML)
```

Note that between these function calls might be a single component interface or a firewalled network between two or more enterprises (Figure 2-10).

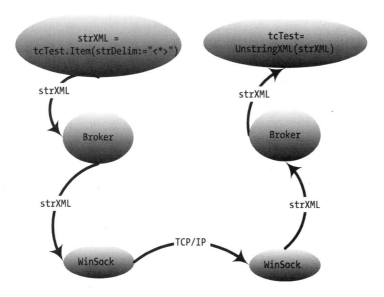

Figure 2-10. Transparent XML-structured parameter exchange

The compound key/value notation also creates the ability to *serialize* the object's internal information. By using the compound parameter syntax for serialization, the object can retrieve, assemble, and report internal values. For example, the following syntax would return the noted values:

```
strItem = objMine.Item("State|City")
    ' strItem is now = "State=Texas|City=Dallas"
strItem = objMine.Item("|")   ' get all the parameters
    ' strItem is now = "ID=14|Employee=David|State=Texas|City=Dallas"
strItem = objMine.Item("<State><City>")    'XML version
    ' strItem is now = "<State>Texas</State><City>Dallas</City>"
```

The pattern's inherent parameter power accelerates the implementation of information exchange capability. While this behavior is necessary for public interfaces, it will also accelerate information exchange and flexibility for private objects. Additionally, we can securely encrypt and transmit textual strings, eliminating the guesswork and attendant liability of letting lower-level connections do it for us.

The Item() and Ref() Interface Definitions

The *Item()* interface definition for Visual Basic (6.0) is as follows:

```
Public Property Let Item(Optional Key as String, Value as String)
Public Property Get Item(Optional Key as String) as String
```

And for Visual Basic .NET:

```
Public Property Item(Optional Key as String=Nothing) as String
   Get
   End Get
   Set (Value)
   End Set
End Property
```

The *Ref()* interface definition for Visual Basic 6.0 is as follows:

```
Public Property Set Ref(Optional Key as String, Value as Object)
Public Property Get Ref(Optional Key as String) as Object
```

And for Visual Basic .NET:

```
Public Property Ref(Optional Key as String=Nothing) as Object
    Get
    End Get
    Set (Value)
    End Set
End Property
```

Key is required unless *Value* is compound. *Key* is a simple variable containing textual tagging information. The Key will identify (or tag) an object's internal Property (for example, "ID" or "Name").

CROSS-REFERENCE *See the project at the end of Chapter 1 for an example of Property manipulation.*

A business-function object could tag business information (for example, "EmployeeID", "EmployeeName", "AccountNum"). A science or mathematics-related object could tag similarly named items (for example, "Species", "Mammal", "Fossil", "Sine", "Cosine", "Hyperbole", "Vector", and so on.). The objective is to hide the actual information behind the *Item()* interface and require the key to identify it for modification or retrieval. How the internal implementation stores, manages, and retrieves the information is of no interest to the consumer.

Value is required. It consists of a "Simple" string for *Item()* or "Complex" object variable for *Ref()* identified by the textual tag.

Parameter Forms

The Property Abstraction has these three possible forms, or actions, contingent upon the tag's context:

- *Let Item* supports simple values.

- *Set Ref* supports complex (object) variables.

- *Get* supports the retrieval of simple values (Item) or complex variables (Ref).

Some simple pseudocode illustrates the usage:

```
Dim strItem as String
    oEx.Name = pEx.Name                    'software-controlled behavior
    strItem = oEx.Item("Name")             'textual parameter value using Item
   pEx.Item("Name") = strItem              'same
```

or

```
    oEx.Item("Name") = pEx.Item("Name")    'direct interface calls with
                                           'no intermediate
```

or even further

```
    strItem = "Name"
    oEx.Item(strItem) = pEx.Item(strItem)  'direct interface calls with
                                           ' dynamic parameter value (preferred)
```

Likewise, with *Ref()*:

```
oEx.Ref("myKey") = pEx                     'Pass in the object by tag
oEx.Ref(strItem) = pEx                     'Or use a variable to hold the tag
oEx.Ref(pRef.Item("ID")) = pEx             'Or retrieve a value as the tag
```

These last examples provide the most flexibility because the notations stand on their own with no contextual information in the code. The value of the *strItem* variable will drive the behavior, and this value could arrive from literally anywhere. The *Key* is always a *Simple* variable, usually just a textual tag or "compound" string. This convention allows us to drop practically any object into the pEx and oEx references, and any parameter tag into the iKey and sKey variables. Doing so leads to abstract, externally programmable, and highly reusable code.

Objects will exchange information using abstract notations like pEx.Item = oEx.Action, *or* pEx.Item(iKey) = oEx.Item(sKey).

The Action() Definition

Here is a pseudocode definition and example of the *Action()* method for VB6:

```
    Public Function Action (ActionID as String,
                Optional ActionData as String,
                Optonal ActionObject as Object)  As String
```

And for VB .NET:

```
Public Function Action (ActionID as String,
                 Optional ActionData as String=Nothing,
                 Optonal ActionObject as Object=Nothing)  As String
```

An example of invoking *Action()* follows:

```
strRetVal = objMine.Action("Load","EmployeeID=129")
```

The *Action()* definition requires the following parameters:

- *ActionID* is required unless ActionData is compound, and is a simple variable containing a textual action, not a numeric value. This is typically an English-language action verb (for example, "Merge", "Load", "Find", "Print", "Compute", and so on). ActionID can also have modifiers (such as "MergeBuffer", "MergeContainer", "LoadBuffer", "LoadContainer", and so on) to provide additional action-level context. It generally behaves like a Key. The *Action()* method uses it to designate internal functions and dispatch work.

- *ActionData* is optional. It's a simple variable containing a behavioral speci-fication. It provides detailed data and instructions to fuel the Action, and is often a compound parameter. If ActionID is null (above) then ActionData must contain the ActionID equivalent.

- *ActionObject* is optional. It's an object variable and may carry an unlimited amount of highly varied information. Many actions require objects as parameters. Some may require more than one, so a Flyweight can wrap multiple, disparate objects and exchange them as a single object.

- *ReturnCode* is required. It's a simple string variable for notifying calling consumers of the action's completion status. The *Action()* and *Item()* will never create an error trap. They will always return a valid completion code. No exceptions. If the *Action()* must return one or more objects, it can use a Flyweight to wrap and return them under ActionObject.

Now, let's revisit the previous example:

```
strRetVal = objMine.Action("Load","EmployeeID=129")
```

This "Load" action could represent a data load for an employee record with the ID of 129, or a data load of 129 Employee IDs. The context and role of the object *combined with the parameters* determines the command's behavior. We can provide practically limitless programmability for the object and activate its capabilities with this simple interface pattern. At the metadata level, we can textually describe the action like a simple sentence, then break it apart for the interface behind the scenes.

XML Considerations

XML enables a single textual message to contain structural and behavioral metadata, embedding information and its own rules for handling directly into the message.

XML can target the message for delivery anywhere in the computing domain, whether a system, a specific interface or component, a server, or any identifiable computing resource. Upon arrival, XML receivers can accept, interpret, and dispatch the remainder of the message. No practical limit exists for how/where an XML message might be forwarded, addressed, replicated, enhanced, or modified as it progresses on its downstream journey.

Interface patterns automatically enable new and existing components for XML messaging. An XML processor can easily transform an inbound message into action identifiers, property values, or compound parameters. This is a powerful and flexible capability for any component.

 TIP Many software companies endure painful redesign to enable XML messaging, but patterns open this door at the architectural level. The .NET Framework's Web services and SOAP mechanisms directly use XML for exchange, which speaks of its power as an information interchange method. If we likewise exploit XML, our data pathways become more seamless.

Implications of Applying the Interface Patterns

Public interfaces have the most impact on delivery, so they must stabilize early. Since private class interfaces affect the structural integrity of internal frameworks, patterns give us freedom to develop private implementation without external impact (they hide and wrap what we do under the covers).

However, behavioral frameworks require structural conformity for efficiency, so don't assume that the interface pattern is applicable to public interfaces only. Full metamorphism is only achievable when all class interfaces conform. We should drive all software development toward patterns, and deviate from them only when the most significant exception arises. Each deviation creates a possible fracture point in the architecture that we will ultimately revisit more than once in the product's maintenance cycle.

We should require a reason to deviate from the pattern rather than make the pattern optional.

The pattern's *interface-neutral* nature provides a window to run-time programmability and offline testability. A testing consumer module can act as *a reusable test data injector*, not a hard-wired testing module. It can pass test parameters and systematically validate the component's interface and its sub-component features without direct connection to a master application.

The specification's flexibility and resilience is derived directly from the pattern of activity and parameter definition prevalent in all interface functions. By reducing these functions to *Item()*, *Ref()*, and *Action()*, the interface rises above the dominance of the technical APIs and software code, and eliminates dependency on application-level definitions.

We can perform regression-testing on every interface with a simple text injector, exercising and validating every object.

Don't miss the significance of this capability. In the common application architecture, whether monolithic or multi-tier, the software hard-wires and controls all behavior. However, when the interface *uniqueness* factor is eliminated, the software code has no hard anchor to wire itself *to*. The code instead must accept the role of *broker*, executing parameter delivery and initiating actions. It can only execute control indirectly, enabled and governed by the availability of parameters and events. These factors drive us toward reaping the following benefits:

High efficiency: Event-driven models use processes as short-term utilities, not driving threads hunting for work to do.

Low footprint: Interface conformity allows us to reuse frameworks and algorithms, radically reducing the code size across the architecture.

Context-sensitivity: When data rides in on an event-wave, we have a means to receive and interpret it, compare it to our current state, and otherwise take the processing opportunity to affect the run-time environment in the context of new and existing information.

Extensibility and interoperability: When adding a new API to the framework, we can quickly expose the new technology and integrate existing technology into it. Application-level features receive the benefit in every area. Software plug-and-play is real.

Fueled by behavioral metadata: When the architecture passively awaits instruction, then activates into structural and behavioral context using metadata, we have the seeds of a metamorphic architecture. Its extensibility and external programmability increase.

Wrap Existing Architectures

Interface patterns wrap legacy interfaces, and we can derive immediate benefit from implementing them.

Wrap legacy interfaces with a pattern-based Adapter, identify all consumers using the existing interfaces, sweep through them once and reconnect their interface calls to the pattern. This is a one-time-only action. The original interfaces under the Adapters may change, but their Adapters will protect the consumers from cascading reconstruction.

 TIP *We can gain immediate benefit from wrapping everything now. We can always go back later and tighten up the underlying implementations, without affecting the consumers!*

Here is a short tour of my personal experience in deploying metamorphic frameworks:

1986: *DataKernel*[2] was configured as an interface pattern broker. It enabled behavioral metadata to drive every aspect of a desktop application. No application-specific code existed in the software. Everything from the database model to the screen layouts and their behavioral rules were defined externally and accessed at run time. This combined the interface pattern with metamorphic concepts.

1990: The interface pattern was commercially proven inside science applications using assembly language, then C language, and then later burned into business-level production using C++, Java, J++, and Visual Basic.

1992: A large-scale, multi-platform, C language implementation used this pattern to separate an entire application layer from its data access layer, providing highly flexible adaptability to multiple data sources (and one of the first multiple-tier implementations in a distributed computing environment).

1997: *vMach*[3] extended DataKernel's capabilities using Visual Basic, ActiveX Data Objects, and various third-party accelerators. vMach users experienced feature-delivery by email, dropped in the same directory as the program, available immediately in the next run-time session.

These examples partially demonstrate a pattern's longevity, power, flexibility and supportability in any language, extensible across platforms.

Design Patterns[1] provides more detail and examples of each primary pattern.

SOAL, Take Two

Let's revisit the original set of Software On A Leash (SOAL) interface stabilization requirements presented earlier in this chapter. Now see how the interface pattern promotes and solidifies them:

1. *No global variables.* For even the simplest data elements, an Adapter can wrap and protect them from being trampled at run time. Access to internal object data is only an *Item()* / *Ref()* call away.

2. *Reduce the count of function calls per class.* The count is now three per class, the *Item()*, the *Ref()*, and the *Action()*.

3. *Reduce the total count of public classes.* Each component should, at the highest public level, expose itself as a single, simplified interface with Action/Item/Ref the only entry points. Ideally, a single proprietary public component should expose only one of each.

4. *Reduce the parameter count and type.* We now have a Key, Value, ActionID, ActionData, and ActionObject.

5. *Ensure that no class interface directly exposes or implements application-level references.* Note how property names like ref.Employee, ref.AccountNum, etc., now vanish, appearing instead as ref.Item("Employee") and ref.Item("AccountNum"). Application-level uniqueness is eliminated. Compound properties (one or many property-value pairs in the same call) further increase power and flexibility.

6. *Ensure that no class has a predetermined place in a business class hierarchy.* By eliminating the uniqueness of the object interface, it can reside transparently anywhere (discussed next).

7. *Identify each run-time object instance with a unique textual tag.* This is the easiest part. It involves simply defining a common textual tag key as the identifier key, and a unique text ID as the value. The key-value pair could be something as simple as "ID=*number*", or as context-sensitive as "ID=Employee" (for a business-specific Employee object). The flexibility remains. A framework will need identifiers like this to organize and find objects after their creation.

The interface pattern is the foundation for building the most flexible and resilient interfaces in the marketplace. Once we stabilize interfaces within their boundaries, we can begin to drive toward constructing resilient, pattern-based behavioral frameworks and have a powerful inventory of building blocks.

Managing Resources

Structural viability is useless without the ability to quickly manufacture and manage objects as resources. Basic object creation—called *instantiation*—is usually covered in the language environment with a *New()* operator of some kind (building the object in physical memory at run time). The class internal implementation can also initialize its own defaults and prepare itself for operation. Creational patterns directly support these activities.

Sometimes the software will create, use, and immediately destroy an object. Perhaps other modules will exchange the object, browse its contents, and share its functionality, even until the run-time environment terminates completely. Creating the object is only half the work; we must keep track of it so we can later destroy it. We also need efficiency to recycle utility objects, because many times we construct an object, use it, and throw it away only to create one exactly like it moments later in a deeper function call.

Classes requiring multiple, even unlimited, instances are typically created in one of two ways: (a) freestanding mode or (b) through a Factory (discussed in the next section and addressed in the Factory section of the Chapter 1 Project).

Dr. Watson, I presume?

In freestanding mode, we simply call the *New()* operator or *CreateObject()* function whenever required. This loose creation control often leads to unpredictable behaviors, memory leakage, and performance drag. When running for long durations, leakage and fragmentation will slowly erode memory resources and performance. Also, a program can crash if an object terminates without permission or if the program terminates with orphaned objects. The proliferation of non-terminated objects causes them to default into the run-time environment's "black hole," will create performance drag, and often can spontaneously combust when the program exits.

The only time a freestanding creation is *usually* acceptable is if it happens as part of the creation of another, controlled object. The same rules apply here: the Adapter's private implementation can do what it wants while it never escapes the Adapter's walls (and the Adapter should not arbitrarily share its spontaneously created objects).

Finally, the program must maintain control of every new instance of an object in memory, and must be able to account for those instances when the program closes. Centralizing object creation and destruction with safety and consistency (especially within a loose framework context) requires a *Factory* pattern.

This section will discuss the following *creational* patterns:[1]

- Factory

- Abstract Factory

- Prototype

Without a Factory as a clearinghouse for memory management, we lose track of valuable resources and invite runaway memory leakage.

The Factory

A *Factory* is a reservoir for managing the creation and destruction of one or more classes, usually in the same functional grouping. You were exposed to the Factory pattern in Chapter 1's project. The Factory counts each time a creation or destruction occurs and provides a statistical way to control memory leakage.

Factories can appear at any level, such as within an object, a subcomponent, etc. We can have so many Factories, in fact, that we can spend as much time managing them as the objects themselves. One solution is an *Abstract Factory*. This Singleton instance can broker creation services for the entire architecture so consumers don't have to directly access a Factory. (Singletons were discussed earlier in this chapter.) Each Factory registers itself to the Abstract Factory with permissions to broker its components.

Abstract Factories

An *Abstract Factory* includes a master structure to contain Factory references and allows the run-time environment to register new ones. Later we can use the Abstract Factory to request an object of an internally registered type. The Abstract Factory will broker the request to the given Factory and return the result. While it delegates the counting of created/destroyed objects to the individual factories, it can still monitor the counts either as a central ledger or as a means to account for all objects prior to shutdown. (Recall the Factory exercise in Chapter 1). Figure 2-11 displays an example of Factory delegation.

A program needs a direct and reliable way to create, count, and destroy objects. This can be a mammoth undertaking for many run-time environments, so don't diminish its importance or impact. Additionally, don't build a creation/destruction engine and later bolt on unrelated responsibilities. Its sole responsibility is creating, counting, and destroying. It's an accounting system where the balances of object counting ledgers must *zero out* before closing the books and exiting the program.

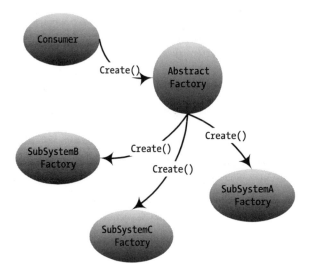

Figure 2-11. An example of Factory delegation

We don't need a central Factory to host the creation details for all objects great and small. We need to control their creation and destruction close to home, as long as we avoid a direct call to *New()* or *CreateObject()* outside the individual factories.

Sowing Fractal Seeds

The Abstract Factory provides a single point of reference to broker objects from other factories, without physically hosting the Factory details.

When a class manufactures one of its own kind, we have *fractal creation behavior* (a good thing). A class is always better equipped to understand its own creation and initialization needs, so we should not externalize them. By driving creational behavior into the class itself, we eliminate the need for any other class to know about or control the details of its creation. Thus, if one object exposes the same creational pattern as another, an Abstract Factory can treat them the same rather than requiring any special object-related initialization knowledge.

This is important, because with fractal creation each class can create its own kind independently, so the only functionality we really need is an Abstract Factory as a reservoir. Very large and complex environments have multiple layers of Abstract Factories. The key is to give a calling consumer a reliable, consistent means to receive a valid instance of any class, regardless of how it is delegated behind the scenes.

Using an interface pattern, we expose a *Create()* abstraction on each class (e.g., *obj.Ref("New")*) and the first instance of it is a *fractal seed*. The fractal seed is a Singleton reservoir to generate all subsequent instances. As such, a Factory can delegate creational behavior into the seed.

The companion to the fractal *Create()* is *Replicate()*. With a *Replicate()* function, the object can both create its own kind and copy (all or part of) itself into the new instance. The plan is to perform a "Replicate" *as the class understands it* (not every class will copy all details between its instances). Replication is also an excellent way to propagate information between computing environments. For example, if a version of the architecture is running on a Sun machine with another running on a Windows NT machine, replicating objects across these platforms provides transparency to consumers within each environment.

If each class can self-create, then we can easily build factories to manufacture them, or Abstract Factories to broker the factories. In fact, each fractal seed is its own factory, so we have options at many brokerage levels as to object creation. We simply must remember that the object as a fractal seed represents a "factory" role, not "deployable object" role.

Of course, using an interface pattern to support this configuration requires an Adapter or FlyWeight for each creatable entity. The interface pattern for *Create()* is supportable with the equivalent *Ref()* key to return an object: *mref.Ref("Create")*. We can also use *mref.Ref("New")*.

```
nRef = mRef.Create()          'extends the interface – not good
nRef = mRef.Ref("New")        'conforms the interface – good plan
nRef = mRef.Ref("Create")     'also conforms the interface –
                              'another good plan
```

Dynamic Object Models

When we place the masterstroke on our carefully woven object model (the draft, that is) we are ready to build it into the machine. The decision we make now will drive the construction process, so wisdom is paramount.

In an application-centric approach, we'll build the object model directly into the software. Once we're finished, we must place it in front of the user, pen in hand, ready to write down their first list of enhancements. The model is already on the chopping block. We just don't know it yet.

The architecture-centric model lets structural metadata drive the creation of the object model at run time, a more responsive and resilient approach, because it moves the user-centric volatility into an externally programmable forum.

Such a dynamic object model requires enhancing the "Create" capability with the reference of the new object's "Parent". Will we have to extend or modify our interface pattern? No, after all, building complex structures sometimes takes several steps. In Visual Basic .NET, for example:

```
oNew = mRef.Ref("Create")
oNew.Ref("Parent") = Me
```

Every Method and Property call should have consistent interface and behavior. This self-contains error control and conforms behavior to a common center.

If the object has siblings/peers, we can add them also. Let's set up a four-dimensional *TimeMachine* reference (WXYZ), where our "oNew" object represents the "W" or *When* hub and three additional objects represent spatial X/Y/Z coordinates. Here's an example:

```
oNew.Ref("PeerX") = mRef.Ref("Create")
oNew.Ref("PeerY") = mRef.Ref("Create")
oNew.Ref("PeerZ") = mRef.Ref("Create")
```

We can create massively complex structures with these patterns, and drive their assembly with metadata. We can build each of the preceding notations with structured text (see Figure 2-12).

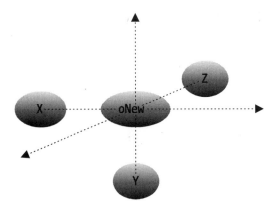

Figure 2-12. A dynamic TimeMachine *structure*

 NOTE *If the object is not aware of its structural position until run time, its internal implementation will have no expectation of parent/sibling relationships or its position in a "tree."*

In the common application architecture, we often find the object model, or *class hierarchy* (as defined by the application level), directly wired into object-level software. When user requirements result in changing the model, we must sift the entire program for impact, rewire it to accommodate the change, and then perform a rebuild and redeployment. Because inheritance and polymorphism enforce structural uniqueness, they actually hinder us in removing application-centric references from the software. However, with the dynamic object model, metadata and run-time context determine an object's structural location, further enabling the building-block theme and opening the door for run-time program-mability.

Within a given object's context, we can navigate immediately to our own parent, siblings, and children. We can automatically navigate to the "top" of our current object chain with a simple recursive *Top()* function. This further extends the interface pattern without changing the interface itself.

The *Top* function will simply return its own *Parent.Top*. If no Parent exists, then the calling thread has arrived at the top member. It will return a reference to itself, cascading this value back through the calling thread. No matter how many levels deep an object rests in the chain, it can always find its *topmost* parent, as shown in the following VB. NET snippet.

```vb
Private Function Top() as Object
  If Parent is Nothing then       'I have no parent, so
    Top = Me                      'I'm the top
  Else
    Top = Parent.Ref("Top")       'else find the top on my Parent
  End If
End Function
'*****************************************
Private Function Parent() as Object
  Parent = myParent               'reference to my parent object
End Function
'*****************************************
Public Property Ref(strKey as String) as Object
  Get
    If strKey = "Parent" then     'if need the parent reference then
      Ref = Parent                'just return it
    Elseif strKey = "Top" then    'else find the Top
      Ref = Top                   'and return it
    EndIf
  End Get
Set (ByVal Value)                 'set my parent
 If strKey = "Parent" then        'accept parm and set local reference
    myParent = Value
    EndIf
End Set
End Function
'*********************************
```

Now let's let the referencing automatically find its way to the top, as shown here:

```
dim oTop as Object
oTop = Ref("Top")        'recursively climbs the model to the topmost reference
```

Dynamic models often appear structurally as object clusters, not one-dimensional trees. Figure 2-13 depicts multidimensional, dynamic object models as clusters of clusters, or frameworks within frameworks. It is highly fluid and dynamic in behavior, structure, and complexity.

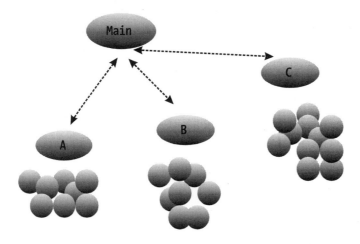

Figure 2-13. Class clusters

With loosely coupled object relationships, we increase our options to create objects anywhere they are useful, rather than part of a wired, predefined model.

The code snippets in Listings 2-1 and 2-2 can be placed in a common Visual Basic .NET class. We'll create three additional classes, TOA.vb, TOB.vb, and TOC.vb, with the required code snapshot in each. This example is included in this chapter's project exercises.

When an object has no predefined parent/sibling relational position or location, it qualifies to become a building block.

Listing 2-1. Dynamic Model Mechanics

```
'TOA.vb code SnapShot
Option Explicit On
Option Compare Text
'We need a place  for properties (Refs and Items)
Private tcProp As New TurboCollection()
'*******************************************************************
```

```vb
'Now let's define the Item() property using the tcProp as the repository
Public Property Item(ByVal strK As String) As String
Get
        On Error Resume Next
        Item = vbNullString                 'prepare if not found
        Item = tcProp.Find(strK).Item       'find the item and return the value
 End Get
 Set(ByVal Value As String)
        On Error Resume Next
        Dim pWrk As ParmNode                 'working storage
        pWrk = tcProp.Find(strK)            'find the property if already there
        If pWrk Is Nothing Then             'if not, then add it
          tcProp.AddItem(Value, strK, strK) 'add the property with the key
            pWrk = tcProp.Ref               'get the property reference again
          End If
        pWrk.Item = Value                   'set the Item to the new value
       End Set
End Property
 '********************************************************************
   'Now let's define the Ref() with the tcProp repository
   '********************************************************************
Public Property Ref(ByVal strK As String) As Object
Get
    On Error Resume Next
    Dim oSeed As Object                     'prep in case "New"
    Dim oNew As Object                      'also in case "New"
'**************************
    If strK = "New" Then   'is this a New request
        oSeed = tcProp.Find("Factory").obj 'yes then get the seed - it was
                                            'added when we built the object
        If oSeed Is Me Then                 'am I the seed?
        oNew = New TOA()                    'yes then make a new one
        'use TOB, TOC as required in each class
        'don't miss the significance of the next statement, because it allows
        'every created object to know where its factory is - so we can build
        'new objects fractally from existing ones without accessing the
        'abstract factory
        oNew.Ref("Factory") = Me           'make this object's Factory = Me
        Ref = oNew    'and return it
Else
        Ref = oSeed.Ref("New")             'otherwise, find the seed elsewhere
        End I
```

```
    ElseIf strK = "Top" Then                    'Asking for "Top" ?
            Ref = Top()                         'call Top() and Make It So
    Else
            Ref = tcProp.Find(strK).obj         'Otherwise, return the
                                                'reference as found
                                                'on the tcProp
        End If
End Get
    '***Define the Set form of the Property*******************
    Set(ByVal Value As Object)
    On Error Resume Next
    Dim pWrk As ParmNode                        'working reference
    pWrk = tcProp.Find(strK)                    'find the Ref if already there
    If pWrk Is Nothing Then                     'else build it
       tcProp.AddItem("", strK, strK)           'add it to the properties list
       pWrk = tcProp.Ref  'get  the Ref
    End If
    pWrk.obj = Value                            'set the Obj to the new val
    End Set
End Property
    '*****************************************************************
'Now let's define the Top function call -
    '*****************************************************************
    Private Function Top() As Object
        On Error Resume Next
        Dim oTop As Object                      'working storage
        Dim oParent As Object                   'local parent
        oParent = tcProp.Find("Parent").obj     'find my parent
        If oParent Is Nothing Then              'if I don't have one then
          Top = Me                              'I'm the top!
        Else
          oTop = oParent.Ref("Top")            'otherwise look on my Parent
          If oTop Is Nothing Then               'not Found?
             Top = Me                           'then I'm the Top!
          Else
             Top = oTop                         'Otherwise use Found Value
          End If
        End If
      End Function
    '*****************************************************************
```

Now that the object-level structural wiring is in, let's build a test case and exercise it.

Listing 2-2. Factories and Dynamic Relationships

```
Option Explicit On
Option Compare Text
'Define the Factory collection
'********************************************************************
'Let's provide a collection as a repository for the Abstract Factor
Private tcFactory As New TurboCollection
'********************************************************************
'Let's provide a place to add our seeds - each its own factory
'********************************************************************
Private Sub AddSeed(strSeedName As String, oSeed As Object)
On Error Resume Next
 tcFactory.AddItem ("", "TOA", "TOA")          'add the element
 tcFactory.Ref.obj = oSeed                     'include seed object
 oSeed.Ref("Factory") = oSeed                  'let seed know it's the factory
 oSeed.Item("Role") = "Seed"                   'let's make a role as well
End Sub'************************************************************
'Now set up a way to make a new object from the factory
'********************************************************************
Private Function FactoryNew(strSeedName As String) As Object
  On Error Resume Next
  FactoryNew = Nothing
  Dim pSeed As Object
  pSeed = tcFactory.Find(strSeedName).obj     'find the seed by name
  FactoryNew = pSeed.Ref("New")               'let the seed create it
End Function
'********************************************************************
'Now let's do a code walkthrough
'********************************************************************
On Error Resume Next
 Dim oNew As Object
 Dim oNewToo As Object
 Dim oNewMore As Object
 Dim oTop As Object
 Dim oParent As Object
'********************************************************************
 AddSeed ("TOA", New TOA)                      'add some objects to the factory
 AddSeed( "TOB", New TOB)
 AddSeed ("TOC", New TOC)
'*******************************************************************
'Now let's add a new TOA to our local environment and play
' around with it
```

```
'*********************************************************************
    oNew = FactoryNew("TOA")          'call factoryNew to get one from the seed
    oNew.Ref("Parent") = Me           'set its Parent to this Form object
    oNew.Item("Role") = "First"       'it's role will be "First" in the chain
    '*********************************************************************
     oNewToo = oNew.Ref("New")        'now I need another object, but I'll
                                      ' manufacture it fractally off one of its
                                      ' own kind - but remember that each object
                                      ' created from the Seed knows where the Seed
                                      ' is to go get more because we initialized
                                      ' its "Factory" when we created it
    oNewToo.Ref("Parent") = oNew      'assign this parent to the "First" above
    oNewToo.Item("Role") = "Second"   'and make its role the "Second" in line
      '*********************************************************************
    oNewMore = oNew.Ref("New")        'let's repeat the above with a third object
    oNewMore.Ref("Parent") = oNewToo  'parent is the "Second" above
    oNewMore.Item("Role") = "Third"   'and this one's role is "Third"
       '*********************************************************************
   oTop = oNewMore.Ref("Top")         'now if we ask for the "Second's" Top,
Debug.Writeline( oTop.Item("Role"))   'we'll get the "First"
'*********************************************************************
   oTop = oNewMore.Ref("Top")         'ditto for this reference
   Debug.Writeline( oTop.Item("Role") 'will be "First" for its Top
'*********************************************************************
   oParent = oNewMore.Ref("Parent")   'But if I ask for the "Third's"
                                      'Parent, I will
   Debug.Writeline(oParent.Item("Role")) 'get "Second
```

Take the code in Listing 2-2 through a single-step and watch how it applies the abstractions to build the virtual object model from thin air. While I am manipulating oNew, oNewToo, and oNewMore as objects in a single context, the reality could be much more dynamic, spanning subsystems and frameworks across the architecture. Once we have our virtual model builder in place, we can enable new and existing objects with the patterns to participate. The .NET Framework provides for true inheritance, meaning we can formulate a pattern and inherit it for greater extensibility and a much thinner code footprint.

Context-Sensitive Creation

Often a *Create()* function will require additional creation-context information, such as special states, initialization parameters, etc. The typical syntax of the *Instruction* contents is a compound property, like so:

```
Key1=Key1Value|Key2=Key2Value|KeynKeynValue…
```

For example:

```
"Term=45|User=2125|FormID=9191|IsModal=False|Startup=False"
```

Or use this XML-compliant syntax:

```
"<Term>45</Term><User>2125</User><FormID>9191</FormID>"
```

In the following example, note how the "Key" parameter carries the "Create" action and the other parameters are modifiers to the action:

```
oRef = myObj.Ref("<Key>Create</Key><Term>45</Term><User>2125</User>")
```

Core versus On-Demand Classes

Two primary class categories are visible to the Abstract Factory. One category is the set of core embedded building block classes within the primary architecture. The other includes classes that *could be* a part of the program's run-time session, but will be registered and created on demand by optional plug-and-play components. The on-demand classes could be anything from an ActiveX Data Object Adapter to Excel/Word or even a connector to an enterprise application. The key is that the program will prepare the core classes for fractal self-creation right away. It will only prepare others on demand.

 CROSS-REFERENCE *The Factory project exercise in Chapter 1 exhibits core and on-demand creation.*

Objects allowing only one instance will always return the master instance rather than creating a new one. The behavior is transparent to the Factory.

At startup, the Abstract Factory will fill its registration collection with the core classes, and then allow external processes to register other classes as needed. It will simply require the *fractal seed instance* of each class plus *its class name* as a search key. This allows all dynamic classes, custom component wrappers, and other non-core classes to gain loosely-coupled access to Abstract Factory services transparently, by exposing a simple "*Create*" interface definition. Thus, it allows all consumers one-stop access to all class Factories. The critical component of the Abstract Factory is the collection of fractal seeds. Its run-time performance requirements need more than a simple language-level collection.

 CROSS-REFERENCE *The run-time performance requirements for the Abstract Factory leverage the TurboCollection, which is discussed in Chapter 4.*

Each Factory should provide *direct* or *soft object destruction*. Direct object destruction means *terminating* it from the run-time environment. Soft object destruction means removing it from use and placing it into an available pool for recycling. This allows the Factory to visit the available pool for recycled objects before building a new one. We then manage memory fragmentation *and* boost performance by eliminating processing overhead for high-frequency create/destroy operations.

The StringAdapter (in the Project Exercises vTools.DLL) is an excellent candidate for soft destruction because of its high utility and frequency of use.

The Prototype

When deploying a new technology, we need a way to jump-start its interface for quick software integration. If we expose programmability, we can inject macro statements and have it translate these into greater detail for its hidden API. Each time we manufacture a new object, we program additional detail to make it unique.

The *Prototype pattern* standardizes and exposes these requirements to quickly wrap, implement and introduce new capabilities with a shortened deployment cycle. This represents a *design-time* use of the Prototype pattern depicted in Figure 2-14.

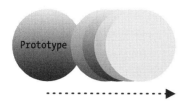

Figure 2-14. The prototype

Another, less pervasive use of this pattern is in predefining a fully structured, complex object for on-demand utilization at run time. The vUIMDemo introduced in Chapter 1 is an example of a Prototype *Form* object in the Microsoft Visual tool set. Its Prototype can represent all Forms, with externally programmable appearance and behavior. Thus, with each instance we can paint an *apparently* new Form, but it's really the same, fully integrated Form with a different face.

We can create prototype programmable objects multiple times in multiple roles. While an infinitely programmable object is not necessarily practical, many aspects of class creation are easily programmable from external sources.

The Prototype provides a way to build the largest percentage of reusable functionality directly into the code. It also maximizes programmability to support run-time demands. With building blocks, robust resource construction, and management and pattern-based interfaces, we are now ready to re-mold the software structure into a more powerful super-pattern: the metamorphic model.

Comparing Application and Metamorphic Models

The common application architecture will address object modeling and class hierarchies from the application-centric, user-driven approach. The metamorphic model considers the user's wishes and supports them without formalizing them as an object model.

To further compare the two models, consider the characteristic of object persistence, an object that saves (or *serializes)* its data and state to a more permanent storage location. In the application model, such an object might expose a persistence reference such as *Save()*. The object then internally wires itself to an I/O model and directly manages its own storage activities (insert, update, delete, etc) at intimate details, usually directly embedding SQL statements. Externally, the behavior might *seem* automatic, but over time this object and various similarly configured objects will step on one another, unable to consistently coordinate database transactions. Adding cross-talk features to avoid collision only increases complexity. Troubleshooting becomes problematic.

The metamorphic model views persistence as just another service. A given object is not responsible for I/O, only for the *serialization* of its internal state. (See Figure 2-15.) A broker can command it to serialize, receive the object's structured information, and pass it on to an I/O service. The given object doesn't know or care why the broker wants the information. Serialization is a derivative of replication, because if we can extract the object's information and state, we can also inject it.

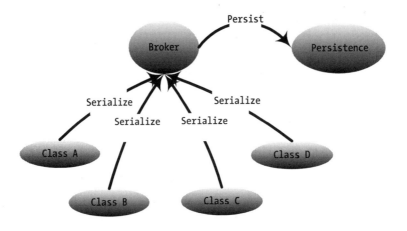

Figure 2-15. Serialization

This pattern of activity is repeatable among all objects requiring I/O, but the objects themselves are passive, not active in the process. Thus, we allow all objects to focus on their roles without clutter or entanglement with details of other subsystems (in this case, I/O).

This aspect of the metamorphic model is scalable, flexible, and reusable; representing one way we can rapidly include objects into a framework and immediately participate in reusable services. This sort of decoupling is the ultimate goal, such that all Adapters and interfaces speak to each other over a common process highway and language, regardless of their role or logical/physical location.

Rather than address the product as a single, cohesive framework, it is far easier to build role-based, thematic frameworks that behave as independent brokers. The virtual architecture illustrated in Figure 2-16, is a collection of loosely coupled frameworks, each providing *organization*, *interpretation*, and *activation*. An Adapter wraps each interface, enabling both transparency and interchangeability within the behavioral control model. Ideally, each framework exposes services through a textual instruction set.

The Figure 2-16 depiction oversimplifies its actual structure; imagine that each of the frameworks can talk freely to one another, and that other—even disparate—frameworks can be dynamically inserted/removed with instant plug-and-play. It's a multidimensional matrix, where each individual framework is a manageable subset, while the whole structure is as dynamic and extensible as our most volatile and demanding users.

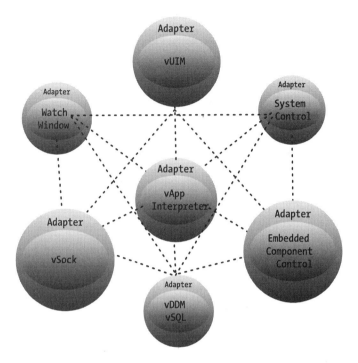

Figure 2-16. The virtual architecture

Metamorphism enables each framework implementation to shift its own identity or role across multiple contexts. Interface patterns allow a behavioral control model to easily manipulate all Adapters, and therefore, all objects, shifting between them transparently without regard to their underlying implementations.

In one-dimensional object models and hierarchies, often a rarified or specific group of objects will enjoy access to carefully crafted algorithms or repeatable processes. Attempting to expose other objects to these algorithms often results in brittle or spurious behaviors. A more systematic approach involves building all object classes with common, repeatable interface patterns. We then extend their individual interfaces later for performance or specific purposes as long as they continue to support the common, interoperable patterns. This opens algorithms and processes to a larger set of objects.

A virtual architecture provides consistent behavioral control across all core architecture objects and components. Each new consumer or component enters the behavioral model speaking a common language and gains immediate access to mature services, algorithms, and processes. Scalability, reusability, and flexibility are therefore the nature of the framework, not the characteristic of a few classes.

Project 2–Structures

To close the chapter, our second project provides a light introduction to some high-speed parsing and dispatch control. It will lead in to the following chapter on best behavior. The primary concepts discussed are as follows:

- StringAdapter class

- Text file manipulation and interpretation

The project listing download includes the VB6 version and VB. NET version. In the download's directory structure, navigate to *VB6* or *VBNET*, then to the *Project2-Structure* directory. Double-click on the ProjectTwo project file or .sln file. All classes mentioned in the following examples are contained within this directory.

ProjectTwo includes a number of class modules and a main module used as a skeleton to browse and manipulate their activity. Double-click on the ProjectTwo project file and it will load the project skeleton. The main modules contain the project examples and some of the program code discussed in the chapter.

StringAdapter

The *StringAdapter* class module wraps all string utilities and streamlines string manipulation in general. Its primary power, however, is the ability to rapidly parse on any token boundary and present a string's contents for browsing.

```
Dim strA As New StringAdapter
Dim strTest As String
strTest = "This is a great string"
strA.Parse strTest, " "
```

These statements will cause the StringAdapter to accept the string, parse it with a delimiter of space (" ") and load an internal TurboCollection with the parsed results. Browsing the results is simple, as you can see here:

```
If strA.DataPresent Then
    strA.MoveFirst()                           'reset to first token
    Do
      Debug.Writeline( strA.Item)              'Output the token value
      strA.MoveNext()                          'browse to the next token
      Loop While strA.More()                   'keep going while more tokens
End If
```

This simple loop will produce the following output in Visual Basic's *Output* window:

```
This
is
a
great
string
```

Conversely, the *Concat* function will put the string back together in its original form, replacing its delimiter with whatever is necessary. Here's the result:

```
strTest = strA.Concat("|")
Debug.Writeline( strTest)
```

Now strTest will contain the following information:

```
This|is|a|great|string
```

Next, let's say we want to browse the string and replace several items with another value. Here's how to do this:

```
strA.Parse strTest, "|"                     'break apart on the "|" boundary
If strA.DataPresent Then                     'check for Info
strA.MoveFirst()                             'move to first one
Do
  If strA.Item = "a" Then strA.Item = "not a"     'swap out the 'a' value
  If strA.Item = "great" Then strA.Item = "bad"   'swap out the 'great' value
    strA.MoveNext()                          'get the next one
  Loop While strA.More()                     'until all done
End If
strTest = strA.Concat(" ")                   'recombine the string, separate with space
```

Now strTest contains:

```
This is not a bad string
```

Another useful feature of StringAdapter involves finding tokens rapidly on an already parsed string. It simply passes through the TurboCollection's *Find* function and returns a Boolean True/False, like so:

```
If not strA.FindToken("Great") then Debug.Writeline( "Not There!")
If strA.FindToken("String") then Debug.Writeline( "Found It")
```

The StringAdapter is a core class, so it will require a high-speed interface but still exhibit the same behavioral and structural consistency promoted by the TurboCollection. Anything the TurboCollection can do (now, or later) will be available to the StringAdapter's internal implementation.

Because the StringAdapter is so pervasive and a complex component on its own, it has its own reserved Factory. This allows consumers to get a new or used object, implement it, and throw it back. Here's an example.

```
Dim strA as StringAdapter          'declare it
strA = glb.NewStringAdapter        'get a new one - go to the glb utility for it
'Actions for string here
glb.OldStringAdapter (strA)         'put it back for recycling
```

Now that we have some basic string parsing and manipulation power, let's go get multiple, structured text strings and play around a little more.

Text File Manipulation and Interpretation

The *TextIO* module encapsulates all activities associated with text file manipulation. It is a Singleton so it can manage *all open text files and references.* Early in programming in both C and Visual Basic I noted that the operating system only allowed a predefined number of text Input/Output streams and each one had to be uniquely identified. I was forever chasing down programmers who would open the same I/O thread ID (i.e., 1, 2, 3, etc.) for utility purposes, only to crash their process because some other thread already had the same ID open. I saw a proliferation of code that would attempt to open a file ID, fail, then increment the file ID and repeat the process in the hopes of getting a *hit*.

The TextIO class manages all open IDs and handles for us. All we have to do is accept the IO Handle it gives us, use it for all I/O stream processing and then close the stream when we're done. TextIO will take care of the rest and guarantee that we will always get the next available stream and that no other process will step on our stream.

How is this different from simply invoking the VB File System object? Recall that the FSO won't have the interface pattern to promote structural conformity. Any problems (or creative uses) of the FSO alone won't propagate automatically when we need it next. The TextIO object will allow us to gather steam, capturing our best ideas in one place, fueling accelerated reuse.

Opening Streams

Let's use TextIO to open several streams at once:

```
Dim oTxt As TextIO                        'allocate it
oTxt = glb.TextIOMgr                      'get the master singleton instance

Dim pHan1 As Object                       'allocate three separate handles
Dim pHan2 As Object
Dim pHan3 As Object
'Open each file inside the current application path
pHan1 = oTxt.OpenInputFile(glb.AppPath & "\..\Snip1Input.Txt")
pHan2 = oTxt.OpenInputFile(glb.AppPath & "\..\Snip2Input.Txt")
pHan3 = oTxt.OpenInputFile(glb.AppPath & "\..\Snip3Input.Txt")
oTxt.CloseFile (pHan1)
oTxt.CloseFile (pHan2)                     'now close all three handles
oTxt.CloseFile (pHan3)
```

This demonstrates the opening and closing of multiple I/O streams.

Now let's open one I/O stream and examine the input. By default, the TextIO object supports a simple forward-read browse. That is, it will read the file one line at a time, allow the loop to examine the current line, but throw it away when moving to the next line.

Note that the return value of OpenInputFile will be a valid TurboCollection object or the value "Nothing". All of our function calls should behave in this manner. They should never trap, error off, or require the consumer to perform any additional work (more on error control and recovery frameworks in Chapter 5). Consider this example:

```
pHan1 = oTxt.OpenInputFile(glb.AppPath & "\..\Snip1Input.Txt")  'open a file
If Not pHan1 Is Nothing Then                        'make sure we have something!
Do
Debug.Writeline ( oTxt.Item(pHan1) )                'print the current text line
```

```
oTxt.MoveNext (pHan1)                               'move to the next line
                                                    ' (throws away previous!)

Loop While oTxt.More(pHan1)                         'repeat until end of file
End If
oTxt.CloseFile (pHan1)                              'close It!
```

> **CROSS-REFERENCE** *See Chapter 6 for a discussion of a more dramatic I/O framework.*

Browsing

Note the thematic *Iterator* behavior of *MoveNext* and *More*. We've seen those references before on the TurboCollection. They apply equally as well here, because they expose similar functionality in the way that they browse information. The two are so similar in behavior, in fact, that the most often used implementation of TextIO is to read an entire text file into memory (a separate TurboCollection) for unlimited, end-to-end, or circular browsing. Rather than build a TurboCollection on-the-fly with the above loop, the function *LoadInputFile()* does it for us. It will open the file, pull the entire file into a TurboCollection, and close the file—all in one call. The following is the most pervasive use of the TextIO object, so it deserves some attention:

```
Dim fWrk As TurboCollection                         'prep a TurboCollection
'Load the file and return the reference
fWrk = oTxt.LoadInputFile("..\Snip1Input.Txt")
If fWrk.DataPresent Then                             'check for data
fWrk.MoveFirst()                                    'reset to top
Do
Debug.Writeline (fWrk.Ref.Item)                     'output the current Item
  fWrk.MoveNext()                                   'go to the next
Loop While fWrk.More()                              'repeat until done
End If
```

Now that we have the file in the TurboCollection, let's browse backwards, like so:

```
fWrk.MoveFirst()                        'start at the top
Do
fWrk.MovePrevious()                     'move to the last one (circular list)
Debug.Writeline( fWrk.Ref.Item)         'output the line
Loop While fWrk.More()                  'repeat until done
```

Adding and Subtracting Lines

When building and reformatting files, it is often handy to add or subtract lines from a textual reference. For example, we might find certain textual cues on a given line (facilitated by StringAdapter) and want to enhance the features or information of the lines after it (or preceding it). In the following example, we will use the StringAdapter to key on specific tokens and add some text after each line. To do this, we will have to add items to the TurboCollection in the middle of the list, not always at the end or beginning.

```
If fWrk.DataPresent Then
fWrk.MoveFirst()
Do
    strWrk = fWrk.Ref.Item              'get the text line
   If strA.FindToken("A80", strWrk) Then 'check for a specific value
 strP = "tcTest.AddItem " & """" & _    'embed a quote
 "A81" & ", " & _
 """" & "A81" & ", " & _
 """" & "A81" & """"
'strP should now be equal to a string containing:
             '  the string  tcTest.AddItem( "A81, "A81, "A81")
fWrk.Add (New ParmNode(), "ToMidAfter")
                                        'add a new ParmNode with Op after curr
                                        ' list member (Insert after)
fWrk.Ref.Item = strP                    'stuff the new string on the Item
End If
fWrk.MoveNext()                         'browse to the next text line
Loop While fWrk.More()                  'until no more lines
End If
```

This demonstrates the ability to insert a new string value in the middle of the list, but also shows a way to manufacture new file values. Let's say we've formatted the changes to the file values. We can verify the list's content now by typing the following into the Immediate Window:

```
fWrk.Dump<enter>.
```

In order to write this as a new text file, all we need to provide is the path and the loaded TurboCollection object (highlighted) using the following notation:

```
oTxt.WriteOutputFile (glb.AppPath & "\..\Snip1Output.Txt", fWrk)
```

Now open the text output file (Snip1Output.Txt) with NotePad and examine the contents. You should find the new text line inserted in the appropriate place.

To radically exploit external structural metadata, we can use the StringAdapter and the TextIO in tandem with reading and parsing and interpreting text files. We can use any entities driven or described by structured text, including XML, Structured Query Language (SQL), system *.INI files, command-line parameters, custom run-time configuration files, even actual source code, and many others.

CHAPTER 3

Best Behavior

In This Chapter:

■ Enforcing behavioral integrity

■ Using metadata as fuel

■ Leashing the development process

■ Utilizing behavioral control models

■ Exploring behavioral patterns

■ Achieving pattern-based behavioral control

■ Building valuable and practical components

■ Obtaining expert advice

■ Applying behaviors

A completed product's behavior is the only outward measure of its viability. The slightest behavioral anomaly can indict the integrity of the strongest, most robust core functionality. So, the software must have complete and consistent control over that functionality.

If we have a tightly wrapped application, changes in technical and user requirements will unravel it rather quickly. If we have lockstep procedures where humans can inject error, the behavioral integrity is constantly at risk. Changes impose themselves from the technology and the users, and always at different frequency and magnitude, but with the effect of rushing water. We try to control change, because it always threatens to destabilize our work. However, if we can break apart behavioral patterns as building blocks, we move toward application development with loosely coupled, highly malleable, *fluid* constructs, capable of embracing—even conforming—to change, rather than dreading it.

We should not use software as a first defense against user requests.

Chapter 2 described structures and patterns to wrap technology, so now we need to enhance them with externally programmable behavior. We need behavioral entities to support and affect our structural entities, and use metadata to dynamically weave their relationships. This will minimize the required changes to software and migrate volatility into metadata, buffering our efforts from the end user's maelstrom. Our product becomes a stabilizing force, an engine for user strength, rather than a source of risk. This chapter will discuss product programmability—the path to changing external behavior without changing software.

Enforcing Behavioral Integrity

Changes in user requirements or changes in available technology affect behavioral integrity. We cannot control the influx and nature of user changes, but we can give the user a more consistent experience by directly controlling the impact of change in these domains. When we start with the assumption that *things could change tomorrow,* we're vowing that we won't build anything that only *works for today.* Table 3-1 shows some risks that are related to this approach.

Table 3-1. How Change Affects Behavior

SOURCE OF CHANGE	FREQUENCY	IMPACT	BENEFIT	RISK
End User	High	External Behavior	Meets current and future user needs and revenue projections	Unintentional breakage of existing features, decreases user confidence
Third Party Component	Medium	Internal Behavior	Extends capabilities, marketability, and thus, future revenue projections	Incompatibility with existing releases, decreases user and buyer confidence
Operating System, Supporting Software	Low	Internal Behavior	Gain portability across multiple operating systems	Increases testing and maintenance workload, costs
Hardware	Low	Internal Behavior, Performance	Gain portability across multiple hardware platforms	Increases testing and maintenance workload, costs

We can apply the most expensive and high-performing technology, but we cannot get paid unless the user is satisfied with its behavior. The user also injects the highest volume and complexity of change, so in many ways, the user controls the keys to our success. We always want to satisfy the user with quick turnaround, but in the heat of delivery we might succumb to symptomatic (quick) fixes or surface-level feature enhancements rather than dig deeper for a comprehensive approach.

Externally programmable behavior provides a product with longer durations between rebuilds, greater stability, and the prospect of longevity without a rebuild. Each time we expose a capability to external manipulation, we remove the necessity to revisit it at the software level, enabling us to meet requirements through metadata. The following are the most powerful products in the market-place and are programmable by nature:

- *Software language compiler* uses predefined semantics (language) and text (code) as metadata. It will interpret text, convert it into another, machine-understood form, and write the product to a file (or execute it in memory).

- *Relational Database Management System (RDBMS)* uses predefined seman-tics (Structured Query Language) and text (SQL commands) as metadata. It will interpret text and convert it into database structures and behaviors.

- *Browser* uses predefined semantics (markup language) and text (HTML) as metadata. It will interpret text and convert it into a user experience.

While I don't propose we reconstruct these capabilities in detail, they provide models for us in building metadata-driven programmability. These products expect their textual fuel to change with each execution or individual statement that arrives on their interfaces. Of course, their customizations are always in context. For example, we cannot customize a database engine into a video game. We cannot customize software in Visual Basic (a Microsoft-only animal) to run on a Sun machine. The hardware and operating systems are completely different, and their respective owners fiercely compete with each other.

Likewise, our programmable program should not attempt to do everything. It has the particular advantage, however, of having access to all the components around it and actively connecting them in abstract, creative ways. Our program can combine the power of the RDBMS, the browser, the compiler, and all their related components and merge them into a more powerful whole.

A programmable program is a broker, a connector across dynamic informa-tion services and behavioral components. It will manage this environment, acting on metadata instructions it encounters during run time. This will not only stabi-lize our overall executable, it will also cause us to think about both data and processes in ways we never used to. As a result, the program will exhibit inter-esting, innovative, competitive, and *reusable* qualities we never considered before.

Regardless of how many underlying technical problems we solve, our development work and the end user intersect on external behavior.

With an end user dragon breathing fire against the back of our necks, why wouldn't we drop in the quickest fix to reduce the heat?

Software built with environ-ment-specific tools cannot port easily from its original home into another type of platform.

Using Metadata as Fuel

The technology around us (even the general world itself) is exploding with information. Not the information we process, but the information *about* what we process. This is the standard definition of metadata, but there's much more.

Meta is a prefix denoting both "change" and "abstraction." Both these meanings directly apply to the changing data around us, and how we can abstract it to more understandable and useful symbolic representation. Not just the structural details, but also instructions acting on the detail. Metadata is both structural and behavioral. Therefore, if we miss the behavioral aspect, we'll neglect how metadata can drive our application behavior in the same way we've always used compiled software to drive it.

Metadata can define structure and behavior.

Looking closer, we find that most behavioral algorithms are just sequences of smaller, more general operations. In pure software language space, we place instructions one after another (von Neumann like) to create an end-to-end process. When we use behavioral metadata, our objective is to abstract these instructions as building block processes. We then mix and match them, assembling them dynamically to create a custom "meta" process with multi-threaded process paths.

We'll need a semantic Interpreter to browse the statements and respond by defining structure and activating behavior, using each statement as a virtual behavioral rule. This allows us to abstract behavior out of software and into metadata. Thus, we can affect structure and behavior without modifying and recompiling binary programs.

Capability modeling (weaving elemental capabilities into application behaviors) transforms application development into an almost artistic endeavor.

Don't assume that this approach drives toward a complexity beyond our reach, because it doesn't. Rather, it drives software into simple behaviors (metadata abstraction) and capabilities that we can easily manipulate, almost like the rendering tools of an artist. If a picture paints a thousand words, so too can we abstract high complexity into simple metadata macros.

....

Application *FX*

An example of a structural metadata repository is an RDBMS catalog containing table and column definitions. We can extract this information and construct an abstraction of it in memory, creating a surrogate data model.

When we combine this data with a behavioral repository, we get powerful application-centric *effects (FX)*: detailed RDBMS information exchange that is totally metadata driven and instantly responsive to database model changes without touching software (We'll dive deeper in Chapter 6).

....

Simply utilizing metadata is not enough. We require a behavioral framework that exploits metadata. The framework's very existence will revolve around it. Metadata will be the program's fuel, and because metadata is externally defined, the program will exist with the expectation of change.

For example, a software language compiler doesn't shrink from changes in code, it devours them. A web browser is unaffected by the HTML and JavaScript constantly changing on its interface; it embraces the change. A database engine does not reject the user's requests to create another table, add another column or definition that never existed before—it welcomes the change.

The program will exist for change, not shrink from it.

NOTE *Gearing our code toward metadata as the standard of operation—structurally, behaviorally, and in its run-time role or configuration—only accelerates the possibilities associated with change.*

Metadata-based deployment will keep us ahead of the curve, and make us able to satisfy users quickly, without changing software. This gives us breathing room to later meet larger user needs that might require new capabilities (and thus software change). Contrast this to the hard-coded model that must brace itself for change and perhaps undergo wholesale rewrite to manage it, while the metadata model will surf on it. Change (even spontaneous change) is no longer something to prepare for or analyze, it's part of the natural equation.

This strategy also supports a true plug-and-play framework. If each component shares a common externally programmable interface pattern, we can more easily introduce new behavioral capabilities and upgraded components, minimizing impact to existing functionality. Components then speak a common language to the framework and to each other.

Not just rapid development, but ad hoc, dynamic applications are the product of behavioral metadata.

Okay, apart from being an interesting and different approach, what does it buy us? It buys us a leash, a harness, to control the two most volatile and perilous forces imposing upon our effort:

- Behavior of the *product* due to user/technology changes

- Behavior of the *humans* (users, developers, testers, etc.) as they affect the change process

All technology and methodology aside, the impact of externally imposed change presents very serious issues in the software development realm. Each of them threatens to derail us, so we must get them on a leash *now,* and the metadata-driven approach provides the path.

Does the quality of change affect the product behavior—or does human behavior affect the quality of change?

Leashing the Development Process

One reason we chose software development as a profession is because it gives us deterministic control over our products. Software both enables and manufactures logical boundaries we can use to affect machine behavior. Few things are more professionally satisfying than watching our technical creation come to life.

When we gain sovereign control over the software, we also acquire dominion over the underpinning technology.

What makes the process ugly is the feeling that it's out of our control. When we see misbehaviors, anomalous data, or processing artifacts—things we can't explain—we experience anxiety. It will either drive us to solve the problems and become better, or cause us to doubt our abilities.

We want to deliver high quality products with short turnaround and effective (but profitable) cost structures. eXtreme Programming (XP) and the cry for *agile* development tools (and agile programmers) attempt to leash our approaches into a "high productivity" model. Many leaders know that when our carefully crafted software fails, the problems are invariably due to process and approach, not our technical ability alone.

Good project management does not guarantee a solid product.

However, while many would drive toward methodology alone, I would drive toward building an architecture that automatically folds the methodology into it. I'm not talking about project-related checklists. I'm addressing how we approach the problem altogether, or as mentioned in Chapter 1, the proper starting point. We can build functionality without deviating from methodology, but if we start in the wrong place, the outcome is still inadequate.

A moth is agile in dancing over a flame, but the outcome is unprofitable.

The following discussion will address how to overcome common pitfalls of every software development project by adhering to these practices:

- Telling the truth about user requirements

- Understanding how change affects product behavior

- Applying an appropriate methodology

- Stalking rogues on teams

- Implementing externally programmable behavior

Read on to discover how the architecture itself will help abate, even leash the problems, so we can finish our work and deliver a quality product (and make some money!).

Tell the Truth about User Requirements

User requirements provide the roadmap for application construction, but once unleashed they are a dangerous and deadly force. Users lay out what they want, expect us to deliver it, and often reserve the right to change their minds completely before we're done.

 NOTE *After a developer spends a year or two in building and deploying applications, one universal truth faithfully emerges: User requirements are volatile quantities. They change faster than the technology alone is able to meet them.*

Our novice ranks often become frustrated and discouraged when first realizing and accepting this truth. We might experience anxiety when our project managers give in to user demands. Naturally, the question arises: Can't we ever tell them no? End users want more functionality in less time and for less money. If users nibble around the edges, we call it *scope creep*. If they request wholesale change, we call it a *new project*! The marketplace is volatile. End users want to keep up with it.

Our experienced ranks accept this truth, but many deal with it according to their individual thresholds. Some stay the course, while others bail out to another software company. It's our way of abating the user-imposed pressure for a while, but it always returns.

Scope rarely creeps. It's usually in a full-bore sprint.

Accepting the challenge of a software development project involves managing the enormous tensions that always manifest themselves. Typically, teams and end users react to change requests in the following ways (outlined in Table 3-2), with predictable fallout.

Table 3-2. Actions and Reactions Related to Change

TEAM RESPONSE	END USER RESPONSE	FALLOUT
Assault the request, challenging the users at every turn, making them pay dearly for suggesting the slightest change.	Find a less combative team. Their requirements must be met, and need kinder, gentler attention.	Breakdown in communication; loss of confidence in the developers; concern over quality.
Manage it, building controls to throttle user requests so each one is accounted for, and thus paid for.	Increased user tension because the development team is unable to meet their requests in a timely fashion.	Delays and user expenses increase; users seek to reduce costs and delays by using contract programmers with higher skills.
Capitulate, embrace, and accept change, learning to operate within its bounds like a cruel master. Morale suffers.	Quality suffers. Overworked developers cannot build high-quality products.	Failure to pay for additional functionality overruns the team's costs. The team must quit or renegotiate. User costs ultimately rise.

If we fulfill user requests shortly after (or even before) they arrive, who could complain?

End users don't view developer productivity as a means to provide relief. They view it as a means to increase the workload.

User: 99% complete, 1% failure = 100% unacceptable. Users view bugs like a tiny drop of poison in the purest water. They just won't drink.

The simple conclusion: what really satisfies a user is when we fulfill their requests! The tighter the time frame from request to fulfillment, the happier users will be and the better we'll look. This is the primary impetus of rapid application development, but we find that in an application-centric model, some time lines (like regression testing) are fixed and immutable.

When we believe the hype that rapid application development will relieve the user-driven pressure (including faster machines, databases, or methodologies, etc.) we fall into another trap: application-centric software does not lend itself to anything "rapid." In fact, our deployment cycles only stretch longer as functionality increases (we must test and verify more). Even when we gain the secret to higher productivity, the pressure to deliver seems to double.

The only place our software development intersects with the end user is in the product's behavior. When requirements alone drive the effort, developers view their work in terms of *percent complete*, the end users view the same work in terms of *percent failure*. It is almost impossible to reconcile the two in an application-centric model because the workload is so intense.

To solve the problem we must address the workload and the user requirements simultaneously. Rapid application development offers the promise, but it's empty. We need traction, and lots of it, to race past the user requirements curve. We need stability, and lots of it, to avoid stumbling, rather, tripping over ourselves, while we maintain momentum. We cannot risk a single bug, because it indicts the integrity of the whole.

We need rapid application *delivery*, but nothing in the application-centric model supports it.

Capabilities versus Features

A *capability* is technical functionality of a product's core software. Examples include anything touching an API, such as screen rendering, operating system support, web, network, and database exchange, dynamic calculation and summarization, etc. Software programmers should build *capability*.

A *feature* is application-level functionality, usually produced by using some combination of *capabilities*. Examples include user screen content, behavior and navigation, detailed database transactions, specific accounting or scientific algorithms, application entity manipulation (Employee, Account, Customer, etc.), display and report contents, etc. Application developers should build *features*.

TIP *Building-block capabilities matter to us, not the user. Only features concern the user, and they don't care about the technology underneath.*

NOTE *One database marketing firm demanded their developers rip out core troubleshooting capabilities because they weren't "user driven". However, these capabilities were "requirements driven," and absolutely necessary to provide good technical support after rollout! Some capabilities are required even if the user never asks.*

A metadata-driven architecture gives us this power, radically decreases our turnaround time, and allows us to fulfill user requirements without compromising quality, and without rebuilding software or exposing it to architectural flaws.

What and How?

While a user cares about the process of how a product is delivered, they don't care how it's technically constructed. At least, we shouldn't let them care. The user's domain is the answer to the *What* question. Users define what they want to do: the feature list.

The technologist's domain is the answer to the *How* question. They define *how* to deliver *what* the users want. If we can get and keep the users firmly seated in the What domain, we will have unlimited freedom to meet their needs in the How domain.

Understanding How Change Affects Product Behavior

The end user expects us to fulfill their change requests without breakage. Users experience frustration when we fix one thing only to break another. Vendors constantly inject the marketplace with hot—even sizzling—interactive offerings. Users see these and drool. They want application fulfillment and sizzle too. They demand the first and expect the second for free.

Our software's behavior has two significant enemies: user-requested changes and marketplace-driven technology change. We can choose to challenge and overcome these enemies or obey them as cruel masters.

When change arrives, we can only brace for impact—or easily absorb the shock.

The application-centric model is a servant to both: artificially injecting volatility and unpredictability, and transforming our technical deliverables into moving targets. We create risk every time we touch the software for a rebuild, whether to fill out an original feature list or include requested enhancements. With each iteration, the software deviates from its original design. At some point, redesign and rewrite are upon us.

Software changes often create *ripple effects,* or *cascading impact.* A small change in one solution area creates behavioral problems in a seemingly unrelated area. In the application-centric model, software controls application-level behavior, so changes in the software code (bug fixes, enhancements, maintenance) create a risk in adversely affecting overall product behavior.

CROSS-REFERENCE *See Chapter 2 for a discussion of the common development model.*

The risks follow this well-known pattern:

1. Changes to software create a possibility of failure.

2. The developer's solution-level understanding drives the change's scope.

3. The developer's skill drives the change's quality.

4. The quality of testing drives the overall integrity.

5. The end user's understanding and expectation drives the change's approval.

Examine the multiple gateways of human-level sifting applied as software changes migrate from the developer's desktop to their target: the end user. Examine also the so-called weakest-link effect. Any given change has a greater chance for success if strong, knowledgeable people execute their part of the process. The result depends directly upon the skill level and understanding of the players.

Again, we address the lesser of evils: will the change affect the product's behavior or will human behavior affect the change? In the application-centric model, these converge to create chaos, so we need an objective means to control them. To boil it down, the application-centric model is a no-win model. We try instead to manage change rather than using a better path: automatic conformity. If we remain application-centric, we'll need to apply an appropriate methodology, and quickly!

If we invoke software to manage require-ments, the entire effort will be no different than the project plan itself: locked down and applicable only to the current effort.

Applying an Appropriate Methodology

In the application-centric model, we have no choice but to pursue a subjective path, to control human behavior as it affects the product. This requires a set of rules, protocols, marching orders—you guessed it—a methodology. It helps us keep everyone in line, right?

But what can we do when we perceive that our ranks have deviated from our carefully crafted methodology? End users like the presence of a methodology because it gives them the right (so to speak) to beat the daylights out of us when we deviate. When we're behind schedule, or features aren't quite up to speed, users need some justification to complain, and the methodology is just the thing.

A primary goal of using a methodology is to focus people on the process, not the personalities. When pressure builds, this aspect is gradually set aside. Personal attacks are commonplace in some environments. Such posturing causes team leads (even CIOs) to rethink their methods. We want to believe that every technol-ogist is *doing it the same way* and that we can set user expectations. However, when invoking a methodology and compliance strategy, we're betting the product's technical integrity on the company's ability to control human behavior. Is this even possible?

Some develop-ment shops swear by *methodologies. Others swear* at *them.*

I've seen user representatives stand up in meetings, point their fingers and shout, "I THINK YOU AND YOUR TEAM ARE INCOMPETENT!" I've seen others very calmly observe, "We need to replace this team and get people who know what they're doing." The professional term for this is: *Yikes!*

In an application-centric approach, our only other alternative is to give various developers the freedom to apply disparate priorities, skills, and methods. We all solve application problems differently and might not have the time to collaborate. We can't use code inspection or run alongside developers with a stick, nor can we expect 100 percent voluntary compliance.

The conclusion: in an application-centric approach, deviations from coding standards are not about architecture. Under fatigue and duress of fire-breathing users, we have succumbed to lapses in diligence, quick fixes, artistic license, lack of skill, outright defiance, and a whole host of intangible issues. Flaws are either injected or passively enter the architecture, but by the time we find them, it's too late. We can tell users we have control over human behavior (compliance) but shouldn't completely believe our own hype.

The real issue is controlling rogue human behavior at *all* times, an impossible task.

Stalking Rogues on Teams

End users decry the presence of "rogues" on our teams. Some people are rabble-rousers—they claim—and should be trimmed out. Actually, every team has two types of rogues: the active rogue and the passive rogue.

The *active rogue* is concerned only for personal success and is uninterested in the team development standards. Active rogues have their own rules, they work just fine, and the rogue adheres to them. The good news: the resulting work is easily corrected and realigned to the team standard because it follows *some* standard. Such a rogue is usually very smart, experienced, and disciplined.

The *passive rogue*, on the other hand, conforms and agrees with all team standards, but sometimes sets them aside in a crunch (or other reasons). Passive rogues introduce flaws accidentally, that are almost impossible to detect. They may not even remember coding them, and upon revisiting their own work might even rewrite it.

While an active rogue might create team-level grief, managers can control the software impact because of the rogue's visibility. The invisible passive rogue, on the other hand, does far more damage. We absolutely require a means to place both rogues in check or we jeopardize the architecture's integrity. Ideally, when we attempt to deviate from standards, the architecture needs an automatic way to guard itself, *from us*.

When the user-centric heat rises, our ability to satisfy their needs through metadata meets these two critical requirements:

- We can meet user requests with high speed, accuracy, and reliability.

- Rogue activity is kept completely in check (we don't, or rarely, touch the software to affect a user-driven change).

Both of these aspects converge on a concept I'll call *active compliance*.

Invoking Active Compliance

Coding[1] and testing standards[2] are important for building solid code at the detail level, abating a multitude of error-proofing headaches. Standards provide significant traction in behavioral control and troubleshooting. Standards alone, however, typically address surgical coding issues. They only lead to product integrity if consistently applied by all players, regardless of skill level.

The user will suffer through surgical fixes, but not pervasive behavioral inconsistencies. Every developer knows that each new or changed line of code represents a failure point, another risk for breakage after product release. Thus the software's quality is directly related to our skill and our diligence. Testing might find behavioral bugs, but only the developer's skill drives the software's *actual* quality. If we can meet the user's goals without changing software, we remove the risk of architectural damage in the heat of user pressure.

A coding standard will not protect the architecture from a developer who is willing to deviate from it.

With an architecture-centric product, only key architects and senior developers directly affect the core software. To deliver features through metadata, we define another role—that of application developer. This role will not affect software, but will invoke the product's programmable capabilities with metadata to achieve an *application effect*. When application developers use metadata in this way, they are automatically in compliance with the product's architecture.

Supporting the user without changing the software product is the primary objective.

Additionally, new product releases should protect existing metadata behavior while propelling new metadata behavior. With new releases, we can fix bugs discovered in the core software that don't affect existing applications.

A database engine uses SQL for metadata, and when we submit a properly formed statement that it can act on, we've complied with its architecture.

Power Plug

Accessing power for a new floor lamp is simple: plug it into an outlet and flip the switch. By "plugging in," however, we have complied with the wishes of the architect and electrical engineer. We *could* blow a hole in the wall, rip out some wires, and twist them around the lamp's plug. We'd get the same effect (illumination) but our lack of compliance would place the solution (and the home) at risk.

Active compliance means automatically embracing the intent of the architects using metadata to meet user-centric needs— and at a breath-taking clip.

Using the plug "as intended" represents our *active compliance*. The application (of the lamp) is not the architect's concern. The plug could be applied to a component stereo or vacuum cleaner. The plug exists as a passive means to provide a reusable power connection. Participating in its use *as designed* precludes the necessity for constant involvement of an electrical engineer.

We have invoked an active compliance mechanism in our software product when application developers and end users alike are in compliance *simply by using the product*.

With active compliance, we enforce architectural and software integrity at one level, then expose programmable capability at another. We meet user needs through metadata-enabled programmability, automatically riding the architectural integrity pathway in the underlying software. Thus, in the heat of battle, the programmable pathway keeps us on track to deliver features without destabilizing the software.

We must enforce compliance where the heat is highest. Within an architecture-centric model, the core software architects will have a much longer release cycle than application developers. They have more degrees of freedom and time to carefully think about their work and craft it with quality. Application metadata developers are in the heat of battle, with users looking over their shoulders and pending delivery deadlines. They *must* solve the application problems in order to relieve the pressure. Required to use the programmable interface, their participation with application metadata constitutes active compliance.

To give an application developer this power to meet user needs without touching software, we need external programmability (through metadata) as a rule, not an ancillary or peripheral capability.

Implementing Externally Programmable Behavior

Externally programmable behavior is sometimes an afterthought. We might implement run-time switches, input configuration files, or just nibble at the edges. Rarely do we consider defining full application-level structure and behavior in metadata, invoking it like dynamic subroutines and interpreting it multiple times through events or conditions.

How do we gravitate toward a metadata-driven, architecture-centric model? We can see that the risk for application-level failure is very high with each release cycle, *but only if it requires a change in the software*. Therefore, it makes sense to establish the following goals from the project's outset in order to burst features from our desktop, protecting working features while deploying new ones:

Goal #1: Minimize or eliminate software-level change with each release.

Goal #2: Maximize quantity and quality of feature rollout with each release.

Goal #3: Maximize the frequency of application-level release.

These goals are impossible to meet with an application-centric product, where our only means of meeting user requirements is changing software.

NOTE *Software alone does not provide a way to avoid a software change (and component rebuild) to meet changing user requests. However, we can use software to build this capability, then rest our remaining efforts on top of it.*

We can either hard-wire application behavior into our products, or take a few steps back and expose application behavior from a carefully crafted, programmable foundation. The difference is dramatic in development, delivery, maintenance, long-term viability, and user confidence.

Consider again a web browser or database engine; do these products themselves require physical binary reconstruction each time we deploy a new application, or even a new application feature? No, in fact their external programmability is something we rely on rather heavily to conform quickly and reliably to our changing application needs.

Product behavior is constrained by many boundaries, largely encapsulated in the language environment. Often the volume and variety of boundaries lulls us into a false assumption that no boundaries exist at all. Vendors and component providers constantly inject the marketplace with supporting products, language extensions, and shareware to enhance behavioral control. Their objective is always to add capabilities, ultimately affecting the value of our final product (because enhanced capability/behavior is the most visible means to express value to the end user).

The key is to focus on programmable capabilities—run-time building blocks—to manufacture features.

DEFINITION *Third-party components, tools and especially development languages provide* lift, *the significant enhancement of developer productivity, product quality, ultimately the user's experience, or (preferably) some combination of these factors. Users and developers alike impose their opinions on what supporting products are "best in class." Users who hear of a given product with poor feature quality will not have high esteem for those delivering solutions with it. With custom software projects and products costing in the millions of dollars, it is not unreasonable to expect the very best.*

We want *lift* and expect our development language environment (and supporting tools) to provide it. Otherwise, we typically select another environment (or another language) that seems more promising. For this reason, language vendors are constantly updating their products to remain competitive. They know we're in search of the ultimate technology to meet all behavioral needs. Our end users are very demanding, constantly changing their own requirements to meet their business goals. These demands are in turn folded upon us, who must merge them into current marketplace software offerings, transform those offerings, or build new ones completely.

Users pay high dollars for custom, technical solutions, and will not suffer second-rate supporting technologies.

In an architecture-centric model, new component introduction is usually under the control and planning of the architects, not due to the request of an end user. In general, we'll support most application-level requirements within a stable technology base. If we lock down this base with structural wrappers and connectors, we can reasonably move toward a more ambitious goal: modify or enhance application features without changing or rebuilding software. Only programmable behavior provides this capability.

Therefore, application developers affecting user-centric behavior are in *de facto compliance* with the architectural, project, and/or enterprise standards.

Programmable behavior puts our technical and human behaviors on a leash. Now let's look at the types of behavior we are actually programming.

Utilizing Behavioral Control Models

Two primary control models are pervasive in the marketplace:

- Flow-based (process-driven)

- Event-based (interrupt-driven)

The Flow-Based, Process-Driven Model

The process-driven model is *active*. Its state is either Running=True or Running=False. It is typically single-threaded and inflexible (although can be parallelized). It will begin operation, take system resources by the throat and burn application logic, business rules, and data until it completes its predefined mission. It exemplifies the input-process-output model (typically used for large-scale "batch" processing).

Process-driven models are resource-intensive (sometimes voraciously so) and require administrative oversight. They (usually) cannot automatically time-slice or share resources, so operators/developers must guard and manage resources for them. A process sometimes finds itself bound by one or more resource limitations, such as being I/O bound, CPU bound, or memory-bound. Whether a given flow-based application reaches conclusion in milliseconds or hours, it *must* complete (and can only suspend/continue or abort). It usually does not have the option to suspend until more work is available.

Some process-driven models include interrupt-driven inputs, providing a continuous processing effect (handy for extracting web logs, queues, or other dynamic resources that "never sleep").

The Event-Based, Interrupt-Driven Model

By contrast, the event-driven model is *passive* (e.g., a common desktop application such as Microsoft Word or Excel, or perhaps an email exchange queue processing thousands of messages as they arrive). While an event-driven program could be running, it could also be disabled, sleeping, waiting, listening, or in any number of other states. It links events to processes through event handlers. A handler's response can trigger other events, merged with its own context, then enriched with the run-time and operating system state and other details. If metadata is part of the response mechanism, we can externally program the event handler's behavior. We can drive an event handler with a real event signal or an artificially manufactured one. Thus, a process only activates and consumes resources when a monitored event requires servicing. This model can also be very selective in which events receive monitoring and response.

Microprocessor-based solutions, both embedded and at the desktop, first popularized event-driven models.

We must package the data associated with the event with the data driven by the event. By combining events with data and treating them both in context, a handler can control both with greater accuracy and flexibility. As a process thread flies through a framework, including multiple tiers and systems, we must keep it packaged in context.

Build first for the passive, context-aware event model. Software can always emulate a process model with an event-driven foundation, but cannot easily emulate an event model with a process-driven foundation.

Software Control

Defining an application-independent behavioral model requires a shift in thinking. We are on a path that *virtualizes* the application rules and their related entities. Rather than build application behavior software, we'll build software that enables behavioral programmability. Rather than build software to define specific application entities, we'll build software that manages virtual entity definition and behavior.

Event models are more complex than process models, but are also more flexible.

This level of abstraction is absolutely key to understanding how we can build resilient software that is practically immune to changing behavioral requirements.

Exploring Behavioral Patterns

This section discusses the four following behavioral patterns and provides some examples of each:

Iterator: Database cursors, text file browsers, summarization, reporting, calculation, collections, lists

Interpreter: Compilers, web browsers, word processors, XML parsers

Observer/Visitor: Database trigger, subscribe/publish queues, web crawlers, email

Template: Mortgage/amortization calculators, reports, publishers

The Iterator

The *Iterator* (see Figure 3-1) encapsulates consistent looping, browsing, and list manipulation functions for simple containers like arrays or collections of common information. The Iterator can control and manage a container's features, moving among its members, finding the beginning or end, adding, removing, sorting, searching, or organizing.

CROSS-REFERENCE *See "Project 1—Groundwork" in Chapter 1 and "Project 2—Structures" in Chapter 2, which introduced the TurboCollection/ParmNode as an Iterator pattern.*

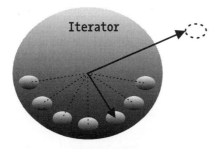

Figure 3-1. The Iterator pattern

An Iterator pattern performs programmable looping functions and enforces a defined entry and terminus. It can invoke the loop, execute a series of functions within the loop, and browse an ordered information source while doing so. Its information source typically provides cues to the loop's behavior controls. Thus, a true Iterator is programmable. It responds to the information it is browsing and behaves in context.

The most powerful Iterator implementations will expose two classes: an Iterator class to perform the looping activities and a node class uniquely suited and optimized for the Iterator's use. (The projects at the end of each chapter use the TurboCollection and ParmNode for these roles.) While the Iterator will manipulate nodes, the nodes serve as anchors for objects of any kind in the run-time environment. This allows a custom class of any type to use the Iterator and nodes to exploit Iterator functions. In fact, the Iterator and nodes do all the work. The custom class is just along for the ride.

For example, if an object wants to create and organize multiples of itself, it can instantiate objects of its own kind, build nodes to anchor them, then add the nodes to the Iterator.

Nodes serve many roles, such as proxies, anchors, and adapters.

The node exposes manipulation properties such as an ItemKey() or a SortKey(), allowing the anchored object to set these keys with its own search or sort values. The Iterator then uses all node key values to provide global sorting and searching. This provides powerful, reusable functionality for objects of any type; an example of applying a pattern to general reuse.

The Iterator is extremely powerful in organizing and manipulating groups of objects. Implemented correctly, it can provide pervasive glue for an entire architecture.

The Interpreter

The *Interpreter* pattern (see Figure 3-2) will browse external content. Typically, the content is textual in nature and is dynamically translated into a structural definition, behavioral action, or some relationship between the two. It enforces simple parsing rules and syntax of textual commands, similar to a language compiler's interpretive functionality. Cueing on keywords and context, it will translate the statements into internal actions, states, or data elements and provide a programmatic interface to the framework's internal domain.

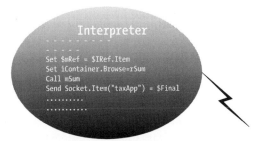

Figure 3-2. The Interpreter pattern

Because the Interpreter must browse and parse, it is directly dependent on the Iterator *pattern.*

The Interpreter needs semantic and syntax rules to insure consistent behavior. Available language definitions provide a rich resource for lexical and syntactic rules. We could use variations on C++, Java, or Visual Basic. We can cherry-pick the best syntax from our own comfort zones. After all, it's only destined for macro-level parsing, not detailed binary compilation. We must simplify, clarify, and rarefy our semantics to provide the most agile, even nimble resource for our own use.

An Interpreter keys specific internal activities to syntax and textual values. It can use contextual combinations (in script form) to dispatch predefined activities, or combinations of activities to reach a desired outcome. Interpreters browse text to define and reference variables, perform actions on those variables, and expose database, system, and third-party component functionality. It can enforce behavioral consistency because it *is* a behavioral controller.

We don't need highly complex lexical rules, just symbolic consistency.

Additionally, the Interpreter will use keywords we define, not just those defined by a surrealistic standards group. We can converge massive amounts of functionality into simple macro statements. The only raw behaviors we need to support are the following:

- *Statements*: A line of text stands alone as a self-contained action

- *Routines/subroutines*: Multiple statements to execute in sequence

- *Definition*: Manufacturing instances of building-block entities

- *Assignment*: Exchanging selected content between entities, or initiating activities

- *Conditional*: Branching to statements based on dynamic conditions

- *Loop*: Repeating statements within a conditional boundary

If we build these rather dramatic capabilities with patterns, we find the following simple themes:

- Each *text line* is an actionable entity we'll call a statement. Its possible variations and syntax really don't require broad flexible boundaries.

- Each statement has two forms: definition or action. We'll use definition to build dynamic *entities* and actions to build behavior between our new entities and any other entities exposed to the Interpreter's internal framework.

- Entities have two forms: *simple* and *complex*. Each, however, is ultimately an *object* to the Interpreter, giving it more freedom in accessing the entity's interface.

- Actions have two forms: *assignment* and *comparison* (derivations of the "=" sign).

We'll use comparison for conditional logic, allowing the Interpreter to decide which statements to use next.

We'll use assignment for two purposes: moving information and initiating activity. This second purpose is the most powerful, because we can invoke huge portions of embedded logic with a seemingly simple assignment. For example the metadata statement:

Simple capabilities and their extensions unlock enormous amounts of power.

```
Set $MyLoadTable.Load=True
```

could perform a simple assignment of "True" to a local variable, or invoke an enterprise information transfer between database systems.

The metadata statement:

We'll leash chaos: tiny actions have dramatic outcomes, only now for our benefit.

```
Set $Warehouse.EmployeeFactTable = $LatestRawFactInfo
```

could easily post a single value (LatestRawFactInfo) into a simple property (Warehouse.EmployeeFactTable). Or, it could initiate an enterprise-level data migration lasting for hours. The point is, now *we* get to decide the meaning and depth.

Routines are groups of statements. We can tag the group with a RoutineName to organize individual statements into a sequence. We make a "Call" statement syntax to invoke a routine from a routine, providing routine reusability even within the macros, even externalize it to other framework entities.

We now decide what symbols, actions, and behaviors to expose within the Interpreter's domain.

For example, a routine could serve as an event handler for a Command Button *Adapter*. We simply submit the textual RoutineName to the Adapter, designated for its "Click" event. Each time a "Click" occurs on the Command Button's

API, the Adapter sees it and hands off control to the Interpreter using the RoutineName. In the final outcome, the Interpreter executes the Routine on the event boundary.

Similarly, we support loops by building Adapter entities with Iterator capability. We then submit a RoutineName to the entity with a command to Browse. The Adapter will call back to the RoutineName once for each node in the iteration.

Within the Adapter's Browse capability, it will initialize itself to its first node (MoveFirst), then call back to the Interpreter using the RoutineName once for every node (MoveNext). The metadata macro statements in the Routine can act on the entity based on its current node, or stop the Browse altogether, like so:

```
Set $ThisContainer.Browse=MyBrowseRule
'*****************************
Define MyBrowseRule as Routine
Set $Wrk1 = $ThisContainer.Item(AuthorName)   'get the current node's info
If $Wrk1 EQ "David" then                       'test the node's info
   Set $ThisContainer.KillBrowse = True        'kill the browse completely
Endif
End Routine
```

These simple capabilities provide programmable behavior in the spirit of a compiler, but with dynamic flexibility.

Ours, Not Theirs

We could have used the Visual Basic Scripting Runtime, invoking VBScript for some of the work. Or we could use JavaScript, even invoke our desktop's Virtual Machine. While doing so achieves the same outcome, it defeats the purpose. We are attempting to unhook ourselves from dependency on technology, including any specific software language. If our Interpreter understands a simple, rarefied lexical syntax, we could replicate its functionality on any operating system, any language environment, without affecting the behavior of the individual statements or the application logic they collectively represent.

All existing products and languages have known limitations, and we don't want to bind our fate to any of them.

Just as the Adapter is the most pervasive structural pattern, the Interpreter is the most visible behavioral pattern. It derives power from associating simple text with internal actions. It invites serious examination because it's the engine of an externally programmable program, extended interoperability, accelerated reuse, active compliance and shockwave delivery. "Project 3—Behaviors" at the end of this chapter gives some specific implementations and examples.

Interpreters drive our compilers, ODBC/SQL interfaces, web browsers, configuration initialization functions (for *.INI files), and XML parsers, to name a few. An Interpreter defines and exposes its syntax-based interface and expects its consumers to adhere to it. Some Interpreters are highly complex. Some will interpret binary information, but most are configured to parse structured text.

The most prominent and often used dynamic Interpreter is the Structured Query Language (SQL) parser on the front end of most popular RDBMS engines. This Interpreter will enforce SQL syntax standards, along with the given engine's proprietary SQL extensions. This keeps the engine's core functionality separated from (but available to) remote applications.

Implemented correctly, an interpretation mechanism provides a programmable interface to expose our product's core features. Ideally, it has an active feedback mechanism to report syntax errors and status.

The Observer/Visitor

Establishing an *Observer* pattern (see Figure 3-3) creates a virtual relationship between two unrelated objects. Observers are lightweight, powerful activation and connection mechanisms to build automatic, event-based management throughout our framework. While wired class hierarchies provide one-dimensional relationships, the Observer provides *multi*dimensional, virtual, and dynamic relationships. ("Project 3—Behaviors" at the end of this chapter shows some examples of observation capabilities.)

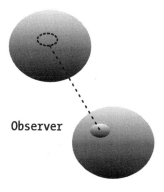

Observer

Figure 3-3. The Observer pattern

The Observer pattern watches things, like changes in data and state, or perhaps tracks a transition across a dynamic threshold. A subscriber establishes the relationship, a publisher accepts and honors it, then the Observer automatically relays and reports on what it sees, usually on designated event boundaries. We will have an *observed object* and one or more *observing objects*. While this approach resembles event-based replication, it is more powerful because the participating objects may have widely disparate roles and responsibilities in the framework, and the Observer can transform a publisher's "data" to a subscriber's "state."

The *Visitor* is an extension of the Observer pattern. The Observer knows exactly what it wants to watch, but the Visitor usually does not. The Visitor can accept dynamic instructions from its owner/subscriber, changing or enabling/disabling its observation behavior on the fly.

We can use Observers to automate screen-level behaviors, such as enabling/disabling controls while a user browses a grid, treeview, etc.

We can initiate simple event and information transfers between objects, or go one step further and provide programmable observation, allowing the inter-object relationship to change dynamically based on instructions from the observing object. The observing object can establish the relationship under one rule and change the relationship using another rule. Because the rule resides inside a given Observer instance, the frequency and number of changes have no limit.

In order to implement observation consistently, we must wrap all third-party components with Adapters. This was suggested in Chapter 2 concerning structural conformity. Each Adapter will in turn support observation and perform the required interface transforms internally. "Raw" component APIs (e.g., third-party products) have extremely limited observation capability, if at all. We can support observation without adapters, but it's tricky and requires maintenance. "Project 3—Behaviors" at the end of this chapter includes an Observer class built for a largely wrapped environment.

As an example, we typically program interdependent screen behaviors, where one control automatically responds when we interact with another control. We might *enable* a menu item or command button based on the state or contents of a drop-down box, a grid, or other browsable source. A typical example is automatic role-based security, where we enable or disable screen navigation based on available screen information or user identity.

Let's say an on-screen grid has a status of "Yes" or "No" in column three. As the user browses the grid, we want to enable menu-based navigation to Screen A if the column value is "Yes," or Screen B if the column value is "No."

We could directly program the grid's RowChange event to examine the grid column and set the enabled value of the appropriate menu item. Or we could set up an Observer between the objects, instruct it to watch the grid's column three and, on a RowColumnChange event, report back a value of True or False depending on column three's value. Observation completely abstracts this behavior.

As another example, we could have two drop-down combo boxes, one using a Country Code as a hidden key value and the Country Name as the display value. The second combo is the reverse of the first, with the Country Name as the hidden key value and the Country Code as the display value. We can set up Observers between the two such that a change in one automatically synchronizes the second by trading Item/Key values on a change event.

The required parameters to establish the relationship are: the participating entities, their properties and values, coupled with a trigger. For the grid example, each subscribing menu Adapter has Observer capability, so each will receive an observation automatically each time the user changes the row, as shown in Table 3-3.

Table 3-3. Observer Structural Requirements

ROLE	ENTITY	PROPERTY	VALUE	TRIGGER
Source	Observed Object (Grid)	Observed Property (Column 3)	Valid Value ("Yes"/"No")	RowChange Event
Target	Observing Object (Menu)	Observing Property (Enabled)	Transformed Value (True/False)	Always listening

What if we could describe this relationship with a simple textual statement? An Interpreter could parse the text, find the named object Adapters identified by their tags, and tell the Adapters to establish a relationship.

A metadata macro statement example like the following assumes a *Grid Adapter* named "Employees" and two menu Adapters respectively named "Send Letter" and "Request Info":

```
Observe $"Send Letter"  Enabled = $Employees RowChangeEvent Column3, "Yes"
Observe $"Request Info" Enabled = $Employees RowChangeEvent Column3, "Yes"
```

Each pattern will key on the RowChange event. The value of Column3 will be evaluated against "Yes." This evaluation (True or False) will be posted to the Menu's Enabled property. A more language-like construct follows:

```
Observe $RequestInfo.Enabled =
$Employees.Item(Property=Column3|Event=RowChange|Value="Yes")
```

The behavior as experienced by the grid user: menus are enabled/disabled automatically as the user browses the grid, and we don't have to specifically program this logic in compiled, binary form.

This is a clean, predictable way to externally program the Observer's behavior, then customize each Observer to act across a broad spectrum of states, events, data, and contexts.

The Template

The *template* pattern shown in Figure 3-4 exposes a common procedure or algorithm, plus an interface pattern to make it a building block. Examples include input-processing-output functions, loop-based functions, browsing or accumulating collected values, reusable utilities, and repeating multi-stage operations. The basic template form will allow an entity to pass itself into the template process, ride its processing thread to completion, and exit with a changed state and contents.

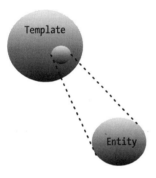

Figure 3-4. The template pattern

When we spend enormous thought cycles and coding on advanced algorithms and solutions, we can either bury them in a specific class or we can make the process itself a building block class (see Figure 3-5). This extends the building block approach discussed in Chapter 2 from structures to behaviors. Structural entities then have access to a pool of behavioral entities and can treat them in macro form, as either elemental functions or abstract methods.

Figure 3-5. Unbinding a process from a specific entity

The *abstract template* shown in Figure 3-6 allows us to string together behavioral entities, with the option of dedicating their behavior to one structural entity, or assembling them in a flexible chain. This creates an *abstract method,* or *dynamic method,* and allows metadata to dynamically designate (and order) entities of any kind for a highly customized, application-centric effect. Now the structures can determine their own fate at run time without a predefined conclusion.

Figure 3-6. An abstract template

Another form of abstract template is a flow-based model, such as the one shown in Figure 3-7. We will always require input-processing-output (batch) support. We could artificially manufacture events to drive a series of event-driven behaviors, simulating a batch-style processing thread. Or we could assemble the processes in a chain and connect the required entities for a virtual flow. Thus, a file of records, web logs, or other unit of work requiring flow-based processing can enter the flow, immerse itself into the various behavioral entities comprising the flow, and exit with a self-contained result.

If we want EventA from StructureB to trigger BehaviorC, we define these entities and their relationship in metadata, not software.

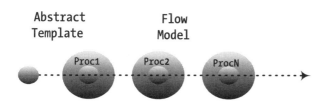

Figure 3-7. The flow-based model of an abstract template

A template can also interface with predefined (legacy) classes if we wrap them with an Adapter or conform their existing interfaces to the template's expectations. Encapsulating building block behaviors provides greater troubleshooting control. We can eliminate behavioral anomalies and give the user a more consistent experience.

A template differs from a *Prototype* (Chapter 2) in that it encapsulates a process or algorithm rather than a structural instance. Templates are often implemented for mathematical functions, parameterized calculations, report formatting, and repeatable decision logic.

To expose the template's functionality, typically one or more seed objects will provide the template with the behavioral anchor (such as simple math, Boolean evaluation, string/date formatting, even high-order calculations). The template will assume the presence of a standard interface such as *Item()* on each seed object. As the template then runs the algorithm, it will use the seed object's interface pattern to access the seed object's properties or methods at appropriate processing junctures.

A simple example is a summarization function for a list of objects. The template would accept the list and browse it from top to bottom with an Iterator pattern, summarizing each object's *Item* value into an accumulator (note that in Listing 3-1 *sSum* is only adding two quantities as a building block). When the template's browse operation completes, it reports the answer. Many template implementations use algorithms with some form of accumulation. Listing 3-1 shows an example of a template function call:

Listing 3-1. A Template Function Call

```
/*********************************************************************
Class sSum
Public Action(ActionID as String, ActionData as String)  as String
   If ActionID = "Add" then
'    Parse ActionData Into ISeed and Addend
     Action = iSeed + Addend                      'add the two parms and return
   Endif
End Sub
/*********************************************************************
Class Calc
'All we want with Browse() is a basic end-to-end browse, to accumulate values
' based on the template algorithm - in this case a sSum() - but we could just
' as easily  accumulate on any object's Action property.
Public Accum ( tcD as TurboCollection, tmp as Object) as Integer
   Dim intSum as Integer
   tcD.MoveFirst                                 'set to browse from first object
   intSum = 0                                    'initialize
   Do
     'call the Algo pattern on the tmp object - pass the accumulator and the
     ' current list item we don't care what Action does, just store and continue
```

```
intSum = tmp.Action("Add", "Seed=" & intSum & "|Addend=" &
                            ,tcD.Ref.Item)
        tcD.MoveNext
     Loop while tcD.More                      'until done
     Accum = IntSum                           'return result now
  End Sub
'/*****************************************************************
Main Body
Dim tcD as New TurboCollection              'workspace
Dim intI as Integer                         'workspace
Dim intSum as Integer                       'results go here
  intI = 0                                   'initialize
'Now build a turbocollection with test data, the numbers  0-9
  do
     tcD.AddItem (intI)                      'put the next value here
     intI = intI + 1                         'increment to the next value
  Loop while intI < 10                       'collection contains values 0 thru
9
'Now make some templates
dim mCalc as New Calc()
dim mSum as New sSum()
intSum= mCalc.Accum(tcD, mSum)    'now accumulate it with sum- answer should be 45
```

In "Project 3—Behaviors" at the end of this chapter, the elements of the ConditionFactory serve as template patterns we can plug into a behavioral model for automatic, transparent conditional/decision capability.

With generalized algorithm components and routines, we can snap together groups of algorithms to achieve complex effects. In fact, most application-level solutions are about gathering information, performing some series of standard processing algorithms on them, and storing them for later. The template provides a clean way to introduce a general processing component for a process-driven portion of the solution, or just to hold commonly used algorithms and calculation logic.

Baseline behavioral building blocks coupled with structural building blocks lead us to powerful architectural frameworks.

Frameworks

Many software development efforts start out defining all the unique characteristics of the solution, its class and object hierarchy, and a host of use-case interactions. Once we get deep into the implementation, finding and exploiting common themes becomes almost impossible.

....

Frameworks at Large

Microsoft's .NET Framework is an example of building a home base for structural and behavioral similarities. The .NET strategy allows Microsoft to promulgate its technology to all developers who are using Microsoft products, increasing the availability and interoperability of all Microsoft technology.

IBM's Application Framework is now a common underpinning strategy for all IBM software, including DB2, Tivoli, Lotus, and WebSphere. IBM drives their e-business strategy from this framework and it increases the interoperability and availability of all IBM technology.

....

A *framework*, simply defined, is a home base for structural and behavioral similarities. Unfortunately, most application-level frameworks are afterthoughts, not part of an architectural foundation. We must critically examine our current application's reuse characteristics. Do we have a set of core utilities available for all developers, perhaps even kept in a global utility module? While most frameworks require utilities, the mere presence of utilities will not create a framework. If such a utility module is a hodge-podge of miscellaneous (and optional) items, it's not our framework, either.

A framework is thematic. It will activate similarities across classes and implementations, expose common constructs with predictable outcomes, provide deterministic trouble-shooting, and ultimately form operational fabric for the entire product.

An architecture can actually self-validate if it opens new options with little additional effort.

A framework is not concerned with application-level intent as a deliverable. It will hold no application-level information or software. Its sole purpose is to define and implement brokerage services between the architecture's programmable entities, and a reliable, consistent compliancy mechanism for their interfaces.

As a concept, most developers agree with the necessity of frameworks. So why don't we see more of them? Why do most solutions tend to have hard-wired application code throughout? Is it because the solution's creators don't have the time to implement a framework? Or perhaps "framework" is a nebulous concept and no two people can agree on its contents or behavior? Perhaps the application itself, not a reusable framework, is the project's priority. For whatever reason, the result (no framework) seems to be the *only* similarity between solutions.

The dilemma: developers agree with exploiting similarities, but differ on how to do it!

....

Frameworks Abound

Frameworks initially emerged as operating systems and real time kernels, largely to provide a common means for application software to control CPU, disk, and memory resources. Vendors placed their own frameworks on these, to support programmable screen look and behavior, interprocess communication and a host of other distributed functionalities.

Vendors migrated toward niche areas, such as suites of products to support limited-scope features (e.g., screen display, information reporting, and data access) all the way to broad-scope products such as Enterprise Application Integration and data warehousing.

The common theme in all these products is the ability to easily assimilate new capabilities because their existing capabilities play on common structural and behavioral themes. Microsoft's .NET Framework is appropriately named because Microsoft has exposed common interchangeable underpinnings. For example, when a new framework-level capability emerges in the Windows operating system, all Microsoft development language environments will have access to it rather than their original state—trapped in separate product-related silos. For example, prior to .NET, Visual Basic did not have the same capabilities as Visual C++, or Visual J++. A technical release for one product had no effect on or benefit for the other products.

The average technologist now comes to a table filled with frameworks, in many ways like a kid in a candy store. What we *can* do is unleash this power on our technical problems (but we'll only achieve one success at a time). What we *should* do is harness this power so we can focus it again and again.

....

Before laying down a single line of code, we should take a deep breath and a few steps back, and ask ourselves: What are the similarities between this effort and the last one? If we want to reuse something from our last effort, did we build it for reuse? If we know we'll need it for our next effort, will we take the steps to make it reusable for afterwards? If not, our ability to reuse will never gain traction.

NOTE *We'll also see repeatable themes in supply-chain, shipping, retail, telecommunications, banking, science, and other market areas. We should build reusable frameworks around and across these areas, exploiting similarities rather than hard-wiring their uniqueness.*

Building a framework requires finding the themes, the similarities, or the patterns of logical behavior and manipulation already present in our product. Application-centric frameworks lead to vertical markets and closed systems, while architecture-centric frameworks lead to horizontal markets, open and interoperable systems. As such, with a pattern-based implementation, each new capability rests on the foundation already built. The effect is not simple reuse, but *accelerated reuse*: each instance of reuse is far richer than its predecessors.

Simple Syntax

If the structural and behavioral details of all templates, adapters, and features are hidden from view, how do we realistically expose them to the outside world for consumption? I have already shown (with the Projects) some examples of textual statements used to dynamically define and access objects, cause those objects to interface and interact, and provide a way to encapsulate data and process in an application-specific context rather than hard-wiring. This requires attention to the syntax of the script itself.

The most flexible syntax for our structural metadata is:

```
Define EntityName as EntityType.
```

Since we've abstracted our types, we only have the following few "actual" examples:

```
Define Wrk1 as Simple
Define cntTest as Complex
Define MyRoutine as Routine
```

These are simple to parse, interpret, and act upon. We can sweep through lines of text, find every definition and create the appropriate entity, or create them on demand as they are encountered (or some combination).

Our behavioral syntax is also simple and flexible. Because we have two entity types (simple and complex), we can further reduce complexity. Behavior boils down to assignment or conditional evaluation. In both cases we have a left side and a right side, plus only four combinations to consider. The majority of dynamic Interpreters use a "$" for parameter or value substitution. Thus, in actual practice, we'll prefix all entities with a "$" parameter to provide quicker parsing, and a *Set* operator to quickly drive the Interpreter toward assignment. Consider this metadata macro example:

```
Set $Simple = $Simple
Set $Simple = $Complex.Property
Set $Complex.Action = $Simple
Set $Complex.Action = $Complex.Property
```

We will further define the Action and Property extensions with optional keys, representing our most complex operation, like so:

```
Set $Complex.Action(Key) = $Complex.Property(Key)
```

And that wraps it up. We can represent our most complex assignments with this syntax because it ultimately drives toward an interface pattern. This keeps our syntax boundaries simple and quickly executable.

Now, let's say we have two entities, a simple *Wrk1* variable and a complex *cntTest* container. The container will hold rows of employee information, including the employee ID and the employee name. Here's the metadata macro example:

```
Define Wrk1 as Simple
Define cntTest as Complex
Set $cntTest.Layout = EmpName|EmpID
Set $cntTest.Load = Select * from Emp
Set $Wrk1 = cntTest.Item(EmpID)
```

The preceding examples show the simple and complex entities interacting to produce an application-centric effect. Here's what really happens in the background:

1. The Interpreter will create a simple and complex object. By default we'll say that the complex type is a browsable row/column container.

2. The container will then connect to a database source (we'll predefine this elsewhere in an INI file) and use ActiveX Data Objects to fulfill the query.

3. The Interpreter receives the RecordSet and unloads the EmpName and EmpID (from the layout) into the container (cntTest), and sets its reference to the first row.

4.   It then accesses the value at the column designated by the EmpID layout label and places it into the simple variable (Wrk1).

5.   We now have a foundation for other operations, including sharing the value of Wrk1, or the entire contents of cntTest with other objects.

These very simple rules and examples show how we can ultimately activate powerful, reusable behaviors with easily parsable textual metadata. Once we start driving all of our application logic into the metadata, we affect behavior (and thus the user's experience) without changing software, and with shockwave turn-around. Where industry leaders cry for agile programmers and languages, our architecture will enable both.

Each time we build a new behavior, we must identify its operant patterns and drive toward them.

Achieving Pattern-Based Behavioral Control

We're typically mentored and trained into an application-centric mindset. Consequently, applying patterns as a basis to drive software construction requires us to re-tune development practices and the thought processes behind them. It's actually closer to a thought transformation, an inversion of our approach. As a developer and designer, we must move away from the practice of hard-wiring application behavior into our software. Therefore, it is important for us to embrace and immerse ourselves in the following realities now:

Reality #1: Nothing "real" exists inside the computer's run-time space.

Reality #2: Use software to transform the statically referenced entities into dynamic entities.

Reality #3: The entities and their behaviors are governed by rules. The default rules (software code) are static.

Reality #4: Through Interpreter patterns, we can use software to transform the normally static governing rules into dynamic rules.

Reality #5: Dynamically manufacture the end-user experience.

Reality #6: The application is external to the software.

Reality #1:
Nothing "Real" Exists Inside
the Computer's Run-Time Space

Every entity is virtual, and the result of a conceptual implementation. Building application-centric interfaces for direct wiring only masks their true nature and creates an illusion of control. (e.g., Employee objects are only real because we wire them so). Hard-wiring is bad—we know that. It inhibits reuse and leads to application logic "leakage" into software to control and maintain the hard-wired object.

The reality is that the machine creates the object in a virtual space totally out of our control, then represents the object to us in the form we've selected. If the machine will treat it the same either way, why not alleviate the application-centric pain and build our entities dynamically?

Every entity is virtual, so hard-wiring is only an illusion of control.

Reality #2:
Use Software to Transform the Statically
Referenced Entities into Dynamic Entities

Software can easily redefine objects into structurally generalized entities that can interoperate with other generalized entities. We'll use patterns (not unique interface calls) for instantiation, identification, activation, and termination.

A dynamic entity has the virtual appearance and behavior of a statically defined entity. However, a dynamic entity is assembled at run time from building blocks. Its behavior results from programmable capabilities. Static and dynamic entities *appear* identical both structurally and behaviorally. One is known at design time, the other is known only at run time. Because a dynamic object can change its structure, behavior, and appearance on the fly, we enable metamorphism.

Software's role now becomes enabling service, but not directly serving, the user.

Reality #3:
The Entities and Their Behaviors Are Governed by
Rules. The Default Rules (Software Code) Are Static

When we want objects to interact, the easiest way is to directly code the desired behavior and deploy it. The static behavioral rules (in software code) will invariably require revisiting for enhancement, rework, even redesign.

If we deploy dynamic behavioral rules in metadata, we will change the role of the software from the keeper of application rules to a broker for metadata rules. We can quickly stabilize software in this role. To meet end-user needs we'll change metadata (often by the hour), rather than software code.

Reality #4:
Through Interpreter Patterns, We Can Use Software to Transform the Normally Static Governing Rules into Dynamic Rules

Interpreters can input metadata to dynamically define structure and behavior. Syntax, keywords, and context all converge on capabilities to bring our application to life.

Behavioral metadata can command screens to commit their information to a database. We can tell databases to retrieve information for screen display. We can command servers to burst predefined reports, or tell screens to display themselves a certain way, with specific controls, command buttons, and labels for user consumption. We can define a physical screen layout with structural metadata, then add behavioral metadata to interact with the user.

An Interpreter uses metadata for rocket fuel, weaving the application into reality at run time.

Reality #5:
Dynamically Manufacture the End-User Experience

We should completely separate the user's application-level experience from the software. If the complete experience resides in metadata, the software will only need to access the metadata, execute according to the instructions therein, and the application will emerge as part of this activity.

The software then becomes a master broker—an engine of sorts. When a user requests a change, it takes place in metadata first (either with technical assistance or direct user input). If the supported metadata syntax will not cover the request, the developer will add the capability to the core software and redeploy it. As the core matures, the time between core changes will slowly increase until the application is fully supported with no software changes at all.

Reality #6:
The Application Is External to the Software

The software, from this point forward, will never again embed specific application logic. If we must include application-level logic for speed, we build a flexible subsystem and wrap it with an Adapter for automatic plug-and-play. Ideally, we can deploy the application-specific code as a standalone out-of-process program connected with a socket.

Migrating the volatile application-level specifics out of the core software at any level is a very profitable venture (even if some application-specific code—though wrapped and leashed—must remain). Separating the two logically will always provide greater reuse of the core. Separating them physically will provide greater longevity for the core without rebuild.

When dynamically constructing an application object, we'll define it by the sum of its building blocks, not by a specifically defined class. Ultimately, we see one level of core building blocks, or basic components, available to the framework as a starting point. We'll then see building-block assemblies to represent virtual application entities.

Using building blocks, the dynamic application object can more easily share information and events with other application objects. We can create structural and behavioral rules for any building block or group of building blocks, increasing their overall programmability. Thus, we guide their behavior by contextual, dynamic behavioral rules (in metadata), not by specifically crafted application software. In fact, nothing about the dynamic application object or its required logic should be embedded into the core software (they are all *realized* at run time).

When an Interpreter inputs metadata to affect structural and behavioral run-time aspects, this is called a *rules-driven* model. Each metadata instruction constitutes a rule, comprised of keywords to define and identify a dynamic structure, connect it to others, and govern their behavior.

The interpreted rules are more than just one-time, throwaway execution parameters for startup configuration alone. Once the rules are received from their external source, they are preprocessed, organized, and optimized for repeatable execution. This allows the Interpreter to rapidly and repeatedly activate on the same rule set. The rules themselves can also define instructions as to events they will observe, tying a programmed event to a particular set of interpreted behavioral rules (like a metadata subroutine or event-handler).

Attempting to establish a virtual model from a legacy, or more traditional model can result in various levels of so-called "technology whiplash" as our architecture transforms into the programmable model. We'll change the way we think about software and its uses, and forsake the application-centric mindset.

The user immerses into a near-magical experience, where needs are quickly met with high quality and functionality.

User requirements = volatility. Manage it with metadata and keep the actual software on a leash.

The application is dynamically realized, not compiled into physical form.

Our challenge is in forsaking software code as the repository for application behavioral rules.

We're trained into believing that the business (or science) implementation—the application—should be inside the actual software. Changing our mind about what constitutes the application (external metadata) and what comprises the software (language-level source code) is a first step—but a big step—toward our ultimate architectural model. We'll create a core architecture to manage and create an experience based on behavioral metadata rules. It dynamically manages different experiences and is not bound to the detailed elements of the experience itself.

How then, do we embrace the structural and behavioral aspects for their true nature (virtual) and rise above them? It's impossible as long as the behavioral rules are in software code. The required steps follow:

1. Change our mind about the physical location and role of "software" and the "application."

2. Commit to conform all structural interfaces to a common pattern with adapters.

3. Identify common behaviors and structures as component building blocks.

4. Build Interpreter logic and syntax to facilitate run-time structural definition and relationship, plus behavioral activation.

5. Transform the software behavioral control itself (which can be seen in Figure 3-8) into virtual behavioral rules in metadata. Only then will we enable a truly dynamic end-user experience.

The virtual model can change its run-time structure, behavior, and role dynamically because it's externally programmable with metadata. Thus, our software architects can build valuable, reusable components while our application-level efforts drive the practicality of our framework.

Building Valuable and Practical Components

Here's an interesting concept: building robust, re-usable components that are valuable and practical, so we can make some money at it. On the valuable side, we shouldn't build objects or components that are only valuable to us. They might be cool concepts but we're wasting our time. We get excited about exploiting some newfound "cool" implementation without regard that critical deliverables are due in days, if not hours (and we've found some time to play?). Whether we might use this toy somewhere, anywhere in the future is absolutely immaterial. It has no value *now*. Our time has value now, and should not be wasted.

Invariably, when the smoke clears on our current project, we might find our newfound implementation available on the internet. We might even receive it in our development tool's next service pack! Don't be one of our starry-eyed ranks racing to the finish line with a marginal innovation. We should save our energy for something more valuable.

On the practical side, don't implement perceived value for impractical results. This often manifests itself in a project focusing major efforts on lightly-used features while ignoring others, even the core of the solution. It also appears when software is injected into a solution, without design or planning, in order to meet a short-term goal. If we do this enough times, the deviations will become the norm and the original design will evaporate. *Practical* will always translate to long-term viability. Otherwise, it's just more throwaway software.

Embracing practical object modeling means developing a healthy skepticism for everything we've been told is the Natural Order of Things. Pragmatists push the edge because we know where the limits are, or aren't afraid to find them. We have often learned our lessons the hard way and are not easily swayed by hype. Many of our innovations are the most dramatic in the industry, but are only realized years later when they finally penetrate the mainstream. At their inception, the innovations are non-standard, so they take time to gather momentum. In software development, good ideas will stand the test of time, but practical innovations find their way into the very fabric of the culture and its tools.

Innovations are borne on the wings of delivery. Implementing an innovation with production strength, consistently and repeatedly, reinforces its value and practicality. Rather than focus on innovation with things we've never done, focus on innovating with things we've repeatedly done, and that we keep returning to. Conversely, if we repeatedly attempt to implement something that consistently fails for the same reasons, we are chasing a rainbow. We should abandon it and save ourselves the grief.

Innovation requires the traction of reuse, or it cannot gain a foothold.

In "Project 3—Behaviors" at the end of this chapter, I expand on the Turbo-Collection structure and show some ways to build automatic behavioral control. The versatility and power of the TurboCollection make it an excellent structural foundation for defining dynamic entities and controlling their behavior. If the TurboCollection enables innovation, it's only because I've used it so many times and in so many places. It qualifies as an example of innovating on what is used most. If we want true innovation to appear in our software, capitalize on what we use the most of—especially those widgets or helper utilities that form foundational structure or behavioral glue.

Innovation requires traction within our technology domains, at the architectural level and the human knowledge level. If we cannot reuse prior work, we spin our tires, generally unable to move forward with innovative ideas. When we gather steam through reusability, we gain the upper hand on leashing the technology and the means to deploy it. Additionally, all of our prior work converges in the software where our hard-won knowledge is available for others—they don't have to repeat the pain.

Obtaining Expert Advice

If mentoring is our best means of knowledge transfer, we reduce the learning process to the lowest denominators. First, we assume our mentors have the time to spend with apprentices, but their time and knowledge is simply too valuable (so we put them into focused, high-intensity delivery). By the time an apprentice is strong enough to deploy, they spend time heads-down on a keyboard, unable to come up for air (even for a few hours). Often, a novice's knowledge and skill increase their employee market value and they bolt for higher pay.

The bottom line: we're often unable (as a rule) to gain traction in knowledge transfer through human interaction, so we must capture it another way.

When we boil down technical knowledge into a reusable software repository, we capture valuable developer expertise. The objective is to let our gifted ranks shine their brilliance into reusable, practical building blocks, then allow our novice/apprentice ranks to learn from the software by proxy. Most developers are self-taught, and find their most valuable learning experiences in the heat of battle, attempting to converge the efforts of others with their own. They might browse sample code, Internet discussion groups, or other self-service outlets to gain understanding. The information must be at their fingertips when they need it, and a reusable repository serves this purpose perfectly. Conversely, if our model is to let them learn from their mistakes, our project and ultimately our shop suffers from their lurches in productivity.

When we combine the capabilities of an Interpreter, fueled by structural and behavioral metadata, we have a programmable, *rules based system*, sometimes called an *expert system*. If we can capture the knowledge of experts and reuse it, we effectively have the expert working for us by proxy. We can package their experience for consistent and reliable redelivery. The software behaves as the expert would, so we receive the repeated benefit of their knowledge (even long after they've exited the project or the company itself). An expert system has the added benefit of building intelligence directly into the software. Over time, it is able to actively think and learn.

Such a framework applies reality-based behavioral rules using an event-driven interpreting engine. It will encapsulate and control architectural components and expose them to the Interpreter. The engine will receive data and rule input, converting their syntax and semantics into internal actions such as connecting components together, initiating communications or processes, manipulating data source components, and other interactions with the computing environment. Many such engines have a series of sub-engines operating as self-contained expert systems in specific computing domains.

Software developers frequently create expert systems for industry, business and science. A few examples include stock trading, accounting, weather forecasting, hospital management, engineering, restaurant management, airline scheduling, architectural design, insurance claims, and human resource management. Whatever the implementation, an expert system has the capability of performing the same actions of the expert as if the expert were present.

Reusable software captures the brilliance of our best developers and deploys their experience by proxy.

The real trick for us then, is to capture the expert knowledge of a senior programmer and expose it to other programmers for their regular use. This allows the senior programmers to attack even larger issues while their expert knowledge disseminates vicariously, without their constant active involvement. If a novice has a concern about a best practice, the master source library will become a rich resource. Thus a novice can "ping" a master developer for mentoring and coaching advice—in context—without requiring the mentor's constant, over-the-shoulder presence.

The behavioral rules of an expert system are expressed in textual metadata. The system's primary engine, the behavioral controller, will accept, interpret, and act on them at run time. The controller can effectively manufacture its own run-time meta-framework and operate it within context of the behavioral rules, unbound by any internally defined or preconceived application-level role. Scalability, interoperability, and flexibility are promoted by such a virtual controller. They are the foundation stones of a virtual architecture, not afterthoughts or bolt-on features.

The expert system model depicted in Figure 3-8 has the following key features:

Seed metadata: The information used to initiate and activate the entire model. It contains structural definition and behavioral instructions.

Interpreter: Inputs metadata to manufacture structural entities and cause them to interoperate according to the behavioral metadata.

Outcome: The application experience, whether driving screens, reports, information, or other application-level quantities.

Dynamic metadata: Additional metadata, constructed or acquired, and understood by the Interpreter at run time, as a secondary outcome of the initial metadata activation. This information is fed back into the Interpreter (back propagation) and commingled with the seed metadata, enriching it and the eventual outcome.

Learning capability: Because the expert system manufactures or acquires its own metadata instructions and enriches its seed metadata input, it exhibits a self-learning, even self-programming capability. An application configured to exploit all of these features is a *learning* system, also called a *software neural node,* the foundation for a *neural network* and ultimately a machine intelligence model.

Metamorphic behavior: As the system learns, it automatically adapts itself to changes in structure or behavior, and allows us to modify its behavior without changing software. The same software can create multiple instances of itself, delegate roles and responsibilities to its peers, and feed them dynamic instructions so they exhibit *application-level behavior that was never realized until run time.*

Expert System

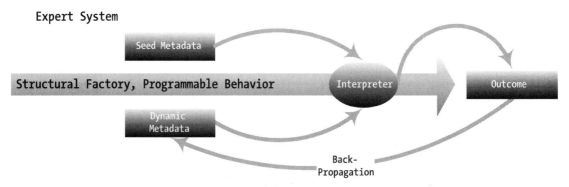

Figure 3-8. Expert system model

NOTE *We could define three separate repositories of application metadata, one for accounting, one for marketing, and one for data warehousing. If the same program can activate and execute all three repositories interchangeably, it is metamorphic.*

How can we apply metamorphism on our current or upcoming projects? Are any existing applications or examples using such a model?

Applying Behaviors

In 1992, the Defense Advanced Research Program Administration (DARPA) received a proposal for military aircraft technology called a *Resource/Duty Framework*[3], described in the following abstract:

> *In a military aircraft, a* Resource *is any instrument connected to the cockpit, whether directly or indirectly. A* Duty *is an unconditional task using one or more Resources. While the pilot is a defacto resource, the pilot cannot substitute for advanced pilot aid technology, such as radar and telemetry. If a military assault from air or ground disables a given Resource, some Duties will not be completed, placing the pilot's life at risk.*

> *An objective is to link the aircraft's Duties to* Interchangeable Resources. *That is, both Resources and Duties are interfaced to a common center, and linked based upon a* best fit *for function and performance. If a Resource is disabled, the Duty has the freedom (and intelligence) to fulfill itself through one or more other Resources.*

> *This provides a means to move toward a* virtual cockpit. *If an aircraft's cockpit Resources are disabled, but another similar aircraft or even a ground source can serve as a surrogate Resource for the disabled Resources, the pilot can get the aircraft to safety. Depending on the severity of damage, the pilot could continue to operate, even engage an enemy, using the surrogate cockpit resources of a wingman aircraft.*

This abstract proposed a dramatic departure in military machine control. A self-contained system (fighter aircraft cockpit) able to instantly integrate to another similar system, sharing resources to empower the pilot. In 1992 this was a proposal, but within 10 years it became a practical reality for a large portion of military vehicles. We now see such features entering the automotive and wireless marketplace.

These practical capabilities also allow people to have virtual presence without physical presence, or attach physical presence to virtual presence. The two are interchangeable, giving busy people such luxuries as a "virtual office," online banking, bill paying, and shopping. We *project* our presence into a virtual environment, where our "virtual self" interacts with greater speed and flexibility than our physical equivalent.

Real-time military applications might benefit from interchangeable building blocks but what of commercial endeavors?

Enterprise Application Integration (EAI)

Enterprise applications can all exist within the same enterprise computing environment. These include legacy or recently installed bases such as human resource packages, manufacturing and retail environments, supply-chain management, accounting systems, and so on. These applications "talk" to each other over a "bus," which is really a graphical depiction of a common network. Each application must be wired to another with specific structural "glue" (software built to interface the applications to one another) through CORBA, COM, or other interface support protocols.

Thus, an accounting package on a Sun platform may only interchange data with a human resources package on a Hewlett-Packard system if a specific piece of software directly links them together. Many software houses, consulting firms, and integrators sell or build these kinds of "glue" software for extraordinary prices.

For example, many EAI architects design and implement a scenario similar to the one depicted in Figure 3-9. This architecture exposes all enterprise resources directly to each other, requiring them to individually understand how to interact with their peers.

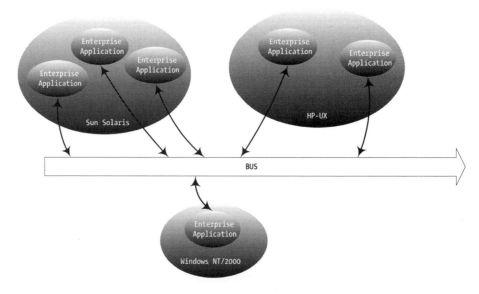

Figure 3-9. Enterprise Application Integration false-start example

This approach continues to represent application-centric architecture, where all software is written for the specific focus of an application. When one of the enterprise applications requires upgrade or replacement, the action directly affects its neighbors. We cannot unhook Accounting on the Sun from the

Reporting environment on the Windows platform without incurring a penalty on both. We will have to restructure, perhaps rewrite software to accommodate changes anywhere on the bus.

Contrast the application-centric approach to the architecture-centric model depicted in Figure 3-10.

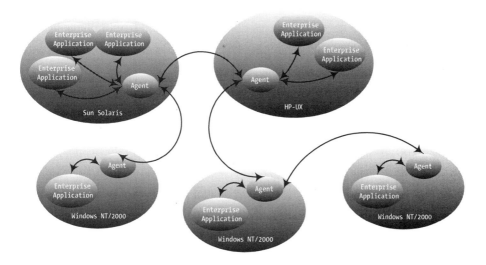

Figure 3-10. Enterprise Application Integration using Interoperable Agents

When we combine the application adapter, a system adapter, and a Visitor/Observer pattern, we see another super-pattern emerge, that of the *Agent*. This pattern is co-hosted with the enterprise application and actively communicates with it. The Agent serves as a broker when we need the application's services. When multiple Agents cross-communicate automatically, we have surrogate connectivity rather than direct application connectivity.

Architecturally, Agents exchange information among themselves with an interface pattern driven by instructions from interpreted metadata. Thus an external subscriber (such as a desktop or web application) interfaces with a local Agent only. The local Agent will broker requests to remote Agents. Thus, Agents are by nature *passive,* and event-driven.

In the example in Figure 3-10, each of the Enterprise Applications and its computing *environment* is hidden, wrapped by the Agent, serving as the gateway for all external entities. Enterprise Applications wanting to interact with other Enterprise Applications need only interact with their local Agent, which will broker the activity. The Agent negotiates all information exchange and creates a seamless, portable wrapper for the computing environment and the applications it contains.

In Figure 3-10, examine the Agents on the Sun, Hewlett Packard, and Windows platforms. Each Agent communicates externally with another Agent, but locally with its cadre of applications. The application behind the agent could be replaced, upgraded, or otherwise modified in a way that, at most, only affects the Agent, not the other applications or computing environments.

Plug-and-play, at the enterprise level.

The overall effect provides the pattern-based illusion of a cohesive operating environment, or a *surrogate computing environment*. For example, we could ship the same metadata instructions to several agents and expect parallel behavior. We could also ship partial instructions to one agent and partial instructions to another, including instructions to cause information exchange between them. This allows one Agent to process asynchronously to another, even though both are completing part of a task. Similarly, we could ship all instructions to one Agent, which in turn could delegate work (if necessary) to other Agents as resources (sending them subsets of the original instructions). The possibilities are limitless. The flexibility and reusability are dramatically different because, depending upon which Agent receives what instructions, a given Agent can behave in multiple, disparate roles.

NOTE *Surrogate computing environments exist in various forms, including parallel virtual machines. This model adapts to both operating systems and enterprise applications such that all entities, custom or otherwise, enjoy interaction within a common computing environment, not a set of "connected" computing environments.*

Multiple Agents can exist in parallel or *multi-present* form (as depicted in Figure 3-10), allowing computing environments to share resources transparently. When we must enhance communication capability, we address the Agents, not applications. New computing environments or applications will require the development and installation of an Agent (or the enhancement of an existing Agent), but this allows it to interoperate with all enterprise applications, not just one. Behavior and control are then based on the patterns controlled by the Agents, not the individual applications.

Because the architecture is externally programmable, no Agent has a defined application "tier." Imagine the same programmable executable running in different parts of the enterprise. One runs on a server in a "service" mode. Another runs on a desktop in a user interface mode, while others exist elsewhere in various roles. If all are programmed to communicate with one another, and even the basis of the communication is programmable, we've enabled virtual integration enterprise-wide. It is not three-tier or even multi-tier, it is tier-less.

With such a possibly dramatic transformation of enterprise integration and interoperability, why don't we see more of it? The answer lies in a perception of value, which is sometimes elusive and intangible.

What Is the Real Value?

In conference with several enterprise technical leaders, they saw the potential of the metamorphic approach, but still could not grasp its overall value. I asked them a series of questions to bring it all together.

- What if you could master reuse in every language, with the ability to start new projects from where the last project left off, not from scratch each time?

- What if you could capture the brilliance of your best developers and deploy it for reuse everywhere, giving them a vicarious presence in every subsequent project (even after they leave your company)?

- Additionally, what if every project could capitalize on the quality and brilliance of every developer in your enterprise, not just the ones attached to the project?

- What if you could mentor novices with this captured repository?

- What if you could meet high-intensity user demands without destabilizing your products or introducing flaws from developer fatigue or inexperience?

- What if you could meet user demands as quickly as they change their minds?

- What if you could change screens layouts, database definitions, user interface look, feel, and behavior, and deploy them for consumption almost *instantly* without compiling a single binary product?

- What if you could deploy and maintain new and existing applications without changing software?

- What if you could deploy the same application on Sun, Windows, and HP operating systems interchangeably, or talk to any resident database without changing software?

- What if you had the deterministic ability to meet the aggressive demands of an end user, knowing you could meet their deadlines without killing your development staff, losing money, or risking your reputation?

- What if your technical environment was so productive, exciting, and fun to use, that you could acquire and keep the best technologists, stabilize your workforce, and gain traction for innovation?

- What if you could wake up each morning with the imminent promise of success rather than a day centered on risk or crisis management?

- What if you could deliver more value than your competitors, charge more money for it, and keep the risks on a tight leash?

- What if your deliveries were more than just on-schedule, on-target, and "complete?" What if they were so wildly (and effortlessly) over-delivered that your end users could only respond with "Wow?"

For each question, I received an emphatic and enthusiastic *YES*. However, it was coupled with caution and skepticism, because it really does sound *so good*, it's got to be either heresy or mythology. Everyone *knows* (don't they?) that software development is painful, expensive, and fraught with risk. But the metamorphic approach transforms the process into fun, profitable, and successful activity—and that's the real value.

We're now in need of some power-tools, especially metamorphic enablers. The following project, and the next chapter, dive deeper into the kinds of tools and capabilities required for highly reusable and re-deliverable software.

Project 3—Behaviors

This chapter concludes with some examples of automatic behavior and building-block behavioral templates. We'll build on the prior projects to maintain momentum, so if you haven't done them in the past two chapters, take a little extra time now to wrap them up. The continuity across these projects builds momentum and increases understanding.

The following examples appear as ProjectThree in either the VBNET/Project 3 Behaviors/ subdirectory or VB6/Project 3 Behaviors/ subdirectory. The examples are in VB .NET but the VB6 listings are identical apart from some minor syntax.

As with all the projects, the software code is in the "main" module, so just single-step and follow along.

Observers and Automatic Behavior Control

When building behavioral patterns, pay careful attention to how much the structural patterns are helping you along. If the structures and interfaces create awkward workarounds or unnecessary wiring and decision trees, simplify them.

Every programming problem has a core set of difficult issues to resolve, along with a host of petty ones that support the user's experience as a whole. Many basic and trivial behaviors repeatedly intersect on every project and product we build. If we can make some of the more mundane behaviors automatic, it allows us to enable them once and move on to the tougher application issues at hand. Let's automate the little stuff so we can put our full attention on the big stuff.

The first aspect of automatic behavior is exhibited in the Observer pattern. This pattern is evident in many queue-based services, such as email servers (such as Lotus Notes, Microsoft Outlook/Exchange, or Groupwise), Queue managers (such as IBM MQSeries), Microsoft MSMQ, store-and-forward servers, and database replicators, to name a few. A common usage of Observation is a database trigger, where a specific data element is keyed to a specific type of event and initiates action when certain conditions are satisfied. An example of desktop Observation capability is when some controls are able to change state (enable/disable) or values based on events and data in other controls. (For example, changing the value of a text box while the user browses a grid, or likewise enabling/disabling menu options based on specific grid data.)

The basic idea behind Observation is to allow one or more objects to participate in the internal implementation of another object, with the least possible impact. Imagine someone from an auditing service arriving in your department to simply observe, take notes, and report back to the home office. The auditor does not interfere with your department's regular operations. When certain events occur during the day, the auditor dials a number on his cell phone, relays information to the person on the other end, and hangs up. The auditor does not ask you to stop, slow down, or otherwise modify your normal pace or activity. If the auditor is efficient, you won't even know he's there.

Let's try a simple example with the ParmNode. Each ParmNode is enabled to participate with Observers by default. If you examine the simple Observer framework implementation in ParmNode and replicate it on any class of your choice, you will automatically imbue that class with Observation capability.

Let's set up several TurboCollections filled with ParmNodes of various values. Here, I'll use a Rainbow, a Western, and a Test TurboCollection:

```
Dim tcTest As New TurboCollection()
Dim tcRainBow As New TurboCollection()
Dim tcWestern As New TurboCollection()
'###
```

```
'Colors of Rainbow
tcRainBow.AddItem ("Red", "R1", "R1")
tcRainBow.AddItem ("Orange", "O1", "O1")
tcRainBow.AddItem ("Yellow", "Y1", "Y1")
tcRainBow.AddItem ("Green", "G1", "G1")
tcRainBow.AddItem ("Blue", "B1", "B1")
tcRainBow.AddItem ("Indigo", "I1", "I1")
tcRainBow.AddItem ("Violet", "V1", "V1")
'####
'####Subjects of Spaghetti Western Classic
tcWestern.AddItem ("TheGood", "TG1", "TG1")
tcWestern.AddItem ("TheBad", "TB1", "TB1")
tcWestern.AddItem ("TheUgly", "TU1", "TU1")
```

Now let's set up some of the ParmNodes to observe others. We'll need to add an element to the tcTest structure, like so:

```
tcTest.AddItem ("", "R", "R")      'add a node tagged "R" to tcTest
```

Now let's tell tcTest to add an Observer on behalf of a ParmNode held by the tcRainbow structure. We'll tell the Observer to observe Item-to-Item ("Item#Item") for simplicity, like so:

```
tcTest.Ref.Observe("Item#Item") =
                    tcRainBow.Find("R1")  ' Red Node will observe
```

With this setup, any modification to the "Item" property in the tcTest ParmNode will automatically be forwarded to the appropriate ParmNode in the tcRainbow structure (in this case, the ParmNode representing the "Red" spectrum. Now let's add another tcTest node to include the tcWestern structure.

```
tcTest.AddItem( "", "W", "W")        ' add a node tagged "W" to tcTest
tcTest.Ref.Observe("Item#Item") =
                    tcWestern.Find("TG1")  ' "the Good" will observe
```

Now we are ready to test the Observer behavior by simply modifying the Item property on each tcTest ParmNode. Note that the TurboCollection's *Find* function will locate and return the ParmNode with the given tag, like so:

```
tcTest.Find("W").Item = "Sergio Leone"    'access the "W" ParmNode and modify it
tcTest.Find("R").Item = "Reddish Tint"    'access the "R" ParmNode and modify it
```

Next, examine the contents of tcTest, tcRainbow, and tcWestern to view the results in each ParmNode's Item property contents.

These are the contents of tcTest:

```
tcTest.Dump()
    "Sergio Leone", " Reddish Tint"
```

The contents of tcRainbow are as follows (change is bolded):

```
tcRainbow.Dump()
    "Reddish Tint", "Orange", "Yellow",
            "Green",  "Blue",  "Indigo", "Violet"
```

Here are the contents of tcWestern:

```
tcWestern.Dump()
    "Sergio Leone", "The Bad", "The Ugly"
```

Note how the modification of the ParmNode object in tcTest automatically propagated to the other ParmNodes in completely separate lists.

Now let's take it one step further and observe it in the opposite direction. We will want to allow modification of a ParmNode in the tcRainbow or tcWestern structures and have it automatically propagated to the tcTest structure, as follows:

```
tcRainBow.Find("O1").Observe("Item#Item") = tcTest.Find("R")
tcWestern.Find("TB1").Observe("Item#Item") = tcTest.Find("W")
```

Next, let's modify these ParmNodes and see what we get:

```
tcRainBow.Find("O1").Item = "Italian Stallion"
tcWestern.Find("TB1").Item = "Orange Apple"
```

After this operation, the contents of tcTest should be as follows:

```
tcTest.Dump
"Orange Apple", "Italian Stallion"
```

The contents of tcRainbow should be the following:

```
"Orange Apple", "Orange Apple", "Yellow",  "Green",  "Blue",  "Indigo", "Violet"
```

These are the contents of tcWestern:

```
"Italian Stallion", "Italian Stallion", "The Ugly"
```

Did you expect to get this result? Why did posting information into a ParmNode on tcRainbow result in modifying another ParmNode on tcRainbow? A similar effect occurred on tcWestern.

The answer is this: Observation is still active from tcTest into tcRainbow and tcWestern *from the first exercise*. Thus, this second exercise resulted in a cascading observation behavior. Posting information to tcRainbow's "O1" ParmNode was forwarded to the "R" ParmNode on tcTest. Since tcTest's "R" was also being observed by "R1" on tcRainbow, it was forwarded there as well.

On your own, try an experiment that sets up two ParmNodes to observe each other (a change in one automatically forwards it to the other). This is not an uncommon requirement and (if allowing external programmability) could actually result by accident (several ParmNodes observing each other in a circular reference). Without the proper controls in place, each ParmNode would be caught in an infinite cascade, a deadlock loop. With the proper controls, each one can happily trade information. The Observers have already been configured with the proper controls.

Note that the Observer provides data interchange by passing the given key (e.g., "Item" or "Enabled") as a property tag into the given object by way of an *Item* property, then lets the object internally resolve the value. This allows the Observer to make a blind, parameter-driven call into an object, retrieve the information and then post it into the observing object with another blind, parameter-driven call. In the Listings 3-2 and 3-3, which is more flexible over the long-term?

Listing 3-2. Structural Hard Wiring

```
Select Case InParm
    Case "Item" :           strW = Inref.Item
    Case "Enabled" :        strW = Inref.Enabled
    Case "Visible" :        strW = Inref.Visible
End Select
Select Case OutParm
    Case "Item" :           Outref.Item = strW
    Case "Enabled" :        Outref.Enabled = strW
    Case "Visible" :        Outref.Visible = strW
End Select
```

Listing 3-3. Structural Parametric Metamorphism

```
OutRef.Item(OutParm) = Inref.Item(InParm)
```

In Listing 3-2, the software must bind itself to a decision matrix. What if a given object wants to implement a property such as "Height", or perhaps "Empty"? Example One will not allow it without a software change in the Observer. Listing 3-3 provides the greatest flexibility (and the least coding change) to implement the observation. This is an example of structural resilience and behavioral automation and simplification *directly enabled by patterns*.

Note that Listing 3-2 essentially externalizes the representations of objects within its behavioral control. Listing 3-3 simply executes the interchange, expecting each object to handle its own representation transparently.

Imagine how difficult our publish/subscribe services would be to manage and maintain if, as a central broker, they had to manage and scrub information as they entered and exited the various internet sites. Such services are simply brokers, managing the store-and-forward behavior without involvement in the actual data format or what it represents.

Automatic information-sharing eliminates an enormous amount of repetitive, tedious coding. However, what if we want to share information conditionally? Don't we need a dynamic way to program decision logic?

Conditional Operators

Dynamic condition testing is another way to provide external programmability. Most programmatic operation is driven by logical decisions, ultimately the result of simple math with *True* or *False* as the outcome. When we compare two pieces of data, they typically fall into one of two categories: strings and numbers. Evaluating one as the other might have value, but we also need a means to evaluate them in context of their actual values. For example, a string value of "0001" is numerically equivalent to "001" but is *not* equal if compared as strings. We need a way to numerically evaluate similar information points arriving from disparate sources.

So we have simple results (True/False) and simple data (numeric or string), so let's simplify the expressions. Only six expression operators are of any consequence (Table 3-4). They are the Greater Than (GT), Greater Than or Equal To (GE), Less Than (LT), Less Than or Equal To (LE), Equal To (EQ), nor Not Equal To (NE). Since any of these could be evaluating raw numbers (by Value) or strings as numeric values, we have an additional suffix "V" for each: (GTV, GEV, LTV, LEV, EQV, NEV).

Table 3-4. Conditional Operators

COMPARISON	STRING OPERATOR	NUMERIC OPERATOR
Greater Than	GT	GTV
Greater Than or Equal To	GE	GEV
Less Than	LT	LTV
Less Than or Equal To	LE	LEV
Not Equal To	NE	NEV
Equal To	EQ	EQV

The first means to execute condition evaluation is to perform an if-then-else decision matrix each time the condition is re-encountered. A second means assumes that each condition will be encountered more than once, (as in a loop) and will require re-evaluation each time. If submitting dynamic instructions to the program, these could come in the form of a loop/Iterator or a multiple-pass subroutine-like script. This means a given condition could be fetched, parsed, evaluated, and executed with each pass (not very efficient). Machines avoid this problem with *caching,* that is, they fetch, decode, and prepare computer instructions, then store them in memory. Many processing instructions are tight loops and decisions, so this strategy allows a processor to burn at high temperature (avoiding the fetch/decode cycle unless absolutely necessary).

We can cache our decision processing also, avoiding the need to parse and evaluate a decision statement with each encounter. To do this, we will have to encapsulate the actual decision point into its own class.

To this end, I have built six classes, each to demonstrate this simple behavior. They correspond to a specific conditional operator, according to the following list:

- EQ: conIsEqualTo

- GT: conIsGreaterThan

- GE: conIsGreaterThanOrEqualTo

- LT: conIsLessThan

- LE: conIsLessThanOrEqualTo

- NE: conIsNotEqualTo

Each of the classes, upon initialization, will be instructed to perform their evaluation either in pure text mode (e.g., standard "EQ" form) or to evaluate members as values (e.g., "EQV" form). Each has a very simple construction, similar to Listing 3-4 used for the "EQ" condition:

Listing 3-4. Example of the IsEqualTo Implementation

```
Public Function Create(iParent As Object, iParm As String) As conIsEqualTo
  On Error Resume Next                      'error check
  Dim oNew As conIsEqualTo
  oNew = New conIsEqualTo()                 'build a new one
  Create = oNew                             'pass it along
  oNew.Init (iParent, iParm)               'just initialize it first
  End Function
'####
Public Sub Init(iParent As Object, iParm As String)
  On Error Resume Next
  oParent = iParent                         'init the object
  blnIsValue = (iParm = "V")                'check for numeric eval
End Sub
'####
Public Function Evaluate(strLHS As String, strRHS As String) As Boolean
  On Error Resume Next
  Evaluate = False
  If blnIsValue Then                        'if check as numeric then
    Evaluate = CLng(strLHS) = CLng(strRHS)  'typecast and evaluate
  Else
    Evaluate = strLHS = strRHS              'else just one-to-one
  End If
End Function
```

To provide fast, factory-based access to these objects, we need to load them into an organized fractal factory for quick run-time access. The code in Listing 3-5 will build a TurboCollection, load it with nodes keyed on string or numeric evaluation (e.g., EQ or EQV) and associate them with the appropriate evaluation object.

Listing 3-5. Adding Conditional Operator Objects

```
Dim tcCon as New TurboCollection
   tcCon.AddItem ("", ".EQ.", ".EQ.")            'account for 'EQ' and wrap with dots
   tcCon.Ref.obj = New conIsEqualTo()            'setup a seed object for the evaluation
   tcCon.AddItem( "", ".NE.", ".NE.")            'do the same for all other evaluations
   tcCon.Ref.obj = New conIsNotEqualTo()
   tcCon.AddItem("", ".LT.", ".LT.")
   tcCon.Ref.obj = New conIsLessThan()
   tcCon.AddItem( "", ".LE.", ".LE.")
   tcCon.Ref.obj = New conIsLessThanOrEqualTo()
   tcCon.AddItem("", ".GT.", ".GT.")
   tcCon.Ref.obj = New conIsGreaterThan()
   tcCon.AddItem ("", ".GE.", ".GE.")
   tcCon.Ref.obj = New conIsGreaterThanOrEqualTo()
```

Initialize the second half of the TurboCollection as follows with "V" Items (for numeric values) and similar keys to above:

```
tcCon.AddItem "V", ".EQV.", ".EQV.")             'equate based on value
tcCon.Ref.obj = New conIsEqualTo()               'add the seed object
tcCon.AddItem ("V", ".NEV.", ".NEV.")
tcCon.Ref.obj = New conIsNotEqualTo()
tcCon.AddItem ("V", ".LTV.", ".LTV.")
tcCon.Ref.obj = New conIsLessThan()
tcCon.AddItem ("V", ".LEV.", ".LEV.")
tcCon.Ref.obj = New conIsLessThanOrEqualTo()
tcCon.AddItem ("V", ".GTV.", ".GTV.")
tcCon.Ref.obj = New conIsGreaterThan()
tcCon.AddItem ("V", ".GEV.", ".GEV.")
tcCon.Ref.obj = New conIsGreaterThanOrEqualTo()
```

Now let's optimize this list into a tree for fast access, like so:

```
tcCon.TreeBuild      'static list - so optimize it all for fast search
```

Next, we set up a StringAdapter to accept three pieces of information: two of them are "variables" and the third is the "operator." Here is the string we will attempt to evaluate:

```
"0001" EQV "001"
```

We separate each element with spaces, allowing the string parser to find them quickly. If the "variables" could also contain spaces, the parser could produce undesirable variables by breaking them apart. I have wrapped the numeric strings with quote characters because many times parameters arrive this way and we'll need a way to show where the string begins and ends (if embedded spaces are present).

In order to load the string with the proper initial value in Visual Basic, we need the following syntax:

```
strWrk = """" & "0001" & """" & " EQV " & """" & "001" & """"
```

Now let's parse the string and have a look:

```
strA.Parse (strWrk, " ")                          'parse on the space
'dump It for viewing In Immediate Window
strA.Dump()
```

The strA.Dump method should display the following in the Immediate Window:

```
|"0001"|
|EQV|
|"001"|
```

Next, we can browse the string and perform the evaluation. For starters, let's browse the string's TurboCollection and set the token EQV's reference to the appropriate evaluation class in Listing 3-6.

Listing 3-6. Set Up the String Adapter Token with Conditional Evaluation

```
strA.MoveFirst ()                                 'reset to beginning.
'####
Do
  ' is the conditional notation it in the list?
  pWrk = tcCon.Find("." & strA.Item & ".")
  If Not pWrk Is Nothing Then                     'yes we found it!
      'use fractal seed to create a new one
      ' using contents of Item to Initialze with "V" or ""
  pOb = pWrk.obj.Create(Nothing, pWrk.Item)
  Set strA.Ref.obj = pOb                          'set the StringAdapter's ref
                                                  ' object to this new
                                                  ' conditional object
```

```
Else
                    'otherwise just strip out the quotes
  strW = strA.ReplaceSubString(strA.Item, """", "")
                    'and replace it without the quotes
  strA.Item = strW
End If
'####
strA.MoveNext()                                'keep looking until
Loop While strA.More                           ' end of string
```

The strA.Dump method should display the following in the Immediate Window:

```
|0001|
|EQV|
|001|
```

Now the token node containing "EQV" anchors an object of type conIsEqualTo, initialized to perform "numeric" evaluations. This StringAdapter is now ready to help perform evaluation on its contents, so let's try one. We'll use the embedded StringAdapter's Find() function that returns the actual node value rather than the string contents of Item(), like so:

```
Dim blnEval As Boolean
  'evaluate left (0) and right (2) items
blnEval = strA.Find(1).obj.Evaluate(strA.Item(0), strA.Item(2))
```

The values at strA.Item(0) (string "0001") and strA.Item(2) (string "001") are presented to the *Evaluate()* function on the conIsEqualTo instance anchored on strA.Find(1). The conIsEqualTo instance is invoked, the parameters are type-cast to integers, evaluated, and since both are numerically equal to 1, the value of *True* will be placed in the blnEval variable.

As a separate exercise, experiment with the same input string, only remove the EQV and replace it with EQ:

```
  strWrk = """" & "0001" & """" & " EQ " & """" & "001" & """"
```

Step through the code again and see what it does. It will evaluate to *False* this time. Can you tell why? (A *string* of "0001" is not equal to a *string* of "001".) Is there a conditional operator you could use that would provide a *True* without using one of the numeric conditional evaluations? (Hint: Try LE or LT.)

Looking Deeper

Can we set up a simple experiment that allows us to replace the strA.Item(0) value and the strA.Item(2) value using Observation? Can we redirect the Observed values into the string's references and then execute a conditional evaluation against them?

In order to reference the token nodes in the StringAdapter, we'll use the Find() functions. An example follows:

```
Dim tcTest As New TurboCollection
tcTest.AddItem( "", "", "")          'add an empty Item to It - placeholder
tcTest.AddItem ("", "", "" )         'add another empty Item to It - placeholder
'###We'll use FindByIndex to locate the nodes on tcTest!
        'observe 1st node of tcTest
tcTest.FindByIndex(0).Observe("Item#Item") = strA.Find(0)
        'observe 2nd node of tcTest
tcTest.FindByIndex(1).Observe("Item#Item") = strA.Find(2)
        'make the 1st  value a numeric 238
tcTest.FindByIndex(0).Item = "238"
        '2nd  value a numeric 238 also!
tcTest.FindByIndex(1).Item = "0000238"
```

Now perform a dump of the StringAdapter. We should get these values:

```
strA.Dump()
|238|
|EQV|
|0000238|
```

Next, execute the evaluation as before. If the evaluation operator is "EQV" as in the first exercise example, the following statement should evaluate to *True* (numeric comparison).

```
blnEval = strA.Find(1).obj.Evaluate(strA.Item(0), strA.Item(2))
If blnEval Then Debug.Writeline( "By Jove! I've Got it!")
```

Pay careful attention to the patterns in action here. The StringAdapter supports a behavioral decision function. The tcTest TurboCollection serves as a holding area for incoming data values (e.g., parameters that are forwarded to the decision controller). Could we label the tcTest nodes with tags (ItemKey) values to allow for more programmatic indexing than just a common integer (0) or (1)? Yes we can, and this is the beginning of a symbolic data and behavioral controller.

The tcTest TurboCollection can be a run-time repository for incoming data (virtual, dynamic variables) and the StringAdapter can provide high-speed interpretation and decision logic *programmable at run time.*

CHAPTER 4

Power Tools

In This Chapter:

- Organizing, interpreting, and activating the metamorphic model

- Examining structural concepts

- Building a programmable application prototype

Every experienced software developer has a back-pocket full of code snippets, utilities, and general shareware collected on previous efforts. While useful, these represent only a fraction of the real power we need for multidimensional metamorphism. What we really need is a set of plug-and-play, predictable and universally reusable building blocks I'll call "power tools."

Power tools provide an initial, thematic springboard *and* long-term architectural stamina. We need power tools with strength at the product's foundation, not the periphery. We must implement and drive structural and behavioral themes, not allow them to emerge as latent artifacts.

Organizing, Interpreting, and Activating the Metamorphic Model

Three factors—organization, interpretation, and activation—provide an overarching theme as we build the metamorphic model introduced in Chapter 1; these factors also apply to every sub-framework we fold into this model. Every subsystem, component, and third-party API will require these factors in order to successfully operate, even power-play.

Generally speaking, these factors are achieved as follows:

- *Organization*—through interface patterns and structural consistency (e.g., Adapters)

- *Interpretation*—by means of behavioral patterns and rules-based interaction

- *Activation*—via metadata-driven, external programmability

At the structural API level, before laying down a single line of code, even before discussing what aspects of an API to expose, we should examine the API for its immediate linkage at the organizational, interpretation, and activation levels. We should determine how an Adapter will serve, what external programmability we'll enable, and what kinds of automatic behavior we'll include in the Adapter "for free." If our goal in building new capabilities rests on these three drivers, we'll always be on target for merging new capabilities and maturing existing ones.

Rather than throw a pile of utilities into a common bucket and call it our toolkit, let's take a look at capabilities providing consistent themes. We've already used the TurboCollection in the Project Exercises at the end of Chapters 1-3, but now its time to dive deeper and explain how the TurboCollection can serve as a master structural class and behavioral glue.

Examining Structural Concepts

In 1983, prior to C/C++ and the advent of objects, Dr. Richard Reese[1] exposed me to the *linked-list* structure as a powerful means to affect structural organization. At the time, the linked list was a most misunderstood animal, and was further complicated by the notion of dynamic variables (new on the scene at that time!). Any student diving into the linked list had a common experience: sink or swim. Personally, I thought it was fascinating.

Linked lists have been a mainstay for decades within Pascal, C, C++, and languages with "true" objects.

A linked list (see Figure 4-1) can dynamically assemble complex information and structure without the nasty overhead of arrays or common collections.

A linked list relies on two actors: one is the Iterator and one is the "node". The Iterator provides specific capabilities to assemble the nodes. Typically the nodes are only loosely connected to neighbors, deferring inter-node navigation to the Iterator. Thus, the nodes exist for the Iterator and don't have direct dependencies on other nodes.

In Figure 4-1, a node on the list has two object references, a *Next* (Nxt) and a *Previous* (Prv). The Iterator assumes, at a minimum, that the Next and the Previous contain a reference to another object using Next and Previous in the same way.

For clarity, "node" in this context is a role, not a specific class like the Node Class in Microsoft Visual Studio.

The resulting structure is a series of nodes, the first of which represents the *Head* or *Top*, and the last represents the *Tail*. Each node has a Next, holding a reference to the next node in the list, and likewise, a Previous, holding a reference to the prior node in the list. Thus, from anywhere in the list we can immediately navigate to a next or previous node. We can cross-connect nodes within and across lists, giving us multidimensional power.

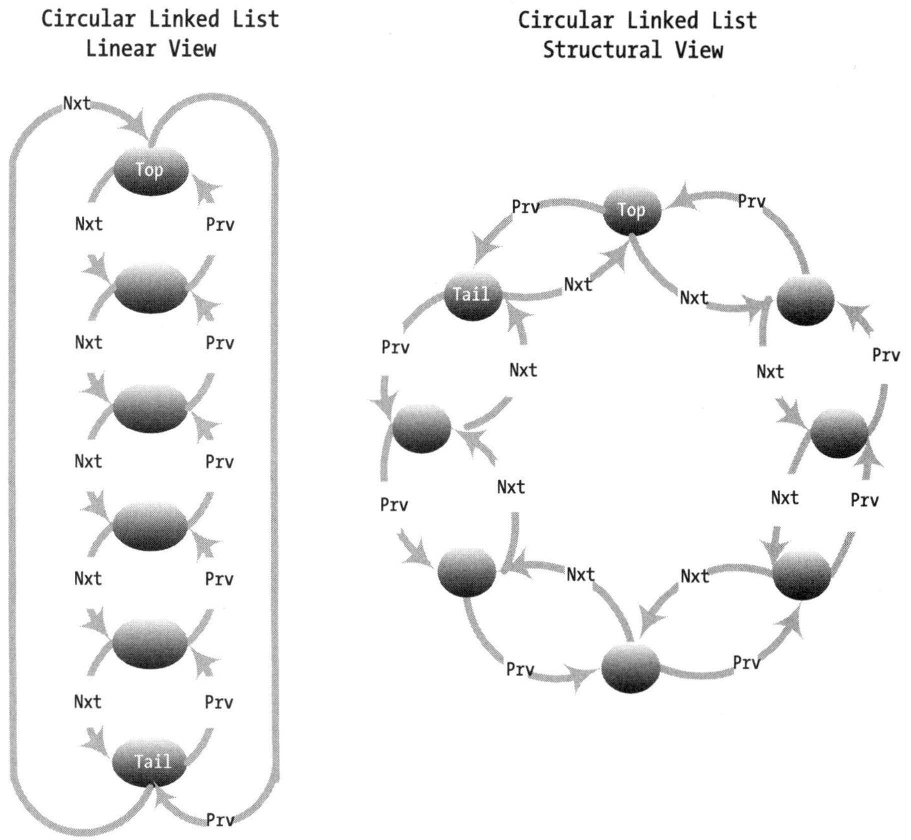

Figure 4-1. The linked list

Figure 4-1 shows two conceptual renderings of the structure. The linear view shows each node pointing to its next and previous neighbor, with the Top and Tail pointing to one another. The structural view shows the list as a circle, where we navigate around the circle until we arrive at the origin. We can use these views interchangeably for conceptual clarity.

Some developers examine this structure and automatically assume it cannot be faster than an array (and for direct indexing of small lists, this is somewhat true). However, arrays cannot compete with a linked list for searching, moving, sorting, removing, and every other aspect of structural organization. Even in areas where the array might be marginally faster, arrays sacrifice flexibility and structural control (a bad trade).

It is impossible to match (or even approach) the TurboCollection's speed and organizational agility with simple arrays or collections.

For example, in adding an item to an array, it's easy to add to the end. Adding to the top, however, requires us to create an empty item at the end, copy all existing items into the item below it (starting from the bottom), and overwrite the first item with the new one. Adding to the middle of an array is equally troublesome, but removing items from an array, especially a large array, takes its toll as we must shift items to compress the structure. If we were only dealing with scalar items or objects, we could probably manage it for awhile. If the array has multiple dimensions, and each "item" is a "row" of information (like from a database source) we would run out of power rather quickly.

Arrays really take a beating on sorting multiple dimensions, because we have to physically move all data around in the array.

The linked list on the other hand, doesn't sort by moving data. It simply reconnects the navigation order of the nodes. Thus, a node containing "David" might have a Previous reference to a node containing "Bryan," and a Next reference to a node containing "Mike" (if sorted alphabetically ascending). However, if we re-sort the nodes in descending order, the node containing "David" will have a Next of "Bryan" and its Previous will reference "Mike." We didn't move any data, we just reconnected their references.

XML folds directly into the TurboCollection's structure, because we can define highly complex structures and serialize them into XML for later reproduction or run-time replication.

The Turbo-Collection derives power from dynamically organizing and reconnecting information without physically moving or copying it.

The linked list beats every structure, hands down, on organization, flexibility, and general performance. Its derivative, the binary tree, can provide blazing search power (later in this section).

Ode to the Node

In building our linked list, the node is the object we'll be punting around. We could enable the Next/Previous capability on every object in our framework, but this only adds to maintenance (and our class interface), and isn't very extensible. For example, if we wanted to extend or augment linked-list capability, we'd have to address it on every enabled class, and that's messy business.

The alternative is to build an "anchor" node. This class will serve all the demands of the master Iterator, but also will provide a way to transparently attach other objects to it. Thus the generic anchor node becomes the object we manipulate most and all other objects are just attached (and along for the ride). We can also use the anchor to hold descriptive information (structural metadata) for the object it anchors.

Generalization Discovers Patterns

I once spoke with a senior programmer who was tearing the remainder of his hair out trying to find a "generic container object" he could use as a placeholder. The goal was to avoid interface exchange protocols or any special coding to connect things. He only wanted to trade information between classes with a commonly recognized class.

Without this, he correctly reasoned, much of his code already written would remain black-boxed. He couldn't re-cast his existing ActiveX controls (or classes with predefined roles) into something more abstract, and all his subsystems had their own interface classes and needed consolidation. His problems loomed larger than he wanted to address.

This programmer tried without success to build a general application-level building block without using interface patterns or other required structural themes. His idea was great, but his approach was flawed. Each time he attempted to scale a new implementation, even with incremental changes, it cracked, sputtered, and failed.

Scope creep usually reveals architectural flaws, so a metamorphic architecture must strive toward malleability, always assuming that change is imminent.

We sometimes reach impasses on defining generalized classes because we're thinking in terms of the application, not structural and behavioral patterns to drive applications. A sure sign that an approach is flawed: when incremental issues dramatically increase complexity.

I approached him with the idea of using a simple flyweight object we could initially define and then mature over time. He said he'd think about it. In the meantime, I clicked Add/Class/New and defined the ParmNode. (ParmNode is discussed in the next section.) Eventually, the ParmNode would be my master building block, and coupled with the Iterator, would propel me toward a metamorphic model.

Incremental changes should always have surgical and simple solutions, otherwise readdress the framework and discover how such incremental changes *could* have been simpler, then head in that direction. Don't get lost in the application features. Building blocks don't (and shouldn't) care about the specific application logic.

Our mental compass must always view patterns, not application features, as Magnetic North, the standard for run-time construction and activation.

179

The ParmNode Flyweight Container

The ParmNode (see Figure 4-2) is a general container, or placeholder, for data and metadata (with a little bit more). An Iterator pattern like the TurboCollection (shown in Figure 4-1) powers and binds the nodes together into a linked list.

ParmNode

Figure 4-2. ParmNode depicted

The ParmNode exposes a very simple set of high-speed, optimized properties. While it supports an interface pattern, its properties and methods exist largely for the consumption of the Iterator. ParmNodes can perform simple information gathering, or serve as an anchor for other objects.

We can also use ParmNodes as Singleton objects (Figure 4-3) outside the context of a list, place any type of information into them and pass them around as a Flyweight. Within interface patterns, ParmNode is welcome everywhere (see the "Generalization Discovers Patterns" sidebar).

ParmNode

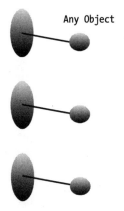

Figure 4-3. ParmNodes collected

I've heard our ranks groan about the inability to characterize information at the elemental level. Our programs manage database rows, or large-scale application objects to hide the data, but nothing applicable to all data elements great and small. Because the ParmNode carries a general *Item*, it can store simple scalar information (see Figure 4-2). Because it carries an *Obj*, it can anchor preconstructed objects. Because it stores a *Row[]* array, it can mimic a file or database row. And because it also stores *ItemType*, *ItemSize*, *ItemKey*, and *SortKey*, plus a number of other metadata-related properties, we can now describe the data held by the ParmNode.

Using this class as a primary Flyweight, we can encapsulate simple and complex information and pass it around as a single object of consistent type rather than multiple objects of disparate type. The structure and behavior of all our interfaces can become more consistent and predictable.

However, having a lot of ParmNodes (by themselves) floating around only defines anchors for data, not how to organize them or snap multiple ParmNodes together to define a logical pattern. For this, we need the Iterator.

The ParmNode can carry data or object references, plus the structural metadata describing their contents.

Microsoft's Simple Collection Iterator

Vendors of language environments like to help us out with predefined classes and widgets to aid in productivity and consistency. The Microsoft Visual Studio environment has tons of built-in functionality for each language it supports. A common theme is the *Collection class*. While I continue to use the Collection (although sparingly), I would only use the *TurboCollection* as a power tool.

While the Collection (I'll use Visual Basic as the example again) is a *linear* linked list (not circular, at least, not in its behavior), it has several limitations. First, it's *Key* must be unique and write-only, meaning we cannot replicate *Items* and *Keys* into another structure. If we want to insert an *Item* to the middle of the Collection, we incur two penalties: first to browse the Collection to find the insert location (by Key), and the second imposed by the Collection to re-index itself when we actually perform the insertion on its API. Performance starts to struggle after 500 items (by contrast, the TurboCollection has unlimited capacity). The Collection may get us started, but it's difficult to sustain any power with it. Because we cannot reclaim the Key value for cross-referencing (searching a collection to find an item-by-key or a key-by-item) we might require two separate Collections. This only increases complexity, leads to brittleness and maintenance headaches.

We don't really have any visibility to the Collection's internal node architecture, or we would have better visibility to its Key and other properties. With the ParmNode, we have this visibility and much more. It's an open, extensible resource that can grow with us.

All that said, the VB Collection is still useful for small-scale, throwaway activities because it has such a low footprint and is very well behaved. We can still balance the use of the Collection inside low-level Adapters and use the TurboCollection as our architecture-level "power tool" of choice.

The TurboCollection Iterator

The TurboCollection activates the organizational structure of the linked list. Using ParmNodes as the primary node, we can optimize the Iterator/node relationship for creative, high-performance, structural innovation.

The focus of object architecture is exploiting similarities, not just accommodating exceptions.

If we can implement a structural, behavioral, and information exchange pattern as a *common currency* to all components and subsystems, we can use it to span every interface, provide search and storage power when we need it, organizational agility without parallel, and be light on memory requirements.

Behavioral consistency is borne on structural integrity, so basing the TurboCollection (a behavioral Iterator pattern) on the ParmNode (a structural Flyweight pattern) is a solid (yet versatile and extensible) approach. They allow us to gel other patterns into frameworks and super-patterns, and provide a consistent means to define, execute, and troubleshoot code and metadata.

The TurboCollection can also serve as a Flyweight (for interface interchange). Additionally, the ParmNode can serve as an Adapter. Thus, both are structural and behavioral foundations for practically every class in our software environment, as well as a dynamic means to organize, collate, and activate metadata from any source.

TurboCollection and ParmNode are ideal structural baselines.

Each ParmNode is outfitted with the optimal hooks for a TurboCollection to connect them together for manipulation. Our program can pull information into memory, attach it as an object or sink it as data onto a ParmNode, then organize multiple ParmNodes into a pattern defined by the data itself, not by predefined application software. We have the immediate ability to input structured information and wrap a dynamic entity around it.

Navigating the TurboCollection

The following example shows how we navigate the TurboCollection. We start with the Head, perform a MoveNext on the list enough times, and we end up back at the Head (More() evaluates to False).

```
Dim pWrk as ParmNode               'define a workspace
tcExample.MoveFirst()              'move to top of TurboCollection
```

```
Do
' get the current reference - do something with it
  pWrk = tcExample.Ref
  tcExample.MoveNext()                       'move to the next reference
Loop While tcExample.More()                  'keep browsing until "no more", (the list
                                             ' reference  is back at the top)
```

Adding Nodes

We can insert a new ParmNode anywhere in the list, including the Top, the Tail, or in the Middle (see Figures 4-4 through 4-6). Some examples of inserting nodes are shown here in Table 4-1.

Table 4-1. Adding a Node

BEHAVIOR	EXAMPLE
Automatic Add to End of List	tcExample.Add()
Automatic Add and Reference Retrieval	pWrk = tcExample.Add()
Automatic Add and Populate	tcExample.AddItem ("Data", "Key", "SortingKey", "Type")
Specific Add	tcExample.Add (pWrk)

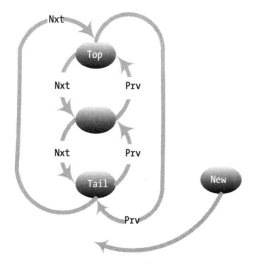

Figure 4-4. Add a node to the Tail.

The following example details how TurboCollection adds a node to the Tail of the list (Figure 4-4):

```
New.Prv = Top.Prv        'Point New back to current Tail
New.Nxt = Top            'Point New forward to Top
Top.Prv.Nxt = New        'Point Tail forward to New
Top.Prv = New            'Point Top back to New
```

This is the fastest way to append nodes. Mechanically, the TurboCollection will unhook the relationship between the Top and the current Tail, reconnect the Tail to the incoming node and connect the incoming node to the Top as the new Tail. Since the TurboCollection is always aware of the Top, we can append to the list with a few adjustments to Nxt/Prv references on three nodes (Top, Tail, New) and we're done.

Managing Operations

Several critical observations are required at this point, the first being that we must manage the first, second, and third Add() operations differently. When adding the first node, no Top or Tail exists. When adding the second node, no Tail exists. When adding the third and following, we consider the Top and Tail. The TurboCollection is already covering these aspects (and much more) for us, so rather than getting brain-freeze trying to implement it on our own, we'll use the TurboCollection and have fun.

Now let's look at adding a node to the top/head of the list (as shown in Table 4-2 and Figure 4-5).

Table 4-2. Adding a Node to the List Top

BEHAVIOR	EXAMPLE
Add node to Top of List	tcExample.Add (pWrk, LLOp:="ToHead")

Adding to the list Top (or Head) is just the reverse of adding to the Tail, and also just as fast. Since we already have the reference to the current Top, we can simply reconnect references to splice the new node into the list. We can build Last-In-First-Out (LIFO) queues with such a construct (Figure 4-5).

Circular Linked List
    Add to Head

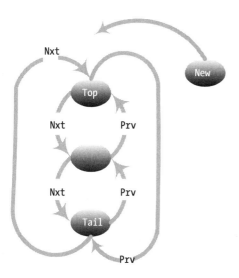

Figure 4-5. Add node to list Top.

Nesting Subroutine Management

Recall the example in Chapter 3 "The Interpreter" about supporting routines and subroutines with the Interpreter. Nested subroutine management requires a Call Stack, and is difficult to implement because we require preservation of the current Routine's state and execution position before jumping off to another Routine. Upon returning, we must restore the calling Routine's state and information, then continue to the next executable metadata statement. A LIFO queue will do the trick.

Inserting Nodes

Many times we'll want to browse a list and insert a node (such as for an insertion sort). Perhaps we'll want to find a given node and add information prior to it (such as XML or HTML tags). Once we complete a find/browse and are ready to insert, we have the option of inserting before the current node (Figure 4-6) or after it (Figure 4-7).

Table 4-3 shows the expected behaviors.

Table 4-3. Node Insertion Behaviors

BEHAVIOR	EXAMPLE
Add Inside the List (Before)	tcExample.Add (pWrk, LLOp:="ToMid")
Add Inside the List (After)	tcExample.Add (pWrk, LLOp:="ToMidAfter")

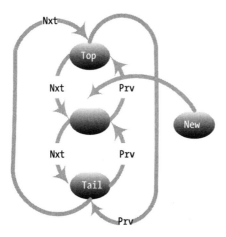

Figure 4-6. Add node to middle before the current node.

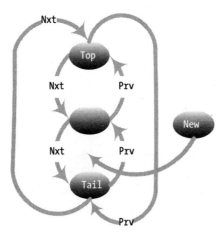

Figure 4-7. Add node to middle after the current node.

These operations are not mechanically different from inserting to the Top or Tail, we simply treat the *insertion point* as a surrogate for the Top reference, and all other behavior is identical.

Removing ParmNodes

Now, imagine removing one row from a large array. To compress the array to its new contents, we would have to copy every subsequent row into the row above it, then throw away the last row. By contrast, the TurboCollection simply removes a ParmNode by surgically disconnecting its Nxt/Prv references and the references of its neighbors (see Figure 4-8).

To accurately remove nodes we need the behaviors shown in Table 4-4.

Table 4-4. Node Removal Behavior

BEHAVIOR	EXAMPLE
Remove the current reference	pWrk = tcExample.Ref
	tcExample.Remove (pWrk)
Directly remove the current reference	tcExample.Remove (tcExample.Ref)
Remove the topmost reference	tcExample.Remove (tcExample.Top)
Clear to empty the TurboCollection	tcExample.Clear()

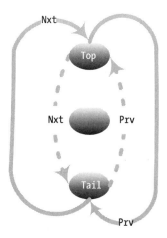

Figure 4-8. Removing a node

Node removal (splicing a node out of any arbitrary location) requires detailed attention to the Nxt and Prv references. We must first reconnect the target node's Nxt/Prv references, then set its own Nxt/Prv references to Nothing before destroying or recycling the node.

We can split lists into several, splice several into one, surgically remove nodes, find, sort, organize, or pass nodes around. We have complete control over them, at both the list and the node level.

Automated Browsing

Imagine a complex Routine we want to execute against every node in a list. If we encapsulate the Routine inside an object with the interface pattern, we can then browse our list and pass each node into it as the ActionObject parameter. Now consider a higher abstraction, where we pass the entire TurboCollection into the object and it performs the browse/execute for us. Next, picture a more oblique abstraction, where we pass the TurboCollection *and* the given object into a browsing behavioral controller, which then browses the list *and* calls the object's interface. We have so many options, each giving us reusable behavioral and interface control. Each time we abstract an interface, we allow other objects (even those we've not defined yet) access to the capability.

Linked lists are inherently simple structures. While I challenge every developer to build their own (for greater understanding) we can have fun in the meantime. So to avoid delay and perhaps pain or injury, use the TurboCollection. Its mechanics are production-tested in a variety of high-intensity environments.

TurboCollection as a Binary Tree

The *binary tree* (see Figure 4-9) is a derivative of the linked list (the TurboCollection supports both). It connects the objects differently by using Parent/Child relationships rather than Next/Previous relationships.

We start with a linked list of ParmNodes in any order. We must then determine the *collating sequence,* that is, a global ordering rule to determine a Sort Key. For example, if the nodes are anchors to employee objects, we might want to use the "SSN", "Employee ID", or "Employee Name" Items as sort keys. We'll browse the nodes once and set their SortKey() properties to an appropriate value, defining the node relationships as a global whole.

The TurboCollection then sorts the nodes and begins the tree construction. It will first find the midpoint of the entire list and use this node as the Tree Top. It then splits the list in two, with half of the list on the high collating sequence (after the Tree Top) and half on the low collating sequence (before the Tree Top). It then performs the same operation on each half. In each case, it will find the midpoint, then split the list into two.

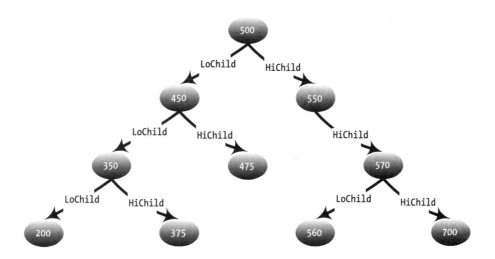

Linked List as
A Binary Tree

Figure 4-9. The binary tree

Upon completion, each midpoint node becomes the parent of two midpoint nodes below it (one for Hi and one for Lo). It also becomes a Hi/Lo child of the midpoint node above it.

In Figure 4-9, note the data organization. Starting from the top, every node below Key=500 is on the *LoChild* side of the top node. Every node above Key=500 is on the *HiChild* side of the top node. Each node in the tree behaves like a new tree, such that the entire structure appears as a cluster of subtrees.

The Tree is a powerful search engine, allowing us to find any element on the Tree with lightning speed. The TurboCollection Find(Key) method accepts a key value (the same key value used to sort and collate it), then enters the tree at the Tree Top, comparing the Key to the Tree Top's key. If the key matches, we're done. If not, it will determine if the key is *less than* the Tree Top's key (and traverse the LoChild branch) or *greater than* (and traverse the HiChild branch). It repeats the same pattern, dividing and comparing, until it reaches an answer. This is the ultimate hybrid between a binary search and a quicksort, both of which perform the same divide-and-conquer algorithm until conclusion.

In a Tree with 10,000 elements, the Find() can locate and retrieve any node within 13 compares, with an average of 11 compares. For smaller lists, one or two compares usually suffices. Regardless of the memory footprint of data in

ParmNode, the TurboCollection can organize and access a breathtaking volume of data. It's great for high-speed lookups without messy array overhead.

With desktop memory affordable and available, we can now leverage it as a high-speed resource for larger volumes of information. At the server level, a memory-based high-speed storage/retrieval capability is extremely valuable.

Browsing a tree in its natural structure is time consuming and somewhat oblique. To mitigate this, the TurboCollection first organizes the list as a tree, then sweeps through the tree and reconnects the nodes again as a list using Nxt/Prv references. Thus, the TurboCollection can use the tree-based navigation to perform searches and use the regular list MoveFirst/MoveNext/More operations to treat the structure like a regular list. The TurboCollection's consumer gets all the required search power for large lists and all the organizational power needed for small, agile data sets. Consumers only add the necessary member nodes with no scrap or spill space (as required with array management), an important efficiency aspect for any solution, especially highly interactive applications.

TurboCollection Interoperability

The TurboCollection's interface has already matured into high-speed methods for Add, AddItem, Remove, Count, Sort, etc. We can use these anywhere in the architecture because the TurboCollection is closest to our own technical action. Just as we need interface patterns as we approach external APIs, we'll also need pattern capabilities on this structure. The primary difference is that the TurboCollection, when exposing patterns, already has highly metamorphic capabilities. If we wrap the TurboCollection with another class, the wrapper automatically inherits its metamorphism.

The TurboCollection's default *Item* property will give two forms of output. When the calling Routine provides a key as a parameter, the TurboCollection will perform a Find() on its list and return the Item property of the node with the same *ItemKey* value as the parameter. For example:

```
strKey = "dbirmingham"
strVal = tcExample.Item(strKey)
```

strVal now contains the Item property information located at the key tag "dbirmingham".

Additionally, if we pass no key into the Item function, TurboCollection will concatenate all Items and ItemKeys and place them into pairs separated by the optional *Delimiter*. The default delimiter is the vertical bar "|" (e.g., "ItemKey=Item|ItemKey=Item|ItemKey=Item"). We can unload a TurboCollection's contents with a single (and simple) call (although for very large lists this is unadvisable!): For example:

```
strVal = tcExample.Item
```

Conversely, the TurboCollection's *Set Item* property will receive two forms of input. The first form includes a Key and expects a single Value associated with it. It will locate the node with the same key and place the value on the node's Item property. Here's an example:

```
tcExample.Item("thiskey") = "thisvalue"
```

The Item will accept a second form of information, a compound parameter including multiple Key/Value pairs without specifying a Key. It will update the items for Keys it finds, then append the remainder to the list, like so:

```
tcExample.Item = "T1=Value|T2=Value2|T3=Value3"
```

While we could use .NET's System.XML object to produce an XML string, the TurboCollection has multi-dimensional power. It also provides for a parameter that will unload the entire TurboCollection into an XML-ready form. Consider this example:

```
'unload basic MOM Item/Itemkey pairs
strXML = tcExample.Item(strDelim:="<>")
'unload detail all Parmnodes in every dimension
strXML = tcExample.Item(strDelim:="<*>")
```

The true value of XML conversion is usually only realized with network-based transfers. For example, if we have a consumer program on a desktop and a service on a departmental server, the consumer can reduce a complex TurboCollection to XML, transmit it over a socket and the server will reconstruct the TurboCollection from the XML into an identical structure. The overhead is light, the operation is highly visible for troubleshooting, and the XML can be encrypted.

Understanding Multiple Dimensions

Simple browsing assumes some linear relationship, but the TurboCollection is also multidimensional. We can attach sub-TurboCollections to each ParmNode, allowing us to browse to a given point in one linear path, then branch to another linear path from that node. The count, direction, even sharing of lists is unlimited.

NOTE *No functional limit exists as to how many dimensions we can support with TurboCollections. Unlike an array, TurboCollection dimensions can* share *and* interleave *multiple dimensions for labyrinthine complexity.*

Figure 4-10 depicts a multidimensional linked list, where the master list (far left) has two more lists (List A, List B) attached to selected nodes. List C is then attached to a node in List A. Finally, both List B and List C reference List D. We can build wildly interwoven structures, creating dynamic cross-referencing and derived relationships.

Figure 4-10. Multidimensional view

Language Integration

An important note about an Iterator's interface pattern: Apart from the standard *Action()*, *Item()* and *Ref()* patterns, it also includes *MoveFirst()*, *MoveNext()*, *MovePrevious()* and *More()*. Every Iterator-enabled class will expose these properties as pass-through capabilities because Microsoft built them into many of the standard looping operations as language extensions. For interoperability with third-party APIs (such as Microsoft's ActiveX Data Objects), we can include these additional methods with the expectation of interoperability.

Mechanics of Iteration

The following discusses some additional highly useful methods and properties directly exposed on the TurboCollection's interface. This is because, unlike the objects it is organizing, the interface drives the behavioral control rather than being controlled by it. The methods listed in Table 4-5 are basic Iterator capabilities, listed in order of significance.

Table 4-5. Iterator Capabilities

METHOD	DESCRIPTION
Ref	Returns a ParmNode object containing reference to the Current Position in the list. As the list is browsed (positional change), the TurboCollection will automatically update this reference to reflect a change in position.
RelRef	Returns a ParmNode reference *relative* to the Current Position (Ref). Accepts a numeric index that is a +/- relative offset of the current position.
Top	Returns a ParmNode reference to the list's starting point. The Current Position (Ref) can be set to the Top using MoveFirst (below).
MoveFirst	Sets the Current Position reference (Ref) to the Top.
MoveNext	Sets the Current Position reference (Ref) to the next node in the list (using the Reference's Nxt property).

Table 4-5. Iterator Capabilities (continued)

METHOD	DESCRIPTION
More	Returns a True if the Current Position reference (Ref) is the same as the Top. (MoveFirst/MoveNext/More browse loop management)
Find	Returns a ParmNode reference if its ItemKey property matches a key (exact or near-match) or by numeric index (absolute position)
SortList	Sorts the nodes on the list based on the values found in their SortKey parameters
Add	Puts a new node on the list at the Top, Tail, or anywhere in between.
Clear	Empties the list
Count	Gives a total count of nodes in the list
Remove	Takes a node from the list, including surgical or key-based removal
Sever	Separates one list into two at a designated node location
Splice	Appends two lists
Replicate	Copies one list into another, creating two
DataPresent	Returns True if the Top reference is not empty; more efficient than a Count to test for data presence.

The primary Iterator behavioral patterns involve building and browsing a list from top to bottom, examining its information and performing context-based actions. The *MoveFirst* method will initialize the Current Reference (Ref) to the Top. Once we examine this node, we execute *MoveNext*. Immediately afterward, we examine *More* to determine loop terminus. More will be True until the list performs a MoveNext on its Tail, the node previous to the Top (setting the Current Reference to the Top, and thus the More will evaluate to False). Here is an example of a simple iteration loop:

```
Dim pWrk as ParmNode
tcExample.MoveFirst()
```

```
Do
  pWrk = tcExample.Ref
  'now examine the information
  If pWrk.ItemType >= "Architect" and pWrk.ItemSize < "TooExpensive" Then
    pWrk.Status = "Hire This Person"
  End if
tcExample.MoveNext()
Loop while tcExample.More()
```

We can also combine MoveNext and More, like so:

```
tcExample.MoveFirst()
Do
   'Examine tcExample.Ref's information
 Loop while tcExample.MoveNext
```

MoveNext can advance the Current Reference and automatically return the Boolean result of More (but subtly mixes the role of MoveNext). If we want to browse remotely, we can reduce a MoveNext/More into a single MoveNext call and remove the overhead for two separate calls.

StringAdapter for Interpeter Support

A power tool like the *StringAdapter.cls* can give us agile, consistent text parsing for our Interpreter engine. This class contains high-speed capabilities for ripping apart and manipulating strings.

The MoveFirst/ MoveNext/More and Ref patterns allow us to export browse capabilities (abstract loop- ing) into application- level metadata.

We often reformat binary, decimal, or other data into a textual equivalent before examining it. HTML, SQL, and XML are text-based representations because a character string is the only form of information with predictable content. Thus, string manipulation and examination (parsing) is a base requirement for any toolkit. We often find ourselves immersed in this activity, with each team member invoking subtle variations.

The StringAdapter pulls all string manipulation under one umbrella, including the native string functions within the language environment. Thus we have a one-stop shop for every string need. As an object, we'll also perform high-speed create and destroy operations with it as we recurse through functional subroutine layers. This makes it a prime candidate for a structural factory to recycle them. Of course, we can also use it as a Flyweight, so once we have the string broken apart we can share it with other entities.

The StringAdapter breaks a string into multiple parts (*tokens),* for consump- tion by an Interpreter. Table 4-6 lists the primary StringAdapter references.

Table 4-6. StringAdapter References

REFERENCES	DESCRIPTION
Parse	Breaks apart the string into tokens on a default or specified delimiter boundary, tokens are placed into nodes on a TurboCollection for quick access
Concat	After parsing, re-assembles into a string (optionally with another delimiter)
MoveFirst, MoveLast, More	Browses the tokens in the underlying TurboCollection. We can use More to determine end-of-list (e.g., Do Loop While More)
Item, Item(*pos*)	By default, retrieves the token at the Current Reference of the TurboCollection, otherwise if using an optional numeric index, returns the token at the requested absolute position. May also update the Item at the designated reference
RelItem	Uses the TurboCollection's RelRef to return the token using a relative index to the current token.
DataPresent	Inquires as to result of the parse, True if the parse was successful
Count	Gives a total number of tokens in the TurboCollection
FindToken	Without parsing, this function will search a string for a given token and if found, report a True, else False. For larger strings, this function is faster than the language environment's equivalent utility. However, the language utility is embedded in the function for interface consistency.
ReplaceSub	Using a target string, find a substring and replace it with another
ReplaceParms	Perform Key/Value matching, replacing $ parameters with their matching values.
RemoveNull	Remove all items with a value of Nothing
StripSpecial	Strip out all non-display characters in the ASCII character set

The StringAdapter exposes an interface pattern but also passes through many of the underlying TurboCollection methods. A TurboCollection is then completely dedicated to leashing a given string for our purposes.

The StringAdapter enforces and activates our structural interface pattern (discussed in Chapter 2) on all objects, allowing us to examine ActionID and ActionData parameters easily, efficiently and *consistently*. Nothing is worse than using string-based parameter passing with each structural entity unable to wrest the parameters from their compound form.

Examples of using the StringAdapter are included in the Project Exercises at the end of Chapters 1- 5. However, Listing 4-1 highlights some of the simple use cases.

Listing 4-1. StringAdapter Behavior

```
'********Parse a string using blank (or white) space as delimiters:
InStr = "This is a good string"
strA.Parse (inStr, " ")
' ********strA now contains
'    This
'    is
'    a
'    good
'    string
'********Note that strA.Item by default contains the first token "This".
'******** Let's replace it with "That"
strA.Item = "That"
' ********Now let's perform a Concat with a new delimiter, the semicolon
inStr = strA.Concat(";")
'******** instr now contains    "That;is;a;good;string"
'******** Let's eliminate all words using the letter "a"
strA.MoveFirst()
do
    if instr(1,strA.Item,"a") > 0 then strA.Item = ""
    strA.MoveNext()
Loop While strA.More
InStr = stra.Concat(";")
'******** instr now contains ";is;;good;string"
' ********to remove the nulls strings (and extra ";")
strA.RemoveNull()
'******** now concat again, this time with spaces
inStr = stra.Concat(" ")
'******** inStr is now equal to "is good string"
```

The StringAdapter's consistent parsing and access behaviors give us the confidence to plug it into place as a building block, invoke its power, and expect predictable outcomes.

mathAdapter

Now let's move to something a bit more advanced. The *mathAdapter* contains interpreted mathematical calculation logic, and leverages the StringAdapter.

We can drop in any arbitrary textual math formula, shoot it to a dynamic calculator and get a consistent result.

First, we'll need to create a mathAdapter object, and a string to calculate from, like so:

```
Dim oMath as New mathAdapter
Dim strWrk as String
strWrk = "(1000 * (40 + 200) ) / 20"
strWrk = oMath.Action(strWrk)
' strWrk is now equal to  "12000"
```

This elemental capability is very powerful. We can dynamically assemble virtually any value or series of textual values and operators. The mathAdapter supports most if not all math computations, because all math ultimately boils down to add, subtract, multiply, or divide.

Knowing exact values to plug into the calculation is great, but dynamic quantities will require parameter substitution in the formula string. We'll let the mathAdapter perform the substitution, but we'll need structured parameter handling (compound parameters or a preexisting collection).

The formula string serves the role of *ActionID*, deferring parameters to *ActionData* or *ActionObject*. The tag/value compound parameter is good for one-shot calculations. However, if we've already defined and manipulated the parameters in another operation, we'll want to pass them along instead of reformatting them into a tag/value string. The ActionObject allows us to maintain raw running results for quick reuse with less preprocessing. The following listing again uses the mathAdapter object's default method as Action():

```
    Public Function Action(ActionID As String,
                            Optional ActionData As String,
                            Optional ActionObject As TurboCollection) As String
    On Error Resume Next
    Dim tcParm As TurboCollection
    If ActionObject Is Nothing Then
        tcParm = glb.UnStringParm(ActionData)
    Else
        Set tcParm = ActionObject
    End If
    Action = Calc(CalcPrep(ActionID), tcParm)
End Function
```

First, let's use compound parameters in ActionData. Parameter substitution will yield the same result as before:

```
inParm = "Parm1=1000|Parm2=40|Parm3=200|Parm4=20"        'parm values
strWrk = "($Parm1 * ($Parm2 + $Parm3) ) / $Parm4"         'parms in formula
strWrk = oMath.Action(strWrk, inParm)
'returns strWrk = "12000"
```

The alternative is a TurboCollection for ActionObject. For visibility, we'll manually fill the tcParm TurboCollection, like this:

```
Dim tcParm As New TurboCollection()
tcParm.AddItem "1000", "Parm1"
tcParm.AddItem "40", "Parm2"
tcParm.AddItem "200", "Parm3"
tcParm.AddItem "20", "Parm4"
tcParm.AddItem "30", "Parm5"
tcParm.AddItem "700", "Parm6"
tcParm.AddItem "80", "Parm7"
```

The following equation calls for only four of the seven parameters in tcParm (Parm1, Parm2, Parm3, and Parm4). We'll pass along tcParm and let the calculator pull the named parameters from it:

```
strWrk = "($Parm1 * ($Parm2 + $Parm3) ) / $Parm4"
strWrk = oMath.Action(strWrk, ActionObject:=tcParm)        'pass the parm list
' strWrk now contains "12000"
```

But since tcParm already contains other parameters, we can instantly request another calculation without additional reformatting or overhead. In the formula, we'll now replace Parm2 with Parm6 and Parm3 with Parm7:

```
strWrk = "($Parm1 * ($Parm6 + $Parm7) ) / $Parm4"
strWrk = oMath.Action(strWrk, ActionObject:=tcParm)
 'strWrk is now = "39000"
```

Calculation Mechanics

Parameter substitution exploits the StringAdapter's Parse power. Note two functions in mathAdapter: one is a *CalcPrep()* and the other is the *Calc ()* function. CalcPrep() simply breaks the incoming string apart to separate each character (such as ")" and "+", etc.) by a *space*. This allows the Calc() function to find things easily.

The Calc() function will then Parse the string on space " " delimiters. At this point, each of the $ parameters will reside in their own standalone token (StringAdapter.Item), and we can easily replace them with an ActionObject parameter value. Listing 4-2 contains the code to hunt them down and replace them follows.

Listing 4-2. Calculator Mechanics

```
Public Function ReplaceParms(strW As String, iParm As TurboCollection) As String
On Error Resume Next
Dim strA As StringAdapter
  ReplaceParms = strW
  If iParm Is Nothing Then Exit Function
  Dim strWrk As String
  If strW <> vbNullString Then            'if incoming string then
    strA = glb.NewStringAdapter           'build a new adapter
    strA.Parse (CalcPrep(strW), " ")      'prep it by separating everything
  Else
                                          'otherwise use Me, that is,
                                          ' the current instance

    strA = Me
  End If
  strA.MoveFirst()                        'start the loop
  Do
    strWrk = strA.Item                    'get the Item
    If Mid(strWrk, 1, 1) = "$" Then       'is it a $Parm?
      strWrk = Mid(strWrk, 2)             'extract it as key
      strA.Item = iParm.Find(strWrk).Item 'Find/Replace
    ElseIf Mid(strWrk, 1, 2) = "@$" Then  'Otherwise an indirect Parm ref?
      strWrk = Mid(strWrk, 3)             'then extract it as key
      strA.Item = iParm.Find(strWrk).Item 'Find/Replace
    End If
    strA.MoveNext ()
  Loop While strA.More
  If strW <> vbNullString Then            'used an incoming string?
  ReplaceParms = strA.Concat(" ")         'then pass the concat'd results back
  glb.OldStringAdapter (strA)             'and toss the workspace
  End If
End Function
```

After substitution, we're ready to calculate. The physical code listing for Calc() is too extensive to provide here, but you can find it in this chapter's project listings mathAdapter. The Calc() algorithm depends on two principles: Left-*Operator*-Right syntax and SubFormulas.

The Left-Operator-Right syntax is how the instruction will appear *textually*, but the Interpreter will have to convert it into an internal method call. Thus, the following metadata instruction represents the human-readable Add syntax:

```
Result = LeftHandSideValue + RightHandSideValue
```

while this next example represents the machine-oriented Add() method:

```
Result = Add(LeftHandSideValue, RightHandSideValue)
```

A SubFormula syntax wraps the parts of the formula with parenthesis "()." We then resolve the formula parts at the lowest parenthesis level and use these results to feed outer parenthesis levels. Note the following two strings:

```
strWrk = "1000 * 200 + 300 / 400"
strWrk = "1000 (200 +  300) / 400"
```

While both strings have the same numeric values and operators, the parenthesis drive toward different answers. The first example will yield this:

```
1000 * 200 = 200,000
200,000 + 300 = 200,300
200,300 / 400 =  500.75
```

while the second example will yield the following:

```
200 + 300 = 500   ' SubFormula executed first
1000 * 500 = 500,000
500,000 / 400 = 1250
```

The SubFormula capability allows an external metadata user to craft the math operation with consistency and reliability. This aligns with mathematical formulas taught from common textbooks, using parenthesis to encapsulate sub-operations prior to conclusion. This obviates the use of a prioritization mechanism for operators.

The complete algorithm is very simple (I've bolded the R*n* result parameters):

```
a) Perform Parameter Substitution
strWrk = "($Parm1 * ($Parm2 + $Parm3) ) / $Parm4"
      becomes
strWrk = "(1000 * (40 + 200) ) / 20"
b)  Break apart into SubFormulas with
    Each providing a standalone result
e.g. R1 = (40 + 200)
c) Line up the SubFormulas in sequential order so
   Elemental SubFormulas feed dependent SubFormulas
R1 = (40 + 200)
R2 = (1000 * R1)
R3 = (R2 / 20)
d) Resolve each SubFormula, passing
   Result to dependent SubFormula
R1 = (40 + 200)                    "240"
R2 = (1000 * 240)                  "240000"
R3 = (240000 / 20)                 "12000"
e) Return Result of final SubFormula
Result = R3                        "12000"
```

Advanced Math

A significant issue with interpreting advanced math functions (such as *atan()*, *cos()*, or *abs()*), boils down to execution order. Do we perform the raw calculations first, the advanced functions followed by the calculation, or some combination? Additionally, some advanced math functions require multiple parameters, which themselves could be the result of another embedded calculation, so we must account for when these parameters are ready for consumption.

Consider the following formula:

```
strWrk = "abs( cos($Parm1) + cos($Parm2) ) * $Parm3"
```

Note the sequential sub-calculations. We cannot perform the abs() function until we finish and sum the cos() functions. In essence, our rules for interpretation just got a lot more complicated, right? Actually, no, in fact, the rules for mathematics are consistent because math is what the machine knows *first*. Everything inside a machine is eventually reduced to the 1's and 0's of math, so we'll ride on that rule as long as possible.

Let's continue with the principles of left-hand side/right-hand side evaluation and SubFormulas. Whether wrapping an operation with parenthesis or with advanced math, the requirements are identical.

The machine knows math first and can apply its rules consistently.

When performing simple calculations, we must first divide the problem into indivisible parts, each one itself a SubFormula with an individual result. We must systematically order each SubFormula in a chained sequence (one SubFormula feeds the next, and so forth). Thus, SubFormulas (Table 4-7) now come to mean *any quantities between parenthesis*.

Table 4-7. Examples of SubFormulas

SUBFORMULA	OPERATION	RESULTS
(a+ b)	*Sum*(a, b)	R1 = *Sum*(a, b)
(a * (b + c))	*Multiply*(a, *Sum* (b, c))	R1 = *Sum*(b, c), R2 = *Multiply*(a, R1)
fn(a)	*fn* (a)	R1 = (a), R2 = *fn*(R1)
fn(a * b)	*fn* (*Multiply* (a, b))	R1 = *Multiply*(a, b), R2 = *fn*(R1)

Note the consistent theme: values between the parenthesis *must* be resolved to numeric values before continuing to the next outer level of resolution (R*n+1*). Each prior result rolls into the results above it until reaching full resolution. A pattern arises in each of the above calculations, but it's not obvious on the surface. Each *method* reference (e.g., *Sum, Multiply, fn*) requires pre-processing to add *null placeholders* to the string. This allows the calculator to treat the function call just like a regular operator.

Note how this:

```
Result = A + B
```

becomes this

```
Result = A Sum B
```

or this

```
Result = Sum(A, B)
```

So if we reverse this syntax with the following

```
Result = Cos(A)
```

we need to provide a placeholder behind the Cos to reduce it to an operator, like so:

```
Result = (PlaceHolder Cos(A))
```

Now see how the Interpreter will reduce this to sub-formulas, as follows:

```
R1 = (A)  - stands alone
R2 = (PlaceHolder Cos R1)
```

Internally, this reduces to:

```
R2 = Cos(PlaceHolder, R1)
```

Thus, we have a consistent external interface for Sum(A, B) and Cos(PlaceHolder, A). At least, their *interfaces appear the same*. The exception is in the *placeholder*. It serves to abstract the Cos interface. Of course, we must wrap the native Cos(A) function with our own Cos(PlaceHolder,A) function, and define its behavior to regard the first parameter (PlaceHolder) only if the second parameter (A) is missing, then make A an optional parameter.

Now any direct call to Cos(A) will have the same behavior as Cos(PlaceHolder, A). We have effectively *leashed* the function call's behavior to play seamlessly with the mathAdapter *and* all internal consumers. The significant conclusion: we don't care what the actual *placeholder* value is. The pattern is in the behavior and structure, not the data itself.

To repeat the prior example:

```
strWrk = "abs( cos(1000) + cos(40) ) * 200"
```

The calculator will pre-format this string to read as follows:

```
strWrk = "(R4 abs( (R2 cos(1000)) + (R1 cos(40)) )) * 200"
```

To ultimately derive:

```
R1 = (40)
R2 = (1000)
R1 = Cos(R1, R1)
R2 = Cos(R2, R2)
R3 = Sum(R1,R2)
R4 = Abs(R3, R3)
```

This construct allows each function call to automatically cascade the results of a SubFormula directly into the next step. We get consistent results with each calculation and we don't have to rely on language references or external functions.

To increase power, we can assign one or more calculators to rows and columns in a *container*, and allow data values to propagate automatically as we include or exclude information.

 NOTE *While this apparently mimics common spreadsheet capabilities, it has more power. Our calculator can use data from anywhere, even across frameworks, because the TurboCollection is multidimensional.*

To mechanically execute this formula, the calculator must first break it up into indivisible SubFormulas, each one feeding the next SubFormula. The calculator will build the structure depicted in Figure 4-11, then traverse it from the top to solve the problem.

```
Calculation Tree  abs( ( cos(1000) + cos(40) ) * 200

(P1 abs( (P2 cos(1000)) + (P3 cos(40)) )) * 200
```

I have included more Rn results in the cascade for clarity.

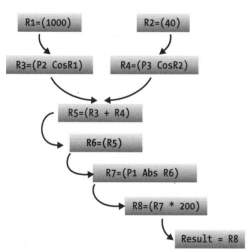

Figure 4-11. Recursive calculator

Parallel threads will initiate the calculation with elemental SubFormulas R1 and R2, each cascading their results into the next formula. Thus, each upstream SubFormula creates an Rn result used by a downstream SubFormula. No practical limit exists for the complexity of a formula using this technique.

Multiple Parameters

What if we wanted to make an additional function call—a custom call—to perform an embedded accounting algorithm, spatial transform, or other advanced multi-parameter function? Clearly, the parse-divide-resolve algorithm above could not handle functions with multiple parameters, because it expects each single-parameter math function to receive a resolved SubFormula result prior to execution, and resolves its SubFormula using left-operator-right logic.

To include multiple parameters, we use a compound parameter. We'll need to use standard syntax and separate parameters with a comma ",". This is somewhat less obvious since we have to systematically concatenate the correct parameters into the compound parameter.

For example, let's say we have a special function of our own creation called *spatial transform*, or *spxfr*. For simplicity, we'll just let spxfr() perform a simple sum of all its inputs and report the results. In reality, it could embed highly complex operations. We'll use just four parameters, but no limit exists if the parsing algorithm consistently evaluates and manipulates them. Here's the sample:

```
strWrk = "spxfr($Parm1, $Parm2, $Parm3  ,  $Parm4)"
strWrk = oMath.Action(strWrk, ActionObject:=tcParm)
' strWrk now = 1260
strWrk = "spxfr(cos($Parm1), cos($Parm2), $Parm3, $Parm4)"
strWrk = oMath.Action(strWrk, ActionObject:=tcParm)
' strWrk now = 220
```

In the next example, the calculator will key on vertical pipes "|". We build a left-operator-right statement similar to the following, where the *right hand* parameter is compound:

```
PlaceHolder spxfr 'P0=1000|P1=40|P2=200|P3=20'
Resolves to
Result = spxfr ( PlaceHolder,  'P0=1000|P1=40|P2=200|P3=20' )
```

Dynamically managing interpreted math formulas stabilizes our software and further removes us from dependency on application-centric math.

Every application has a need for parameter-driven mathematics. It is often the one element of solution development *most* driven by user needs (and whims).

After that short tour of handling text strings and advanced parsing, it's time to turn up the volume, of *text*, that is. A programmable program is a voracious, high-volume consumer of external structured text.

TextIO as Text Stream Manager

We've looked at one-liner instructions to build calculations, individual statements, and macro text. For a high-speed Interpreter, this amounts to spoonfeeding. If an Interpreter requires sequential text statements as fuel, it's time to invoke a high-volume fuel injector with swift, accurate, and consistent text file access.

We'll also need to manipulate the text at various levels, including paragraphs, lines, and individual characters. The StringAdapter handles individual characters and tokens, but the TextIO facility can access and prepare text files for high-speed *in-memory* browsing and manipulation. We can abstract the APIs of any file system manager, no matter what the operating system, and standardize its structure and behavior.

Table 4-8 lists some common behaviors, ordered by frequency of usage.

Microsoft provides the File System Object and Unix C++ provides similar I/O facilities. However, these are primitive and non-portable I/O windows.

Table 4-8. Text File Access Behaviors

REFERENCE	DESCRIPTION
Handle	Provides an object references for an open file. Returned by OpenInputFile and OpenOutputFile as an "open file handle" for use by other TextIO methods
OpenInputFile	Accepts a path and returns a Handle if the file was found and opened. Positions the file at the first record.
OpenOutputFile	Accepts a path and returns a Handle if the file was opened successfully. Automatically creates new files or overwrites existing ones.
Item	Returns the text line of the current input record, or puts (and writes) a text line as an output record.
MoveNext	Moves current input reference to the next record in the file. Only valid for files using OpenInputFile.
More	Tests for end-of-file marker; only valid for files using OpenInputFile.
CloseFile	Closes a file, whether for input or output
LoadInputFile	Accepts a pathname, opens an input file, loads it into memory, closes the file and returns the result as a TurboCollection (each Node.Item contains one line of text)
WriteOutputFile	Accepts a pathname, opens an output file, sequentially writes a TurboCollection's contents (Node.Item values), then closes the file.

TextIO will quickly get the file into memory and present it as a TurboCollection, with an open passport to any area of the framework.

Program modules can easily step on each other when accessing or manipulating text I/O streams. We'll see a crash on a seemingly arbitrary boundary associated with opening or closing a stream. The culprit, an inconsistent use of *file handle* references, leads to an inability to open or close a stream without accidentally colliding with another stream. The file *handle* is the program's only anchor to the I/O stream, so if we corrupt the handle, we lose the stream.

Our Interpreter will need fast access to huge amounts of structured text. Consistent text file I/O is an absolute necessity.

Some clever programmers will open a file stream and, if it fails, retry until successful. Others may change stream access parameters and retry, eventually getting a "hit." None of these solutions is consistent or workable for high-speed file consumption, so we need a central switching station to keep every processing thread honest.

TextIO is a *Singleton* object (created once at run time and globally referenced thereafter). Any thread can request file access (read/write), manipulate the file as a stream, and close it, all with consistency and reliability. The TextIO object maintains track of which file streams are available and which are already open. When we open a stream, it dedicates a *Handle,* and using it is our only means to manipulate the stream. No other process has visibility to the Handle unless we allow it. Thus the TextIO never gets confused as to which stream needs service.

As such, when opening a file for read or write, the TextIO needs only a pathname of the file's location (any valid URL will do) and it will return a Handle when the file opens successfully. When opening a file for read or write, an error in the "open" will automatically return an empty Handle. For example, let's open one Handle for input and one for output:

```
Dim iHandle as Object
Dim oHandle as Object
iHandle = txtIO.OpenInputFile("inputPathName")
oHandle = txtIO.OpenOutputFile("outputPathName")
```

Upon opening the file for input, Item() will contain the *first* line of the file (and will always contain the "current" line). It will not move to the next line without a call to its *MoveNext* to advance the file's position. When the file has exhausted all input lines, its *More* function will return *False* (our Iterator pattern). The following loop structure will access a file one line at a time:

```
Dim iHandle as Object
Dim strLine as String
iHandle = txtIO.OpenInputFile("inputpathname")
```

```
If not IHandle is Nothing then
  Do
     strLine = txtIO.Item(iHandle)          'now contains the current line!
     txtIO.MoveNext( iHandle)               'get the next line
     Loop While txtIO.More(iHandle)         'until no more lines
     txtIO.CloseFile (iHandle)
  End If
```

When opened for output, the *Set Item()* property *writes* the text placed into it. The following loop will unload a TurboCollection (tcData) of string text values into a file:

```
  Dim oHandle as Object
  oHandle = txtIO.OpenOutputFile("pathname")
  If not oHandle is Nothing Then
  tcData.MoveFirst()
  Do
     txtIO.Item(oHandle) = tcData.Ref.Item    'write the value to the file
     tcData.MoveNext()
  Loop While tcData.More()
  txtIO.CloseHandle (oHandle)
End If
```

The fastest way to deal with file I/O is to pull it all into memory at once, thus the above patterns will repeat themselves many times. For this purpose, we have encapsulated them into the *LoadInputFile()* and *WriteOutputFile()* functions.

LoadInputFile()

LoadInputFile() accepts a pathname and returns a populated TurboCollection, loaded such that each sequential node contains one line of text. This is a perfect tool for metadata input, and on most systems (especially desktops) is extremely fast even for large files. The following code will pull an entire file into memory using a targeted TurboCollection.

```
Dim tcLoad as TurboCollection
tcLoad = txtIO.LoadInputFile("pathname")
```

All handle overhead, file open, close, and browse are self-contained in a single, reusable call. If we move toward external programmability, where run-time instructions are held in external text files, we'll use LoadInputFile a lot.

WriteOutputFile()

The counterpart to LoadInputFile() is *WriteOutputFile*, also encapsulating the handle and all open, close, and browse functions into a single, reusable call. It accepts a file path name and a TurboCollection ready for output. Thus, we can simply populate a TurboCollection with a text line for every node, then send it to the file system with one call. Here's an example.

```
txtIO.WriteOutputFile ("pathname", tcData)
```

Using these basic functions, we can easily input, output, and control our text I/O. Additionally, if we always expect a TurboCollection to contain the I/O results, we have an I/O pattern. For example, isn't the LoadInputFile simply a system request for data, returned as a TurboCollection? Higher abstractions can send I/O calls to it, or to other sources accessing a database, socket call, internet HTTP call, or other input source. The abstraction, in every case, will expect a loaded TurboCollection as the return result, and the TextIO provides the file access resource for this purpose. In short, we really don't care if TextIO accesses the file system or any other source of textual data—we only want our request for data dynamically fulfilled.

Container as Row-Column Data Cache

The TextIO provides a filled TurboCollection of text-file information, and is a transparent I/O building block in this role.

Desktop applications deploy container-style controls to hold and expose large blocks of organized information. These include grids, combo/dropdown boxes, tree views, list views, and others. Manipulating their contents only becomes more complex over time.

In application-centric deployments, team members typically use a variation on a common theme: loading text lines or database rows into memory, ultimately destined for the container-style controls. Unfortunately, many of the drop-down boxes, such as those for countries, zip codes, area codes, and the like, use an I/O call *each time* they appear. We really need a *common* caching mechanism, · allowing us to fetch information once and reuse it in multiple places.

Various third-party components provide this sort of caching (such as Microsoft ActiveX Data Objects Recordset) but none can give us the right balance of speed and control over the information. We need a turbo-charged (and ultimately portable) approach that makes our desktop really scream.

No Direct Linkage, Please

I would counsel against becoming too dependent on components providing direct linkage to their data sources. For example, some components allow us to embed connection, SQL, and other instructions directly into the component's properties, allowing it to act as a free agent in database information exchange. Regardless of what we've heard, using such features can be our own product's greatest weakness for the following reasons:

- Brittleness creeps in because the component is not "hardened" against network noise, database overloading, workstation limitations, etc.

- Departmental deployments experience marginal success, but enterprise-level deployments sputter and fail.

- The component encapsulates the linkage, but obfuscates the errors and disconnects. Troubleshooting is difficult.

- Intimate details about the information source are embedded in the component to enable its run-time conversation, making it difficult to switch information sources later. We are now dependent on the component's API, defeating our objective of reducing our dependence.

- Direct linkage rarely supports all information sources (often favoring a discrete subset), so we'll have to build workarounds for others (e.g., text streams, internet sources, socket-based I/O, etc.).

- Direct linkage inhibits information sharing, because the component is doing its own thing.

- If we have an outcast component, one that does not support direct linkage, we'll have to build workarounds for it anyhow.

Our end is worse than our beginning, because now we have some components in an information silo and some on the information periphery, with all sorts of glue and bridge software to keep them talking because they don't naturally share with others. We need a common center of activity.

If we build a *container* class, we can assign it the sole responsibility of exchanging information with all possible data sources, coupled with a consistent internal data organization, topped off with an interface pattern.

Data drives behavior, so inconsistent data access leads to inconsistent behavior.

Container Patterns

A container class can be an interchangeable building block to all consumers, and provides caching capabilities (avoiding repeated calls to data sources for relatively static information). We can then soft-link our information-based components to the container as the primary source of I/O. The container can encapsulate calls to ActiveX Data Objects, the TextIO class, and every imaginable form of I/O available to the framework. Doing so stabilizes every potential I/O failure point and generally provides more consistent behavior. If we need more I/O capability, we can add it to the container. Bugs in the access layer? Fix it in the container and it's fixed everywhere.

Centralize the container as a structured information cache, buffering the architecture from behavioral I/O anomalies.

More importantly, the day will come when we need to port to (or include) another data source entirely. Do we review every component to examine their portability, or do we use a single object (the container) as the data source manager with all components depending on it? The second option is far more flexible and portable. At run time, our information container can access any number of sources, but our internal consumer components are oblivious to the *actual* source.

Another hidden reality: If the container is well behaved and available via remote control (TCP/IP or otherwise) we can replicate it on servers and hosts to provide transparent, remote data power with a consistent and reusable interface. Whether the container runs embedded, in-process, out-of-process, or remotely, the effect is the same: consistent, reliable data access with no interface surprises, software breakage, or behavioral inconsistency.

Mechanically, run time components will access a single object, a container, for all information needs. The container will not only wrap the primary classes of ActiveX Data Objects, but also flat files, internet sources, XML sources, socket-layer interchange, run-time Active Server Pages interchange, *custom business objects*, and a host of others.

This capability has *extreme* power when integrating custom business objects from legacy applications. We first enhance a legacy business object to expose its information as a container-friendly source. Then our container can simply include it as one of many sources, further opening legacy accessibility and availability. With the .NET framework, Microsoft's XML Web Services lets us interface container roles seamlessly and get on with other integration issues.

A container can hide ugly database or data access details, and pulls all information sources into a common form.

Pushing data manipulation power into the container and allowing it to manage a variety of sources on demand, frees our application layer to simply call on it for services. The details (ugly, elegant, or otherwise) are hidden, as they should be.

Layout Capability

The container's foundational capability is the *Layout*. As the container's internal structure is row/column oriented, the members of the Layout describe a column. The container can hold one or more rows of information, but the individual column definitions in Layout can also contain the metadata to describe the information.

Consider the following simple row/column organization shown in Table 4-9.

Table 4-9. Simple Example Data Set

EMP ID	USER	OFC LOC	ROLE	START DATE
01234	David	Southwest	Author	12/20/1999
43210	Valerie	West Coast	Editor	08/01/2000
12345	Grace	West Coast	Publisher	03/01/2000
81818	Karen	West Coast	PowerBroker	01/01/1998

With this structure, we can derive some other metadata information about each column, which in turn will drive how we'll process or view it. Think now in terms of database columns and rows (Table 4-10), and their identifying information.

Table 4-10. Container Layout Structure

USAGE	PARMNODE	COLUMN 0	COLUMN 1	COLUMN 2	COLUMN 3	COLUMN 4
Display	Item	Emp ID	Name	Ofc Loc	Role	Start Date
DB Column	ItemKey	PUB_ID	PUB_NM	PUB_LOC	PUB_ROL	PUB_DT
Type	ItemType	Numeric	String	String	String	DateTime
Size	ItemSize	5 Digits	15 Chars	20 Chars	15 Chars	Default
Format	FormatStr	"00000"	"#"	"#"	"#"	MM/DD/YYYY
Order	ID	0	1	2	3	4

We can add any number of information descriptors and roles, but the ones listed are encountered most often and will serve any application quite adequately. At a minimum, the Layout will require the column names. We can manage a surprising amount of information with column-name information alone, but with

The container is an Adapter/ Iterator super-pattern, combining multiple behaviors for a more powerful whole.

Because many information sources have large layouts, we can define tcLayout as a binary tree for fast access to column-level information.

more detail, we gain more control over column formatting, display, manipulation, and other processes. Thus, if the information in the Layout structure changes (columns are deleted, added, or modified at run time), the software simply conforms its behavior to the new Layout description *as it happens.*

The container supports complex XML structures. We can use the Layout to define complex structures, then exchange them with XML

The TurboCollection naturally lends itself to the Layout implementation, largely because it provides for a varying-length list (no more or less columns than actually required) and the ParmNode already supports each of the descriptors that appear in Table 4-10.

 NOTE *We'll need one TurboCollection (tcLayout) to control the Layout and one TurboCollection (tcData) to actually contain rows of information described by the Layout.*

If the Layout can describe one or more columns of information, we'll need a place to store a *row* of information described by the columns (again, in terms of a common database system's row-column orientation). The column names (Layout) are static, describing the data in each row (see Figure 4-12).

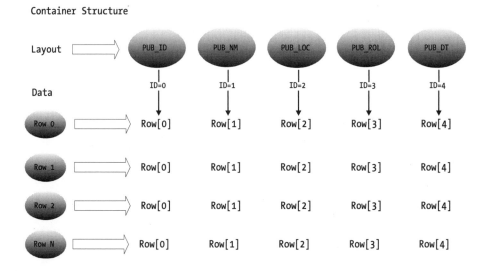

Figure 4-12. Container row/column layout

We'll use the Layout to represent a row's columns, and use another list of ParmNodes to actually contain a row's worth of column information. Thus we have two TurboCollections: *tcLayout* to hold the column layout, and *tcData* to hold the actual rows of data conforming to the Layout. In the description of ParmNode (earlier in this chapter), note the presence of a variable-length string array (Row[]).Each element in a ParmNode's Row[] will correspond to *a column* entry in the Layout.

If we use the Layout node's *ID* property to define a given column's index in the Row[] array, we effectively have a quick map into row-level information. This provides two levels of power in retrieving a given piece of data. First, we can directly index it (e.g., Node.Row[3]). Or, we can derive its index from the Layout (e.g., PUB_ROL's ID is 3). Both capabilities enhance information retrieval.

Two separate containers with similarly described information can now exchange, overlay, or merge their contents using the column names or perform raw transfer using numeric identifiers. They can also use column aliases to align information (e.g., CUSTOMER_NUM and CUST_NUM meaning the same thing on different information systems). Thus, the container is a *data integration* engine, and can reside on either desktops or servers, depending on the workload. In many applications, we find that the data we need is already in our hands, just not connected or all in one place. The container allows us to merge the information without resubmitting it to the database for this capability.

The container can perform in-memory join and rollup without accessing the database for this capability.

Benefits of Using the Container

The container is especially handy for caching often-used application information such as canned lists of countries, cities, zip codes, user names, business hierarchy descriptions, accounting information, and the like. Scientific developers like to store the results of calculations, math tables, charts, transformation algorithms, images, maps, etc. Anything cacheable is a candidate for container management.

The user can experience near-instant multi-key sort and re-display of containers with thousands of rows.

Most applications will use a large subset of these capabilities. Note that each positioning method (MoveFirst(), FindFirst(), etc.) uses *tcData* and regards a *row* of information, while the Item() uses *tcLayout* and returns a *column's* worth of information *in the current row*.

In keeping with the container's building-block use of the interface pattern, each left-hand tag in Table 4-11 is an ActionID, not a traditional interface reference (e.g., "Layout" represents Container.Action ("Layout"), not Container.Layout()). Doing so stabilizes every potential I/O failure point and generally provides more consistent behavior. The following capabilities are listed in their order of usage.

Table 4-11. Container Capabilities

ACTIONID	BEHAVIOR
Layout	Defines the column layout of the container. Each layout node will have a corresponding data element in the Row() array of each data node.
AddRow	Accepts a compound variable with one or more columns of data identified in it. Inserts a data node and populates it.
GetRow	Retrieves the information in all columns for a given row
PutRow	Accepts a compound variable with one or more columns identified in it, and updates the current row's corresponding columns.
RemoveRow	Removes the current row node
Row(Index)=Value	Gets or puts information on a current row's designated column (Index)
FindFirst/FindNext	Finds a row node based on column-wise information matching. Allows for repeat of the search from the current position.
Item(ColumnTag)	Accepts a column identifier and retrieves the column's information from the current row
Trigger	Declares an event to watch and instructions on its handling
Observe	Watches events in the container and automatically relays results or state
Load	Accepts loading instructions, clears the container and loads it with new information from a designated source (file, database, etc.).
LoadAsync	Executes a load but does not wait for results before returning to the caller. Allows other threads to have priority while waiting for the load to complete.
Format	By providing a column identifier and a format string, the format can be applied to the column's raw information each time it is accessed. Common usages include transparent screen display (percentages, dates, currency, etc.).
Calculate	Column-wise variation on the mathAdapter(), using individual columns as parameters for an embedded algorithm. Used for automatic row-level calculation into a designated result column.

Table 4-11. Container Capabilities (continued)

ACTIONID	BEHAVIOR
LoadAdapter	Loads selected information from an existing browse-enabled Adapter
LoadPrep	Prepares the container for loading with predefined instructions. Does not execute the actual load until another process requests the container's information.
LoadContainer	Loads selected columns from another container
MergeContainer	Merges selected columns from another container into common rows based on common key/column values (like an in-memory database "join")
MergeFilter	Merges selected columns from another container based on a column-wise filter
DbAction	Executes any arbitrary database action, with no load expected
DbActionAsync	Executes DbAction without waiting for results
Concat	Concatenates columns in a given row
AsyncStateWait	Waits for a particular async state to occur.
Path	Sets a path for loading flat files
Save	Saves the container's row/column information into a comma-delimited file or database table (and optionally the file's layout as metadata)
Browse	Examines one row at a time, calling back to a designated object with each row's contents
KillBrowse	Externally kills a browse operation (call back procedure can kill the browse controlling it)
MoveFirst, MoveNext, MovePrevious, More	Positioning methods transparent from the Data TurboCollection

Containers have enormous versatility in loading, manipulating, and organizing information for application-level usage. A container is akin to an Adapter for the application's data sources, whatever (and wherever) they may be.

No matter a container's size, we'll want to find rows based on column-level information. These are functionally equivalent to a text editor's find/find-next operations. They accept wildcards and more advanced forms will support synonyms, antonyms, and soundex (sounds like) search parameters.

The find functions may search all columns, or allow column designation. The container's Current Reference will hold the found row, and provide the starting point for a FindNext.

The following highlights show some of the container's feature-level versatility.

Layout, Load, AddRow, GetRow, PutRow, RemoveRow, Item

These functions define the Layout, then perform a raw AddRow of textual information, or directly call a Load() defining an external data source to pull multiple rows. We can update a current row (PutRow), take it out (RemoveRow) or just retrieve the row's information (GetRow). We can get a single column's worth of information with Item(ColumnName).

MoveFirst, MoveNext, MovePrevious, More

These functions allow us to navigate and browse the container's data. We can position the container's "current row" to the first row with a MoveFirst, then advance the current row one at a time with MoveNext (or reverse this with MovePrevious) and test for list terminus with More.

Browse, KillBrowse

These functions allow us to automatically browse the rows in the container in both directions (unlike a common file pointer or database cursor). The browse sets up and activates the end-to-end iteration (the equivalent of a *Do-While)*. The KillBrowse stops the iteration (the equivalent of an *exit Do*).

These functions allow us to initiate an automatic browse of the container's data, with the option to kill the process in midstream. It assumes that Browse() will accept a callback function to perform actions on each row.

FindFirst, FindNext

These functions allow us to search for a given row in the container and use it as the container's Current Reference. The FindFirst will find the very first occurrence of the search criteria while the FindNext will locate subsequent rows using the same criteria. The FindFirst/FindNext combination are the equivalent of a filtered browse. While the container will still examine each row, it will only stop on rows meeting the search criteria.

MergeContainer

This function performs an in-memory *Join* or *Rollup*. Applications invariably find themselves in possession of two containers with similar information. Rather than push it back into a database to join or summarize the results, the Container can merge the contents of another container.

The typical parameters include a "key" column to match each container's rows, the columns to copy in case of a match, and/or the columns to insert in case of no match. Using the Layouts from each container, we can map columns by common tags without worrying about their physical positions. We can also alias column tags such that uncommon tags can still find a match (e.g., EMPLOYEE_ID and EMP_ID).

LoadPrep, LoadAsync

Most applications will load and cache a wide variety of information references. We know that pre-loading the information will cause downstream processes to run faster, but what is the best time to load it? If we load large references when the user demands it, their first-time wait might be longer. If we load everything at once, we risk loading up data that the user may never use during their current session.

Additionally, we often like to set up these sources with initialization scripts in central locations (and call them all at once!). How can we break up their operations for optimum performance?

LoadPrep will allow us to initialize the container with everything it needs to load up the information, but does not perform the load. When we first browse or query it for information, it will execute the load automatically (ideal for small information sets). If the user never asks for the information, it never performs the load.

A container can setup or pre-stage information sources in background, stealing spare cycles to avoid inconveniencing the user.

For larger information sets, *LoadAsync* will accept all load parameters, then execute the load in asynchronous background. Thus the users can continue about their business while this function steals empty cycles to complete the load. Even if the user never asks for the information, the overall apparent performance hit is negligible.

If the user asks for the information, it's already loaded and ready. If the load is not quite complete, the user's initial access is throttled with the AsyncWait function, which forces the load to complete its work as quickly as possible.

These two capabilities give the user the best balance of performance and information management.

Case Study: Business Object Linkage

One company wanted to provide linkage to their new common container class and their legacy business objects. To test their strategy, the development team enabled a primary legacy object with the interface pattern, using it as a window to the object's internal data, state, and methods. They configured the container to derive its Layout and data from the business object's properties (each column would describe one property).

Finally, they made the business object's Action() method visible to the container. The container served the role of broker to the business object, and transparent, seamless integration to the remainder of the framework, and ultimately the enterprise.

Business objects that once had wired, closed interfaces were then open and reusable.

Power Tool Checkpoint

The power tools discussed so far form the primary foundation for our architecture-centric framework. They provide structure, behavioral control, interpretive power, information availability, and organization, and a strong, thematic interface for interoperation. These include the following:

- *TurboCollection* and *ParmNode* for structural glue and high-speed organization and activation capabilities

- *StringAdapter* for reliable high-speed parsing functions

- *MathAdapter* for dynamic calculation capabilities

- *TextIO* for consistent access to external structured text from any source

- *Container* for data loading, integration, and caching for flat file, database engines, XML, third-party, custom legacy, or any external data source

As we build an application on top of these tools, we'll need some common application-level patterns as well. When larger components are sums of smaller components, the reuse capability picks up speed, and we become more productive—both as software developers of an architectural product and as application developers of the metadata using the product.

Building a Programmable Application Prototype

Let's take a look at the capabilities needed for an *Application Prototype* super-pattern. In project exercises at the end of Chapters 1 through 3, I've shown how to build generalized structures and behavioral control using simple interpretation. Now let's review an application class we can expand to control all of our application-specific logic.

The important objective: Don't build a class that *uses* application-level functions. Rather, build a class requiring building blocks such that, when dynamically woven together, collectively *exhibit* application-level functions. The prototype must provide a means to dynamically manufacture structure, behavior, and active relationships throughout.

Our primary behavioral controller will be an Interpreter coupled with an Iterator. We'll need all the power tools for performance and the interface pattern for interchangeability and structural conformance. We'll have to build toward this final destination, so let's focus now on the *starting point*.

Structural Reference

To begin the journey, remember it starts with the interface. We first need to abstract the plethora of information types into a smaller set under our symbolic control. The primary abstract structural types are listed in Table 4-12.

Table 4-12. Abstract Structural Types

TYPES	DESCRIPTION
Simple	String (default) represents all simple data types. If all data ultimately reduces to strings, we have higher visibility and can troubleshoot them in the field.
Compound	String (only) represents one or more Tag=Value pairs. Complex structured text appears on many major interface specifications, including HTML, XML, ODBC, and SQL.
Complex	Object (only) is a custom object or general container/flyweight class. We can also use ParmNode objects as surrogates, or TurboCollections as Flyweights.

Interface Patterns

In Chapter 2, we took a detailed look at how an interface pattern can give us unlimited structural extension and behavioral control. In order to fully support a metamorphic application prototype, we'll need to apply this pattern (shown in Table 4-13) and use it as the original and primary interface for all our building blocks.

Table 4-13. Interface Pattern

PATTERN	DESCRIPTION
Action	Activates, initiates, or terminates the internal implementation
Item	Inserts or retrieves simple or compound property and state information
Ref	Requires a key parameter to find and return internally stored objects
Create	(Internal via *Ref()*) Uses class internal rules to manufacture one of its own kind (fractal self-creation)
Parent	(Internal via *Ref()*) Represents the owner or creator of an object
Top	(Internal via *Ref()*) This property represents a virtual recursive path to the top of a dynamic object chain / hierarchy or cluster.

The pseudocode interface descriptions for *Item()* and *Ref()* follow:

```
Item(Optional strKey as String, strValue as String) as String
Ref(Optional strKey as String, oValue as Object) as Object
```

Using Item() and Ref(), our prototype can dynamically manufacture new internal properties. Since any given property is simply a key/value pair, we can store infinitely more in an internal TurboCollection. The prototype must create a set of default "starter" properties. Then, if Item() or Ref() automatically create a property's key/value pair when they are first encountered, we can add infinitely many more through external means (including external objects and metadata). The pseudocode follows:

```
Property Item(strKey as String, strValue as String)
If Found Property Reference With strKey then
  Replace Property Reference Value with strValue
Else
  Add Property Reference,
  Update Property Reference with strKey and strValue
End If
End Property
```

A common objection to this approach is that we apparently cannot take any specific action on a given property. However, we could simply intercept it inside the Item call, or we could tie the Item to the Action() (since the Action() already behaves as a "Set" operation). The following notation allows all Item "Set" calls to pass through to Action:

```
Property Item(strKey as String, strValue as String)
  'Perform update operation like above
  '…..
  Action strKey, strValue
End Property
```

For a "Get" operation, however, we'll need more information:

```
Property Item(strKey as String)  strValue as String
If Found Property Reference With strKey then
  Item = Property Reference Value
Else
  Item = Action ( "Get" & strKey,strValue)
End If
End Property
```

Now we can automatically defer to the Action() method. If we define an ActionID and all its parameter detail, we can still drive the Action() through Item with this pass-through scenario. Why is this useful? When we get to Observers (below) we'll see the ability to automate inter-object transfer between Item() properties, allowing us to initiate an Action through the Item call.

What is not so apparent is that external objects can insert their *own* properties (and objects) *inside* our prototype's implementation, establishing a dynamic, virtual relationship. Let's suppose we have an object (ObjectB) that wants to take ownership of the prototype (ObjectA). Let's also assume that all objects in the framework have a metadata-driven understanding that every object's "OwnerID" is unique. Examine the following notation:

```
ObjectA.Item("Owner") = ObjectB.Item("OwnerID")
```

Or perhaps another object already owns it, so here's something a little safer:

```
If ObjectA.Item("Owner") = "None" then
  ObjectA.Item("Owner") = ObjectB.Item("OwnerID")
Else
  Debug.Writeline( "Object " & ObjectA.Item("OwnerID") & " already has owner")
End If
```

Note how this allows any object to arbitrarily *stamp* another object with its own internal information, establishing (in this case) the same sort of relationship as primary/foreign keys on a relational database system. And we do it all without changing the interface or the software.

Imagine now having multiple sub-objects with identifiable owners, floating around in a sea of objects. A behavioral controller can manage the relationships at a framework level, ultimately driven by metadata-based rules. These are simple examples of how dynamic property sharing provides virtual and programmable linkage between otherwise disparate objects. We can now dynamically, without software rebuild, allow objects to remotely control the behavior of other objects.

Next, we'll look at textual metadata as a foundation for interpreting structure and behavior into dynamic existence.

Structural and Behavioral Metadata

The post-chapter Project Exercises have already introduced metadata in basic forms. If you've followed them, you now have an operating framework within which to extend and expand capabilities for additional power.

Metadata is useless without the capacity to rapidly parse and interpret it. However, it is equally useless without syntactic and lexical interpretation rules. We can draw on a number of sources, including a combination of several, to get a best fit. Table 4-14 contains some popular sources for basic structural and behavioral syntax.

Table 4-14. Popular Sources for Basic Structural and Behavioral Syntax

LANGUAGE	ADVANTAGE	DISADVANTAGE
Java	Web extensions; pervasive on the Internet; Java Virtual Machine provides native run-time Interpreter	Complexity must be cordoned into manageable subset. Java Virtual Machine is not always available.
C/C++	Most pervasive language in operating systems, especially in distributed computing. High availability of powerful, inexpensive, and *portable* components.	Complexity must be cordoned into manageable subset
Visual Basic	Simple to understand and "macro-izes" many complex functions. High availability of powerful and inexpensive components. Run Time Interpreter available for VBScript.	Scripting Runtime can hamstring portability and performance. Best to use internal Interpreter.

I've chosen Visual Basic for examples and projects in this book because it pervades the marketplace. It's not portable like C++ and Java, but it doesn't have to be. I've given the above languages as examples of *templates* from which we'll build metadata Interpreters, not the underlying software language used to interpret and act on the metadata script.

These language definitions have breathtaking complexity, but we're not really interested in re-implementing a language compiler or Interpreter. Our desire is to replicate, at a high level, their capacity to define structure and activate behavioral *patterns*, comprised of several highly useful categories. I touched on these patterns briefly in Chapter 3, now we'll dive deeper.

If we build compiled software to broker application-centric metadata, we can implement it in any language without affecting the application metadata.

Structural Metadata Categories

When building metadata to represent structure, we can reduce its syntax to several simple categories. Table 4-15 shows the structural metadata categories.

Table 4-15. Structural Metadata Categories

CATEGORY	DESCRIPTION
Statements	The most pervasive textual pattern. Represents a line of structured text. Requires repeated parsing and interpretation, and is subject to material and contextual change with each subsequent interpretation. A statement typically reads like a sentence with a noun (Entity Definition), verb (Action) and modifiers (Parameters).
Definition	A statement used to build a dynamic entity (e.g., simple or complex)
Routines	Groupings of statements which are labeled for quick reference and execution.
Rules	A Routine bound to a component event by a Trigger (below). Rules can call routines, are prioritized to their events and can be interrupted by a higher-priority rule.

Statements

Statements appear in several forms but will almost always abstract multiple common compiler-language statements. This allows an Interpreter to view each textual line as a standalone, self-contained operation. Structural statement syntax could include:

```
Define ObjectA as Complex
```

Some behavioral statement syntax follows:

```
set ObjectA.Property(Key) = ObjectB.Property(Key)
```

Every line of textual metadata is a statement, divided into two broad categories: structural definition and behavioral activation.

Definition

The DEFINE statement constructs the TARGET as an entity of TYPE, like so:

```
'Simple variable type for holding strings, numerics, dates, etc
DEFINE CurrDate as Simple
'Complex type stores structured row/column information
DEFINE BizCities as Complex
'Modify behavior for Parallel extensions and multiple threads
DEFINE MathAlgo as Complex:Parallel
'Modify behavior to use OLEDB data sources
DEFINE AddressLoad as Complex:OLEDB
'Modify behavior to use Socket/TCP/IP as data sources
DEFINE PeerComm as Complex:Socket
```

These examples show how we can default the definition of "Complex" to a canned internal object (such as the Container mentioned earlier). We can also extend the definition to include other types of complex objects such as Sockets, even legacy or third-party Adapters.

The pattern uses the notation of "Complex" in the definition and treats it interchangeably with other entities defined as Complex. The metadata describing and activating their relationships will not require any additional extension no matter how many (or how many kinds) of complex types are available to the Interpreter.

Routines

Only the Interpreter will have access to all forms of complex types, and will bring them all to a common table through metadata definition.

A *Routine* is a grouping of statements, similar to a language-level subroutine. In an interpretive framework where routines and their statements are fed serially, we must guard against uncontrolled interruption. For example, if one Routine is browsing the contents of a complex variable, we must protect it from interruption to avoid accidentally resetting its contents. Thus, the Interpreter must obey all applicable threading rules, such that each Routine should complete all of its statements within a single context. Individual statements have visibility to other contexts by permission.

This is not an especially difficult capability, considering that Interpreter-friendly languages (such as C++, Java, and other visual development environments) are event-driven and automatically handle threading through a generous set of process and interrupt controls. For our Interpreter to ride on this carpet, external events must eventually cascade their threads into its domain, coupled with contextual information as to the event's source and its meaning to the Interpreter.

We can invoke Routines spontaneously from events, or call them from other Routines, including invoking itself with recursion. Once the Routine has control of the thread, it typically executes statements serially. We define a Routine as follows:

```
Define LoadCheck as Routine
   StatementA Here
   StatementB Here

   ….
End Routine
```

For multi-threaded performance, we can use parallel syntax and exploit (or simulate) multiple threads:

```
Define LoadCheck as Routine
   StatementA Here
   Define ThreadA              'thread A starts now
       StatementB Here
       StatementC Here
   End Thread
   Define ThreadB              'thread B starts now
       StatementD Here
       StatementE Here
   End Thread
End Routine
```

In the above example, a multi-threaded environment can execute StatementB and StatementD simultaneously. If no multi-threading is available, the statements simply execute serially.

We can chain statements together in a logical sequence for application-level effects. Since subroutine calls are also statements, we can mix, match and perform highly custom groupings of elemental statements. The result is application behavior *emergence* as described by the metadata statements rather than specific software code.

The ability to define and execute Routines is the heart of metadata-based behavioral control. While elemental statements perform one small part of a behavioral effect, they cannot formalize application-centric behavior without Routines. The metadata statements *and* Routines weave the application into existence at run time.

Routine and Statement Framework

To define Routines effectively, we must build a TurboCollection list of Routines (each node has the Routine Name). Under each Routine node, we build a sub-list of the Routine's actual statements (each statement is therefore a node on a sub-list). Thus, we can submit the Routine's sub-list to a statement Iterator, which in turn calls a statement Executor once for each statement-level node. The simplest hierarchy follows:

```
Routine Executor -> Routine
              Statement Iterator->Statements
                            Statement Executor (Statement)
```

The following layout defines three simple Routines:

```
Define myLoader as Routine
   Statement A Here
   Statement B Here
End Routine
Define myReader as Routine
   Statement C Here
   Statement D Here
End Routine
Define myWriter as Routine
   Statement E Here
   Statement F Here
End Routine
```

The Interpreter will convert the above metadata into the structure shown in Figure 4-13. This structure is very simple and easy for software to interpret and navigate.

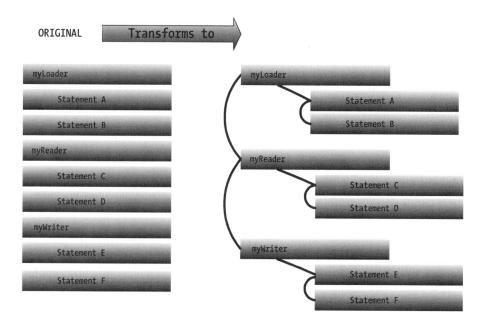

Figure 4-13. Routine logical structure

Events Rule

A *Rule* is just a Routine *bound* to an event on an external object. If we desire to share a Routine outside of the Interpreter, we must convert it to a Rule. This means we concatenate the Routine Name with the Interpreter ID. We'll now use both descriptors as a unique ID (Routine Names by themselves are unique inside the Interpreter, but rarely globally unique). Once the Routine Name leaves the Interpreter's domain to bind to an event, it becomes a Rule.

```
interpreterID:RoutineName
```

Using metadata definitions, we will identify the Rule with an event and send it to an entity. When the event fires, the entity will use the Rule to locate the Interpreter and ultimately invoke the Routine. We'll look closer at Rule definitions shortly.

Behavioral Metadata Categories

To guide our Interpreter's behavior, we'll classify statements into the types and roles listed in Table 4-16. This list, though small, provides an enormous amount of application-level power when we combine, mix, and match them for a specific feature deployment.

Table 4-16. Behavioral Metadata Categories

TYPE	ROLE
Trigger	Binds Routines (as Rules) to external events (asynchronous signals from components)
Observer	Creates a virtual relationship between unrelated objects and automates their information exchange
Assignment	Moves information from one variable entity to another
Subroutine Call	Calls another Routine from within a current Routine (and returns execution control when completed); supports both parallel and asynchronous execution
Iteration	Loop control, browses information sources
Decision	Interrogates information and context; executes or ignores statements based upon dynamic, contextual decisions
Environment	Access to environment variables, system-related information, and language environment features/functions
Input/Output	File I/O, database exchange, socket I/O, etc.

Trigger

A *Trigger* is the behavioral mechanism for a Rule (above). It establishes and activates a virtual, event-driven relationship between an external Adapter and an internal, interpreter-owned Routine. No logical limit exists as to how many rules we can tie to a given Adapter. However, practical limits on performance may preclude their unlimited proliferation.

Rather than specifically programming a CommandButton's Click event, we'll simply define a Routine and attach its Trigger to its Click event.

For example, we'll use an Interpreter, bind one of our Interpreter's Routines to an external Trigger-enabled component Adapter and cause it to watch a specific event. The example below has an objective: to hand off process control from a screen-level command button to the Routine LoginUser whenever the user "clicks" the button.

We identify several players in all this: the Interpreter ("txtLogin"), the command button Adapter ("cmdOk"), the Routine ("LoginUser") and the event ("Click"). Table 4-17 reviews the required entities, along with unique identification tags.

Table 4-17. Summary of Trigger's Requirements

ENTITY	IDENTIFIER
Application ProtoType / Interpreter	txtLogin
Routine/Rule	txtLogin:LoginUser
Adapter for a Command Button	cmdOk
Screen containing Button	frmLogin
Event Name	Click

We can expose any building-block object to the Interpreter as "Complex" because they all look and behave the same.

Now to bridge the gulf between the application prototype and the other entities, we need a statement to define the relationship. The Trigger's parameters only require an owner (the ScreenName and command button) and the event to watch, as follows:

```
Define Trigger:Routine=LoginUser|Owner=cmdOk|Event=Click
Define LoginUser as Routine
   Statements Here
End Routine
```

We can now register the Routine as a triggered Rule at any time during the Interpreter's execution. The Routine, Adapter, and event are loosely coupled through the Trigger (and each entity has its own identifier). Defining the Trigger initiates the following processes:

```
The interpreter will locate the frmLogin:cmdOk Adapter Object
The interpreter will insert a Trigger into the
      Adapter's Event Path,  using the Interpreter's ID,
      the named Routine and Event
The Adapter will now watch for the named Event (Click)
When the event fires, the Adapter will
      Locate the Interpreter (txtLogin)
      Pass to it the named Routine (LoginUser)
      Also pass event-based contextual information
The interpreter will accept the processing thread from the
      Adapter's event, along with the named Routine
The interpreter will locate the Routine and invoke it.
```

The final effect: the user *clicks* a command button with a mouse (or hot key) and the Routine (LoginUser) automatically executes. If application-level instructions are in the LoginUser, we now have a way to manage the event's behavior (in the application script) without changing the binary event-management software associated with the user's screen.

Does all this sound like a lot of handshaking and overhead? In fact, the primary overhead is in the setup (locating the Adapter and installing the Trigger at run time). Once the structures are in place, they passively listen for the correct event. From there, dispatching the Rule to its Interpreter happens rather quickly. It is important to view the setup (initially establishing the relationship) and activation (executing the thread) as separate elements of the process. The setup will occur once and will enable the activation to occur as many times as the event fires. Thus if we pre-process the Trigger setup to optimize the Trigger action, we get high-speed response.

Interpreter optimization tip: pre-process each statement on its first encounter so if we encounter it again, we don't repeat prior parsing.

Observer

The *Observer* provides a powerful means to define dynamic virtual relationships between objects that otherwise share nothing. For example, consider the following regularly appearing application-level features:

- One control's update automatically initiates behaviors in another control.

- A command button is enabled only when certain screen fields contain valid information.

- Navigation to certain application areas is only enabled based on specific conditions elsewhere in the application (including role-based security).

- Browsing a grid, treeview, combo-box, etc. causes update or enable/disable of other screen elements based on the view's information or state.

- Part of a screen is enabled/disabled based on a user's navigation or action elsewhere on the screen.

These special effects are standard application behaviors, and are often the product of specially-crafted software to enforce them. Our core architecture must support and enable this behavior automatically, through external programmability. Do we have access to a mechanism that can enable these behaviors automatically with a simple metadata statement?

The Observer provides a means to dynamically define these behaviors (and many others) by describing the relationship as a programmable pattern. Observer patterns appear in enterprise-level behavior management through publish-subscribe services, store-and-forward systems, replication, and triggered, event-based data exchange (including MQSeries, MSMQ, MAPI Servers, RDBMS Replicators, etc.). We can directly wire this behavior at an application level, or build the highway upon which this behavior will ride. The second path gives us external programmability.

The command to invoke an Observer between two entities includes identifying the following elements:

Automatic observation enables components to share information and state when no other apparent relationship exists.

- Source and target entities

- Properties on target/source entities exchanging information

- Source entity's event to Trigger the exchange (optional)

- Property values (or conditions) to watch for (optional)

A simplified syntax for the Observe directive follows:

```
Observe Entity.PropertyName = Entity.[EventName].PropertyName
                [Condition][Value0[,Value1,ValueN]]
```

The *observed* source (Right-Hand Side) has the most complex syntax, allowing us to observe its properties with these complex options:

- Specific event occurs

- Specific condition exists

- Specific property meets a condition against one or more values

- All of the above

Observation occurs in various forms, but the simplest is initiating information exchange from source to target regardless of the event. For example, let's update a command button's *Enabled* property based on the value in a grid's designated *Role* column. Every update to the grid's column will initiate the observation, like so:

```
Observe $cmdNew.Item(Enabled) =
    $gridProgram.Item(Property=CellValue|Key=@Role)
```

However, the overhead for this activity might be unwieldy, (especially considering how event-intensive a grid control can be). We can therefore throttle the Observer by binding it to an event (with the assumption that the RowChange event is the only one we're really interested in as the user browses the grid). Here's an example:

```
Observe $cmdNew.Item(Enabled)=
    $gridProgram.Item(Event=RowChange|Property=CellValue|
                                Key=@Role)
```

The preceding statement will Observe on a predefined grid event (RowChange). Thus, if the grid experiences a RowChange event, its context will be relayed into the Observer for examination. If the Observer matches up its observed event and an inbound event, the Observer will immediately access the grid's *CellValue* property on the current row, in the *@Role* column, forward the *@Role* column's information to the awaiting property (cmdNew.*Enabled*).

We can further throttle the return values (programmed filtering) by converting specific values to True/False based on conditions tested in the source, prior to forwarding them. We can effectively enable/disable the command button based on a specific column value ("*PowerUser*") in a specific column ("*Role*") on the grid. The observation will occur each time the user browses the grid (RowChange). The following syntax reads "When a RowChange Occurs, If the Value In @Role Is Equal to PowerUser, Return True, Else False":

```
Observe $cmdNew.Item(Enabled)=
    $gridProgram.Item(Event=RowChange|Property=CellValue|
                        Key=@Role|Op=ValueIs|Value=PowerUser)
```

Now let's observe the same column, only for values within a certain set of defined values (we use the IN rather than the IS to maintain a semblance of SQL syntax, e.g., *Value* is in *ValueSet*):

```
Observe $cmdNew.Item(Enabled)=
    $gridProgram.Item(Event=RowChange|Property=CellValue|
                        Key=@Role|Op=ValueIn|Value=PowerUser,ReportUser)
```

This sample reads: "When RowChange occurs, If the Value in @Role is one of PowerUser or ReportUser, Return True, Else False".

Here's an example of using a variation for wildcards, where the IN operator serves equally well:

```
Observe $cmdNew.Item(Enabled)=
    $gridProgram.Item(Event=RowChange|Property=CellValue|
                        Key=@Role|Op=ValueIn|Value=Power*)
```

It now reads: "When RowChange occurs, If the Value in @Role is Prefixed with "Power", Return True, Else False".

The Project Exercises at the end of Chapters 1 through 5 include examples for initiating observation between entities. The mechanics for enabling observation are identical for each participating entity, and when they expose all properties through their common Item property, no practical limit exists for interchanging information (embedded, automatic publish and subscribe) for any entity, great or small, at any level, throughout the framework.

 NOTE *The production version of Observer exchanges information with lightweight MOM XML templates (Tag/Value pairs), providing unlimited extension in programmable behavior. It also supports multiple sources, rules and Boolean operators to tie rules together.*

Assignment

In-memory data movement is such a common and elemental part of computing that significant hardware resources (burned into the silicon chips and its driving firmware) are *totally* dedicated to blasting data around inside the CPU's domain. Software languages exploit this capability to infinite extremes, so practically every tool will provide a complement of powerful data movement capabilities.

The primary issue with *assignment* is not one of data availability, or even accessibility. It rests in the consistency of the interfaces and their data interchange behavior. Just because a component shares its interface with other components does not make it automatically interoperable. Linking and automating data interchange is often difficult, even with hard-wired, carefully crafted software.

While the Observer (above) performs passive, automatic exchange, the assignment capability will perform active, deliberate exchange. However, the mechanics of both are very similar.

In the discussions on structural consistency in Chapter 2, the ability to interchange information is a paramount concern and consideration when crafting component interfaces. However, like all marketplace quantities, interface consistency is not something to expect from the constellation of component vendors screaming for our attention. They want to capture us as a long-term user, so will build as much uniqueness as possible into their interfaces, hoping that we will take the bait and inextricably link our implementation to theirs.

Consider the following hard-wired model using a grid control from ACME, purveyors of software to the world (and various Warner Brother's cartoon characters):

```
Set mGrid =New acmeGrid
MGrid.Columns(0).ColumnHeader = "User ID"
MGrid.Columns(0).DataField = "UserID"
MGrid.Columns(1).ColumnHeader = "User Name"
MGrid.Columns(1).DataField = "UserName"
```

If we hard-wire the implementation this way, we will *never* enjoy the option of easily installing a better, faster grid component. This simple example of software code betrays a common theme, that we are directly accessing component interface methods and properties to affect behavior. This is exactly what the component vendor wants, and exactly what we must avoid.

It is our mission to thwart the vendor's marketing objective, wrap their component with an Adapter, and plug it into our framework as a seamless, interoperable, and indistinguishable player. When Adapters provide interface consistency, inter-object assignment is simple and reliable. The Item() and Action() patterns provide all the interface power we'll ever need.

The framework requires an instruction syntax to exploit the interchange capability. For this we'll use a *Set* directive, performing assignment from the "source" result into the "target" property. In keeping with most parameter-substitution engines, we'll require a "$" prefix on all internally "tagged" entities or those constructed with the metadata macro Define statement. Assignment also assumes presence of some predefined functions such as string conversion, date/time, and environment information. Each of these will appear as an embedded complex entity, metadata macros syntax follows:

```
'Get the date using the embedded System entity
Set $SysDate.DateFormat=YYYY/MM/DD
Set $CurrDate=$SysDate
```

The Interpreter will hunt down the variables, convert the strings to tags or parameters and make a transparent assignment call. The assignment will always work for variables using an interface pattern.

Because these are metadata instructions first, they provide portability across platforms and products. As long as the Interpreter recognizes the script and executes it consistently, it doesn't matter what the underlying software language or computing environment is.

Subroutine Call

The logic behind a subroutine call rides on the software language's native ability to invoke and recurse subroutines. In fact, when we are parsing sequential text instructions and encounter a subroutine call, we simply call the parsing engine again with the Routine Name designated in the call. The software language will immediately begin parsing the Routine until completion, then return control to the original calling thread, which takes up right where it left off before the call.

This strategy also directly exploits *recursion,* the ability of a software Routine to call itself. Consider the following statement, a variation on the example used for Routines earlier in this chapter. I'll use bold text to identify the metadata macro Routine Name.

```
Define myLoader as Routine
   Statement A Here
   Call myReader
   Statement B Here
End Routine
'/////////////////////////////////////
Define myReader as Routine
   Statement C Here
   Statement D Here
End Routine
```

The myLoader macro Routine includes a *call* directive, with a macro Routine Name as its only parameter. Could we include multiple parameters with call? We absolutely can, using the following interpreted abstraction of the interface pattern. I'll use bold text to identify the macro's parameters:

```
Define myLoader as Routine
   Statement A Here
   Set $aID = $STR("DB2:Read")
   Set $aData = $STR("Table=EmpTable|Cols=EmpID,EmpName,EmpDept")
   Call myReader aID, aData, myContainer
End Routine
#########
Define myReader as Routine
   If $ActionID.EQ.$STR("DB2:Read") Then
      Statements to Call the Database using $ActionData, $ActionObject, etc.
End Routine
```

This construct depicts implied parameters of ActionID, ActionData, and ActionObject. As such, when the Interpreter invokes the subroutine, these three parameters are made available to the called Routine in context. If the called Routine accesses these parameter variables, they will contain the values placed there by the calling Routine. When the subroutine terminates, the Interpreter can optionally return the variables as modified by the called Routine, or restore their original values. We must verify that the Interpreter stacks/unstacks these values just like a language compiler.

Iteration

We'll always need to loop, rapidly repeating a series of statements in the context of browsing an information container (such as browsing the return result of a database query, or examining the contents of a text file, and so on.)

A complex variable can embed browse capability but must expose a browsable structure to the Interpreter. Typical usage follows, with bold text to highlight the Routine designated for per-node callback.

```
Define myContainer as Complex:ODBC
Define myBrowseExample as Routine
    Set $myContainer.Layout=AcctID|AcctName|Dept
    Set $myContainer.Load=$STR("SQL:select * from Accounts")
    Set $myContainer.Browse=myBrowseRoutine
End Routine
'////////////////////////////////
Define myBrowseRoutine as Routine
  Set $Wrk1=$myContainer.Item(AcctName)
End Routine
```

By invoking browse on *myContainer*, this will invoke myContainer's internal browse method, start at the top of its result set and examine each row, calling back to myBrowseRoutine once for each row found. Thus, the myBrowseRoutine is always invoked in context of a single row of information. The myBrowseRoutine can then access column-level information through myContainer's Item() property.

Note also how the Interpreter invokes myBrowseRoutine in the same manner as an event handler (rule). It rides on exactly the same logic. When we first invoke the browse, the Interpreter ID and Routine Name are provided to the browsing object, which in turn calls back to the Interpreter once for each row.

Interpreters can call other Interpreters, even invoke another metadata Routine remotely in a separate instance of the program. The TurboCollection's multidimensionalism provides us with dynamic, symbolic linkage to any source of metadata instructions.

The Interpreter requires consistent, thematic, and rock-solid iteration capabilities because it leverages them so heavily for its own work.

NOTE *Virtual Machine Intelligence also uses metadata instructions to write text files of dynamic metadata instructions, then pulls these into memory and executes them—a self-programming program.*

Decision

Statement interpretation and execution requires constraint, such as the capacity to make decisions within the surrounding context, information contents, or state. Typically we'll want selective execution of a series of statements.

"Project 2—Structures" and "Project 3—Behaviors" demonstrate decision logic factories using the *StringAdapter*. The objective is to bundle statements out of their sequential order and build IF-THEN gateways to them. The most complex construct follows:

```
If Value-Condition-Value Then
   Statements Here
Else If Value-Condition-Value Then
   Statements Here
Else
   Statements Here
End If
```

This construct supports an initial condition (IF), multiple secondary conditions (ELSEIF) and a default condition (ELSE). We're intimately familiar with this construct, but probably never considered abstracting it into an interpreted form.

Bundling statements under their conditional operators is simple: we just define each branch as an embedded Routine, with a name visible only to the decision tree. When a given condition resolves to *True*, we execute the Routine.

Our real concern is the *possible* complexity of the conditional statement itself. It can be as complex as the most intricate assignment statement, but this is not the most efficient use of it. We really want to avoid over-complicating the conditional syntax, or the Interpreter will get bogged into logical parsing complexity rather than reaching its true goal: to decide what to do *and do it*. As such, building the capacity for infinitely complex conditional statements, while "kinda cool" is not very practical. Consider the following condition statement:

```
If $MyContainer.Item(AcctID) EQ $gridContainer.Property(Column=UserID) Then
```

And compare it to the following statements:

```
Set $Wrk1=$MyContainer.Item(AcctID)
Set $Wrk2=$gridContainer.Property(Column=UserID)
If $Wrk1 EQ $Wrk2 Then
```

The second example, while requiring more statements, simplifies the implementation of parsing and executing the conditional statement. We'll get better overall performance from the second example, but more control with the first. The goal is to balance their usage so we can optimize their interpretation.

An Interpreter can rip through simple, building-block statements faster than a few highly complex statements.

The vMach framework optimizes complex variable evaluation for metadata if/then and select/case, as well as complex conditions. Used in balance, we get significant leverage over application logic. The project exercises at the end of this chapter take a deep headfirst dive into dynamic conditional logic. We'll look at deeply complex conditions and select/case statements.

Environment

Every computing process requires access to its environment, such as operating system information, time zone, current date, user name, computer name, computer network/IP address, and a host of hardware, registry, and component metadata, to name a fraction.

In each case, we'll format the return values or quantities into simple strings, thus the return result will always be a simple variable. The shortest path to automate this capability is to expose a single complex pseudo-variable within the Interpreter's scope we'll call $GLOBAL. The $GLOBAL is actually a predefined metadata keyword and references a *Singleton* (which we discussed in Chapter 2). It accepts a simple or compound parameter as a key, and also returns a simple or compound value.

The GLOBAL Adapter is the interpreter's view of the *glb* object (discussed as part of the Singleton in Chapter 2). It keeps a local list of all "global" parameters added during run time. If the parameters don't exist, the GLOBAL function will look for them externally.

The following demonstrates GLOBAL's pass-through capability to system environment variables, in this case "UserName" under Windows NT.

```
Set $Wrk1=$GLOBAL.Item("UserName")
' Wrk1 now contains dbirmingham, derived from the operating system environment
```

We can also cause certain elements to interoperate, such as setting the application's DateFormat, and causing all date functions to use this format as default. If we internally bind the text value to the Visual Basic Now() function, modified by the DateFormat environment value, we can achieve the following effect:

```
Set $Wrk1=$GLOBAL.Item("SystemDate")
'  Wrk1 = '01/01/2001'
Set $GLOBAL.Item("DateFormat")=$STR("YYYY-MM-DD")
Set $Wrk1=$GLOBAL.Item("SystemDate")
'  Wrk1 now = '2001-01-01'
```

Basically, the $GLOBAL variable is the Interpreter's *program-level* property reference. Thus, if our framework is running as a single instance called PROG.EXE, the $GLOBAL variable would be conceptually similar to invoking PROG.Item().

....

Abstraction or Distraction?

Are we just building another language on top of Visual Basic? Perhaps we're using C#, Java, or C++ and each language has its own flavor of Now(), Today(), or other functional constructs. We might like to transport application-level script between environments without changing it, but cannot if the language or system level calls are not themselves abstracted.

We might want to upgrade from VB6 to VB .NET, but find now that even a simple call to Format() is radically different between the two versions. Do we painfully change the software everywhere that Format() is used, or do we build our own abstraction to protect ourselves from the differences?

 TIP *When in doubt, abstract.*

....

We can now see how the structural patterns fall into place for *every entity*, at every level, whether specifically defined or even considered as part of the original implementation. Holding fast to the patterns will allow seamless and almost instant extensibility into new capabilities—bounded only by our imaginations.

Input/Output

The most critical aspect of application development and solution deployment is the ability to manage and organize huge amounts of complex information. Regardless of size or complexity however, if the structural and behavioral metadata manipulation is sound, we can enhance performance under the covers (in the software) without impacting the framework's behavior. The objective is to expose better and deeper data capabilities. The metadata-based capabilities are late-bound and can exploit newer, faster technology within moments of its availability.

Experienced developers have touched upon various forms of input and output, but most application-centric programs hard-wire these capabilities directly into the software. Abstracting input/output as a general, multipurpose capability requires forethought.

One objective is to build our Interpreter with enough intelligence to assign a resource, or entity, appropriate for a given duty. For example, the following syntax will manufacture a complex entity suitable for OLEDB access to a database via standard SQL commands:

```
Define myContainer as Complex:OLEDB
```

The Interpreter will need a container-style class (see "Container as Row-Column Data Cache" above) to handle the row-column return values. Will the Interpreter select a general purpose container that supports many forms of I/O, such as flat file, OLEDB, socket and other data sources? At the application level, *we don't care*. The instruction requires an OLEDB container resource and the Interpreter must fulfill it.

Generally speaking, the container pattern (and any objects defined to support it) must follow common behavioral patterns to be completely interchangeable. In fact, the following notation should exhibit the same behavior (if not provide the same information) as the prior notation:

```
Define myContainer as Complex:TCPIP
```

This example will send/retrieve socket-oriented information. After we define the entity, the remaining application script accessing it should not have to know which. If we further parameterize it, we can say that the source is totally unknown until run-time, such as determining the input source and assigning it to a GLOBAL property (InfoSource), then later accessing it as follows:

```
Set $Wrk1=$GLOBAL("InfoSource")
Define myContainer as Complex:$Wrk1
```

All definitions, instantiations, and behaviors are now determined at run time and will follow consistent, interchangeable patterns. Application-level I/O should be transparent as to its source and destination, and the application could use one source to retrieve and another to store.

Consider now the following notation:

```
Define myContainer as Complex:Custom:MyBizObject
```

This notation opens the door to expose a specific, custom business object to the Interpreter, so subsequent statements can interact with it like any other container. Will the Interpreter select a standard container that is *aware* of MyBizObject, or will MyBizObject be the actual interface behind the complex definition? Again, the metadata instructions don't care. All the instruction sees is a resource with supported behavioral cues. It is the Interpreter's duty to bind those cues to real objects and actions. It is the object's duty to conform to the Interpreter's interface pattern requirements.

In whatever way we support and expose the input/output behavior, the types of sources and destinations—while deep, wide, variant and disparate—have at their core a common pattern that the metadata instructions can mimic and exploit. Most, if not all, of these behaviors are examined in this chapter's earlier discussion on containers.

Application Prototype Checkpoint

The application prototype has significant capabilities, exposed by the building blocks and leveraged by behavioral patterns. Once we start thinking in terms of programming *the application* using metadata instructions, and building capabilities using compiled software, we will automatically shift our efforts to higher reuse and productivity.

When the compiled software behaves as a metadata broker, its role is separated from the common application architecture, and is no longer a slave to the whims of the user. Developing applications with metadata instructions likewise has faster, even blinding turnaround speed compared to compiled software. Thus, we have more stable software, a nimble, responsive platform, and happier, even satiated users.

How did we get there? By wrapping all the potential component misbehavior into Adapters, exposing them as building blocks, then binding behaviors into interface and behavioral patterns. We achieve organization, and through interpretation achieve behavioral activation. All these aspects serve to place the technology, the capabilities and every risk-laden aspect of software development on a leash.

Project 4—Interpreters

Now that we've put more flesh on the prototype's bones, we need to wrap it up with a project exercise for greater understanding. This chapter's project exercises dive into detailed mechanics of interpretation and activation. They'll give you a taste for what it means to handle behavior using structural classes as a foundation. With these strategies, we can build powerful, externally programmable software that stabilizes quickly and gathers strength over time. While the exercises show how to post data in and out of variables, they don't show any real connection to the outside world. We'll get to that in the next project.

Be careful to observe the foundation, not just the operation of the software. Performing conditional execution, creating dynamic routines, and setting variables is great for an example, but remember that we are trying to build patterns. Each of these variables and its attendant tags can mean many things to the underlying software. Moving a single piece of information from one variable to another can be a simple way to represent a full email blast from a database, or launch the generation of business analysis cubes to our end users, or initiate database replication across an entire enterprise.

The key is this: the superficial metadata operation is simple, but the underpinnings can be extremely detailed and complex. The objective is to encapsulate the detail and expose its programmable parameters to the outside world. Text-based scripts will not replace the software, nor should they become a detailed language surrogate. They should exist in the *gulf,* the twilight zone between binary programs and end-user requirements (and all their volatility). Protect our software and our career from the chaos while continuously providing the end users what they want.

 CROSS-REFERENCE *See Chapter 1 for a discussion of the physical, abstract, and virtual components of the Cyber Gulf.*

Interpretation Mechanics

Interpretation is not about sifting huge amounts of textual tokens in the hopes that we can somehow sense or discern a pattern from them. Interpretation focuses on deliberately linking textual tags and cues to key features in the base software. This sort of "soft linkage" requires *keywords* that the Interpreter expects to find in the text (as prompts to perform predefined actions) coupled with syntactic ordering. The more predefined actions available in the core, the more programmable it is.

We don't want to expose every possible capability at the Interpreter level. For example, a grid component might perform a "load" while a text box only performs simple assignment. The objective is to push capabilities into the components and allow the Interpreter to broker the instructions rather than being intimately aware of them.

A common language compiler uses keywords such as Set, Dim, Define, While, If, EndIf, and the like. The keywords provide both structure (defining variables) and behavior (controlling action) as well as modifiers to each. In fact, each interpreted statement acts like a sentence, with nouns (variables), verbs (actions) and variations on dealing with each (modifiers, adverbs, adjectives, etc.), comprising a language pattern with a syntactical and lexical foundation. The beauty is that we don't have to endure the pain of creating a language, because this is already mature in the marketplace (compiler languages, markup languages, etc.), only language *patterns*. We'll look at these in this project.

In the prior chapter, the project exercise dealt with some basic mechanics of string interpretation. In fact, any interpreted (and thus programmable) environment will start by using structured text. Each line of structured text is a standalone string, hence the requirement for high-speed string manipulation. With a string manager such as the StringAdapter, and a text line manager such as a TurboCollection, we can easily build a sophisticated Interpreter.

Defining Variables

The first example includes a call to access the text file *Snip1Input.Txt*. At the highest level, only two data types really interest me. One is the simple data type (dates, strings, numeric quantities, etc.) and the other is a complex data type, which we'll look at in detail in the next project.

The contents of *Snip1Input.Txt* file follow:

```
'  Define the workspace
Define Simple Wrk1
Define Simple Wrk2
Define Simple Wrk3
' Perform operations on them -
Set $Wrk1 = "David"
Set $Wrk2 = "Built"
Set $Wrk3 = "This"
```

These macros "define" three simple variables, followed by three "behavioral" macros to assign their values. We could very easily accomplish this in hard-wired software code similar to the following:

```
Dim Wrk1 as String
Dim Wrk2 as String
Dim Wrk3 as String
Wrk1 = "David"
Wrk2 = "Built"
Wrk3 = "This"
```

But this would be *forever* hard-wired into the compiled code structure. What if we wanted to add a fourth variable (e.g., Wrk4)? Or perhaps modify the contents of the second variable (Wrk2) to "Made" instead of "Built"? We need a way to manipulate these values without rebuilding and redelivering the code.

On another level, let's assume that the tag "Wrk1" and its companion data variables are part of the *application*, and are subject to change at the whim of the user. Wouldn't we like to have these tags externally programmable rather than having to rebuild the binary program each time the user(s) changed their minds? For this, we'll need the capability to manufacture variables from metadata instructions.

Setting Up Workspaces

First, let's set up some workspaces. We'll need a way to input the file *Snip1Input.Txt* for later browsing, so we'll need a TextIO and a TurboCollection we'll call tcFile.

```
Dim oTxt As TextIO
Dim tcFile As TurboCollection
oTxt = TextIOMgr
tcFile = oTxt.LoadInputFile("Snip1Input.Txt")
```

Creating a Holding Area for Variables

Now we've got the entire file loaded into the tcFile TurboCollection. Next we'll need a holding area to anchor each variable (such as Wrk1, Wrk2) we find in the text, as well as a means to parse each line as it arrives. We'll need a StringAdapter (strA) as a workspace, and a TurboCollection (tcVar) as the holding area.

```
Dim strA As New StringAdapter()
Dim tcVar As New TurboCollection()
```

Walking Through the Text File

Now let's walk through the text file a line at a time. Note that we'll parse each line, then examine its first word. If it's a *Define* we'll jump to the DefineLogic() subroutine. If it's a *Set* we'll jump to the SetLogic() subroutine.

```
tcFile.MoveFirst                        'start at the first
Do
        'parse It, break the string on the space character
    strA.Parse (tcFile.Ref.Item, " ")
        'If the first word Is a "Define" then to DefineLogic
    If strA.Item = "Define" Then
      DefineLogic (strA, tcVar)
    'else If the first word Is a "Set" then do the SetLogic
    ElseIf strA.Item = "Set" Then
      SetLogic (strA, tcVar)
    End If
tcFile.MoveNext ()                      'keep going to the end of file
Loop While tcFile.More
```

Reviewing DefineLogic()

Now let's take a look at the DefineLogic() function. It accepts the pre-parsed StringAdapter strA structure and the current tcVar TurboCollection. Note that each call of DefineLogic() makes no assumption about the pre-existence of any given variable. It explicitly tests for the variable's existence prior to adding it. This avoids any confusion if the creator of the text input file accidentally declares the same variable twice. We can even send a "developer" warning message that the variable is already present.

The DefineLogic() function browses the StringAdapter assuming that the structure of the string will be the keyword Define, followed by a type-name, in this case simple, followed by the variable's name. If *each* Define declaration uses the same syntax, we can define as many entities as we want in the text file. Here's an example:

```
Private Sub DefineLogic(strA As StringAdapter, tcVar As TurboCollection)
  On Error Resume Next
  Dim pWrk As ParmNode
  strA.MoveNext()                       'Move to the next Token
  If strA.Item = "Simple" Then          'Should be the keyword "Simple"
    strA.MoveNext()                     'then move to the next Item
```

```
      Set pWrk = tcVar.Find(strA.Item)          'try to find the variable name
      If pWrk Is Nothing Then                    'not there, so proceed to add It
'add an Item, using the variable name as the ParmNode ItemKey and SortKey
        tcVar.AddItem( "", strA.Item, strA.Item)
      End If
    End If
  End Sub
```

With DefineLogic() structured this way, we can build as many run-time variables into tcVar as required. The Interpreter will add each one as it's encountered in the textual input. If we later remove or add variables from the instructions, it only affects the dynamic content of tcVar, not the software. We can also link tcVar to other areas of the framework, such as elements of other Interpreters, Adapters, or any available object instance. Thus an interpreted behavior (next) can access variables not explicitly defined.

Examining SetLogic()

Now let's take a look at SetLogic(). This function will interpret a string in similar fashion to DefineLogic, with the exception of requiring the existence of a given variable name before proceeding. The SetLogic() function accepts the same parameters as DefineLogic, the StringAdapter, and the tcVar TurboCollection. It will parse the string to find the target variable, then further parse the string to determine what value the variable should receive. By marking the variable in the metadata macro text with a "$" character, we help the parser to treat it differently than another keyword. Here's an example:

```
Private Sub SetLogic(strA As StringAdapter, tcVar As TurboCollection)
  On Error Resume Next
  Dim pWrk As ParmNode
  strA.MoveNext()                          'skip the "Set" keyword
  If Mid(strA.Item, 1, 1) = "$" Then       'does the next Token start with "$"
      Set pWrk = tcVar.Find(Mid(strA.Item, 2))  'yes, then strip the $ and find
      If pWrk Is Nothing Then Exit Sub     'Is It there?
      strA.MoveNext()                      'yes so move to Operator
      If strA.Item = "=" Then              'Is an "=", so redundant
        strA.MoveNext()                    'move to next value
          pWrk.Item = strA.Item            'and put It In the Var's
                                           ' Item property

      End If
  End If
End Sub
```

Executing tcVar.Dump

Now let's execute a tcVar.Dump. It should yield an output similar to the following:

```
S[Wrk1] K[Wrk1] I["David"] T[] Stat=[]
S[Wrk2] K[Wrk2] I["Built"] T[] Stat=[]
S[Wrk3] K[Wrk3] I["This"] T[] Stat=[]
```

> **NOTE** *The shorthand is for the ParmNode properties on display:
> S=SortKey Value, K=ItemKey Value, I=Item Value, T=ItemType Value,
> and Stat=Status Value).*

Enhancing DefineLogic and ItemType

We have now effectively created a means to define an unlimited number of work-space variables at run time, along with a simple means to modify their values. Could we enhance the *DefineLogic* function to recognize more than simple variables? Could we also include *ItemType* functionality?

What if we needed to modify one variable with the value of another, and still maintain the original functionality? For example:

```
Set $Wrk3 = $Wrk2
```

This would mean a relatively minor enhancement to SetLogic(), one that would look for the $ characters in the second (right-hand side) variable rather than always expecting text. Consider this example, and I'll use bold text for the additional code for SetLogic:

```
Private Sub SetLogic(strA As StringAdapter, tcVar As TurboCollection)
  On Error Resume Next
  Dim pWrk As ParmNode
  Dim pWrkR As ParmNode                       'need another temp variable
  strA.MoveNext()
  If Mid(strA.Item, 1, 1) = "$" Then
    Set pWrk = tcVar.Find(Mid(strA.Item, 2))
    If pWrk Is Nothing Then Exit Sub
    strA.MoveNext()
    If strA.Item = "=" Then
      strA.MoveNext()
```

```
        If Mid(strA.Item, 1, 1) = "$" Then          'If $ Is present
          Set pWrkR = tcVar.Find(Mid(strA.Item, 2))  'find It
          If pWrkR Is Nothing Then Exit Sub
          pWrk.Item = pWrkR.Item                     'set target to source value
        Else
          pWrk.Item = strA.Item                    'otherwise just use the text
value
        End If
      End If
  End If
End Sub
```

Now the results from tcVar.Dump will be as follows:

```
S[Wrk1] K[Wrk1] I["David"] T[] Stat=[]
S[Wrk2] K[Wrk2] I["Built"] T[] Stat=[]
S[Wrk3] K[Wrk3] I["Built"] T[] Stat=[]
```

We now have the primitive beginnings of a text Interpreter (with dynamic definition and assignment capabilities) that can grow to do much more. In the next example let's expand on this theme. We'll now build routines and decision logic into the structure of the text.

Routines and Subroutines

Typically two types of routines exist in a run-time Interpreter's domain. One is an event handler (rule) and one is a subroutine. An event handler must be tied to an event of some kind (e.g., click, load, change, etc.), so requires linkage to the source of the event. A subroutine could be invoked at any time (either as a call from the event handler or as an actual event handler itself). The primary difference in the two is this: we want to allow subroutines to execute whenever invoked, but not necessarily event handlers. We must queue some events to avoid stepping on others. For example, if a user hits the form's "X" button to close it, but the form's routines are at a critical execution juncture, we'll want to queue the *Close* event until a more appropriate point. These aspects can be managed in *behavioral* operation, so we will need a strong structural foundation to support them.

We've already set up some primitive decision handling, so let's expand on this also. This example's data file is *Snip2Input.Txt*. But first, some housekeeping. Recall the conditional logic we set up in Chapter 3's project exercise. Now we'll encapsulate this logic into another class we'll call *conFactory*. I'll need a global Singleton (like the *TextIO* manager) to provide us with fractal seeds to the original conditional operators. Like before, each of the conditional operators will be placed in a TurboCollection, only this time wrapped in the *conFactory* class. I'll define a Singleton of this type as *ConditionFactory* object as follows:

```
Dim ConditionFactory as New conFactory()
```

Anytime I need a new conditional operator object, I simply access the *ConditionFactory* with notations similar to the following

```
Dim oCon as Object
oCon = ConditionFactory.Ref("EQ")
```

Now the value of *oCon* is a new, properly configured *conIsEqualTo* object). We'll use late binding because at the Interpreter level, we need transparency. If we've appropriately minimized the references and parameters on the object's interface, we don't take a performance hit. Additionally, while the Interpreter will connect Adapters with later binding at their interfaces, the Adapters themselves will use early binding under the covers, so we get the best of both worlds.

Next, I will migrate the *SetLogic, DefineLogic* and their supporting structures from the project's *Main* into a text interpretation class called *txtTerp.cls*. We'll use this class to define a framework for subroutines, decision logic and ultimately, looping control.

The following statements will create a text interpretation object, initialize it and command it to execute its Main Routine.

```
Dim oT As New txtTerp()                          'declare the variable
' now load and Initialize the Input script file
oT.Init(Nothing, "File=" & glb.AppPath & "..\Snip2Input.Txt")
oT.Action("Execute", "Routine=Main")    'command to execute the Main routine
```

Housekeeping out of the way, we'll now need to expand the *DefineLogic* lexical rules to include the subroutine. Because each subroutine will form a list of statements, the objective is to create sub-lists, also TurboCollections, for each subroutine. In the following example, the input file divides the actions into the subroutines *SubExampleOne* and *SubExampleTwo*. The contents of *Snip2Input.txt follows:*

```
Define Simple Wrk1
Define Simple Wrk2
Define Simple Wrk3
```

Now call these defined routines:

```
Call SubExampleOne
Call SubExampleTwo
```

Define the first Routine like this:

```
Define Subroutine SubExampleOne
  Set $Wrk1 = "David"
  Set $Wrk2 = "Built"
  Set $Wrk3 = "This"
End Subroutine
```

Define the second Routine as follows:

```
Define Subroutine SubExampleTwo
  Set $Wrk3 = $Wrk2
End Subroutine
```

The two primary subroutines have names, encapsulating their own statements. However, some statements exist *outside* of these subroutines (the statements between the variable definition and the first subroutine definition). What is their "subroutine name," if any? For clarity and consistency, we'll cordon all these statements into their own subroutine and call it "Main" by default. Listing 4-3 shows the routines in these logical and physical divisions.

Listing 4-3. Dynamic Variables and Routines

```
************************Variable Definition begins here**************************
Define Simple Wrk1
Define Simple Wrk2
Define Simple Wrk3
***********************Subroutine Main() begins here**************************
Call $SubExampleOne
Call $SubExampleTwo
***********************Subroutine SubExampleOne() Begins here ******************
Define Routine SubExampleOne
  Set $Wrk1 = "David"
  Set $Wrk2 = "Built"
  Set $Wrk3 = "This"
End Routine
```

```
***********************Subroutine SubExampleTwo() Begins here*******************
Define Routine SubExampleTwo
  Set $Wrk3 = $Wrk2
End Routine
```

Now we'll build a software loop that divides the file into three separate grouping-ings. The groupings will be by subroutine name and will be the anchors for the text included in each Routine. We'll call this TurboCollection tcSub.

Anchoring Sub-Lists

The ParmNode has a reference property on it called *tc,* of type TurboCollection. This allows the ParmNode to anchor sub-lists with clarity. Using the ParmNode's *Ref* or *Obj* properties is handy for anchoring single objects, but using sub-collections, or collections-of-collections, it is easier to follow and maintain our own logic by using a specifically typed reference, and also enhances performance. In the following listing, I have included only the section that defines the Routine sub-lists. This complete code snippet from Listing 4-4 can be found in txtTerp.Init().

Listing 4-4. Routine Organization with Sub-lists

```
TcFile.MoveFirst()
Do
If strWrk <> vbNullString Then
    strA.Parse(strWrk, " ")                      'parse the line on spaces
    If InStr(1, strA.Item(1), "Routine", vbTextCompare) > 0 Then  'is it a routine?
        'yes so add it to routine list
        tcSub.AddItem("", strA.Item(2), strA.Item(2))
        'and build a sub-list on it
        tcSub.Ref.tc = New TurboCollection()
    End If
    If Not (strA.Item(0) = "End" And
            InStr(1, strA.Item(1), "routine", vbTextCompare) > 0) Then
            tcSub.Ref.tc.AddItem(strWrk)         'otherwise add to sub-list until
                                                 ' end of routine
    End If
tcFile.MoveNext()
Loop While tcFile.More
```

Place a breakpoint right after the loop end, and upon arrival execute a *tcSub.Dump* in the Command/Immediate window. This will yield the following values:

```
S[Main] K[Main] I[] T[] Stat=[]
S[SubExampleOne] K[SubExampleOne] I[] T[] Stat=[]
S[SubExampleTwo] K[SubExampleTwo] I[] T[] Stat=[]
```

This example illustrates the three entries that exist in the tcSub TurboCollection, but not what each entry actually contains. To show this, we'll need to expand on the *Dump* function for use on each of the TurboCollections we added to the tcSub references, along with the lines of text added to each TurboCollection. Here's an example:

```
tcSub.MoveFirst()
Do
  Debug.Writeline ( "*****Start of " & tcSub.Ref.ItemKey & "******")
  tcSub.Ref.tc.Dump()                         'dump the sublist also
  Debug. Writeline( "*****End of " & tcSub.Ref.ItemKey & "******")
  Debug. Writeline()
tcSub.MoveNext()
Loop While tcSub.More
```

This code will yield the following information, to tell us that the lines of each subroutine have been organized and stored correctly.

```
*****Start of Main******
S[] K[] I[Call $SubExampleOne] T[] Stat=[]
S[] K[] I[Call $SubExampleTwo] T[] Stat=[]
*****End of Main******
'
*****Start of SubExampleOne******
S[] K[] I[  Set $Wrk1 = "David"] T[] Stat=[]
S[] K[] I[  Set $Wrk2 = "Built"] T[] Stat=[]
S[] K[] I[  Set $Wrk3 = "This"] T[] Stat=[]
S[] K[] I[End Subroutine] T[] Stat=[]
*****End of SubExampleOne******
'
*****Start of SubExampleTwo******
S[] K[] I[  Set $Wrk3 = $Wrk2] T[] Stat=[]
S[] K[] I[End Subroutine] T[] Stat=[]
*****End of SubExampleTwo******
```

This is an example of using a TurboCollection (tcSub) to anchor more Turbo-Collections (in this case a two-dimensional TurboCollection). We may add as many dimensions as needed to describe highly complex and sophisticated structures. A single pass will set up the structures once and for all, later allowing us to browse and execute their statements as separated subsets.

The final form throws away the original text statements to define the variables. This is because the remaining text is not for definition, but for *action*. Each Routine is designed to act on predefined variables, and assumes that the variables are already in place from the original pass.

To run the textual script like a program, we would set up a loop to browse the Main subroutine for action statements. In this case we have two, the "Set" and the "Call". The Set behaves as in the previous exercise (assignment). The Call will transfer control to the named subroutine, then return.

We'll define this method as ExecRoutine(), and include *recursion*. It will call *itself* to execute another layer of subroutine (and further subroutines, as many levels deep as required). It will pass on parameters it first received to protect its current thread of execution. The logic demonstrated in Listing 4-5 will parse the Set and Call to respectively assign variable values or follow a dynamic execution thread. This method is in the txtTerp class.

Listing 4-5. Executing the Application Script

```
Private Sub ExecRoutine(tcRoutine As TurboCollection)
  On Error Resume Next                            'error trapping off
  Dim strA As  StringAdapter                      'dim the adapter
  Dim pWrk As ParmNode                            'and some workspace
  If tcRoutine Is Nothing Then Exit Sub           'nothing to do? get out
    Set strA = NewStringAdapter                   'workspace adapter here
  '////////////////////////////
  tcRoutine.MoveFirst()                           'start at the first statement
  Do
    strA.Parse (tcRoutine.Ref.Item, " ")          'parse on the space character
    If strA.Item = "Set" Then                      'Is It a "set" command?
      SetLogic (strA)                              'pass It on to perform
SetLogic
    ElseIf strA.Item = "Call" Then                 'else Is It a call command?
      strA.MoveNext()                              'move to the next token
      If Mid(strA.Item, 1, 1) = "$" Then           'should be prefixed with "$"
                                                   ' for sub call
        Set pWrk = tcSub.Find(Mid(strA.Item, 2))   'find the subroutine
        ExecRoutine (pWrk.tc)                       'call recursively to execute It!!
```

```
        End If
    End If
  tcRoutine.MoveNext()                         'keep going until we're done
  Loop While tcRoutine.More
  '/////////////////////////////////////
OldStringAdapter (strA)                        'reclaim workspace without
                                               ' destroying It

End Sub
```

Now, to start the action, we'll execute the ExecRoutine() function using the Main subroutine as the starting point. When ExecRoutine() interprets the line values in Main, it will cascade into the other subroutines. We don't need any other workspace. We'll use the tcSub.Find function to get the node containing the Main subroutine, then navigate into the TurboCollection anchored on this node's tc property. Note that the subroutines and variables are local to the instance of txtTerp, so we don't have to pass them around in subroutine calls (tcVar and tcSub). A single call will initialize the activities and events (later) will drive others.

```
ExecRoutine  tcSub.Find("Main").tc
```

This notation is entirely internal to txtTerp and as such, cannot be exposed to a txtTerp consumer; it's too specific to the internal implementation. To further encapsulate access to the subroutines managed by txtTerp, let's enhance the txtTerp.Action method to include an "Execute" action.

```
oT.Action("Execute", "Routine=Main")   'command to execute the Main routine
```

In order to support compound parameters, we'll need a function call to snap apart a parameter string into key/tags and their values. The assumption is that a long parameter list may arrive, commanding the txtTerp object to, among other things, execute a Routine. To do this, it will have to find the Routine's name in the parameter list as follows—we've already defined the syntax for it:

```
"Key1=Value1|Key2=Value2|Key3=Value3|"...
```

Now let's build a function to break this string apart into key(s) and value(s). For our purposes, a string will arrive containing text to designate a given Routine, in the following case, the "Main" Routine:

```
"Routine=Main"
```

The function *UnstringParm* (found in our *glbAdapter* class) will accept a raw string and break it up into key/value pairs, placing the results in a TurboCollection as follows:

```
Item="Main", ItemKey="Routine", SortKey="Routine"
```

The Routine shown in Listing 4-6 is a global utility in the *glbAdapter* module of the project.

Listing 4-6. Unstringing a Compound Parameter

```
Public Function UnStringParm(strIn As String,
        Optional strDefaultKey As String) As TurboCollection
  On Error Resume Next
  Dim tcL As TurboCollection
 Set UnStringParm = Nothing                      'preset return values
  If strIn = vbNullString Then Exit Function     'no work, then exit
  Set tcL = New TurboCollection()                'build a new collection
  Set UnStringParm = tcL                         'set the return value now
  Dim strD As String
  Dim strA As StringAdapter
  Dim strB As StringAdapter
  Set strA = NewStringAdapter                    'workspace
  Set strB = NewStringAdapter                    'workspace
  strD = strDefaultKey                           'allow a default key,
                                                 ' In case of no key=
     ' no value, need one anyhow for consistency
  If strD = vbNullString Then strD = "Default"
  strA.Parse( strIn, "|")                        'break apart on pipe symbol
  Do
    strB.Parse (strA.Item, "=" )                 'break on the "=" symbol
    If strB.Count = 1 Then                       'only one value here?
      tcL.AddItem (strB.Item, strD, strD)        'then no key, use the default
    Else
        'othewise use the value and key
    tcL.AddItem (strB.Item(1), strB.Item(0), strB.Item(0))
End If
'
  strA.MoveNext()
  Loop While strA.More                           'repeat until done
'
  OldStringAdapter( strA)                        'reclaim without destroying
  OldStringAdapter (strB)
End Function
```

A power tool variation on glb.UnstringParm() is glb.UnstringXML(), which will break apart an XML string into a TurboCollection.

With the return value of this function (a formatted TurboCollection), we now have the ability to quickly find and correlate parameter keys to their values. For example, the following notation would perform a *Find* on the TurboCollection using "Routine" as the key. Since the value associated with "Routine" is "Main", the final value of *strWrk* will be "Main".

```
Dim tcP as TurboCollection
StrWrk = "Routine=Main"
tcP = glb.UnStringParm(strWrk,"Routine")         'Unstring the Parameters
StrWrk = tcp.Find("Routine").Item
```

Note that the default value of "Routine" is passed into the *UnstringParm* function. This will allow the following two strings values to create similar behavior:

```
StrWrk = "Routine=Main"
StrWrk = "Main"
```

This practice increases the flexibility of the parameter management while maintaining common structural (and thus behavioral) control when browsing the resulting TurboCollection.

Now let's take a look at the final form of *txtTerp.Action* in Listing 4-7.

Listing 4-7. The Final Form of txtTerp.Action

```
Public Function Action(ActionID As String, Optional ActionData As String,
                Optional ActionObject As Object) As String
    On Error Resume Next                         'error traps off
    Dim tcP As TurboCollection                   'get workspace
    Dim strK as String
    Dim strA As New StringAdapter()              'more workspace
    Action = vbNullString                        'valid return values set
    Select Case ActionID                         'examine Actions
    Case "Execute"                               'Execute?
      ' Unstring the Parameters
      Set tcP = UnStringParm(ActionData, "Routine")
      If tcP is nothing then Exit Sub
'
  ' simplified version of the find / execute
    strK = tcP.Find("Routine").Item              'find the routine's name
    Set tcP = tcSub.Find(strK).tc                'find the named routine's lines
    ExecRoutine (tcP)                            'Execute it
'
```

```
' shorthand version of the find / execute
'      ExecRoutine (tcSub.Find(tcP.Find("Routine").Item).tc)
     Set tcP = Nothing
   End Select
End Function
```

    I've used bold text to highlight the simplified version of the three statements that actually reference the tcSub list and execute the Routine. I've also highlighted (commented-out) a single-line shorthand version of the same execution. The first will give you a feel for the required collection navigation steps. The second will give you a feel for how easy it is to consolidate the code into a single statement. Be careful with this kind of flexibility because you can obfuscate the code's intended purpose. You be the judge on your own coding style, priorities, and comfort level of TurboCollection's behavior.

    Single-step through these functions to get a feel for how the software will cue on the textual information in the *Snip2Input.txt* file. Notice how we've built dynamic variables, execution logic, and the ability to structure specific, identifiable routines of statements. The required structures are very simple, tightly controlled, and share behavioral similarities.

Decisions, Decisions

To further show behavioral control patterns, let's add some decision logic into the mix and see how we can programmatically control a Routine's execution. We'll add the following script to the *Snip2Input* file:

```
Define Subroutine SubExampleThree
  If $Wrk3 EQ $Wrk2 Then                      'compare dynamic variables
    Set $Wrk1 = "Wrk2 is Equal To Wrk3"       'perform the statement
  Else                                        'otherwise
    Set $Wrk1 = "Wrk2 is Not Equal To Wrk3"   'perform this statement
  EndIf
'
Set $Wrk3 = "This"                            'this statement Is unconditional!
End Subroutine
```

    We'll dynamically compare the variables *Wrk3* and *Wrk2*. Based on the outcome, we'll reset the value of *Wrk1*. Note that the final Set statement for the variable *Wrk3* is unconditional.

The objective is to configure the Routine so we can invoke it multiple times and have it execute in the fastest, most optimized path each time (and produce a dynamic outcome based on the condition logic). Requiring the Interpreter to browse for the if-else-endif cues on each pass will eventually affect performance, especially for large numbers of statements within a nested "if". Ideally, we would like to shortcut the interpretation so it will only examine the required lines and no further. This maximizes the caching strategy discussed in "Project 3—Behaviors," so now we'll apply it.

The first task is to set aside every instance of an if-then-else combination. The most complex of the combinations follows:

```
IF Condition Then
          Statement(s)
    ELSEIF Condition Then
          Statement(s)
    ELSE
          Statement(s)
ENDIF
```

Thus the pattern here is to use the first IF and the final ENDIF to define the completed structure, with a single ELSE or multiple ELSEIFs in between. The ELSE is the default condition in case all other IF/ELSEIFs fail. Each IF/ELSEIF will evaluate two and only two variables for a given condition. This also easily translates to a select/case structure (in Project 7—Screen Prototypes).

In the following example, the Conditions will be compound (multiple conditions in a single line) such as:

```
IF Condition or Condition Then
                Statement
ENDIF
```

When interpreting text, we find that compound IF/ELSEIF conditions are often accommodated with multiple nested IF statements. However, to build more clarity and conciseness into our scripting rules, you are free to experiment in expanding the provided decision logic to a compound capability once you see the examples given. A word of warning, however: the more complexity we drive into the decision syntax parsing, the more time it will take to resolve the decision. The vMach product provides for unlimited count and nesting of dynamically interpreted conditions.

To construct sub-blocks of conditionally controlled statements, we need some structural enhancements. In prior examples, we saw a subroutine constructed as follows:

```
Define Subroutine Name
   Statement
   Statement
   Statement
End Subroutine
```

In the next example, all statements are executed, but now with condition logic, only some statements will be executed. Thus, we need to compress the entire Routine into its basic statements.

```
Define Subroutine Name
   $Set Statement
   $Call Statement
   If Condition then
      $Call Statement
      $Set Statement
   Endif
   $Set Statement
End Subroutine
```

Now the tcSub structure will compress these elements into subroutine items. I've bold-faced the automatic in-line modification to tag the condition following:

```
Define Subroutine Name
   $Set
   $Call
   $Condition
   $Set
End Subroutine
```

All of the statements between IF and ENDIF have been compressed into another structure and tagged with the $Condition keyword. When the Interpreter browses these routines, it will know to perform a set, then a call, then execute a conditional series of statements, then finish up with a final set statement. All statements outside of the $Condition are *unconditional,* so execute as-is.

To support this notation, and the structures behind it, we'll need some more background setup. During the initialization, after all the subroutines, variables, and structures are in place, we'll make another pass on all the subroutines, starting with Main. This pass will be used to resolve the decision trees and logical branches, so let's call it ResolveDecisions(). We'll need to call it for each subroutine, because ResolveDecisions() might need to recurse into itself for nested condition logic. Here's an example:

```
tcSub.MoveFirst()                                'begin browse of all subroutines
  Do
      'execute resolve with the current subroutine list
    ResolveDecisions (tcSub.Ref.tc)
  tcSub.MoveNext()                               'get the next one
        Loop While tcSub.More                    'until done
```

ResolveDecisions() then looks like this:

```
Private Sub ResolveDecisions(tcRoutine as TurboCollection)
  On Error Resume Next
  Dim tcList As TurboCollection
  Dim pWrk As ParmNode
  Dim oCon As Object
  Dim strA As New StringAdapter
  Dim strK As String
  Dim intNesting As Integer                      'count the nesting level
   intNesting = 0
  tcRoutine.MoveFirst()                          'start at first of routine
  Do
    strA.Parse( tcRoutine.Ref.Item, " ")         'parse It with spaces
    strK = strA.Item                             'hold the keyword
```

The first Case in Listing 4-8 will break out the statements underneath each IF or ELSEIF header into another list. The entire IF-ENDIF block will be compressed to a single Routine reference labeled "$CONDITION". In order to compress the list, I will move the information from some nodes into their sub-list equivalents. Rather than remove the copied nodes as I go, I will mark them with "REMOVE_ME_NOW". This will keep me from revisiting the lines and will allow me to remove them all at once at the end.

Listing 4-8. Converting Textual Conditions into a Structure

```
    Select Case strK
    Case "if", "elseif"                        'Is It a decision (If or elseif)
'make a new routine
 If tcList Is Nothing Then Set tcList = New TurboCollection
'add the condition  statement to It
      tcList.AddItem(tcRoutine.Ref.Item, strA.Item, strA.Item )
      'get a condition operator object
      oCon = ConditionFactory.Item(strA.Item(2))
      If Not oCon Is Nothing Then
         Set tcList.Ref.Ref = strA              'take the entire parsed string
         strA.Find(2).obj = oCon                'put the operator object on It
         strA = New StringAdapter                'get a new adapter
      End If

      If strK = "if" Then                       'If It's an "If", not "elsif"
        intNesting = intNesting + 1             'nesting level Increments
       ' add the new routine to the current routine
        tcRoutine.Ref.tc =  tcList
        tcRoutine.Ref.Item = "$CONDITION"       'mark It as a $Condition
      Else
       'otherwise If It's an "elseif", remove It
        tcRoutine.Ref.Item = "REMOVE_ME_NOW"
      End If
```

The next Case in Listing 4-9 will examine the ELSE and also add its statements to a sublist as though they are a separate Routine. The ENDIF will remove one level of nesting.

Listing 4-9. Nesting Multiple Conditions

```
    Case "else"
'add the routine line to the sublist
     tcList.AddItem(tcRoutine.Ref.Item, "else", "else" )
'remove It from the original list
     tcRoutine.Ref.Item = "REMOVE_ME_NOW"
   Case "endif"
'add the routine line to the sublist
     tcList.AddItem (tcRoutine.Ref.Item, "endif", "endif")
'remove It from the original
     tcRoutine.Ref.Item = "REMOVE_ME_NOW"
'decrement nesting level now
     intNesting = intNesting - 1
  'If nest Is done, back to main level so this condition block Is done
     If intNesting = 0 Then Set tcList = Nothing
       '

   Case Else                               'otherwise It's any other statement
     If intNesting > 0 Then                'If Inside a condition block then
       Set pWrk = tcList.Ref              'get the current reference
       If pWrk.tc Is Nothing Then
            Set pWrk.tc = New TurboCollection()  'build another list
  'add the current routine line to It
       pWrk.tc.AddItem (tcRoutine.Ref.Item )
       tcRoutine.Ref.Item = "REMOVE_ME_NOW"    'and remove the original
     End If
   '

   End Select
 tcRoutine.MoveNext()
 Loop While tcRoutine.More
```

Now that we've shaped the lists and sublists, I can now remove the vestigial nodes we have already marked, like so.

```
tcRoutine.RemoveItemContaining ("REMOVE_ME_NOW")    'remove all marked nodes
 End Sub
```

Follow the structures as created and you will see a new TurboCollection added to each IF/ELSEIF/ELSE tag, with their respective statements inside it. Each of these TurboCollections constitutes a Routine on its own, and each is anchored to the condition block's master TurboCollection.

This master TurboCollection is then anchored to the original Routine's first "if" nesting level, and it's Item value is overwritten with the value "$Condition". Once all the Routine lines are copied into these substructures, they are removed from the original structure. Figure 4-14 depicts the layout.

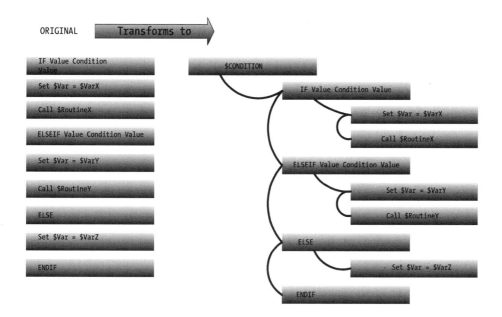

Figure 4-14. Conditional logic structure

Note that the ResolveDecisions() logic has the inherent ability to build nested levels of decision logic automatically. Here is the additional logic for ExecRoutine() to account for the $Condition keyword, with bold-face text to highlight the specific operations:

```
Private Sub ExecRoutine(tcRoutine As TurboCollection)
  …
tcRoutine.MoveFirst
  Do
    …
    …
    If strA.Item = "Set" Then
      …
    ElseIf strA.Item = "Call" Then
      …
    ElseIf strA.Item = "$CONDITION" Then
        ConditionLogic tcRoutine
    End If
  …
  …
```

We've added the ConditionLogic() method cued on the keyword "$Condition".
Now let's see how ConditionLogic() browses the new structure layout. Listing 4-10
provides an example.

Listing 4-10. Nested Conditional Execution

```
Private Sub ConditionLogic(tcRoutine As TurboCollection)
  On Error Resume Next
  Dim strWrk As String
  Dim tcR As TurboCollection              'anchor for condition block
  Dim tcList As TurboCollection           'anchor for conditon block sublist
  Dim strA As StringAdapter               'workspace
  Dim blnEval As Boolean                  'evaluator
  Dim pLHS As ParmNode                    'left side variable
  Dim pRHS As ParmNode                    'right side variable
  Dim oEval As Object                     'evaluation object anchor
  '
  tcR = tcRoutine.Ref.tc                  'get the condition block
  tcR.MoveFirst()                         'get the first one, the "If"
  Do
  strA = tcR.Ref.Ref                      'get originally parsed routine line
  If Not strA Is Nothing Then             'If there, then an "If" or "elseif"
    strA.MoveFirst()                      'move to the first part (If or elseif)
    strA.MoveNext()                       'move to the next part, LHS var
    pLHS = FindVar(strA.Item)             'find It
    strA.MoveNext()                       'move to the next part
    oEval = strA.Ref.obj                  ' evaluation object anchored here
    strA.MoveNext ()                      'and the next - RHS var
    pRHS = FindVar(strA.Item)             'and find It too
    blnEval = oEval.Evaluate(pLHS.Item, pRHS.Item)     'evaluate them!
    If blnEval Then                       'If Its True, then
        ExecRoutine(tcR.Ref.tc)          'execute routine anchored here
        Exit Sub                          'and get out
    End If
  '
  ElseIf tcR.Ref.Item <> "Endif" Then     'otherwise, It's a plain old "else"
        ExecRoutine (tcR.Ref.tc)          'so do It
        Exit Sub                          'and exit
  '
  End If
  tcR.MoveNext()                          'keep going until we get
                                          ' a true eval or "else"
  Loop While tcR.More
End Sub
```

Notice that if any condition block evaluates to "True", it will perform ExecRoutine() again with the sub-list on the condition block just as though it's a subroutine. Could the Routine in this sublist's condition block have another embedded IF/ENDIF block? Of course, and this logic would recurse through it seamlessly. In fact, we could have as many IF/ENDIF nestings as we want and ConditionLogic() would follow them (the function DumpRoutine will also recurse through the levels of list structure and display their contents for verification).

As a supporting capability, the $STR statement notation will wrap a string into its own simple variable and use it rather than re-parse the string each time. Take a look a the following:

```
Example One: "This Is A String"
Example Two: $STR("This Is Another String")
```

While the second notation requires additional metadata coding, it also allows the Interpreter to reduce it directly into an internal variable without further guessing as to its intended purpose. When you single-step through such a conversion, you will find new variable names created that uniquely identify and encapsulate a static string's data.

Another supporting feature is an additional function call to encapsulate the management of variables. While it is good to parse flat text and find a variable, what of the variable's contents? What if we have loaded a variable $Wrk1 with the value "$Wrk2"? Which value do we want to retrieve: the text value "$Wrk2" or the actual *contents* of $Wrk2? A simple example follows:

```
Set $Wrk2 = "Howdy"
Set $Wrk1 = $STR("$Wrk2")
Set $Wrk3 = $Wrk1
```

In this case, should the Interpreter assume that the contents of Wrk3 should now be the value "$Wrk2" or the value "Howdy"? The Interpreter, with no other guiding information, will load Wrk3 with the value "$Wrk2". It is handy, however, to load variables with information about other variables and access them indirectly. We therefore need an indirection cue (such as the standard "@") as follows:

```
Set $Wrk2 = "Howdy"
Set $Wrk1 = $STR("@$Wrk2")
Set $Wrk3 = $Wrk1
```

In this example, the FindVar() function will load the value "Howdy" into Wrk3. This will proceed to as many levels of indirection as required until the Interpreter no longer encounters a "@$" combination.

But Wait, There's More

The production version of the txtTerp.cls has a more dramatic capability, that of allowing us to open up a *Watch* window to view the metadata instructions. We can see our defined variables and manipulate their values, even set breakpoints and single-step through instructions—*in the field*. How can we do this? When we expose various internal variables to txtTerp, along with routines, statements, and so forth, then couple these with the external variables visible to txtTerp, we can easily populate TreeView and other standard screen views to display and manipulate values just like we would from the original development environment.

When instructions, variables, and their context are symbolic, we can represent them any way we please, and organize them for our own productivity and troubleshooting. The big advantage here: We can debug and perform single-step of application logic and variables without the aid of the development environment. How valuable would this be? Only a metadata-driven architecture can provide this power in the field, at the seat of the end user.

The vUIMDemo includes the basic *Watch* capabilities. Go to the vUIMDemo/ directory and double-click on the vUIMDemo.exe file. When the first ProtoMe screen appears, hit Shift/Alt and the Watch window will appear (see Figure 4-15). This is a simplified version of the production Watch window.

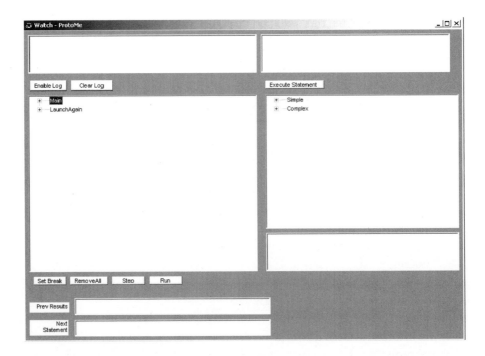

Figure 4-15. The Watch window

In the box just above the Execute statement button, type the string:

```
Set $Wrk1 = myname
```

Then hit the Execute statement button. Note the text that appears in the Log window on the upper left. Now, in the execute box, type:

```
Set $Wrk2 = $Wrk1
```

And hit the Execute statement button again. The log shows that the variable Wrk2 now contains the contents of Wrk1.

In the TreeView just under the Execute statement button, note the branches for "Simple" and "Complex". Open the "Simple" branch and it will reveal a list of all the Simple variables visible to txtTerp. Scroll down to find the $Wrk1 and $Wrk2 variables. By clicking on these nodes, the box below the TreeView will reveal their contents. The contents of $Wrk1/$Wrk2 reflect our assignment activity above.

Continue to scroll down to the complex branch and click to open it. We now see all the complex variables visible to txtTerp and their types. We can likewise reference them in the Execute statement window and affect their behaviors. All of the controls on the ProtoMe form have adapters exposed to txtTerp, and appear in this list. For a simple example, let's put the following statement in the Execute statement window:

```
Set $txt0.Item = HowdyFromTexas
```

Now go back to the running ProtoMe form (find it in the task bar at the bottom of the Windows desktop). The second textbox now has the value "HowdyFromTexas", which you just typed. Let's use another example:

```
Set $Wrk1 = $txt0.Item
```

Go to the Variables Treeview, find the Simple/Wrk1 variable, and click on it. The contents will be revealed in the window below (value HowdyFromTexas). Go back to the ProtoMe screen and type any value you want into the same text box, then repeat the above statement and examine Wrk1's contents in the TreeView.

We did not have to define *txt0* as complex anywhere in the metadata. This is because the ProtoMe structural definition already knows how to wrap the textbox and expose it to the Interpreter as a complex type. We only have to specifically define others (e.g., containers) when we need dynamic workspace.

Take a look at the TreeView on the left-hand side containing the behavioral metadata (in vMach, this is called *vScript*). Click on the branch labeled LaunchAgain and see the statement that will be executed whenever we click the LaunchAgain button. This instruction simply tells the current form to launch another form, in this case itself: ProtoMe.

Double-click on the statement beginning with *Set $Form*. This will highlight the statement. Now go back to the ProtoMe screen and click on the LaunchAgain button. The display will immediately jump back to the Watch window using the Set $Form statement as a breakpoint (note the Next Statement window at the bottom of the screen). If we now touch the Step button, the statement will execute. We now have two ProtoMe screens on the desktop.

Let's try something more interactive: In the vUIMDemo directory you'll find ProtoMe.txt. Open this file with Notepad. Add the following statements to the top of the file:

```
set $cboTest.AddItem=A|Adam
set $cboTest.AddItem=B|Bob
set $cboTest.AddItem=C|Callie
set $cboTest.AddItem=D|David
```

Save the ProtoMe.txt file and go back to the running application ProtoMe and hit the LaunchAgain button. Click the dropdown button of the top right ComboBox and it will reveal the new ComboBox values.

Now go back into the ProtoMe.txt file and add the following statement after the cboTest statements:

```
Observe $Txt1.Item=$cboTest.Item(Event=Changed|Property=Item)
```

Save the file, then go back to the running ProtoMe application and hit the LaunchAgain button. Now perform the dropdown like before and select "Adam". The value "Adam" will appear in the Combo Box *and* the uppermost TextBox.

Now add the following statement to ProtoMe.txt:

```
Observe $Txt3.Item=$txt1.Item(Event=Changed|Property=Item)
```

This will cause any value posted to the *txt1* TextBox to be forwarded to the *txt3* TextBox. Save the file and once again hit the ProtoMe's LaunchAgain button, then select "Adam" in the ComboBox. Note how the value of "Adam" is now propagated to *two* TextBoxes. However, if you simply type some values into the upper-left Textbox, only these are replicated in the second observing TextBox.

Each time the ProtoMe form was loaded, the form's behavior wrapped itself around the new statements. Imagine sitting next to a user, modifying the application, and the only thing they need to do to experience it is to close the form and reopen it (without leaving the program itself!)

Note the following macro in the ProtoMe.txt file:

```
Observe $cmdLaunchAgain.Item(NotEnabled) =
    $txt4.Item(Event=Changed|Property=Item|Op=ValueIs|Value=NoLaunch)
```

If you type the text value "NoLaunch" into the last text box on the screen, the cmdLaunch button's "Enabled" property will be set to "False". The button will consequently gray out. If you type any other value, or just add another character to this value, the button will enable again. For this demonstration, you can use other operations (Listing 4-11) on the left-hand side (such as Enabled) and on the right-hand side (such as ValueNot, ValueIn, or wildcards) for more effects (note that each Observe macro should appear on a single line of text:

Listing 4-11. Additional Observation Behaviors

```
Observe $cmdLaunchAgain.Item(NotEnabled) =
        $txt4.Item(Event=Changed|Property=Item|Op=ValueIn|
        Value=NoLaunch,NoLaunch2)
    Observe $cmdLaunchAgain.Item(Enabled) =
        $txt4.Item(Event=Changed|Property=Item|Op=ValueNot|
        Value=LetsLaunch)
    Observe $cmdLaunchAgain.Item(Enabled) =
        $txt4.Item(Event=Changed|Property=Item|Op=ValueIs|
    Value=Launch*)
```

Note also that the ProtoMe form is set up for Application ShutDown because the ProtoMe.txt file contains the statement:

```
Set $ShutDown=ShutDown
```

If we remove this statement, then we can close each subsequent launching of the ProtoMe form without shutting down the program. This lets us define multiple other forms in the application, we can open and close them without shutting down completely (default behavior).

These are just simple examples of how we can build powerful, agile, and metamorphic applications with rapid delivery and shockwave turnaround.

CHAPTER 5

Virtual Frameworks— Error Control

In This Chapter:

- Leashing the computing environment

- Controlling the chaos

- Implementing chaos rules

A *virtual framework*, like the one illustrated in Figure 5-1, is actually an assembly of frameworks, each with a role or scope of responsibility, and ideally integrated to the remainder with an interpreting behavioral controller. The application proto- type and project exercises in Chapter 4 show how interpretation provides the virtual glue to bind these elements together.

While each framework can (and often is) part of the same executable program, their co-location is not required. In fact, none of the frameworks are directly aware of the others. We'll expose them to the interpreter and allow it to broker the relationships symbolically rather than directly. This enables both plug- and-play and distributed computing.

A virtual framework adapts to resources from the surrounding computing environment (desktop, server, combination, and so on), conforming itself in context. It also adapts to the available I/O resources, including text and database sources, provides a dynamic user experience, is seamlessly interoperable to other frameworks, and keeps it all under tight control with error and exception handling.

Any framework can appear as an entity, as well as any of its parts, because to the interpreter they are only symbols.

The first objective is to get the surrounding computing environment on a leash. Everything else in the framework will avail itself of various computing resources, including simple things like current date and time, logon user name, the computer's network name or internet address, even the computer's current time zone. More advanced aspects include the machine's operating system, actual and available capacity, special on-board resources such as telephony, web serv- ices, special peripherals, or designated enterprise applications.

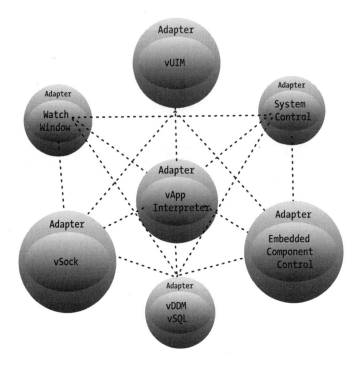

Figure 5-1. Virtual framework

The next objective is to get error management and exception handling on a leash, which I'll cover in this chapter. An unstable error recovery model allows havoc to reign across all the frameworks. Consistent and thematic exception handling generally stabilizes behavior and provides external consumers (and troubleshooters) with a common window to all internal activity and status.

Next it's on to the data management model, which is covered in Chapter 6. This framework needs access to database instances, physical locations, tables, columns (and their descriptions), and an automated, non-application-centric means to activate and seamlessly manage I/O.

The final objective is to get the user interface on a leash. In Chapter 7, we'll look at a thin, powerful, externally programmable, and reusable screen presentation system that does not require HTML for dynamic effects. In fact, the screens will have every appearance of application screens with the ability to change into *any* application-centric appearance on the fly without program reconstruction. Don't miss that statement: we can manufacture Visual Basic application screens that *only* exist in offline files, *not* a part of the compiled executable, yet behave *as though they are.*

Leashing the Computing Environment

Portable software knows no true boundary. Building a 100 percent portable program is practically impossible, because each new and existing computing environment has such subtle differences. When leashing the machine, we are very close to the science of computing, and will encounter aspects that are specific to hardware, operating systems, or their configurations. In computer science, the three pillars of science must guide us:

Repeatability: We can reliably reproduce behavior for troubleshooting or exploitation.

Observability: We have deep visibility into the operational issues encountered by the software, and can quickly resolve problems and understand processing flow.

Falsifiability: We can build and test hypothetical scenarios (including test data generation) that will reach consistent and deterministic conclusions.

With these pillars in place, we'll have a common point of reference (in this book and especially on our teams) for prioritizing the construction and testability of our software products. Thus, when we approach issues such as portability and compatibility, we have more understanding of the types of issues to address as we build products across platforms.

Portability and Compatibility

If we're building applications that are "all Microsoft, all the time," portability into Unix, Mainframe, Linux, and other environments is not a priority. However, portability across Microsoft environments *is,* so should we build specifically for Windows NT Service Pack 4, or for any version of Windows we might encounter on any desktop or server? Should we build for the Windows desktop only, or also for multiprocessor Windows servers, perhaps Windows CE users as well? Clearly, even Microsoft-centric products need compatibility resolution across versions and systems.

However, as desktop users become more voracious for information and automation, our products will require interoperability with multiple computing environments. Should we build highly robust desktop presentations with one language and high-performance back office systems with another language? The questions surrounding the "simple accommodation" of computing environments versus their abject exploitation are in our faces every day, and we ignore them to our disadvantage. No, we won't lose career options, opportunities for advancement or even significant salary increases, but we will lose ground in the race for technical excellence and we most certainly lose the traction required for accelerated reuse.

100 percent portability is rarely practical.

The computing environment is our servant, not our master.

We must symbolically separate our program code from the computing environment. Even if we're writing in a non-portable language such as Visual Basic, we'll still need to wrap and hide ourselves from the entanglements of the machine. This practice gives us the freedom to wrap ourselves around the operating system and hardware. Thus changes in technology will have less impact on our core software.

System Classes

System utilities, including everything from message boxes, system function calls, date/time/time-zone, and connectivity information, etc., deserve their own *System Class*. The language environment typically provides a complement of such objects, but we should wrap them with our own interface. This will provide every framework consumer with consistent and reliable access to the system environment. Architecturally, it provides an Adapter to the various system functions, treating them as an API.

Consider the following notations:

```
mObj.Item = Format(SystemTime(), "yyyy/MM/dd HHmmss")
mObj.Item = sysObj.Item("SystemTime")
```

In the first example, the software accesses the *SystemTime()* function directly. The second example uses a system object as a broker for the information. Is there a difference between their behavior? What if we want to define a system-wide default display format for the system time as MM/DD/YYYY? We can universally control output formatting with the second, but not the first. The objective is to control behavior from a central structural focus. The first notation provides no control at all.

If we find ourselves returning to a piece of code even once in response to an application-level need, we must find a way to never return again.

Apart from system-level features, are there any other quantities we can reduce to a single tag=value equation like "SystemTime"? We'll begin a search with anything that appears within our software as a textual string constant. The first ones to fall should be those we must modify when user requirements change. The program code should absolutely never embed application-centric string constants. These should be migrated into external repositories (at the very minimum in *.ini or *.ksh files). After all, the primary reason we use strings is for potentially volatile information. More often than not, when software change is required, we modify string constants first! Let's just get them out completely.

For example, a database connection string is a prime candidate. Many applications directly embed DSN constants, USERNAME/UID, and PASSWORD/PWD information into the compiled program. Each time a database administrator changes the passwords for security reasons, our applications will not only go offline, they'll require a *rebuild*.

As an extension, many applications directly bind themselves to a physical data model at compile-time (early binding). When even so much as a column is added, or extended, this invalidates the program and necessitates a rebuild.

 CROSS-REFERENCE *See Chapter 2 for a discussion of avoiding rebuilds.*

Controlling Startup and Initialization

If it's text, it's metadata. Get it out of the compiled software.

This chapter's project exercises show some direct and effective ways of accomplishing the following tasks:

- Moving volatile quantities into an external forum (e.g., a text file) as tag/value pairs, and fetch them at run time.

- Exposing global variables through a Singleton object for global value references (e.g., a global class).

- Providing a means in this object to pass-through to system environment variables.

Wrapping environment variable access gives us the option to override them with our own equivalent values instead of their system defaults.

Consider the following pseudocode notation:

```
Public Function GlobalValue(strKey as String) as String
    Dim pWrk as ParmNode
    Dim strWrk as String
    pWrk = tcGobal.Find(strKey)          'find the reference with the key
    If pWrk is Nothing then               'not found so
      strWrk = SystemEnviron(strKey)      'is it in the system environment?
    Else
      strWrk = pWrk.Item                  'got it - return the value
    Endif
GlobalValue = strWrk
End Function
```

In this example, the tcGlobal container will provide the first gateway to the requested information before jumping to an external source. If the value is not defined locally, it accesses the external environment. At any time during program execution, consumers will experience consistent access to the applicable environment values, whether system-level or overridden with local equivalents.

One sure way to obviate rework is to adopt run-time configuration as a consistent "first offense" in addressing any problem, that of cordoning off the "volatile" activities and sequestering the solid, repeatable ones. Upon first considering this, we might instantly think of a few unique candidates inside our own software. That's great, because we should build our candidate list from the application needs as much as the technical needs.

Run-time configuration: using external (usually textual) startup parameters to immediately affect the product's behavior and define its role.

For example, let's say we have an application subsystem with 100 feature points. I can predict that over half of them will change in scope and nature before production rollout. Could I tell which half? Of course not, so I assume that all of them are prone to change. This in mind, I start out by finding ways to migrate their volatility into an area I can manage in one place—outside of the binary executable.

Sound like a daunting task? Consider the Windows operating system—most of it is built around "detecting" and "conforming to" its computing host. It makes some basic assumptions, such as the presence of a CPU and a hard drive (maybe!), but when the operating system installs, it "self-configures" based upon a wide assortment of variables with unimaginable permutations. When completed, the operating system continues to provide a largely consistent experience for most users, from platform to platform, regardless of the vendor, the components, or peripherals, and other volatile "unknowns." In addition, vendors are able to train support people on these consistencies to provide their own consumers with assistance.

Begin with the overall expectation of change, not the blind assumption of stability and momentum.

We must carefully examine our executables, especially since it concerns startup and initialization. What can we do to migrate some of the embedded "parameters" into something like an *.INI file, or a textual script representing often-changed parameters? We only have to load the INI file into memory once at startup, not each time we need its information.

Here's a summary of how to leash the computing environment:

- Move volatile or programmable values out of the program code and input them at run time.

- Encapsulate standard "language level" system and utility calls.

- Wrap often-used utilities with an Adapter and put them on a leash: opening a file, displaying a MessageBox, requesting the system date or environment variables, obtaining detailed registry information, or deep system API accesses.

The project exercises include the glbAdapter, presented to the run-time framework as a global singleton called *glb*. We'll use this class as both a springboard and focus for discussion. One area in particular, error management, needs global in-memory tracking.

Controlling the Chaos

The most important behavioral leash ever invoked to master a framework, or an assembly of frameworks, is a consistent error control and exception recovery model. For clarification, a *bug* is not an *error*. A bug is an apparent misbehavior in an application feature. An error is a failure in the software to complete a processing operation.

 NOTE *Language vendors tout "global error control," but never speak in terms of the whole application, only that control is available "anywhere we want it." Well, I want it everywhere, but I want to view it from only one place.*

Bugs versus Errors

Common examples of bugs include missing or incorrect data on reports or screens, inconsistent look and feel, unresponsive or disconnected interfaces, incorrect data storage and retrieval, and more. These are all surface issues.

Typical examples of errors include network or database connection outage, an I/O operation failing to complete, dirty data entering the program, a third party component raising a *trap*, a function call failing, an operation exceeding memory or disk capacity, or the operating system hanging. These are all subsurface issues. Table 5-1 lists the key differences between errors and bugs.

Table 5-1. Differences between Bugs and Errors

ERRORS	BUGS
Capability failure	Application misbehavior
Acceptable and expected	Unacceptable and unexpected
Controllable	Shows lack of control
Root causes	Symptomatic
Directly connected to source	Disconnected from source
Traceable	Nebulous origin

Many developers find themselves in the role of slayer, *because without error control the bugs arrive at a blinding clip.*

We should draw one conclusion from this comparison: that "bug fixing," a.k.a. *slaying,* is the wrong approach to eliminate misbehavior. We can only control misbehavior by invoking a strong, predictable harness on error-control. Bugs will then diminish and eventually become exceptional occurrences. To accomplish this, we must record and recover from each error in context, as close to the source as possible, not hand off to a consumer. This provides visibility to the error's source and increases the troubleshooter's proximity to (and ability to eliminate) the error's cause.

Often we cannot directly reproduce errors. They are products of chaos, data or process collision, or other mathematical anomaly and, as such, are elusive to the most experienced troubleshooter. Thus, one critical aspect of computer science, *repeatability,* is not consistently available. The only fallback to this is something that *is* consistently available, that of *observability.* If the framework can record the error when and where it occurs, we'll have a vapor trail for the detectives.

Harness, record, and dispatch errors as close to the source as possible.

We can more easily drive out the repeatable (observable) errors, but intermittent errors with no apparent cause make the hunt difficult. The more we build framework logic into our solutions, the more discrete the paths are for process threads, and the fewer places exist for errors to hide from us.

Casual interviews with master developers and troubleshooters (slayers) reveals a consistent pattern. Many of them have the same story, so while the secrets of a strong error recovery model are neither special nor original, they always work.

Slaying Bugs with El Jefe De Insectos

The work of a slayer is never done. Without an error recovery approach we treat the concepts of bug and error interchangeably. We spend lots of time fixing bugs in one place only to find the same bugs in another part of the program. Functional application misbehavior issues are not errors. They don't require recovery. An end user might find that a grid control is not populated with the right data, or that screen navigation is not what it should be. These are *symptoms,* but not errors.

I spent an entire summer blowing away bugs in a highly complex application. No sooner than a bug list would arrive at my desk than I would attack it and dispatch them within the hour. The first month of this was challenging. The second month, I gathered steam with repeatable methodologies. The third month, I realized I was spinning my wheels. By this time, the development and Q/A staff had offered me the *Golden Scarab Award,* a tongue-in-cheek reward for my bug-slaying effectiveness. My nickname had become *El Jefe De Insectos*—BugMaster.

They did not realize that I could slay bugs more effectively because I kept encountering the same bugs and repeating the same efforts. Why were these bugs returning, unaffected and impervious to my hail of virtual bullets? Did I need a better tool? Better processes? These wouldn't help, as the following story illustrates.

My parents once told me of a man who came to a nearby town with a "universal bug killer." The town had a problem with cockroaches (what town doesn't?) and this man had a product that would "Kill every cockroach, guaranteed!" People turned out in large numbers to order this product, and for lots of money. The salesman left town after selling more of these than people wanted to admit, then a few months later the product started arriving in the mail. It was essentially two pieces of wood labeled "A" and "B". The instructions read: "Place bug on block A, then forcefully bring Blocks A and B together with bug in between. Repeat as necessary."

While the joke was on the buyer, and all of us get a good laugh, there are parallels in the world of fixing buggy code that are astonishingly similar. The novice slayer spends endless hours hunting down bugs, reproducing behavior, and closing in on the target. When the source is found, the slayer places the bug on block A, examines it further to make sure it's a bug and not a "good insect," and when satisfied, slams down Block B, checks the bug off the "bug list" moves on to the next battle. Did the slayer fix the bug or just address the symptom? We'll only know if it shows up again in another form, and he happens to be the slayer again. Unfortunately, the bugs are still breeding in the application's basement. They'll be back, and with greater force.

Reducing Error Recovery Options

We must view bugs as symptoms and attack their true source. Otherwise, they'll always return.

Ever been hovering over the shoulder of an end user and witness a message box containing something like:

```
ODBC Runtime Failure in line 89 timexpl(), ORA2000,
          Request Canceled, Administrator 3345:2134
```

I've seen developers, while sitting alongside an end user, casually write down the error, as though it meant something, or as though it was supposed to be there, and continue as though nothing happened. This sort of error really frightens the end user. It makes them feel quite helpless, and it should.

There's a reason why "Abort, Retry, Ignore" was the mainstay desktop error message for years. It was only replaced later with a more pleasing user screen "Ok, Cancel." The primary difference in the two: fewer choices in the second. Anything we can do to reduce the error recovery options for the user, do it. In fact, only float options to the user when we absolutely have no other choice.

Many applications will offer a message like: "Application Failure, Unable to Continue," inside a simple "Ok" message box. When the user clicks "Ok," the application closes. While some developers view this as rudeness, the alternative is to let the application continue, limp along, and provide an even more egregious user experience.

Get out while we can.

That's because within the domain of our solution, no matter how simple the error, the user is absolutely helpless to do anything else. Take a look at the verbose ODBC message that you saw at the beginning of this section. Is there *any* information in it? Anything the user can actually act on?

Now take a few steps back, and think of our internal components. Begin viewing a calling procedure (consumer) as an end user, to the called procedure (service). If the service call returns—or can return—an extensive domain of error messages and codes, the consumer will still have to boil them down to a smaller set of actionable codes.

Our consumer processes are the end users of the capabilities behind our interfaces. Like a desktop end user, we should limit the type and count of errors they immediately see.

If the error recovery model allows all possible codes, messages, and flags to pervade across the framework, then we have no control over errors—there is no error management. Getting the framework under control without directly addressing this issue is like trying to pour a cup of coffee in an earthquake.

Anytime I've had the unfortunate role of slayer for a solution I did not build, I usually find a pervasive "growl" in the solution's infrastructure, especially one that causes intermittent mayhem. The first thing I attack is the error control environment.

Chaos Concepts

College and university classrooms are, in large part, the domain where chaos management, chaos science, and other chaos-related issues are taught or discussed. Chaos has many implied meanings, from a "formless void" to theoretical discussions and some example-ware with fractal programs or, for the advanced classes, neural networks. Most of it is theoretical and presented in a context that makes it seem far, far away. It's detached from "real" computer science, something we will be fortunate to experience, someday, if we're into that sort of thing.

What a shocker it must be to encounter the science of *chaos control* within our first few months of professional programming. Of course, that's not what it's called. We're told to do some "troubleshooting," perhaps some "tightening" of a buggy piece of code. Or worse, we're given a list of bugs recently encountered by the Q/A staff or end user and told to find and fix them. Like the majority of software projects on the radar, one bug fix is as good as the next. Most are very surgical and incomplete fixes. Many address the symptom, not the root cause.

An error recovery framework provides the benefit of addressing errors as they occur, rather than encountering their side effects in the visible behavior. Chaos control is about patterns emerging from discrete sources rather than hunting for superficial flaws and killing them. This approach is deterministic and predictable, so when I say "chaos control," think in terms of logical patterns; it's how our computer will present them and how our software will be able to best deal with them.

Now, we'll run down to our local computer bookstore and get several of the two-inch-thick tomes on all the different kinds of errors, types of recovery schemes, presentation mechanisms, and error logging implementations. When our brain is full, let's come back and let's take a look at the practical side of error recovery. I'm not disregarding or demeaning all that research, we'll probably need some of it. I am asserting that without a framework to deal with errors across the board, it doesn't matter what we know about their details.

The rest of this section discusses the following chaos concepts:

Patterns and primary sources, not details.

- Closing in

- Chaos as a rule?

- How tiny events affect outcome

- Events are not repetitive

- Chaos, by definition, is not predictable

- Testing versus usability

- Finish simple, not complex

Closing In

Focus on error control within a closed system, because that's what a computing environment really is. Regardless of how interconnected we are, it's not limitless. We'll reach hard or virtual walls within our computing domain. And, while some errors may come from the dark corners of those boundaries, some from the high process of our distributed environments, and some from the deep crevasse of our core/legacy systems, physically we are still in a *closed system*. All sources of error can be known and *should* be known. The source of our woe is not fire, flood, or earthquake (although these make impressive statements in damage control meetings).

Address the source.

It's not the error itself, it's the *source* of the error that counts most. We must take vendor and technology-specific error codes and messages and transform them, adapt them into our framework, and ultimately into the application riding on it. Don't focus on "all possible errors." If we think about it carefully, all of our errors in a closed system will fall into only a handful of manageable buckets. I'll help you find them.

Focus on errors as a "pattern," not discrete quantities.

Chaos as a Rule?

This is an oxymoron, to be sure. Chaos has no rules, right? Actually, a program exists in a closed environment driven by universal physical and virtual rules, electricity, carefully manufactured silicon wafers, BIOS, operating system, IEEE standards, the list is endless. The very platform containing the development environment is practically welded to a set of operational rules.

It's amazing that *chaoticians* or others who attempt to study "open system chaos" do all their modeling on computers. They come up with distorted conclusions, and breathless statements, "Look, chaos really does have order!" Nah, you're just modeling in an ordered, closed system. Finding "order" surprises you?

The rest of this section discusses some of the chaotic, repeatable, and observable conditions that we must address within our error control framework, unless of course we want to buy stock in Maalox. These topics are followed by a list of five chaos rules.

How Tiny Events Affect Outcomes

We watch an application crash hard and leave an incredible mess in its wake. Rolling back the failure might take hours, or days. When we trace it to a root cause, it's something simple. A file ran out of disk space, a counter rolled over, etc.

> **NOTE** *Many years ago, an American fighter jet crossed the Equator for the first time. Its auto-pilot system had never encountered negative latitudes. It flipped the aircraft, crashed, and killed the pilot.*

A tiny event in an obscure piece of code can cause application failure, general protection fault, server crash, etc. A seemingly innocuous one-liner, and our whole world is toast. And aren't objects like that? We work so hard to centralize behavior to get consistently good behavior (and sometimes get consistently bad behavior with it).

The good news: it's all from the same source so fix it once. The primary reason such hard-crash errors occur is that there is no framework, no safety net to catch all the "spurious" errors that otherwise escape. If the framework provides general buckets for categorizing errors plus a default home for those as-yet-to-be encountered ones, then everything has a place. If it allows all errors to fly out totally unchecked then, yes, we are in for a bumpy ride.

The tiniest events often have significant impact. If our framework or programming practices leave holes in areas we consider insignificant, the computer's natural chaos will find them. If our program is a balloon, and errors are needles, it will only take one to pierce the tiniest hole. If it gets through, the results are certainly more significant than the attention we paid to the needle. If, however, we have controlled the source (such as eliminating access to a needle at all), the balloon's environmental safety factor rises several notches.

The first robot landing vehicle mission to Venus ended in spectacular failure, crashing on the planet's surface. The culprit was a single, misplaced dash "-" in the software.

Events Are Not Repetitive

No sooner did we code for that very specific error condition on the database, (or that evil business subsystem from the guys across the hall) than another one arose. We seem to spend our life bulletproofing our software, there is no end to the combinations of events that can produce errors. However, it's precisely because they're *not repetitive* that we must build error categories.

Think of it as a swarm of insects, bugs, flying in mass quantities with no direction or purpose. Then think in terms of building traps, mechanisms that will suck them in and destroy them long before they reach us. We don't care which barrier stopped and destroyed them, only that they will never arrive.

Repetitive errors are predictable. Where's the fun in that?

This is a critical point, because the framework *must* condense the "all possible errors" into a smaller, controllable subset. The calling consumer only understands one thing: it didn't get what it asked for. It did not succeed—it failed. "Yes" and "No" are a very limited subset of information, and about all most consumers can deal with.

Exploit the patterns, tame them, make them work for us. "Fuzzy" relationships also exist, meaning that just because an operation failed, it may also have partially completed, so we have use for "warning" messages.

Behavioral patterns emerge because, scientifically speaking, we are always in a closed system.

Chaos, by Definition, Is Not Predictable

While chaos is not predictable, its effects are. We burn in a multi-tier solution for weeks in a development environment. When it migrates to a testing environment, it fails in the first five minutes of operation. It then takes time to stabilize it. I can predict this scenario; I cannot predict how, why, or at what magnitude the errors will occur. So why assume that it won't happen?

We can either build additional time into our project and make sure our team is steeled for the delivery event, or we can build a framework to give us *in situ* mastery of the errors generated in the delivery environment. The difference is simple: a framework is a weapon to tame a new wilderness, while the lack of a framework is like standing helplessly in a desert.

Testing versus Usability

We present a solution to a user, they love the screens, the flow, everything is perfect. The first time they call up data, or try to save it, it fails. "Didn't you test this?" they ask.

We typically test things at the unit level, the functional/technical level, not at the integrated or operational level. There is a world of difference in the two. Additionally, we are psychologically predisposed not to break our own code. If a particular hot-key does not work properly, we tend to avoid it. Consequently, we forget it's an issue. According to Murphy's Law, this hot key will draw the user's finger like a moth to a flame.

Regression testing is your friend.

Hire (or rent) people who will learn the operational aspects of the application and test it like a user. Cherish their feedback. For complex applications, invest in automated testing software to provide hands-free shakeout of the majority of testing tedium.

Finish Simple, Not Complex

Every procedure (any level) will finish with one of two states, success or failure. In most cases, our options to recover from failure are also binary—we can send a message to the user asking for recovery options, or we can attempt to recover automatically. In most cases, we must recover automatically because (like the user) our calling consumer is helpless to take action apart from the standard "abort, retry, or ignore" presented in whatever form is appropriate.

Success or failure (binary values) drives to the core of the machine.

If a component can detect the reason for a failure (for example, incomplete information on a screen or an attempt to insert a unique value that already exists), and these are within the user's ability to control, then by all means float an intelligent message and allow for a retry. If the component must report failure status to the user, use adequate, user-friendly information, as to what happened and why. If the user cannot affect the outcome, don't include the user in the recovery process.

Users come in three different flavors:

- *Developers*, who may want huge, verbose blocks of error information burst to the screen

- *Testers*, who may want a repackaged subset of this same information

- *End users*, who couldn't care less about "Oracle error number 25" and "ODBC recovery failed in tstMainUser." In fact, such errors can *viscerally* shock end-users, so avoid inflicting pain where possible.

In one solution, I saw some of the strangest errors, some totally unrelated to the current operation. How were such messages escaping their subsystem domain? A casual code examination revealed that each subsystem attempted to trap and repackage errors into "buckets," with the express purpose to "intelligently bubble" a useful message to the user. I saw progressively complex error handling routines rising out of the subsystems, the most complex in the user interface. The whole system was possibly 30 percent over-coded in error management alone. Unfortunately, it was easy for a "new" (or unpredicted) error code to escape this multi-tiered error sifter.

Identify the user type and report accordingly.

This above is an example of addressing "every possible error," which is an impossible task, rather than addressing the source of the error, a task easily handled by modular coding.

The "bubble" reached a "boil" in no time!

Implementing Chaos Rules

Without an error recovery model, chaos does in fact rule our entire run-time domain. It is merciless and cruel. If we really think we can start at the 80 percent architecture mark and race to the finish line, deploy our application, and go home happy, we're fooling ourselves. When a program starts up, the entire computing environment starts bombarding it with events, information, and other noise. The program must buffer itself from this onslaught and slog through them, bringing itself into a stable, run-time mode.

This section provides the five following rules to help you combat chaos:

Rule #1: Standardize, and do not deviate from valid result values.

Rule #2: Log it—if it's not recorded, it never happened.

Rule #3: Recover at the source, not the consumer.

Rule #4: Never raise error traps.

Rule #5: Provide for a run-time log.

Rule #1:
Standardize, and Do Not Deviate
from "Valid Result Values"

What is a "valid value?" I'll boil it down to simple terms. There are only two contexts: functions returning *values* and methods returning *state*. Methods returning state codes are easy, the method either worked or it didn't. Functions return two types of values, simple or complex (e.g., objects).

For a simple value, we always have a default—a null string ("") for string return values and a "0" for numeric return values. For an object request, the only valid values are the object itself, or Nothing. There is no third choice. An "undefined" or "unknown" object type is *totally* unacceptable. The following pseudocode example shows how to frame an object request so that it's output is never undefined. In the following example, I'll highlight the point where the return value is set to a valid value:

```
Public Function myObjBroker(strKey as String) as Object
On Error Resume Next                 'never, ever trap an error to a consumer!
Dim pWrk as Object                   ' set up a local workspace
myObjBroker = Nothing                'set the default return, no undefined values!
pWrk = objSubRequest(strKey)         'go get the real information
If pWrk is Nothing or err.Number <> 0 then Exit Function  'we can leave now
myObjBroker = pWrk                    'otherwise set the return value
End Function
```

To return state, for most method calls, we can return a simple Boolean TRUE or FALSE. It finished favorably, or it didn't. Most component consumers are helpless to recover against any other options.

For more granular status requirements, return long integer values. A successful result always returns the value of zero, no exceptions. An unsuccessful result then has the remainder of the long-integer's non-zero values to delineate the error. If we choose to use this method, we should build some general intelligence into the 32-bit result. For example, we may want to declare all error values below the value of 1000 as super-critical, requiring immediate attention, while those below 10,000 are warnings, and those above 10,000 are simply debug reporting messages to be ignored, etc. This will allow our error handlers to perform intelligent recovery and aid to the troubleshooter.

This practice reduces the output of every error source to a small set of intelligent values (three possible outcomes for perhaps thousands of error codes). We'll probably see more localized patterns emerge from these as the framework matures, so be creative and exploit them.

The application level must also define a small set of error categories and messages. These categories will be the only "valid values" recognized across the application itself. If error codes enter the system from a sub-component, we must drive them into and standardize against one of these application error categories (allowing for consistent error recovery application-wide). This does not mean we throw away the actual error information (see Rule #2 below), only that our return codes to the consumers will be standardized as a category.

For a popular database API, we reduced 1000 error return codes to three values: success, failure, and warning.

We'll map all errors to something like this:

```
Public Enum ActionReturnCodes
  ActionSuccess = 0
  ActionFailed = 1
  ActionNotFound = 2
  ActionIncomplete = 1000
  ActionQuit = 1100
  ActionWarning 10000
End Enum
```

If we use dynamic messages attached to these values, we should store them in a flat file or database table and pull them into a TurboCollection of message Items, keyed by their integer identifiers. Now our code can manage categories of errors, have useful, application-specific messaging, and allows us to set aside detailed error management. When we need to report an error to the user, access the message collection and fire off a message box. Adding more intelligence to the message object allows us to govern behavior through external values rather than coding changes.

Table 5-2 illustrates the subset of error control parameters we'll drive every error event into. The "discrete category" denotes the enumeration shown in the ActionReturnCodes structure.

Table 5-2. Valid Return Types for Most Components

GENERAL TYPE	SPECIFIC TYPE	VALID VALUES
Value	String	Discrete category (ActionSuccess, etc.)
Value	Object	Object Reference, or "Nothing"
State	Boolean	True/False
State	String	"True", "False" or other discrete category

Rule #2:
Log It—If It's Not Recorded, It Never Happened

Error recovery requires in-context recording. The error management framework needs a way to record and report the "actual" errors in context but without being spread out all over the place. In effect, each component needs to have access to an error log for its own use, but we need central error repository for troubleshooting and intelligent recovery at higher levels.

 NOTE *In Operation Desert Storm, recon units were trained to report issues everywhere, regardless of context. At HQ, the reports were woven together in context, providing patterns of enemy troop movement.*

So now we need to build an error management module (or class) and provide a self-contained instance of it in each tier (or subsystem) of the framework. Where we may once have raised the error up, now we'll push the error down, into the handler. Because the handler is centrally recognized, we get the benefit of an application-level log with the power of the component-specific handler.

The error handler, however, should be a universal adapter. It should not be specifically coded for each context, there's no reason for that. This will force the issue of packaging the errors where they occur rather than sending them up to the calling routine, or out to the ether, for someone else to deal with.

Troubleshoot by viewing intersecting patterns in the log.

A Log on the Fire

Let's take a look at three levels of function calls, one to initiate an activity, another to wrap more context around it, and a third to deal with dirty details. Say we have a report/screen level to initiate the call, a Merchandise level to wrap context, and ActiveX Data Objects to handle details. This message was posted from the screen-level:

```
Unable to complete action.
```

This message was posted from the Merchandise-level:

```
Merchandise Component, Inserting Record With Content "Casual Slacks"),
        Error Number = 500, Error Description = Operation Failed.
```

While this message was posted from the ActiveX Data Objects level:

```
ADO component, dbEngine Class, During Execute Operation with SQL Statement =
    Insert Into Mds (Mds_ID, Mds_Description) Values (10804, "Casual Slacks"),
    Error Number  3724, "Data value cannot be converted for reasons other than sign
    mismatch or data overflow. For example, conversion would have truncated data."
```

For any given level, the individual error message is meaningless. However, if they arrive in sequence to a central repository, we can reconstruct the entire context of the failure. The objective is not to package and re-package error information, but to record it so a troubleshooter can easily reconstruct it. If cascading errors occur in various contexts, there is one and only one way to track them as they occur, by having recorded them in space and time regardless of their context or source.

We can build several cross-reference lists from this information. The first is the running list of errors at the subsystem/component level, using the component name as a key. The second is the list of errors associated with the object name/object type where the error occurred, and the third is the time sequence of the error. When the troubleshooter accesses the time sequence, the error's source and vapor trail reveal themselves, like so:

Did you see that? There it goes again . . .

```
Error Log #1, Time Sequence #1
ADO component, DBEngine Class, During Execute Operation with SQL Statement =
    Insert Into Mds (Mds_ID, Mds_Description) Values (10804, "Casual Slacks"),
    Error Number  3724, "Data value cannot be converted for reasons other than
    sign mismatch or data overflow. For example, conversion would have truncated
    data."
Error Log #2, Time Sequence #2
MainBiz Component, BizTemplate Class, Merchandise Handler, Inserting Record With
    Content "Casual Slacks"), Error Number = 500, Error
    Description = Operation Failed
```

From this time sequence we can piece together what actually happened. Note that we cannot automatically recover from these errors. We can only use it as a running log of out-of-context operations that we can now see as a pattern. The ADO error did not occur in the Merchandise object, so we did not send it there. The Merchandise error did not occur in the screen or other consumer, so we did not send it there. We sent them both to the error recovery log so they could be seen as time-sequenced operations even though they are, at first glance, out of context with one another.

This information allows the developer to see all errors as a whole, rather than out-of-context snippets. We are no longer restricted to just the screen-level error, for example, the insertion did not occur so the screen is not displaying anything. Nor are we restricted to the merchandise-level error where we know what we were trying to do, but it didn't happen that way. Finally, we're not restricted to the ADO-level error where somebody asked for something, but we couldn't make it happen.

Observability is a pillar of science.

Since the screen-level operation attempted something with Merchandise that did not work, the recovery options are further limited. All we can do now is send a simple message to the user, "The operation was unsuccessful." While this may frustrate the user, the user is helpless to correct the real cause.

Note also how the error's context becomes more nebulous the farther we get away from the original consumer. Packaging all of these for the original consumer is difficult and ultimately useless. A better approach is to leave a trail for the troubleshooter.

Include the user only when you have to.

What Just Happened Here?

The Merchandise object knows it was trying to perform a database operation against the ADO model, so if the operation failed it only needs to call up the last ADO operation(s) to determine if self-correction is possible. Since self-correction is usually not possible, the objective is to capture all of the events in their sequential occurrence so the true nature of the error can be dealt with (in post-mortem comprehensive context) rather than symptomatically.

As a developer I can tell that the above Merchandise/ADO errors occurred for one of two reasons, either the database column receiving the information is the incorrect size, or the information being posted to it is in the incorrect format. Either way, I can correct the problem and it will never happen again.

I can also build developer support in the framework to capture this condition automatically before it ever leaves the shop.

The primary benefit of having the errors all in one time-sequenced contextual log is that we can query the log's contents from a distance, over the network, even over the Internet. We get the errors in context, as they happen, without having to reproduce them!

For very rapid turnaround, package the error log into a textual message and use the workstation's or server's onboard MAPI interface, then send email messages to our help desk or support site. Optionally, dump ErrorLog entries to the client machine or server event log. Either strategy (or both) will help us in analyzing run-time failures without having to reproduce the context at our site.

Error logging gives us information as it happened, not as we reproduced it. Our corrections will be more accurate.

Rule #3:
Recover at the Source, Not *the Consumer*

Fix and recover all errors at the level where they occur. Never require a calling procedure or consumer to handle another component's errors.

The method/function/property should only return a valid value. The following code example guarantees that the return value will be a valid object, or the value of Nothing:

```
Public Function GetThisData(Key as String) as Object
  Dim oData as DataClass
  On Error GoTo ErrHan            'Jump out if error encountered
  GetThisData = Nothing           'Set valid return value first!
  oData = Nothing                 'init the variable
  oData = oADODB.execute(Key)     'if it traps, it will jump to ErrHan below
  GetThisData = oData             'return the result
 Exit Function
ErrHan:
  ErrorHandler Me, "Component", _
        "GetThisData With Key= <" & Key & ">" , Err.Num, Err.Description
   Exit Sub                       'exit now is Ok, return result already
                                  ' set - optionally Resume Next
End Sub
```

The .NET Framework provide a new construct, the *Try/Catch,* allowing us to wrap the error control within a structured statement rather than "crafting" it as in the VB6 example above. Try/Catch syntax would look like:

```
GetThisData = Nothing               'Set valid return value first!
oData = Nothing                     'init the variable
Try
    oData = oADODB.execute(Key)     'if it traps, it will jump to Catch
Catch
    ErrorHandler Me, "Component", _
        "GetThisData With Key= <" & Key & ">" , Err.Num, Err.Description
End Try
```

The Try starts a structured exception handler. We then put executable statements that might possibly generate an exception trap after it. Catch will run if a statement in the Try block fails. We can add additional "optional" filters on the Catch block to further screen its execution.

I've seen this scenario facilitate proactive analysis and recovery before the end user even gets a chance to complain.

Never trap errors to a calling consumer. Just because third party components do this does **not** *make it a best practice.*

Note how this wraps the ADO call, because ADO can raise a trappable error when it fails. In this scenario, the consumer only wanted a single, populated object (no bulletproofing overhead to avoid error traps). In fact, this strategy eliminates error trapping completely for all consumers. The following code shows a call to the GetThisData function with no error control overhead in sight. It's already under control inside the call:

```
Public Function GetMyData(Key as String) as Object
  GetMyData = GetThisData(Key)
End Sub
```

Now if our consumer asks for an object, we either return the object reference or return Nothing. The consumer can easily handle this binary situation, and of course can examine the error log afterwards. Success/failure values will follow a similar rule: reduce them to Boolean if possible.

Rule #4: Never Raise Error Traps

Never raise an error trap unless you have an extreme scenario—the database has crashed, the network is toast, fire, flood, earthquake, you get the picture. Floating trappable errors upward, or directly raising them, is a last-resort strategy and should not be installed as a default.

Many third-party APIs have trappable errors. That's fine, it's a requirement of the physical separation of our framework from theirs. It does not, however constitute a best practice for our internal exception handling. We should not bubble these errors upward. Wrap them and log them, then return a valid value to our calling procedure. If the error is serious enough, the calling procedure is helpless to fix it. If the error is not serious enough, it does not warrant floating trappable errors. Block the traps and gracefully return with a valid value.

Invoking an error trap means we intend to hijack the calling routine's processing stream.

Here's the real issue: if we raise an error, the calling routine *must* provide error recovery for our service, or to put it more bluntly, the routine must allow for the fact that we intend to *hijack* its processing stream. Trappable errors are invasive to a consumer, and should be used only in the extreme. Calling consumers should enjoy the benefit of function calls that behave correctly always, never returning invalid values and never, as a rule, raising an error trap as the default recovery strategy.

Rule #5:
Provide for a Run-Time Log

When all else fails, it's handy to have a running operational log of each major step of our application's logic. The underlying product driving the application can provide strategic messaging points whenever an application invokes its interface. While this can be verbose and unwieldy without a switch to turn it off, having the ability to turn it on can be a lifesaver.

While most developers like to use the visual point-click values on their data and process variable in local toolbar windows, it is often very easy to unload those variables on-the-fly with inline print-output statements. These are simple, text-based statements that dump information to the screen about contents of variables, error codes, procedural entry and exit, etc.

This mimics a visual development environment (e.g., the Visual Studio *Immediate* window). Unfortunately for the developer as troubleshooter, the visual development environment is rarely up and running at the user desktop. So if the troubleshooter needs more application-level or contextual information than what is provided in the error logs, a run-time log is the only way.

NOTE *The vMach[1] product provides a* Watch *window to breakpoint and single-step through abstract metadata instructions and variables, providing more power than a simple log. (see Project 4—Interpreters).*

What this means is that we need to provide a wrapper to the common *Debug Output* function to our visual environment (e.g., Visual Basic's Debug.Print/Debug.Writeline). Every call to this function will write debug information to our language environment screen and also to a flat text file. This log file will be our window to our application's primary procedural steps. If the application produced buggy results, the log should provide enough information to reveal where it jumped the tracks.

What if all of the operations succeeded without error but the information in the database is still wrong, or the processes did not navigate or respond as we thought they would? Only a run-time log will tell us this.

So plan to put a hook into the program code, visible at every level, with the syntax of:

```
DebugOut (iStr as String)
```

We can attach this reference to the aforementioned global object, allowing us to call it from anywhere:

```
glb.DebugOut ("Found An Error Here!")
```

Under the covers, we'll shoot the message string to the immediate/output window (in development) and, if enabled, the output log file (for production). This is an internal-use function only, so we can make its interface as simple or as complex as required. Word to the wise, however, the output will go as a single line to a flat text file, and everything we want to output in that line can be represented in a single string of information. So how complex does the DebugOut interface need to be? Not very—a single string parameter will do the trick.

Now go back to our Startup.INI file (above under Controlling Startup and Initialization) where we might have other run-time configuration parameters. Here's a new one for Startup.Txt:

Wherever it makes sense to install a DebugOut statement, do so. Once in place, leave it there. We'll have no reason to remove it later.

```
DEBUGOUT=TRUE/FALSE
```

When the program starts, it will detect whether the variable "DEBUGOUT" is enabled. If True, it will open a log file and start streaming information to it. If False, it will ignore the file output and all other DebugOut statements.

This allows us, at a distance, to turn on Debug print statements even though we cannot see them until they're done. We can turn it on remotely, allow an end user to step through the misbehaving features, then turn it off and examine the detail. It's a powerful means to log application logic as it executes, but also to turn it off once "all is well." As with the error recovery log, we can instruct the application to email this log file to us directly from the source.

NOTE *Mabry Mail© is a software component allowing us to instantly package an email (with attachments) and fire it off without opening a user dialogue. It will support any SMTP gateway, and we can configure its on-site proxy requirements with metadata.*

The extension of this strategy is to pass the current object context into the debug statement, such as using an interface pattern like so:

```
DebugOut (sMsg as String, sContext as String, oContext as Object)
```

This allows consumers recording debug information to offer themselves in context of the debug statement. Thus, a consumer need only extend the DebugOut call with:

```
DebugOut  "My Debug Statement", "What I was trying to do", Me
```

Doing so segues into another area of debug output control: that of using *levels*. This capability includes suppressing or releasing messages based upon an externally programmed level indicator. In the example for Startup.Ini, we would include another notation near the DEBUGOUT:

```
DEBUGOUT=TRUE
DEBUGLEVEL=1000
```

We then have the option of including a level number in the DebugOut statement. If the context object (above) provides a level indicator, we can determine if the output should be released or suppressed. Here's the example:

```
Public Sub DebugOut (sMsg as String, sContext as String, oContext as Object)
On Error Resume Next
Dim lngLevel as Long                           'workspace
Dim lngGlobal as Long                          'workspace
lngGlobal = CLng(glbAdapter.GlobalValue("DebugLevel"))  'get the DEBUGLEVEL
lngLevel = lngGlobal                           'set default
if not oContext is nothing then                'if object is present then
    lngLevel = oContext.Item("DebugLevel")     'get the object's level
End If
If lngLevel  > = lngGlobal Then                'if they enable output
    'Output the Debug Statement Here           'output the debug information
End If
End Sub
```

This example provides several levels of power, especially considering that we can install "default" levels in all objects. For instance, let's say each time we create an object we give it a default DebugLevel of 1000, like so:

```
pNew = pFactorySeed.Create(pParent)
pNew.Item("DebugLevel") = 1000
```

At a minimum, this provides, the creation of a universal debug level that is greater than zero. Thus we can automatically suppress all debug output from all objects by setting the global DebugLevel to 999 or less, like so:

```
DEBUGOUT=TRUE
DEBUGLEVEL=999
```

In addition, we could provide programmatic instructions to a given object, increasing its debug level to release its output. Here's an example:

```
pObj.Item("DebugLevel") = 1500
```

Thus, any debug statements issued by the object from that point forward would be surgically visible in the DebugOut log until the DebugLevel for the object (or for the framework GlobalValue) changed to suppress them again.

The slayer will have direct control over the level of verbosity, whether at startup, during run time, or some combination, and in context of the failing object. The slayer can suppress noise from well-behaved objects and focus only on the troublemakers. The objective is to get more information into the hands of the slayer in context so errors are brought under control and bugs are driven out.

Simple valid-value operations will keep our code moving and minimize our error-recovery coding at every level. Error logs and point-of-origin control keep all consumers safe. Debug logs provide a window to the run-time environment. This framework provides a predictable and deterministic means to isolate and slay problems (and problem areas) long before they are visible to the user—a beautiful thing.

Project Five—Error Control

This project will deal with a number of advanced topics, again building on the projects that came before it. The Project5 Frameworks Error Control directory contains the necessary modules. Pop open ProjectFive and find the *main* module.

I've provided a "bonus" section for the .NET projects centering on date/time formatting as an example of global behavioral management. The VB6 version of Format(Now,"YYYY/MM/DD") does not yield the same result as the .NET version of Format(Now(),"YYYY/MM/DD"). On February 2, 2001, the VB6 result would be "2001/02/02", whereas in .NET the result would be "YYYY/02/DD". Why is this true? In the .NET Framework, *case matters*. Thus to derive the VB6 equivalent, the appropriate .NET format string should be "yyyy/MM/dd".

Unfortunately, case is completely insignificant in almost every other area of date/time integration, including database engines. Microsoft has also chosen to use HH as the 24-hour version of time and "hh" as the 12-hour version of time. Thus we can affect behavior by modifying upper and lowercase of the letters. If, however, I require transparent integration across multiple environments, this scenario is too language-dependent for metamorphic reusability. Therefore, I have programmed our *glb* class to understand and translate for us, complying with Microsoft's needs under the covers while giving transparency to our application-level functions.

Thus a call to glb.DateFormat(Now, "YYYY-MM-DD") will yield exactly what we need. What's more, the function call is portable to other machines and operating systems. We can now let our internal functions use the *glb* class as the broker for such technology-specific idiosyncrasies. Single-step through these date-time conversions and see how they conform transparently to a standard we can use, while translating the .NET handling behind the scenes for a consistent outcome.

Now it's time to put some more building blocks to work. In the prior project, we leveraged the container pattern, so let's use its functionality internally to help us capture and control information. We'll do this through the *cntAdapter*, which is the default class for the container pattern.

We'll first need a layout for our dynamic error log, and the following format seems to provide the widest scope:

- *Date/time stamp* to capture the actual point in time of recording

- *Component* to capture the component where the error first occurred

- *Class* to capture the name of the class where the error occurred

- *Context* to capture what the operation was trying to do at the time of the error

- *Message* to record the actual error number and message produced by the operation (if applicable).

What if we need more? No problem, as we'll soon see. Let's define a container for the error log and set its layout:

```
Dim cntErr As New cntAdapter()
cntErr.Action("Layout", "ErrTime|ErrComponent|ErrClass|ErrContext|ErrMsg")
```

Note how all of the recording columns are soft, defined in a single compound parameter. If we need to extend it later, we simply add more to the end inside the parameter string. If we need to shoot this to a file or database, the column names help to easily serialize.

Now let's set up some workspace to clarify adding an entry to the container:

```
Dim strTime As String              'hold the time stamp
Dim strComponent As String         'hold the component name
Dim strClass As String             'hold the class name
Dim strContext As String           'hold the context
Dim strMsg As String               'hold the message
    Dim strDat As String           'hold the concat of all the above
```

Next we'll fill them with some test information:

```
strTime = glb.DateFormat(Now(), "YYYY-MM-DD HH24:MI:SS")
strComponent = "Program"
strClass = "Main"
strContext = "Example"
strMsg = "0 - Here is an Error Message"
```

Then we concatenate them on the delimiter boundaries expected by the container, using the vertical pipe "|" as separators:

```
strDat = strTime & "|" & strComponent & "|" & _
    strClass & "|" & strContext & "|" & strMsg
```

Now we just add the row to the container:

```
cntErr.Action("AddRow", strDat)
```

The container's automatic behavior will use the layout and the vertical pipes to slice the string into the appropriately formatted columns. If we want to see what we just added, let's do a GetRow:

```
Debug.WriteLine(CStr(cntErr.Action("GetRow")))
```

Let's add two more error messages:

```
strTime = glb.DateFormat(Now(), "YYYY-MM-DD HH24:MI:SS")
strContext = "Another Example"
strMsg = "35 - Here is an Error Message 35"
strDat = strTime & "|" & strComponent & "|" & strClass & _
          "|" & strContext & "|" & strMsg
cntErr.Action("AddRow", strDat, Nothing)
' And Another
    strTime = glb.DateFormat(Now(), "YYYY-MM-DD HH24:MI:SS")
strContext = "Yet Another Example"
strMsg = "481 - Here is an Error Message 481"
strDat = strTime & "|" & strComponent & "|" & strClass & _
    "|" & strContext & "|" & strMsg
cntErr.Action("AddRow", strDat, Nothing)
```

Note the only changing values: the *Context* and the *Message*. Everything else remains the same. This tells us that the Date/Time, Component, and Class information can be derived (and we could derive these from system calls like *Now*, *ExeName* and *TypeName*).

Now that we've recorded all this data, how do we get back to it? The container provides these simple browsing functions just for the occasion:

```
cntErr.Action("MoveFirst")
Do
  Debug.WriteLine(CStr(cntErr.Action("GetRow")))
Loop While cntErr.Action("MoveNext") = "True"
```

This operation combines the MoveNext/More capability into a single call so we can reduce the total count of calls to the container. This is important if we ultimately intend to browse this structure over a network or other remote troubleshooting venue.

Now we have the primitive features to help us log and track errors. We need a way to package it up, leash it, and make it easily available to all our developers. Let's next migrate this functionality into the glbAdapter. We'll initialize the container and its layout automatically, then expose an ErrorHandler action on the glbAdapter, which will invoke the glbAdapter's internal ErrorHandler() function. Note how now we only need to address the error Context and Message, while all other information is automatically derived, like this:

```
Private Sub ErrorHandler(ByVal strErr As String,
                             Optional ByVal oAction As Object = Nothing)
       On Error Resume Next
       Dim strTime As String                    'define our workspaces
       Dim strComponent As String
       Dim strClass As String
       Dim strContext As String
       Dim strMsg As String
       Dim strDat As String
       Dim tcp As TurboCollection
       strTime = glb.DateFormat(Now(), "YYYY-MM-DD HH24:MI:SS")
       If oAction Is Nothing Then               'no object info available?
          strComponent = "Program"              'just default both
          strClass = "NA"
       Else
             'else get the reference's Top
          strComponent = TypeName(oAction.Ref("Top"))
          strClass = TypeName(oAction)          'and the class name too
       End If
        'decompose the compound message
       tcp = glb.UnStringParm(strErr)
        'find and pull the context and message
       strContext = tcp.Find("Context").Item
       strMsg = tcp.Find("Message").Item
       strDat = strTime & "|" & strComponent & "|" & strClass & _
              "|" & strContext & "|" & strMsg
       Ref("cntErr").Action("AddRow", strDat, Nothing)
       tcp = Nothing
End Sub
```

Next let's add some information, then go back and get it. We'll need to either expose the error browse capability on the glbAdapter or expose the cntAdapter itself through the *Ref* property. For simplicity, let's use the *Ref* property. I've already included the following statement in the glbAdapter's *ErrorHandler* method. This will allow the glbAdapter to configure and register the local cntErr reference on the very first call of the ErrorHandler:

```
If Not cntErr.DataPresent Then
    cntErr.Action("Layout", "ErrTime|ErrComponent|ErrClass|ErrContext|ErrMsg")
    glb.Ref("cntErr") = cntErr
End If
```

Now all we do externally is get the cntErr reference and browse it:

```
cntErr = glb.Ref("cntErr")                          'get the reference
cntErr.Action("MoveFirst")                          'browse as before
Do
    Debug.WriteLine(CStr(cntErr.Action("GetRow")))
    Loop While cntErr.Action("MoveNext") = "True"
```

If we're browsing the glbAdapter remotely and don't really have handy access to a cntAdapter, look at soft-wiring the cntErr's interface to the glbAdapter. It's really pretty easy, since all we have to do is pass-through the actions for the cntErr. We simply tell the glbAdapter that it's "BrowseContext" is the "cntErr" and every call to MoveFirst/Next/GetRow is totally transparent. We simply configure the glbAdapter (internally) to log errors to the target called "cntErr". While in this context it's a local container, it could just as easily be a similarly interfaced socket adapter, MAPI adapter, or other error-capturing object. The objective is to let "cntErr" be the *tag keyword* recognized by the glbAdapter. Here's the example:

```
'This time, Insert a container to the global adapter
glb.Ref("cntErr") = New cntAdapter()
glb.Action("BrowseContext", "cntErr")               'set the context
glb.Action("MoveFirst")                             'move first and browse information
Do
    Debug.WriteLine(CStr(glb.Action("GetRow")))
    Loop While glb.Action("MoveNext") = "True"
```

The .NET project includes an example of Try/Catch. I've already described this earlier in the chapter under *Rule #3 Recover at the Source*. Single-step through this example to show how we can capture errors close to the source and not raise them to our calling consumers.

This form of parameterized and "contextual inheritance" is easily propagated across languages, computing environments and the internet for one simple reason: it obeys interface patterns and soft logic rather than hard-wired inheritance rules. Why is this important? Because we know that the error reporting and recording requirements could change down the road and we'd rather not revisit all this. We might like to initialize and browse other logs from the *glbAdapter,* so we simply set the BrowseContext and go get the information. Using the *cntAdapter* and the *glbAdapter* with interface patterns, changing the error reporting format is as easy as changing the initial layout—and because it's already text we can define it externally to the program as well.

By keeping the error log in the cntAdapter, we have high visibility to it, along with a simple way for developers to log errors in context. However we choose later to expose it to a troubleshooter (e.g., a Watch window), the framework itself is simple.

CHAPTER 6

Virtual Frameworks– Modeling Data Dynamically

In This Chapter:

- Developing the data model

- Performing dynamic aliasing

- Implementing the vDDM Adapters

- Leashing the power of dynamic integration

- Exporting application logic

A universal truth of any solution is that the *data model* describing the user's storage and retrieval activity is perhaps the most application-centric of any construct in the developer's domain. At the elemental level, the developer must wire access to specific database columns (such as price, quantity, markup, and cost). A screen developer must gain access to these elements and present them to the user, effectively creating an interactive relationship between specific database columns and their corresponding on-screen entry points (drop-downs, grids, text boxes, etc.).

Our goal in this section is to create a framework that allows our executable to dynamically wrap itself around the data model description and expose the model as a structural and behavioral control resource. The next chapter will integrate this framework with a more dramatic one: treating screens as information resources in the same way. We'll be able to describe and activate the data model and the screen layouts, navigation, and behavior at run time, without changing software. Let's look at the data model now.

Developing the Data Model

The data model exists at two levels: the *logical* and the *physical*. From a database perspective, the logical model is the description of the database tables and their primary relationships. If the logical model is the "bones," the physical model is the "flesh," the specific columns and attributes to describe data's details. The complete model, of course, is termed a *schema*. When we focus on these elemental descriptions and implementation details, we lose focus on a higher goal, as the following story illustrates.

A small strike team of architects spent many days working on a data model for an application-centric solution. The object modelers burned hours in brutal detail over the various elements of their carefully-crafted class hierarchy, only to watch it crumble as the data architects picked it apart using hard-won knowledge of database storage requirements. The data modelers said they couldn't build a schema without knowing what the operational object model looked like, yet the object modelers could not conceptualize the classes and their data storage requirements without knowing database management details. The team was in a fog.

Object and data modelers often deadlock because their require-ments are so interleaved and interdependent.

In fact, achieving consensus from the team to get a "persistence" model seemed like a hard-won victory. The final focus of the debate was whether to build a data model and then fashion the object model against it, or fashion the object model and then build a data model to "persist" it. This debate is common in many application development environments, and rarely abates even for years after production release.

The debate obfuscates the real problem. While the team members swatted the irritating modeling insects, drinking coffee while debating the *elegance* of their models, the lion of user change awaited just outside the door, already hungry and ready to devour them. No sooner would they place a masterstroke on their carefully painted rendering than new user requirements would enter like a sandblaster.

By the project's midpoint, the impatient application developers had already hard-coded over half the data model into their software, with specific references to columns, tables, and their various dependencies. Each time the end users changed their focus, or some additional requirement imposed itself, the event caused a tremor in the data model and the application code, and a few times caused a quake. While the data model (and its attributes) eventually stabilized (somewhat), the application never did. Every release of software seemed to require a rebuild and shakeout of various areas of storage management.

Figure 6-1 depicts a simple starting point for a data model. We'll reference this data model for examples throughout the chapter and the project exercise. The Employee Table (EMP) holds foreign keys for Address (ADDR), and Site (SITE), which in turn hold keys for City/State/Zip (CSZ), Country (CTRY), and Security

(SEC). Will this schema be sufficient for our application needs? What if we need more fields in the ADDR table, or the CTRY table? Can we add them without affecting existing application logic? Can we surgically apply new database changes without addressing a large part of the application? We can, but not without careful planning.

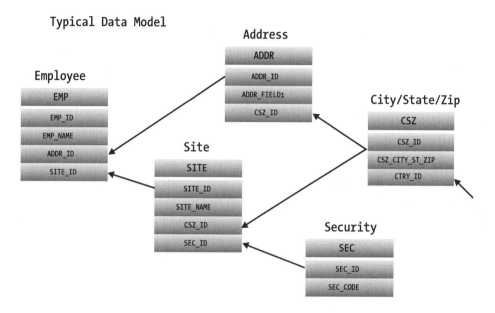

Figure 6-1. Basic data model example

 NOTE *Configuration management spans software, operating systems, hardware, data models and anything touching the application's behavior. If even one part is out of sync, the behavior of the whole is jeopardized.*

Managing Changes to the Data Model

In a shop experiencing major configuration management problems, a senior architect lamented that a data model change, no matter how minor, would break software all across the enterprise. He and several others had built a *sniffer* function to perform impact analysis (with the help of some third-party tools). The sniffer would discover the affect of data model change on production software. When changes hit, the sniffer would automatically find and rebuild the affected modules or programs to re-synchronize everything. They were so proud of their model, but could not have known they had institutionalized *cascading reconstruction*! (See details on cascading reconstruction in Chapter 2.)

Data—and its description– is always on the move.

In Chapter 2, I proposed a dynamic application object cluster, not a predefined hierarchy. In fact, a predefined object model creates an artificial constraint for the *data architect*. The architect will make presuppositions about which objects to persist, rather than viewing data as information, and as such, a fluid, moving resource. Data architects often complain about the volatile demands of the application programmers, who in turn complain when data architects must shift or enhance the data model without the developer's consent or involvement.

If a CIO had to choose between data or applications, data would always win.

Reports, data queries, data mining, user application screens, and a whole host of user-driven behavior, all press on the data architecture. A programmer's application is only one star in the constellation, alongside third-party tools, products, and enterprise applications. Reality sets in on the programmer: the application is suddenly "along for the ride," not the focus of the effort.

Information is not a static, persistable entity; rather, it is a fluid, moving resource.

Object modelers want ultimate control because it makes their lives easier (they can push nasty issues off on the data architects). The data architects want ultimate control because they are nearly always the first ones called onto the carpet to explain degradations in performance. Both groups want the best solution. Both groups want to minimize their own maintenance workload. Either way, the application itself is caught in the middle.

Applications come and go, but data is forever.

We also know that an application's data model experiences the same flux and volatility as the application software. The two models are often on a parallel path, but are rarely in complete synchronization. In an application-centric approach, this condition directly affects the stability of the software code.

Rather than sweep the debate under the carpet, or engage in endless confrontations, address it head-on. Wouldn't it be great to have a framework that actually accommodates both object and data models? Such a framework would be flexible toward the changing needs of the user community but would also respond quickly to changes, even wholesale reworks, of the database structure. Therefore, if the objective is to eliminate data model dependence and cascading reconstruction from a data model change, a programmer absolutely cannot afford to embed any part of the data model definition into the physical software.

For full metamorphism, early binding of database tables, instances, or schemas is prohibited. Keep your hands and feet inside the vehicle at all times.

I Like It, I Just Can't Use It

The Microsoft ActiveX Data Objects .NET offering includes the new DataSet class with a breathtaking amount of new functionality. One in particular is the ability to specifically define tables and columns, complete with their type descriptions and definitions, and compile this information directly into the software. For an application-centric effort, this is perfect. For maximum cross-application reuse, however, we can't leverage these features.

TIP *Keep the application out of the compiled software.*

Realizing the Benefits of a Dynamic Model

Using a dynamic application model, loosely coupled to a dynamic data model, the application and data architects are free to run on separate tracks, because their capabilities don't converge until run time. The real effort then, is to certify accurate and consistent convergence. In essence, using dynamic models for each domain frees their owners from artificial constraints of a predefined, application-centric model.

This requires forethought and abstraction from us, the software developers, not the data modelers. The data modelers are irreversibly lashed to the database engine's structural modeling requirements, and the data model's run-time behavior will not deviate from the capabilities of Structured Query Language. The database engine strictly enforces table, column, and relationship rules. The software developer can only request accommodations from the data modeler within this narrow corridor of capability. While a database engine is very powerful, its structural constraints are rigid and immutable. At run time, however, the software developer can wrest the structural information from the database and further activate it with behavioral metadata, creating virtual structure and behavior unavailable in the database engine.

We are the masters of our realm, so let's wrap it around the database constraints rather than binding ourselves directly to them.

The software needs a way to access the data model that does not hard-wire the model's table names or column names/descriptions/relationships into the compiled software. It also needs a way to access the most recent changes in a data model without breaking or reconstructing major portions of code. Finally, it needs a way to transparently link disparate data models to make them appear as one to the application. All this, and more, can be derived if we approach the model(s) as though they are moving targets, with the assumption that they could change, and radically so, between run-time sessions of the program. Note that I did not say between design sessions, code migration, or other methodology-driven milestones. I said *from execution to execution*, quite literally that the model could be in flux even as we are in a run-time session, and it will not affect the software's behavior.

We need software-driven, abstract, and multidimensional behavior that is unavailable in a database engine.

The next section introduces you to some useful modeling tools.

Modeling Tools

Oracle Designer 2000, ERWin, Microsoft's Visio for Enterprise Architects (VEA), and other modeling tools allow us to manage whole enterprises from a desktop. As data architects, we can shape data models into anything we want, but can the applications keep up with us? Realistically, what is the typical turnaround time for the design, implementation, and availability of new database changes coupled with the time to integrate and deploy them in an application? Days? Weeks? What if we could do it in *minutes?*

The VEA architecture provides for an integrated enterprise view, along with some really hot hooks for allowing a program to "sense" a database change in real time and respond to it. Not just for Q/A and troubleshooting as was originally intended, but also for exploitation at the moment the change is available. Take a look at the VEA currently at the following web site:

http://msdn.microsoft.com/library/en-us/dnvs700/html/vseamodelingp3.asp.

Once we finish this discussion, our minds will be racing on how we can integrate and exploit these ideas.

Changes in the data model (arbitrary or wholesale) should not affect compiled software in the slightest.

One DBA arbitrarily changed database column and table names overnight, then announced his work to the team. While his changes did not affect the software, they did affect the application metadata using the original names. We'll see shortly how to prepare for and minimize the impact of such an event. Of course, correcting (or replacing) such an inconsiderate and maverick team member is your problem.

The software needs an internal means to access the application data model as is, without any assumptions as to what tables or columns are present. In practice, the software must reconstruct this model in virtual memory as a dynamic structure, and it must use the database catalog's information as the metadata for this structure. Thus, the software creates a memory-resident (virtual) data model, and is dynamic, because it can change at any time before, during, or after the program is invoked. Additionally, we can store it on the client, a server, or both. This describes a *Virtual Dynamic Data Model (vDDM)*, which is discussed next.

The Application Data Structures

The vDDM has a singular duty, that of moving information systematically between the application and the database. It requires structural metadata from both domains to construct its virtual framework, but uses predefined template objects and interpreters to manage behavior.

vDDM for ADO

The application data structure and its behavior are primarily constrained by the structural and behavioral rules of Structured Query Language (SQL). From the application's perspective, these include Insert , Select (Read), Update, and Delete statements, each of which ultimately finds its way to a SQL interpreter interface (brokered by drivers such as ODBC or OLEDB). For Microsoft language products, this means using the ActiveX Data Objects (ADO) model shown in Figure 6-2. By default, the Windows version of the vDDM wraps the ADO model in order to better control and layer it with additional functionality.

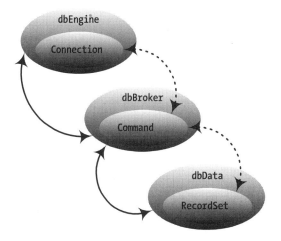

vDDM Connection
Model

ODBC/OLEDB connections support high-frequency/ small-size operations while batch loaders support low-frequency/ large-size operations.

Figure 6-2. Wrapping ADO objects: dbEngine *wraps a* Connection, dbBroker *wraps* Command, dbData *wraps a* RecordSet

In other environments, such as Sun Solaris Unix, Hewlett-Packard Unix (HP-UX), Apple Macintosh, and Linux, the three wrappers (dbEngine, dbBroker, and dbData) remain the same in both relationship and behavior because they wrap or emulate the Windows ADO equivalent. Thus, a portable program linked to the vDDM for data brokerage will not change a single line of code for data access as it migrates and is reconstructed in another environment. The vDDM for ADO is simply unplugged and the vDDM for the target environment is plugged in. The vDDM won't even care if the original database was Oracle and new one is VSAM. The access patterns are consistent and the vDDM consumer interfaces don't change.

The vDDM is an example of a building-block framework, comprised of smaller building blocks.

The basic operation of the vDDM connection/access model illustrated in Figure 6-2 uses dbEngine to build a Connection object for a given database. More than one dbEngine can exist at a time, but for simplicity we'll discuss only one. The dbBroker then uses the Command class to execute ODBC statements against the dbEngine database connection. The dbData wraps the Command's resulting RecordSet if, for example, the command was a SQL *select* statement to return database rows.

The connection string (for the dbEngine.cls) I have provided for this chapter's project exercises contains the following information (see file *DBSPEC.txt*). It is represented as tag=value pairs. The "[]" will enclose optional predefined keywords while the "{}" will enclose an externally-defined value description.

- DBVENDOR=[Oracle, Teradata, DB2, SQLServer][1]

- TABLEPREFIX={such as DB2's Creator ID, Teradata's table prefix, or the database instance name if connecting from a system manager level in Oracle}

- DSN={The ODBC Data Source Name defined for accessing a particular database (e.g., defined in the Windows Control Panel ODBC Manager)}

- UID={User ID for authentication on the named database}

- PWD={Password for authentication on the named database}

The following are optional to support IBM DB2 and NCR TeraData

- DBNAME={Actual name of the database, required to download the proper catalog information}

- DBOwner={Owner of the database, also required to download proper catalog information}

The dbEngine will require some or all of the preceding information to accurately connect a target database. A fully populated connection string is not always required. An example, provided in the DBSPEC.txt file of this chapter's project, follows:

```
CONNECTION=DBVENDOR=Oracle|TABLEPREFIX=|DBNAME=VMACH|
    DBOwner=VMACH|
    CONNECT=DSN=VMACHDVL;UID=VMACH;PWD=DOVERPRO
CONNECTION=DBVENDOR=MSAccess|TABLEPREFIX=|DBNAME=MSAccess|
    DBOwner=NONE|
    CONNECT=DSN=testaccess
```

Why all the effort in wrapping the ADO interface? Can't we just use the interface as-is and move on? Sure, we could expose the ADO raw to the remainder of the software, but apart from violating what I've already told you about wrapping everything, such exposure would not benefit us at all. By wrapping ADO, we can push an enormous amount of programmable power into the ADO wrappers. In the next sections, I'll explain more about what each wrapper does to enhance ADO's power and to hide its implementation from the vDDM's consumers.

vDDM Construction

The ADO connection model will access the application data model's *schema* (table and column definitions) through the database catalog functions. For Oracle or SQLServer, this is as simple as a call to the Connection object's *OpenSchema*. For DB2, we'll need to execute a SQL statement against DB2's system tables and use the resulting RecordSet to unload the given application schema. In either case, the objective is to derive a set of application-level table names, column names, and their descriptors. Figure 6-3 shows the schema information and construction flow.

Wrapping ADO allows us to extend, stabilize, and customize its behavior all at once.

vDDM Construction

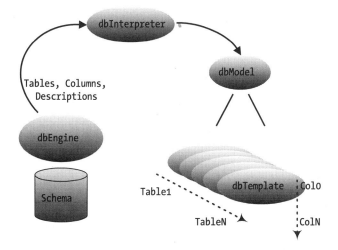

Figure 6-3. vDDM construction

The *dbInterpreter* will construct in memory one *dbTemplate* object for each table it discovers in the schema. It will load each dbTemplate with the column names and column descriptions particular to that table.

The dbInterpreter's results include a memory construct called *dbModel,* containing one placeholder for each table found in the source schema. Each placeholder will anchor a dbTemplate object, in turn containing the table's detailed column-level information. Thus, if any external process has the textual name of a given table, the dbModel can derive the table's column-level information from the table's assigned dbTemplate.

Each column-level reference not only holds information about the column, but provides a placeholder, or *Item*, for the column's actual data. Thus, whether a process wants to gather information about a column, or actually stage the column's data, it will use the same interface for both.

dbTemplates represent tables and contain columns, complete with placeholders for staging data.

The dbInterpreter then sifts the distinct column names among the tables. From this, it creates a master table of all distinct column names. It then builds an alias for each unique column name and makes the alias *synonymous* with the actual column(s). Thus, one alias can serve multiple tables and columns. The distinct column aliases are then treated as active *publishers* while the actual column references are treated as passive *subscribers*. Figure 6-4 illustrates the resulting virtual data model.

This configuration assumes that columns with the same name on different tables form a relationship between the tables, and contain referential information. Thus the publisher/subscriber relationships provide *active referential integrity* to the entire model. The relationships are enforced through *Observers*. We can always disconnect aliasing globally or surgically, but using it provides enormous power.

Synonyms create an automatic cascading effect for staging information into like-named columns. If any consumer updates a column's staging data element (using the alias), the Observers will propagate the information to all other columns of the same name. Thus, the default alias declares synonymous relationships between tables through like-named columns. All of this happens locally, in memory so as the software interacts with the vDDM, we are actually preparing it for a single blast to the database of one or more records.

Name Duplication

The bane of this sort of model is the use of non-unique names. For example, the Emp table might contain a column called Description, as might the Site table. Such columns are not intended to share the same information, but the vDDM will enforce it this way by default. We can include additional metadata to disconnect these synonyms to avoid undesired behavior. Of course, our calling consumer will then have to use fully qualified column references (e.g., Emp.Description). However, if we take a short look at our current data models, we'll find the vDDM merging right alongside them with few changes.

Virtual Data Model

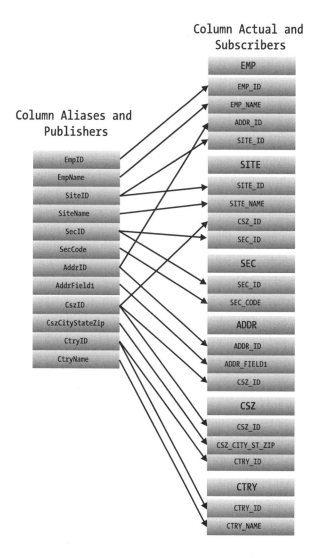

Figure 6-4. Virtual data model

Computer Associates ERWin©, Oracle Designer 2000©, and Microsoft's Visio for Enterprise Architects (VEA)©, and many other data modeling tools provide significant warnings against duplicated column names that are outside the referential model. They often suggest column names such as Emp_Description and Site_Description to manage uniqueness, because it's a best practice. As I speak to enterprise data architects wrestling with structural metadata mapping, uniqueness in name, location, and source provide enormous benefits in troubleshooting, dependency analysis, and tracking.

Unique column names primarily serve us for referential connectivity.

315

Creating inter-column synonym relationships with Observers provides us with a synchronization mechanism when posting information to columns in the vDDM. After all, each column placeholder is more than just a tagged reference, it actually wraps a staged data point for later preparation in a Structured Query Language statement (see Figure 6-5). By posting information points to their various column locations, we can then command the vDDM to manufacture an execution-ready SQL statement using the table/column metadata and the data itself.

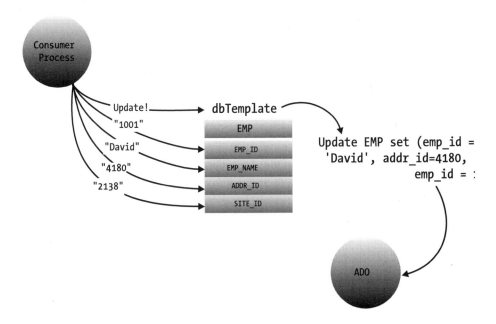

Figure 6-5. dbTemplate facilitating automatic SQL generation and database update

The vDDM can contain both the data values and column descriptors, so it can automatically manufacture an execution-ready SQL statement.

While unique (and standardized) column identifiers are ideal, they're not always realistic, so we need a powerful aliasing capability to keep them all honest.

Performing Dynamic Aliasing

An application can define more aliases in a variety of forms, each one benefiting from the vDDM's aliasing rules. Many applications must integrate data across components, third-party applications, and computing environments using disparate names for the same information. This often requires careful software handcrafting to verify that the information remains in sync, almost always requiring referential enforcement at the application level. The vDDM makes this aspect automatic and transparent, through the publish/subscribe relationships of the aliases.

The alias creates these three modes:

- *Synonym* relationship between two existing column references

- *Surrogate* name for a single existing column reference

- *Pseudonym* column having no initial relationship with other column references.

All of these relationships are available at run time with no additional intervention from data architects or administrators. They will appreciate these features but should not abuse them by relaxing their best practices for data modeling.

Synonym

The *synonym* connects two existing columns such that they behave as one. For example, an Employee_ID on one data model's tables might be the same information (and role) as the Account_ID in another data model. Or perhaps the Customer_Num in one data model corresponds to Account_Num in another model, Customer_ID in another, and Cust_Num in yet another. The synonym allows the application to tell the vDDM which ones should be treated the same, and the vDDM then automatically enforces their relationships without the application's regular intervention.

Of course, if all your data lines up correctly, ignore this . . .

Surrogate

The *surrogate* provides another, perhaps more meaningful name for an existing column. Many database column names have meaningless or obfuscated names, such as *Rev00* and *Rev01*, which may mean, respectively, a revenue amount for the first and second quarters, or may also mean a revision level for software, or even the reversed or rolled back placeholders in a repository.

Of course, if none of your column names are obfuscated, and all are stable, ignore this . . .

When ambiguity exists, a *surrogate alias* can impute meaning between the application and the data model. Perhaps an alias of *FirstQuarterRevenue* could be assigned to *Rev01*, providing detail that is under our control. In addition, if First Quarter Revenue should find its way into a more meaningful reference, such as *RevenueQ1*, we only need to redirect the alias, not modify the application. Also, if a data architect removes or renames an existing column name, a surrogate can reconnect the application to the data's new home without changing application code. A surrogate is similar to a synonym only in its data-sharing role.

Pseudonym

The *pseudonym* is an additional column placeholder with no particular associated database table or other relationships. In database systems worldwide, we're in constant need of placeholders and staging areas to keep information handy for later SQL construction (e.g., a Select statement) without committing or over-writing current work. SQL queries and commands often require data points that are similar to but not quite exactly the information in a particular column (e.g., ranges of data, "like" queries, or phonetic matching). Another example includes providing a constant prefix, environment variable, pre-computed value, or external parameter for inclusion in a seamless SQL query construction simply by referencing its synonym tag or value as though it's any other column. As we'll see later in component-SQL, we can use these placeholders as keywords for the vDDM's automatic SQL-generation behavior.

The pseudo column provides this placeholder capability. Like any multi-use variable, however, it's global to the virtual data model and has all the attendant woes of global variable management. We can also use it to hold intermediate data, or we use dynamic variables in the localized interpreters.

A side effect of these roles includes the ability to declare a *pseudonym* as a placeholder, then making it a *synonym* to another column. We could also declare a *surrogate* for a given column, then declare a *synonym* relationship between the surrogate and an existing column.

Automatic Behavior

These types of aliasing are all virtual, dynamic relationships providing automatic behavior otherwise carefully crafted and connected in software. The vDDM provides the framework for the relationships on demand. The behavior is consis-tent and more importantly, programmable.

NOTE *The vDDM's aliasing capability effectively provides an interface to the application consumer level, because the application logic will only reference the aliases, with no knowledge of the underlying column information or real table/column names.*

SQL Statements

All of these data relationships ultimately wrap the construction processes for Structured Query Language (SQL). As such, the vDDM contains a solid foundation for enforcing how and when to include aliases, keywords, data values, etc. to automatically assemble or enhance a functioning SQL statement.

The vDDM uses the dbEngine and dbBroker to pass SQL statements to the database, and uses dbData to accept any return results. A *Select* statement almost always returns a result, even if it's a dbData with no records found. The *Update*, *Insert*, and *Delete* statements, for the most part, only return success/fail status.

The vDDM extracts the data model (metadata) from the database catalog and configures it as an engine for application assistance.

For example, the following SQL statements represent typical versions of Insert, Update, Select, and Delete statements on the aforementioned EMP table depicted in Figure 6-1.

```
Insert into MyDevDB.Emp (Emp_ID, Emp_Name, Addr_ID, Site_ID)
     Values (21, 'David', 834, 921);
Update MyDevDB.Emp Set Emp_Name = 'DavidB' where Emp_ID = 21;
Select Emp_ID, Emp_Name from Emp where Emp_ID = 21
Delete from Emp where Emp_Name = 'DavidB';
```

Note the specific use of column names, tables names, and embedded values. A database engine largely requires this SQL statement form, or it will not recognize the column names, data types, or destinations.

While many database applications support wildly complex SQL statements, they must all follow the same rules. Like the structural model discussed in Chapter 2, SQL statements come in two general flavors: simple and complex.

Exploit the "structured" in Structured Query Language.

The *simple* statement typically accesses a single database table. The vDDM automatically supports simple SQL through the *dbTemplate* class. We can affect a table update with a single macro command to the template with no additional SQL details required. For example:

Simple SQL generally pushes data, while complex SQL generally pulls it.

```
Table=EmpTable|Action=Update|Using=EmpID
```

provides all the information the dbTemplate will need (execute an update on the EmpTable using EmpID, and automatically include all the data already resident in the template).

The *complex* statement usually spans multiple tables, (left, outer, anti-join) merging their results for a consistent outcome. Through a *synonym engine*, the vDDM supports externally-defined, packaged SQL skeletons containing a mixture of keywords, values, and column aliases.

Automation Patterns

Our objective is to give the database exactly what it wants, but to avoid having the hard-coded SQL statements be our starting point. Rather, let's take a few steps back and look at the following patterns in the SQL and the ways we can exploit them:

Pattern 1: We can hold staging data *values* in the same context as column *aliases*.

Pattern 2: We can replace column names with aliases.

Pattern 3: Using the column's descriptive information, we can wrap a staging data value with quotes (for string types), with special functions (such as char() or to_date()) for specific data types, or leave the data value as-is (for numeric types).

Pattern 4: Table names sometimes require prefixes defined at run time (such as a similar table name existing in both a development database instance and a production database instance). A table alias allows us to conform the name to one expected by the database, such as prefix/creator/owner IDs required by engines like DB2 and Teradata.

Pattern 5: We can represent complex SQL statements, functions, and stored-procedure calls in skeleton form, using aliases, by treating them as building-block snippets of reusable SQL.

Now let's examine each of the preceding patterns in context.

Patterns 1 and 2: Staging and Describing Data

A vDDM consumer can execute the following to associate data values with column names. Note that in each case, the consumer only knows of the alias, not the underlying column identifier, as shown previously in Figure 6-5.

```
'###### Setup the initial values in the respective column references:
dbModel.Item("EmpID") = 1001
dbModel.Item("EmpName") = 'David'
dbModel.Item("AddrID") = 4180
dbModel.Item("SiteID") = 2138
```

Each of these statements sets a staging value in the vDDM's column location for the given alias (EMP_ID, EMP_NAME, ADDR_ID, and SITE_ID) and also propagates the same value to every occurrence of the same column name regardless of the table it resides in.

Now that we've set the staging values, let's set up the same SQL statements as in the preceding example, only this time using aliases for everything. This is a *virtual SQL* statement, or *vSQL*:

```
Insert into @Emp (@EmpID, @EmpName, @AddrID, @SiteID)
        Values (@EmpID, @EmpName, @AddrID, @SiteID);
Update @Emp Set @EmpName = @EmpName where @EmpID = @EmpID;
Select @EmpID, @EmpName from Emp where @EmpID = @EmpID
Delete from @Emp where @EmpName = @EmpName;
```

Because the vDDM uses the aliases for a *functional equivalent*, it knows where to substitute a column name or the column's staging value. For example, the vDDM replaces each alias in a *column-name* position with its associated column identifier (@EmpID replaced with EMP_ID). It replaces each alias in a *data-value* position with the *properly formatted equivalent* of the staging data found at the column's location (@EmpName replaced with 'DavidB'). Example conversions follow:

```
Insert into MyDevDB.Emp (Emp_ID, Emp_Name, Addr_ID, Site_ID)
        Values (21, 'David', 834, 921);
Update MyDevDB.Emp Set Emp_Name = 'DavidB' where Emp_ID = 21;
Select Emp_ID, Emp_Name from Emp where Emp_ID = 21
Delete from Emp where Emp_Name = 'DavidB';
```

Patterns 3 and 4: Data Types and Engine

We might have a need to access more than one data source. RDBMS engines have different APIs, but we can transparently overcome these with OLEDB/ODBC drivers. What we cannot transparently overcome are the various subtle extensions from each vendor. Some engines require an instance name as a prefix to each table reference (e.g., DB2© and Teradata©). Some column references might require additional "wrapping" with embedded query functions (e.g., Oracle© and MS SQLServer©).

The vDDM can automatically replace each table-name alias with a properly formatted equivalent (based on connection information and minimum database engine requirements). Inside the vDDM, we can align vendor-specific behaviors (the vDDM is structurally an Adapter after all). We can program the vDDM with API-level details (such as to format a date string) each of which has subtle differences (for example, to_date(), to_char() and so on). The vDDM uses the database engine identified in the original connection string to automatically align the required extensions.

Thus, the application can provide a vSQL skeleton that is consistent and *portable* between databases. This capability has enormous power, especially when jump-starting or restarting a project with the intention of accelerated reuse.

....

Case Study: Shifting Gears

In a large, retail data warehouse project, a desktop application interfaced the user to warehousing rules and reporting functions. The team building the warehouse back-end had not yet decided which database system to use, but the front-end team was under pressure to produce the desktop functionality.

The front-end team installed Oracle on a small, departmental device and began their construction efforts using the vDDM and the vSQL syntax. Two months into the effort, the desktop application was already in multi-user beta testing when the back-end team announced their choice of DB2 (on an IBM mainframe) for the primary application storage. While this was not unexpected, such an announcement could have been devastating in any other context.

The vDDM had the team integrated from server-side Oracle to the mainframe DB2 environment *within a week*, and within another week they could seamlessly and transparently talk to either. While the entire development team ran Oracle on their laptops, they could still build and deploy application functionality for mainframe DB2. The vSQL was 100 percent portable between the two engines. The vDDM was a consistent bridge.

Could we have used stored procedures? Sure. And maintain their synchronization in two separate database engines? I would rather let the vDDM do it all it one place.

 TIP *The chief objective—and most significant challenge—of building transparent data access falls into the same realm as reusable software for applications. From the user's real world, build a rich symbolic bridge across the Cyber Gulf to link the application realm and information realm to its ultimate consumer (the user). The vDDM's synonym engine and the application prototype's interpretation engine are primary examples of this bridge in action.*

....

Pattern 5: Component SQL

Every project, especially on an enterprise scale, has a need to reuse existing SQL in various forms. In many cases, an application developer will cut-and-paste existing SQL statements (as a "template"), tweak them to fit the problem at hand, then deploy them.

Invariably, this practice leads to SQL inconsistency (and thus behavioral bugs) as we must enhance the original template or fix errors. We might fix the original, not knowing that one or more other features used it as a starter template. We'll chase down the errors with each SQL change, and the problems will get worse over time. Burying this problem into stored procedures does just that—buries the problem—it doesn't go away.

Ideally, we need to build our SQL statements dynamically from reusable SQL snippets, or component-SQL. For example, if a SQL *Select* statement is broken into two or more components, such as a main body, a table list, a *where* clause, and perhaps a sub-select clause, we can mix and match components without affecting other areas of the application. If my *Select* statement needs additional filtering in the *where* clause, I simply transpose my *where* clause component for the existing one, and off I go. (More on this in a later section on *Packaged SQL*.)

Implementing the vDDM Adapters

The vDDM derives its power from its ability to do the following:

- Create SQL statements automatically from standard SQL rules

- Shape SQL statements from packaged skeletons

- Snap together fully dynamic SQL syntax in the application layer

You can find examples of each approach in this chapter's project.

In each case, the vDDM will merge application-level information into the SQL statement prior to execution. The dbEngine will also provide general brokerage for totally dynamic (raw) SQL statements, but can manage all others through predefinition or default behavior. Ultimately the dbEngine will receive and process the SQL statements generated at any given level, but we still want to maintain the freedom to bypass the preprocessing or default levels and drive a raw SQL statement directly into the interface. Table 6-1 shows the levels of complexity and their handlers:

Whether abstract or raw SQL, we have complete control.

Table 6-1. Typical SQL Usages and vDDM Handling

PATTERN	COMMAND	HANDLED BY	TYPICAL USAGE
Default SQL	Single-Table, Simple SQL	dbTemplate.cls	Update/Delete/Insert
Predefined Complex SQL	Multi-Table, Packaged SQL Skeleton	Synonym engine	Select/Update/Insert
Dynamic Complex	Any SQL Statement	dbEngine.cls	Select

The following sections discuss these key vDDM Adapters:

- dbEngine

- dbBroker

- dbData

- dbInterpreter

- dbTemplate

The dbEngine Adapter

The dbEngine is an Adapter to the Microsoft ActiveX Data Objects (ADO) *Connection* object (and thus the window to an ODBC/OLEDB provider). It will connect to a schema on a designated database engine/platform and then use this connection as the basis for all following operations. The dbEngine effectively wraps the dbBroker and dbData as resources on the dbEngine's Connection.

The dbInterpreter (discussed later in this section) uses the dbEngine to manufacture the vDDM's data model—including all dbTemplates—from the visible schema/catalog information. The vDDM can easily manufacture multiple dbEngines and point them to different database connections. This includes different database engines as well; a connection to Oracle, SQLServer, and DB2 could all reside simultaneously within the same run time, each with its own dbEngine wrapper. We can manage dedicated connections, connectionless, or connection-on-demand through the dbEngine.

The dbBroker Adapter

The dbBroker is an Adapter to the ADO *Command* object. Consumers can manufacture multiple brokers sharing the same dbEngine connection. If using multiple dbEngines, the consumer need only request a dbBroker from the appropriate dbEngine. The dbBroker can automatically provide connection pooling and management because it's constantly in contact with its dbEngine.

If a dbEngine has multiple connections to the same database, the consumer can specify which connection to use. For example, transactional processing often requires read and write operations to finish a transactional update. Unfortunately, some engines do not support both activities with the same connection. We can deploy brokers for these multiple purposes for several connections to one database or to multiple databases.

The dbBroker executes, manages, and closes SQL commands. Its return value is a dbData object (next).

The dbData Adapter

The dbData is an Adapter to the ADO *RecordSet* object. The dbData exposes general and Iterator interface *patterns (Item, Action, DataPresent, MoveFirst, MoveNext,* and *More).* It uses Item(Key) where the "Key" is the name of a retrieved database column.

  The dbData performs best in a read-only role, deferring outbound data behavior to the dbTemplate (later). Thus, consumers have a more controllable, predictable, and flexible interface than driving everything only through dbData.

  The dbData adapter is directly linked to the vDDM's synonym engine, so our calling consumer can use @EmpID or EMP_ID interchangeably and the dbData will know how to translate the column reference in context of its RecordSet results. This allows us to use aliasing even in the query itself (e.g., select emp_name ename from emp) for maximum flexibility.

dbData can automatically and transparently translate aliases to their actual column-name equivalents.

The dbInterpreter

Once the dbEngine connects, it opens visibility to one or more application database tables in a catalog/schema. The dbInterpreter pulls the visible application schema into memory, parsing its information into elemental parts. It then reconstructs the complete application data model in "virtual" space.

  The dbInterpreter will manufacture one dbTemplate (next) for each application table represented in the schema. It will then load each dbTemplate with the column references found on the table. It uses Observers to connect like-named columns between tables as synonyms. Lastly, it manufactures cross-reference collections so consumers can post information to any database "column" in the schema, or gain access to a dbTemplate for table-level I/O.

Interpreters are key to organizing and activating metadata, in this case, the structural database catalog information.

The dbTemplate Class

At its basic level, we can describe any data model with tables and columns. The dbTemplate class is designed to represent—in memory—the attributes and required operations for a single database entity, or table, including columns within the table and their descriptions. The table will have a Name, then each column will have an associated Name, Type, Primary/Foreign Key descriptor, Nullable, Size (if a string or numeric), and other information available about the column. Each column also has a placeholder for data.

  Since we use SQL terms to standardize each element, the vDDM has many degrees of freedom in implementing the dbTemplate to automate almost all standard database operations, and certainly any operation required by an application-level consumer.

For instance, let's say we have a table named EMP with the columns EMP_NAME (String), EMP_ID (Numeric), and EMP_START_DATE (Date). Let's also say we post their respective staging values as "David", "3185", and "11/17/2001". (These values appear in bold text in the following example.) The dbTemplate now has enough information to automatically manufacture valid SQL statements, as shown here:

```
Update EMP set EMP_NAME = 'David', EMP_ID = 3185,
    EMP_START_DATE = to_date('MM/DD/YYYY','11/17/2001') where EMP_ID = 3185;
Insert Into EMP (EMP_NAME, EMP_ID, EMP_STR_DATE) Values
            ( 'David', 3185, to_date('MM/DD/YYYY','11/17/2001'));
Delete from EMP where EMP_ID = 3185;
Select EMP_ID, EMP_NAME, EMP_START_DATE from EMP where EMP_ID = 3185;
```

The vDDM has all the metadata required to automate many of the mundane and breakage-prone aspects of SQL generation and execution.

In each case, we are able to correctly "cast" the column staging content because we already know the data type (strings wrapped with quotes, numerics left "as is," date value properly formatted, etc.). This example wraps the Date for Oracle, but only because the connection designates Oracle. If the dbEngine designates another product, we could just as easily "sense" this and automatically factor it in. The vDDM and its subclasses are all Adapters, and can wrap any database-specific behavior and abstract it from our immediate view. Anytime we find a new database extension, or want to integrate a new database entirely, we can account for its subtleties under the covers and the vDDM will handle all the details without the application's knowledge or regular intervention.

This strategy allows us to abstract our SQL statements into vSQL, making them portable across many databases and information sources without changes. The application metadata stabilizes quickly and we remove dependency of the software on database model specifics and the subtle differences between engines.

Interpreter Mechanics

The first objective of the interpreter is to "sense" the data model information from the external environment (e.g., database catalog, ERWin models, or just flat text descriptions etc.), then systematically download and configure the remainder of the model.

The dbInterpreter class will need the two following basic types of information with two additional options:

- Names of the tables

- Names *and* descriptions of the columns within those tables

- (Optional) constraint relationships (primary/foreign key) definitions.

- (Optional) any designated synonyms, pseudonyms, or surrogates to include (or disconnect) while manufacturing the model. (We can always designate more later.)

Table Names

The vDDM defaults to all tables visible to the logon connection. If the total table count is large, or if the application only needs a subset of the schema, the vDDM can use a specific subset of the table names. This is especially helpful for large and complex data models where the application only needs a small fraction of the whole. If we have the luxury of modeling our own data, we can build patterns into the table names as informational cues, such as prefixes or suffixes, that the dbInterpreter can easily key on. Some database engines support additional table description or attribute information we can leverage toward this purpose. Whatever the additional filters, get them into metadata.

The vDDM ultimately needs a list of table names to expose within the framework, in use for the duration of the run-time session. Of course, we could set up refresh capabilities, to get a "new" definition without closing and re-opening the program. Such a feature usually only has benefits during development, so take care before burning this feature into the production version.

Now that we have all the table names in our hands, it's time to manufacture some objects dedicated to managing a table in a general sense. This is the dbTemplate object. The dbInterpreter will manufacture one dbTemplate object per table name. This dedicates the object to the table and allows the vDDM to manipulate the objects as though they are associated with one, and only one, table.

The multidimensional TurboCollection class is a key foundation to manufacturing virtual relationships and automatic behaviors between tables.

We'll organize all the dbTemplates into a master structure for fast access, in this case the TurboCollection, optimized into a binary tree, called dbModel. By using a binary tree, every column and table reference is practically at our fingertips.

Columns are elemental windows to the actual data.

Column Names

After organizing dbTemplates, we add column names. Each dbTemplate will receive a full compliment of the column names associated with its designated table, and also acquire the additional metadata per column, such as data type, is-null, any engine-specific formatting information, and the column's size and/or precision. Of course, the ParmNode already supports this information (and more), so we can store the column metadata as ParmNodes on a TurboCollection inside the dbTemplate. Once acquired, the dbTemplate converts its TurboCollection to a binary tree for fast run-time access.

Data Model Visibility

How does the dbEngine "sense" the data model? Two means exist. The first alternative is to use the model "as designed" inside a tool (e.g., ERWin©, Oracle Designer 2000©, or Microsoft VISIO EE/VEA©). These tools typically burst execution-ready SQL statements that can create the required database structures ("create scripts"). Because they produce standard SQL, the dbInterpreter can read it as text, then parse it for table, column, and relationship distinctions. This is a "silo" approach but can be effective in very large or complex environments requiring strict change control.

When reading "create scripts", we still can't activate them if the scripts have not been applied to the database.

The second alternative is to access the RDBMS's run-time system tables and catalogs to glean information about the table names, their columns, and relationships. The ADO function *OpenSchema* works for most ODBC/OLEDB sources. For those it does not, we will have to write a SQL statement to access the system catalog tables. This means perform a raw connection and issue a canned SQL statement directly against the catalog "system" tables for what we want.

We only have to access the catalog once at startup, but we could extract it "on demand" multiple times to enable iterative development.

The IBM DB2© database is a typical example of this requirement. All ADO will need is the connection string, and DB2 will need the name of the database to access. Recall that "startup" DBSPEC.txt file I mentioned for storing our database connect string? (See "The dbEngine Adapter" section, earlier in this chapter.) For DB2 we need some additional information—the name of the database, which we'll tag as DBNAME and the following SQL string stored in an INI file (I've applied bold text to the DBNAME for clarity):

See how we can also "alias" the results of the DB2 query to match the OpenSchema return fields, so the results are transparent to the vDDM interpreter.

```
DBNAME=DBHPRQ1
DBVendor=DB2
CONNECT=DriverName;Pwd=XY;UID=WX
DB2METASQL=SELECT COLS.TBCREATOR, COLS.TBNAME, COLS.NAME, COLS.COLNO,
        COLS.COLTYPE, COLS.LENGTH, COLS.SCALE, Cols.NULLS FROM
    SYSIBM.SYSCOLUMNS COLS, SYSIBM.SYSTABLES TABS WHERE
    TABS.DBNAME = '@DBNAME' AND (TABS.CREATOR = COLS.TBCREATOR AND
    TABS.NAME = COLS.TBNAME) ORDER BY COLS.TBNAME, COLS.COLNO
```

The vDDM will simply replace '@DBNAME' with its tag/value equivalent in the startup script. Each time the vDDM needs to connect to another instance of DB2, just change DBNAME in the startup script. The rest is transparent for all DB2 connections.

Once we've wrested this information from DB2, it's a totally transparent resource.

Note that we should not embed the DBNAME value in the actual SQL skeleton because the DBNAME is more volatile than the skeleton itself. An application may have many instances of a database, one for development, Q/A, training, production, and so on. All will use the same SQL skeleton but different DBNAMES. We could even put the different DBNAMES into a separate file for loading into a drop-down box for access at user login time. Keep it flexible.

The vDDM can use the following notations to determine easily which DBNAMEs are valid, which one is the default, and display them for user selection on a login screen:

```
DBNAME=MNPPRD1
DBNAME=MNPPRT2
DBNAME=MNPPRP1 (Default)
```

We can instantly and transparently connect to and exchange with multiple database instances, versions, even separate engines without modifying vSQL or program code.

This approach is flexible, simple, maintainable, and increases the longevity of the binary software. The executable will not require rebuild for a new database instance, only for a new vendor product. Using this file, we can add as many database instances as required (testing, training, user acceptance, etc.). If the data architects choose to build a new database instance for any reason, this startup file can make it visible simply by adding a new entry.

This approach moves "volatile" issues to the periphery (such as data model changes and SQL generation to accommodate them) into external text parameter files, and moves static, solid functionality into the core. This example has another stage of that practice, in moving "more volatile" features (DBNAME) away from "less volatile" features (the SQL skeleton using it!).

We'll only integrate a database once, then access it thereafter (quickly gaining traction on information integration).

I provided this example for DB2 specifically because *some* environments don't seamlessly integrate DB2 with the MSADO components, specifically with the ADO *OpenSchema* function. Regular queries, however, are generally supported, so this DB2 query will operate like any other ODBC/OLEDB call.

Static Scripts versus Live Access

We have two ways to supply catalog metadata to the dbInterpreter: as a static script of create-statements or by providing "live" access to the catalogs. A static script assumes the vDDM will always have a script to work from and that a modeling tool will always reflect any changes. A static script also provides faster integration with a new database environment and is more portable than live access.

Live access assumes that the vDDM will always dynamically download the schema information from the online catalog and that the physical model actually exists in the database (not always true at the start of the project). Live access is far better for more mature applications, maintenance, and ongoing enhancement.

I like the flexibility of both methods. Plan to use either one, but keep your options open. For simplicity however, the vDDM model provided with this chapter's project exercises only exposes the live access option—the online catalog version.

Before diving deeper, let's talk about a few items we can negotiate with our data architects to make the entire development process smoother and the schema itself more elegant and robust.

Surrogate Keys

It is a best practice in any data model to provide 10-digit (or more) *binary* unique identifiers (surrogate binary keys) as the primary referential key in each table. Such identifiers make our model crisper, cleaner and more agile. A 10-digit binary key takes up (typically) between 4 and 8 bytes of storage, and can be manipulated and compared/sorted/indexed faster than its textual equivalent. The use of text-based keys is fine for searching in a transactional system, but not for referential integrity. To support fully robust Create, Read, Update, and Delete features of all application entities, the surrogate binary key is a critical element. It will pay for itself many times over at every level of the solution, not just the database level. The surrogate key is so important because it allows us to interconnect our tables with crisp relational boundaries that do not depend on the volatility of the application data itself.

We need a way to uniquely identify information separately from its application-level information.

A case in point, I have a very popular financial software package on my desktop. One day I found that I'd fat-fingered the name of a Payee in the online check-writer. If the misnomer were only visible to me, I wouldn't care. But the online payee will see their name misspelled each time they receive payment from me. Could I change the name to reflect the real value? No, the package uses the textual name as the primary key, and it's connected to lots of other embedded stuff as the foreign key. To change the value would disconnect it as the parent of other table entries. If the accounting package had standardized on surrogate binary keys, this would not be an issue. The Payee name would simply be a reportable display value, not the value used for referential connectivity.

Now, are binary surrogate keys *required* for the vDDM? No, in fact the vDDM engine is just as robust without them. The physical application data model is a different story, it will be more robust *with them*. The vDDM engine only enforces what it finds in the catalogs. My suggestion here is to provide your *application* with the freedom to treat all of its application information as "simple attributes" to the physical model, not for referential connectivity in the logical model.

The vDDM is flexible either way for connectivity to legacy/core data models without constraint. Be aware, however, that as we move forward, the surrogate key is a best practice that will increase our application's resilience and our physical model's overall flexibility.

So, if you are in the middle of heated negotiation with your data modeling crew, the things you should lobby for the hardest are the following:

- Use binary surrogate keys as primary unique identifiers and keys

- Use globally-unique names for all columns, allowing primary and foreign keys to "naturally" intersect wherever they are found. This is the simplest, most flexible, and elegant means to help the application logic conform to referential integrity rules.

- *Never* enforce referential integrity with the application logic. Always use database-level integrity and require the application (through the vDDM) to conform.

When surrogate binary keys uniquely identify every row in the data model, we have more freedom to change application-level information without fear of referential disconnection.

We should be able to list all tables and columns on a page and not see any repeating values in the column names (apart from key relationships). Barring this, a fallback option is to uniquely identify all the columns ourselves with fully qualified identifiers, using the table name, the column name, and, in some cases, the actual database name. This will ultimately prove to be an inflexible and cumbersome fallback, so try to avoid it from the beginning.

Spend your energy lobbying for these three features to be consistent and pervasive within the model, or at least your domain of the model. We'll find that most data modelers/architects are more than happy to accommodate these requests, and many will impose them on us. Data modeling tools automatically enforce it. Data architects are often swamped with a host of special requests from application designers, so if we limit ours to these we'll all be happier for it!

These practices serve to simplify the primary vDDM mapping structures, so in the long run they will make our lives easier.

The vDDM creates a synergy between data modelers and object modelers that otherwise can be a very tense relationship.

Mapping Structures

Within the vDDM are two master mapping structures, one of the column names dbColumns and one of the table names dbModel. For fast access, the vDDM converts both of these collections to binary tree structures. The dbColumns collection is hidden from the vDDM interface behind the dbModel shown in Figure 6-6, so that any reference to *Item* on the dbModel automatically cascades to the dbColumn.

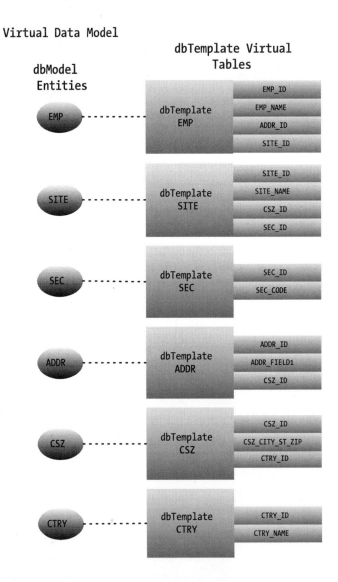

Figure 6-6. Table alias mapping structures

The dbColumns collection contains a unique alias synonym for each *column name*. Thus, placing information into an alias affects all columns of the same name. So even if several tables have the same column name (sharing of primary and foreign keys), only one alias will represent them.

What I've just described is a model that automatically and dynamically supports our model's referential integrity without any further work from the application. Let's say the application needs to insert a new EMP record plus relational information in another table (such as ADDR). The ADDR table needs an EMP_ID, but the parent EMP record and its values don't exist yet. When creating the new EMP record, we must assign a new EMP_ID prior to insertion. This action automatically cascades the new EMP_ID value to the ADDR table (see Figure 6-7).

Virtual Data Model

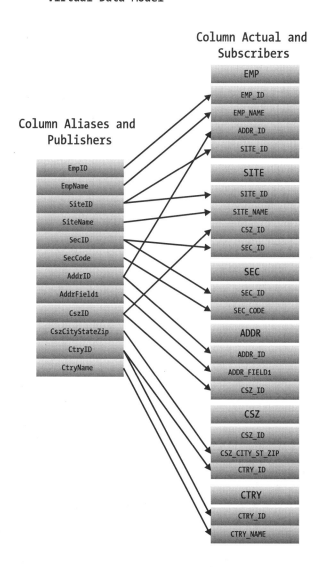

Figure 6-7. Column alias relationships

ADDR is then ready for insertion and is automatically tied to the just-inserted EMP row. Each time we insert a new record, its identifier is added to the dbModel and cascaded to the proper location. We can effortlessly create and manage table information. This is especially handy when navigating screens that follow a data hierarchy (typical), because the vDDM automatically enforces and publishes new information to its child tables as we generate the information.

We've achieved automatic, transparent, and reliable referential integrity, based on the data model, and we've only scratched the surface!

Flexibility

Let's say we have a database instance with a hundred tables, each with delicately interwoven relationships for database integrity. In a typical implementation, even minor changes to the database structure could initiate a full-scale impact review for the software. Not so for the vDDM, it automatically senses the changes at the next run-time session. I've seen wholesale changes of database entities, relationships, and additions of new tables and columns all within a matter of weeks, sometimes even days. Most of the time, this kind of rapid change is devastating on the momentum of the application development effort.

The vDDM exists with the expectation of change on each execution.

With the vDDM however, the software enjoys a loose, not tight coupling to the data model. The application metadata is also more malleable and flexible to change. In fact, the addition of whole tables and columns in the data model has *zero impact* when first initiated. We then have time to exploit the new tables and columns systematically, instead of in a crisis.

The vDDM is a firm, reliable resource with high longevity. It wraps itself around changes in the data architecture, so application-level changes won't affect it. When we have to change vDDM software, we'll largely address technical database extensions or differences rather than data modeling issues.

Our alternative is to let the database access framework off the leash and have a hodge-podge of different implementations, approaches, and methods (bound to the styles and whims of individual developers) that must undergo meticulous review with each database change.

With the vDDM, we abstract the data model so that we can activate it with metadata-driven logic. Data model changes will now only affect the metadata, not the program code itself.

Packaged SQL

Every application has a need for custom, complex SQL statements. Typical examples include joining multiple tables on specific criteria and application-derived parameters, including those provided by the user.

We'll have a deployed executable that never requires a rebuild after a structural change to the database.

 CROSS-REFERENCE *This subject was foreshadowed earlier in this chapter under Automation Patterns,* Pattern 5, Component SQL.

Invariably, the application developer will finish a carefully crafted SQL query for one application area, only to require the same query, with subtle differences, in another application area (stored procedures also have this weakness).

Maintaining two (or more) is difficult. What if a maintenance programmer changes one without the awareness that the change should be included in the other? We need a way to define SQL macros and snap them together dynamically. This requires another level of abstraction logic, that of assigning synonyms to logical groupings of synonyms. Each logical grouping is a snippet, and several snippets form the entire statement. Consider the following examples in Table 6-2.

Table 6-2. Component vSQL

SYNONYM TAG	SQL SNIPPET
EmpWhereID	@EmpID = @EmpID
EmpWhereName	@EmpName = @EmpName
EmpWhereAll	@EmpID = @EmpID and @EmpName = @EmpName
EmpAddrJoin	@Emp.@AddrID = @Addr.@AddrID
EmpAddrSiteJoin	@Emp.@AddrID = @Addr.@AddrID and @Emp.@SiteID = @Site.@SiteID

We can assemble macros of vSQL statements using their macro package tags (component synonym in bold):

```
SQL:Select * from @Emp, @Addr, @Site where @EmpWhereID
```

yielding the result:

```
SQL:Select * from @Emp, @Addr, @Site where @EmpID = @EmpID
```

Ultimately being converted to the following:

```
Select * from Emp, Addr, Site where EMP_ID = 8154
```

Often, the SQL join criteria (*where* clause) is the most significant variable. However, some SQL statements have sticky details inside the *Select* clause. Consider that the DB2 *timestmp* (timestamp) type is actually 27 text characters representing date, time, and microseconds, and is used by DB2 for unique record identification. Consider also that, without any defined control of its representation, the Microsoft ADO model will pull the timestmp into the RecordSet and *truncate* the microsecond information, which for the timestmp is the most critical and significant. The only way to pass it through the ADO truncation is to convert it to character with a char() function in the SQL statement. If in the package macro we include another notation such as:

```
EmpTmstmp    char(@EmpID)
```

We can then use the following:

```
Select @EmpTmStmp from @Emp
```

Then the vDDM will first resolve it to:

```
Select char(@EmpID) from @Emp
```

And finally resolve it to:

```
Select char(Emp_ID) from Emp
```

We can snap together individual macros and synonyms as pseudo-components, including the ability to use a single synonym for a complete (and sometimes very complex) statement. For example, at the statement level we can use:

```
Set $myContainer.Load = SQL:@EmpSelect
```

where @EmpSelect has been previously defined as:

```
Select * from @EMP
```

What if we later change the EMP table, adding a special include/exclude flag for use everywhere we access the EMP table? Rather than hunt down every EMP table access, we simply change the value of @EmpSelect and the change applies globally and automatically on the next execution.

Synonyms provide a single point of maintenance for complex vSQL application-wide.

The primary benefit is the reuse of vSQL logic in building blocks rather than performing a cut/paste of existing vSQL to make a new skeleton or statement. With packaged vSQL, we simply assemble the existing parts we need through predefined synonyms, then flesh out the remainder with specific vSQL syntax, more synonyms, or some combination thereof.

Because vSQL ultimately wraps and configures an existing SQL skeleton, no limit exists for the structure of the skeleton itself, including sub-selects, complex joins, and other SQL capabilities.

This framework gives us another level of power over disparate data, to transparently integrate it, simplifying our application levels.

Leashing the Power of Dynamic Integration

The reuse factor of vSQL statements rises, and we experience reuse within yet another language: Structured Query Language.

Can developers use this synonym/text strategy for other dynamic languages, such as HTML, XML, or Java? Of course, and many industry leaders have done so (although their algorithms and methods are proprietary). Whether at a departmental level or full scale product release, the capability of snapping together binary or textual parts into interpreter-friendly streams is extremely powerful.

This strategy is a quantum leap in competitive advantage. While other shops are programming the old-fashioned way with application-centric models, vSQL teams will arrive with the pre-integrated parts in hand, ready for assembly and deployment.

....

Case Study: Component Business Capabilities

What's that? You told us Oracle© over the phone but you really meant Teradata©? No problem.

One direct marketing firm is a leader in loyalty management (frequent flier, frequent diner, frequent hotel stay, and so on). Each client enjoys a completely customized loyalty management system, and has no idea that under the covers, each one is running the same basic system (the same component parts) assembled to appear customized. The reuse factor in this environment is extremely high.

The firm can acquire and deploy new client systems with breathtaking speed, far outclassing their competitors with feature strength, consistency, reliability, and response to changing business needs. None of their programmers are overworked, and their operations staff can administer all the loyalty campaigns in the same way, across all clients. The back-ends of every program run exactly the same. The customizations enter the picture at run time, through interpreted metadata.

....

vSQL Configuration Management

The vDDM needs a quick way to access and load packaged vSQL at run time. It also requires strict version control on the vSQL itself because it's so tightly mated to the application metadata using it. Some developers like to store vSQL snippets in a database, where the snippet's synonym is the key and the snippet is just a string of text. Others like to use a simple text file to list all synonyms and snippets as tag=value pairs and pull them all into memory at run time.

The text file method is better for configuration management, and whatever benefits we might realize from putting them into a database are eclipsed by this reality: we need strong version control and audit/rollback of vSQL just like source code. In an application-centric model, engineering this in a database context (whether by using specific tables or stored procedures) is simply too much overhead to be worthwhile.

Here is a list of the factors involved in using text files and database storage:

Version control: Most changes to vSQL are in context with application scripts, and both must be modified, tested, and then applied simultaneously. This is very difficult to accomplish if the vSQL is stored in a database table, or even through stored procedures.

Localization: Text files will be stored on a server, invariably in ASCII format, while database storage has character formats subject to the host platform. One production implementation of vSQL was on a mainframe using DB2, limiting the available character set to IBM's EBCDIC. We quickly restructured the implementation to use server-side flat text—it simply removed one layer of variability.

Changes applied by accident, like accidental behavior breakage, should be visible only to the developer, and nobody else.

Auditability: In version control we can roll back changes or throw away bad software simply by reverting to a prior version. What if one version includes several vSQL changes along with some application script changes? How will we audit this—to roll it back, correct it so it really works, or avoid irrecoverably destroying our working vSQL? Database storage, including stored procedures, make this aspect problematic.

Testing: Text file storage means a developer can get a local copy (just like application instructions) and test them together in context before applying them (by checking them in to the master source control). If using a database, we would actually need a separate database instance for each developer so they would not step on each other.

When moving rapidly to inject change and meet user needs, we need a foolproof way to apply changes that keep us moving forward, not stumbling on each other or accidentally applying changes out of context to other supporting software elements. vSQL version control has requirements identical to source code control. We can check out the vSQL text file with other metadata scripts, make changes alongside other metadata changes, and check them all in at once. We won't have to migrate changes from multiple places, like stored procedures. Everything will be available and synchronized at the next run time execution. The vSQL file content is consistent and won't magically change when moved from one storage platform to another. As metadata, vSQL text files will be co-hosted with the binary executable, or at least on the same networked file system, so the solution is self-contained.

Additionally, we can store feature-centric vSQL in separate files, then identify these files in a common Startup file. This allows us to include or exclude files of vSQL snippets without stepping on other features. Doing so also provides more portability for a feature, keeping SQL logic and application feature logic in sync without keeping all vSQL in a common, unwieldy file (one project had over 800 vSQL entries across the entire application!). (More detail on vSQL in this chapter's project exercise.)

NOTE *The vDDM loads vSQL as either a standalone statement or as another file containing more vSQL statements. Thus we can unit-test vSQL by placing feature-centric portions into their own files.*

Maintenance support and remote fixes are easier to execute. We can make a fix and ship it to the user in a single zip-file transmission. The fix is applied by the administrator with a single *unzip* or file copy.

Like a database entry, vSQL is retrieved at run time on demand. However, vSQL in a flat file can be retrieved with less overhead and simpler run-time maintenance.

Wrapping the Engine Itself

The vDDM is effectively the rich-featured wrapper for our database engine, not just the physical data model. Even though our company or shop may have "standardized" or even institutionalized on a given database engine product, things change. We typically don't see customers swapping out databases, but we do see them acquiring different ones for specific uses. Multiple database vendors are especially common in large enterprises.

Troubleshooters can beta-test and deploy surgical fixes from text files. This yields simplicity to administration that will become legend for you and your team.

We can stage, integrate, and deploy upgrades to components (like ODBC/OLEDB drivers for another database) with more systematic and deliberate Q/A processes than the volatile application features. If we have a CIO or other technical leader, or even a business leader, who assumes we can switch whole database engines to a different one with no impact whatsoever, there is a disconnect in their understanding.

Educate others.

However, don't be fooled. That same CIO will pay for porting the system to a different database engine. What they won't like paying for is porting it *again* to the *same* database engine, even if it's on a different operating system. They know the port should only occur once, regardless of the source and target platforms.

Get educated.

With the vDDM, once we work out the integration issues for one database engine product, such as DB2, SQLServer, or Oracle, we're done for that engine. Everything past that is just vSQL programming.

vSQL built for DB2 will behave identically for Oracle (or any other product), because the vDDM will broker similarities and hide differences.

The vDDM facilitates exchange of database information in the context of the target engine's ODBC/OLEDB and persistence requirements. If we nail these issues down along with any other engine-specific extensions, we'll never have to re-integrate the engine again. Our only enemy will be product upgrades, but we can handle them outside of application deployment. Thus, we migrate the expert knowledge of our best SQL programmers into vSQL and database engine expert knowledge into the vDDM and its SQL script generator.

One of the more robust aspects of this framework is its ability to mature and become stable very quickly within our development environment. Persistence errors, constraint violations, and other pesky problems sift out early because we have automatic enforcement and detection within the vDDM.

Additionally, the column-level metadata is often associated with actual user-level screen controls. This means we can use the column's information (such as its data type, its size, and whether it is required—not null) and other important points to control our screen behavior. For example, we can detect the "Nullable=False" status to place an asterisk (*) next to each screen-level "required" field. We can set a Text Box *MaxLength* property to the width of its target data field (*Itemsize*), etc.

Now we have some real data power, and if any aspect of a column should change, our program is automatically aware.

Refining Data-Awareness

Consider the two following definitions of *data awareness*; the first is general and the second is the vDDM explanation:

Data awareness (general): Capability of a *specific* component to link to and be interoperable with our favorite database engine. *Specific* means: grid control, drop-down control, menu control, etc. A team has to buy one or more components and only acquire the capability for the individual controls, not the application as a whole.

Data awareness (vDDM): Capability of a *single* component (vDDM) to broker data-aware metadata to *any* control or component inside a product or application framework. The vDDM provides information as to the description of data plus a means to interchange data with *any* target database engine (and automatically conforms to database changes).

"Data aware" components claim to link directly into our external data sources and automatically handle information exchange. Personally speaking, after long weekends integrating "cool" data-aware components, and receiving marginal (if any) support from the vendors in our efforts, our team had a weary discussion on the viability of data awareness. We were spending more time tweaking and tuning the data aware components just so they would work than we were customizing them to meet application requirements. No sooner would we migrate a carefully integrated data-aware component into Quality Assurance than the screen would load, the grids and other components would appear, and they would all be empty. No explanations, no errors, and we were completely blind as to the true source of the problem, because it was failing inside the data aware component.

Many vendors shorten their time to market and deliver unstable or brittle data aware components. The vDDM, however, breaks "data awareness" out of the specific third-party domain and extends it to all of our controls, not just those we purchased with a "data aware" feature. Therefore, subtle nuances of a database environment are under our control, in one place. No more embarrassing spontaneous combustion of that cool data-aware component we just installed.

"Data aware" can turn into "better beware."

Let's examine the pitfalls and priorities of exporting application logic versus centralizing it.

The container discussed in Chapter 4 and the vDDM create a powerful two-pronged weapon in ultimately mastering information and its flexible, multivariant representations.

Exporting Application Logic

Many database engines allow us to build specific application-centric logic and install it directly into the database engine, in the form of stored procedures. This tactic, while useful in maintaining control in a single place and providing shortcuts at the application level, also poses a danger that is not so obvious.

Stored Procedures

Stored procedures are optimum for binding high-speed, multi-stage input operations into a single transaction, but don't serve well for general application and reporting logic.

It boils down to revenue stream, and you're standing in it.

Using stored procedures binds our application to a specific database engine product (and sometimes a specific version of a database engine). If we ever want to port to another database engine, we must consider porting the stored procedures. We'll have to take one engine's specific flavors and syntax and carefully convert them and test them under another syntax. In some development shops, the magnitude and scope of such an effort totally dwarfs any benefit in the migration/porting itself. Of course, the database vendor *knows* that. They have every incentive to find ways of keeping us tied to their product (more licenses, renewals, support, etc.).

Integrity Considerations

All that aside, after porting data models across multiple database engines, I know that I may want stored procedures to enforce integrity for the sake of batch import, complex transaction, date/time stamping, or other non-application needs. But I really want to avoid stored procedures to enforce desktop application integrity. It creates too many go-betweens for the application's error recovery, frustrates the user, and adds to our maintenance headaches.

 NOTE *Referential integrity is the domain of database constraints. Application data integrity, especially the virtual connectivity available within the vDDM, should not be exported. It requires a nimble, memory-resident model to provide a robust user experience.*

The vDDM's role is to assist the application in the activity of database information exchange. The information itself rides on metadata that defines and wraps it. The vDDM energizes and automates the metadata, providing more practical power to the application than the database engine alone.

Impact Review

When we migrate application logic into the database, or keep it anywhere but the application itself, we incur the penalty of impact review each time the application or database model requires a change. When application-centric models decentralize database access, a number of false themes arise and start to pervade the framework. These themes include the following:

- Installing Save or Load methods on class interfaces, with the assumption that invoking the Save method will magically *persist* or *populate* the object's internal data according to embedded application-specific code

- Application logic leaking from class to class as they attempt to share (often delicately so) the referential relationships required by the database model

- Tremors in the class model with each change in database definition— because an object *absolutely requires* binary reconstruction, regardless of the central, peripheral, or marginal importance of the database definition change. Thus, any change in the database model can initiate a full application impact review.

None of these issues arise when using the Virtual Dynamic Data Model. The vDDM will provide flexibility and freedom to an entire framework, as a resource for both architectural or application-level support. The vDDM covers persistence logic so other objects don't have to embed and manage it on their own.

Apart from plug-and-play database connectivity capabilities, the vDDM has the added power of exposing multiple database engines and adapting their various extensions. If the application scripts consistently use vSQL as their SQL standard, the vDDM will translate it and use it correctly and consistently for all integrated database engines. Thus, the application developer can build features against one database engine, test them on another, and deploy them on yet another with *no vSQL impact*.

We must eliminate embedded SQL logic (especially raw SQL statements) directly in the compiled software. Whether SQL is bound to a database definition or to the *expectation* of a definition, embedded SQL logic dooms a programmer to reconstruct binary database logic with each change in user application requirements *and* each change in database definitions. Without the vDDM, moving toward a dynamic application prototype like the one discussed in Chapter 4 would be impossible.

We cannot, on one hand, abstract some instructions (application behavior) while embedding others (SQL). We must abstract it all.

The vDDM assumes first that all data models are application-centric, but that the brokerage services for accessing the model are not. It provides a resilient, reusable brokerage without any embedded knowledge of the data model or its intended purpose.

Project 6—Data Integration

This project will deal with a number of advanced topics of interpreted subroutine definition and execution, complex variable initialization, control, assignment and iteration, run-time configuration parameters, and database management. It builds on the projects that came before it. The Project6—Frameworks—Data Model/ProjectSix file contains the necessary modules.

In the VB6 project version you'll find separate DLL components for the vDDM and vTools. The .NET version, however, combines the vDDM and vTools together into a single DLL. The txtTerp class and cntAdapter class are a subset of the vMach^2 framework.

NOTE *Set a breakpoint on the* FactoryInit() *function call in Main(). When starting up the vDDM, it collects a wide array of information points (in StartupInit()). You'll see this information appear in the Output/Immediate window, and the output is different between the VB6 and .NET versions.*

Some vDDM and interpreter operations might fly past without appropriate breakpoints. You can place a breakpoint on the glbMain.DebugOut function call to throttle this output. The vDDM always reports running debug information to its calling consumer through glbMain (another example of globalized messaging, but enough to fill another book!). Thus any local or embedded messages will arrive through this gateway.

Perform a walk-through of the software managing and executing the interpretation. It's simple, effective, and easy to extend. When using a pattern-based approach, we avoid over-coding any given part because we're not concerned about parsing every character or token, only breaking them apart and dispatching them as early as possible to a downstream component or Adapter.

The Interpreter only exists to evaluate and dispatch work as a "broker." It's not really focused on interpretation for its own sake. In fact, the objective of the Interpreter is to limit the total time spent on evaluating a given statement. The time spent between receiving the statement and dispatching it must be *very* short.

At a hardware level, a CPU receives machine instructions and performs a fetch, decode, execute cycle on each software statement. At the metadata level, the Interpreter performs the fetch and decode, then dispatches the action and parameters to the designated entity in the statement. Thus, there is no functional difference between the software interpreter and CPU, except that the CPU uses precompiled instructions from a binary source while we are using dynamic instructions from a textual source.

The abstraction capabilities of the Interpreter are another primary advantage, because both simple and complex variables can serve as facades or Adapters to highly complex interfaces. The Interpreter has the ability to simplify and dynamically expose these interfaces for higher availability and accessibility to consumers. One component could ultimately represent a complete data warehouse while other components represent complete data marts used by the warehouse as a source. A simple assignment in script such as `Warehouse.Item = Mart.Item` could launch the entire transfer process, with the Warehouse and Mart components covering all the necessary bases for the information exchange. Another likely syntax is:

```
ReturnVal = Mart.Action ("Load" "March 2001",  Warehouse)
```

Where the Mart component internalizes the Warehouse component and both go into deep information exchange at the appropriate implementation level.

The primary objective is to abstract and interpret components at a much higher level than their software equivalents. As each component matures, its interface remains stable and thus available for use by new components, and is a reliable resource for existing components. The overall software capability will increase with more accelerated reuse at every stage.

How will this affect our deployments, managing our people, computing resources, and other aspects supporting the development effort? Will we require process transformation, training, or technology infusion? All of the above and much more, but the result will be an answer to the industry's cry for agility, and the competitive edge to attain success and accelerate our reuse in every area of application deployment technology.

Rapid application delivery.

Iterators and Container Patterns

Database and file I/O rests on the ability to access multiple physical instances of information (rows, records, or lines, etc). As such, Iterator patterns are pervasive in software development, largely to support I/O activity. They appear primarily in input/output operations to drive file and database information exchange. Anytime software performs a Select statement in Structured Query Language, it initiates the possibility of returning more than one row (or record) of information. With multiple rows, software must navigate through them (browse) or input them one (or more) at a time into a processing stream. Either way, software will *iterate* inside a loop of control, where the loop terminus will be the detection of the last row of information.

Pseudocode for this activity follows:

```
Access Multiple Information Rows
Set Browse Reference to First Row
Do
    Access Current Row
Move Browse Reference to Next Row
Loop While Not Last Row
```

To manage large sets of information, software needs a way to put it all into a high-functioning, high-performance object geared for structured information control. This object, embedding multiple Iterators, state flags, metadata control and special manipulation code, is a container pattern.

The TurboCollection provides us with a streamlined Iterator framework. How do we encapsulate it so we can derive even more organizational power? The answer is in configuring multiple TurboCollections so we can quickly access, organize, and describe information to external consumers.

To set up the environment, open up the Main5.bas module and find the method FactoryInit(). Add the following highlighted line to the end of the block:

```
Private Sub FactoryInit()
  On Error Resume Next
  FactoryAdd ("StringAdapter", New StringAdapter())
  FactoryAdd ("TurboCollection", New TurboCollection())
  FactoryAdd ("ParmNode", New ParmNode())
  FactoryAdd ("Observer", New Observer())
  FactoryAdd , ("Container", New cntAdapter())
  End Sub
```

This will add the container class to the factory. Now let's set up the container in the following code. We'll need a new one, so let's call factory for it. I've already set up a cntAdapter to provide a place to work on container activity. It has the standard configuration for Create. I will use Nothing as the new container's parent, since we are in the top Main level.

```
Dim cnt As cntAdapter
cnt = Factory("Container")
```

However, when creating a new container from within another object, we can transmit the container's Parent by including a reference in the Create(). In this case, the new container's Parent will be the calling object:

```
cnt = Factory("Container", Me)
```

Before loading any information into the container, it needs structural organization. If the primary purpose of the container is to maintain and access rows of information in a column/row format, we will need to define the column layout. Two types of column tags exist: the actual display value (for a grid or report), and the alias into a data source. (See the discussions of aliases and synonyms earlier in this chapter for details.)

The first exercise deals with flat text files, so we will use the following column alias tags: *Column0 – Column4*. Keep in mind, these column names could just as easily be UserName, or EmployeeID, or AccountName. The names will be separated with vertical bars "|" for delimiters, as shown here:

```
cnt.Action ("Layout",   "Column0|Column1|Column2|Column3|Column4")
```

All we're really doing is loading up the container's tcLayout TurboCollection with the column names. Now we're ready to load up some information. Let's call the container's Load method. For now, we'll use an embedded text file name. Later we'll set up a dynamic one. The Load command needs the following code:

```
cnt.Action ("Load", "Source=Text|Path=File:Snip1Input.Txt")
```

This will tell the container to regard the source of the input, a file (as opposed to an ODBC source, TCP/IP source, etc) and the full URL for the path. While we could overload the URL for some of this information, it would not be compatible with dynamic sources of the same information and we might have to scrub it or modify it to fit.

Next, consider the following notation:

```
cnt.Action ("Load", "Source=Binary|Path=File:Snip1Input.dat")
```

This gives a similar story, only this time it tells the loader to expect a binary file at the file in the path. Similarly this code:

```
cnt.Action ("Load", "Source=ODBC|SQL:select * from myTable")
```

tells the loader to access an ODBC connection and use the remaining information as the SQL statement for accessing the ODBC information. We can thus internally program the loader function to behave according to the parameters rather than hard-wired paths or access methods. We'll dig deeper into this a little later.

Now we've loaded the container with information and we're ready to access it. Let's browse it like we did in Chapter 5 project:

```
cnt.Action("Movefirst")
      Do
            Debug.WriteLine(cnt.Action("GetRow"))
      Loop While cnt.Action("MoveNext") = "True"
```

The following code will access the second column's information for the entire information set. Note that it will use the column's name and the column's index for examples. This shows the power of extracting the information with either its column tag or its column position.

```
Dim strWrk As String                              'workspace
cnt.Action ("MoveFirst")                          'move to the first node
Do
  'get second column's data by "tag"
  strWrk = cnt.Item("Column1")
'concat with second column's  data by "position"
  strWrk = strWrk & "     " & cnt.Item(1)
  Debug.Writeline (strWrk)                         'show it
  Loop While CBool(cnt.Action("MoveNext"))        'repeat until done
```

Sorting

Now let's try sorting the information based on a given column. I've shown how to sort the TurboCollection in prior projects, but now we can use the container to encapsulate more power for this capability. When performing general sorting activity, some issues arise which must be handled gracefully and consistently. They deal with guaranteeing an accurate collating rule so any and every selected key will yield consistent ordering.

Natural collating for a sort uses left-to-right (string-based) examination. A simple data reformat will therefore yield consistent results, so if a data column is designated for sorting, we'll reconstruct its data for the key.

Keys of type "date" must be reconstructed in Year, Month, and Day format, specifically YYYYMMDD. This will guarantee that every date will naturally collate.

Because we are collating string-type information, the value "2000' and "21" will not sort correctly (2000 will appear before 21 if compared as strings). Unless we re-cast the value as numeric or pad the numbers with leading zeros (e.g., 002000 and 000021), we will not receive accurate results. How then to program the container's behavior to mask these details from us? We really don't care how much the container hides, we just need consistent results.

The container requires more information at the column level, so we need to give it the data type. In the Layout, we can default the type to "string" for convenience, then customize as needed. The data file *Snip10Input.txt* contains the following information:

```
01234,David,Southwest,Author,01/01/2000
43210,Valerie,West Coast,Editor,08/01/2000
12345,Grace,West Coast,Publisher,03/01/2000
81818,Karen,West Coast,PowerBroker,01/01/1998
```

We have an ID, Name, Location, Role, and Date. Let's reset the container's Layout to reflect these values. We'll need more information than the plain Layout description used before. This time we'll need data type information. A plain Layout description follows:

```
cnt.Action ("Layout",  "PUB_ID|PUB_NM|PUB_LOC|PUB_ROL|PUB_DT")
```

The enhanced Layout looks like this:

```
cnt.Action ( "Layout",  "
   "Tag=PUB_ID,Type=N|" & _
   "Tag=PUB_NM,Type=c|" & _
   "Tag=PUB_LOC,Type=c|" & _
   "Tag=PUB_ROL,Type=c|" & _
   "Tag=PUB_DT,Type=d")
```

This example allows the Layout function to extract specific descriptors from the command and apply them for the proper effects. Layout can further extend this notation to include other information such as size and default values, if necessary. We can bind any descriptor we want (Format=, Size=, etc.) and the Layout knows what to do with it.

Using this approach provides more programmability but does not change the binary interface for cntAdapter, only its internal parameter handling. By extending the parameter definitions like this, we extend the capability of creating a Layout from a database definition with little effort. In the following section of database management, we will see more fruit of this strategy.

With the Layout enhanced, we can now form a Sort algorithm that will correctly format the keys and order the information correctly. The Sort algorithm can collate on one or more column tags in the Layout (for example, by PUB_LOC and by PUB_DT). This requires several operations, described in the following pseudocode:

```
Accept the column identifiers for sorting
Provide for an additional Pseudo-column in the sort directive,
    called Descending, which will command the Sort function to
    perform a descending sort.
Assemble a sort template, identifying only the designated columns
Browse the container's data, beginning at the Top
With each row, use the sort template to extract the information from
    the selected columns in the row
Format the columns according to their row type:
For strings, truncate them to 10 characters, or pad them to 10 characters,
    left justified
For numbers, expand to ten characters, with leading zeros, right justified
For dates, reformat to YYYY/MM/DD form
Concatenate each column's information into a key
Put the key on the row Node's SortKey
```

When completed with all rows, invoke the container's tcData TurboCollection's Sort method (it will automatically regard the SortKey for collating each Node). The syntax and result for a single-key sort follows:

```
cnt.Action ("Sort", "PUB_DT")
```

Browsing will yield this output:

```
81818|Karen|West Coast|PowerBroker|01/01/1998
01234|David|Southwest|Author|01/01/2000
12345|Grace|West Coast|Publisher|03/01/2000
43210|Valerie|West Coast|Editor|08/01/2000
```

However, if we want to sort on multiple keys, the syntax should be consistent with other parameter usages, such as the following Sort directive (and result):

```
cnt.Action ("Sort", "PUB_LOC|PUB_NAME")
01234|David|Southwest|Author|01/01/2000
12345|Grace|West Coast|Publisher|03/01/2000
81818|Karen|West Coast|PowerBroker|01/01/1998
43210|Valerie|West Coast|Editor|08/01/2000
```

The use of SortKey rather than ItemKey is deliberate: SortKeys are dynamic and malleable while ItemKey usually shares a predefined relationship with their associated Item.

With these elemental constructs, (and those exhibited in "Project 5—Error Control," AddRow and GetRow) we can quickly include database, socket, or other information sources within the container's implementation. Each one can use the internal equivalent of the AddRow to populate an empty container. Then external consumers can browse information (using MoveFirst/MoveNext), reference information by column (using Item) or by row (using GetRow). The preceding examples in this chapter use *Text* as the load directive, but could just as easily use *SQL* and pass a SQL query (rather than a file name) to an awaiting data access component.

Container and the Interpreter Mechanics

The ability to demonstrate the container's text-driven mechanics and interface is of no value unless we can plug the container into interpreter logic. The exercises in "Project 5—Error Control," included an interpreter *txtTerp* to draw structural and behavioral metadata from a text file source. Let's examine how the container's behavior plugs into this model.

The file *Snip1Input.txt* (Listing 6-1) contain example metadata macros for this section.

Let's instantiate the txtTerp to load the metadata script contents.

```
Dim oT As New txtTerp
oT.Init Nothing, "File=Snip2Input.Txt"
oT.Action "Execute", "Routine=BrowseDemo"
```

The contents of the *Snip2Input.txt* file are shown in Listing 6-1, fashioned as metadata macros.

Listing 6-1. Interpreted Metadata Logic

```
'## DEFINE ONE SIMPLE AND ONE COMPLEX VARIABLE
Define Simple Wrk1
Define Complex cntWork
'
'### SETUP THE LAYOUT FORMAT
Set $Wrk1=
    STR("Tag=PUB_ID,Type=N|Tag=PUB_NM,Type=c|
         Tag=PUB_LOC,Type=c|Tag=PUB_ROL,Type=c|
         Tag=PUB_DT,Type=d,Format=YYYYMMDD")
```

```
'
Set $cntWork.Layout= $Wrk1
'
'DEFINE A ROUTINE TO INTIIATE BROWSE
Define Routine BrowseDemo
  Set $Wrk1=$STR("Source=Text|Delim=,|Path=file:Snip1Input.txt|Delim=,")
  set $cntWork.Load=$Wrk1
'
'## BROWSE THE FIRST ROUTINE
  set $cntWork.Browse=BrowseExample
'
'## BROWSE THE SECOND ROUTINE
  set $cntWork.Browse=BrowseExample2
End Routine
'
'## ROUTINE TO CALL WITH EACH ITERATION OF cntWork
Define Routine BrowseExample
  Set $Wrk1=$cntWork.Item(PUB_NM)
  Set $Wrk1=$cntWork.GetRow
  Set $cntWork.Item(PUB_NM)=$STR("This")
End Routine
'
'## ANOTHER ROUTINE FOR EACH ITERATION OF cntWork
Define Routine BrowseExample2
  Set $Wrk1=$cntWork.Item(PUB_NM)
End Routine
```

Listing 6-1 performs the steps of setting up two variables (one simple and one complex). It also initializes the variables and the three routines used to demonstrate the browsing capability. The first routine (BrowseDemo) performs a load of information, then executes a browse of the loaded container, first with BrowseExample and then with BrowseExample2.

The Interpreter and internal parser will bind the cntWork label to a container object and use it as a resource for the remaining scripted operations. While we've demonstrated in software that we can directly drive the container's activity, we must now demonstrate the same functions as driven from the script, with the software acting as a broker.

The key is in the lexical rules for assignment to complex variables (see Chapter 4, "Structural Metadata Categories/Statements"). Assignment to simple variables is straightforward, but now we have a more complicated set of rules. Table 6-3 illustrates the various assignment combinations, based on the left-hand side (target) and right-hand side (source) of the assignment (let column), and their functional complexities (right column).

Table 6-3. Property/Method Patterns

PATTERN	ACTION
Simple=Simple	oTgt.Item = oSrc.Item
Simple=Complex	oTgt.Item = oSrc.Property(Tag)
Complex=Simple	oTgt.Property(Tag)=oSrc.Item
Complex=Complex	oTgt.Property(Tag)= oSrc.Property(Tag)

Table 6-3 reveals three elemental patterns on each side of the equation, an entity, a property/method, and a key. Table 6-4 shows each element with a highlighted example.

Table 6-4. Property/Method Details

ELEMENT	EXAMPLE
Entity	***oTgt***.Item = ***oSrc***.Item
Method/Property	oTgt.***Item*** = oSrc.***Property***(Key)
Key	oTgt.Property(***Key***)=oSrc.Item

The objective for parsing each side of the equation is to quickly find the *entity*, the *property*, and the *key*.

 NOTE *The entity is the major designated object involved in the action. The property is the element of the entity to address. The key is an optional part of a complex property (such as a tag, index, or a grid column identifier).*

We first resolve the right-hand side (RHS), then use the right-hand result as part of the resolution of the left-hand side (LHS) (Table 6-5). For example, consider the most complex assignment, two complex variables with property and key references:

```
cntWork.Item(PUB_NM)= cntWork.DateTime("YYYYMMDD")
```

The first step is to separate them into their elemental parts, which is shown in Table 6-5.

Table 6-5. Elements of Left- and Right-Side Entities

TAG	LHS	RHS
Entity	cntWork	cntWork
Property/Method	Item	DateTime
Key	PUB_NM	YYYYMMDD

The second step is to resolve the right-hand side result. Recall that the property/method will go into the ActionID parameter, while the key will go in the ActionData parameter. The ActionObject will default to the interpreter object's reference *txtTerp*, shown here with the value *Me*:

```
strRHS = cntWork.Action("DateTime", "YYYYMMDD", Me)
```

Now use the right-hand side result *strRHS* as part of the parameter set for resolving the left-hand side. If a key is present (in this case PUB_NM), we will provide a notation that assigns the *strRHS* value to PUB_NM as a key=value pair, like so:

```
strResult = cntWork.Action ("Item", "PUB_NM=" & strRHS, Me)
```

By resolving the right-hand side, followed by resolving the left-hand side, we mimic the mental and physical patterns used in mathematical assignment outside of the machine. Inside the machine, this approach serves equally well and provides us with several stepping-stones during the process to back out or rollback if necessary.

For example, if any part of the right-hand side fails to execute, we can default *strRHS* to a null string. We can do the same with the left-hand side, and at any point bail out of the evaluation and report an error or otherwise discontinue. We can also use the statement's result (or lack thereof) in metadata decision logic to negotiate further statement control.

NOTE *See the* txtTerp.SetLogic *function for a more detailed code overview of dynamic assignment.*

Performance Configuration Strategies

A run-time programmable product will behave in a variety of roles. The product may start on a server and provide inter-client brokerage services. It may start on a client and immediately search for a local or remote version of itself to acquire brokerage services. It may launch multiple copies of itself to farm out work units in multiple threads. These are a few of the run-time roles that allow a single programmable program to *morph* either at initial launch or during execution. It is far easier to develop a software program that talks seamlessly to itself than to build separate programs with intersecting communication features.

In the absence of an integrated metadata repository environment (a subject that could fill volumes), our primary external sources for configuration parameters are environment variables and external parameter files (that essentially mimic program-specific environment variables), and command-line parameters. We can also use secondary, less nimble sources such as databases, Internet sources, or in the case of Windows, the Registry.

 NOTE *"Project 5—Error Control" in Chapter 5 showed how we could use a container as global persistent memory storage for error logging.*

The objective is to fill a Startup file with key/value pairs that can be loaded into a globally available TurboCollection. The glbAdapter exposes the Ref() and the Item() property to capture global variables (as seen in such a startup file). All we have to do is parse the file, separate it into key/value pairs, and post the information to the glbAdapter with the simple notation. Here's the example:

```
glb.Item("Key") = "Value"
strValue = glb.Item("Key")
```

The glb.Item() function can perform pass-through to the system environment variables or command-line parameters as *defaults*. The Startup file can be used to override the defaults or provide application-specific values that internal scripts will request and evaluate.

Some uses of the Startup file include various forms of startup instructions, such as the following:

- Startup screen (logon, splash, and so on)

- Startup role (service, client, broker, application Adapter, and so on)

- Security signature (verify authorization to execute)

- Communication (IP config, computer name, network neighborhood)

- Connectivity cues, such as names of specification files for database connectivity, third-party products, network-related utilities, etc.

- System parameters (memory, disk space, available hardware and drivers)

- Component references and registry info

- Similar system tasks, such as programs in queue and interprocess control

The software product must have the ability to initialize in more than one mode, and also co-exist as multiple instances of itself in various roles. For example, the product could instantiate itself as a screen-based consumer, then replicate itself as a service. It could then command its service to pre-load data from a variety of sources (acting as a cache) while the screen-based consumer continued to provide a responsive experience to the user. When the user required cached information, the consumer could request a transfer from its service. If the consumer closes, it can opt to leave the service running, especially if the service's cached information will not likely change soon. This strategy provides the consumer with a nimble, responsive appearance while replicating its own functionality in parallel.

Does this seem too complicated? What's far worse is to physically build and deploy different programs with separate, predefined roles that could possibly get out of sync on any release, or fail to communicate with separate but intersecting protocols.

The optimum strategy is to allow the same physical executable to start up in a variety of roles and with a variety of input parameters. Whether the program loads to execute a parallel thread locally or remotely, the result is the capability of doing multiple things at once without being lashed into the confines of a single program thread, but simultaneously sharing an integrated framework among all participants.

The Virtual Machine Intelligence *vMach*[1] framework can instantiate in multiple roles across multiple machines and leverage multi-tier or parallel operations. Running as the same binary executable, it can share information with itself as instances of an active agent, client desktop, or back-end application server.

vMach[1] = *metamorphism in action.*

These capabilities are impossible if we embed application-level logic. Only an interpreter, coupled with vDDM, vUIM, and other metadata-driven frameworks, will power this model and give us a creative and competitive marketplace edge.

Database Management

Working with flat files of structured text has general usefulness in every application, but most applications use a storage engine, usually an OLEDB/ODBC (Open Database Connectivity) compliant engine, or other RDBMS (Relational Database Management System). The most marketplace-prevalent engines are such engines as Oracle, Microsoft SQLServer, NCR Teradata, Sybase, Informix, and IBM DB2/UDB, to name just a fraction (in no particular order).

I made an extensive—but not exhaustive—list of RDBMS engines to make a simple point: even though all of them are ODBC-compliant and support standard Structured Query Language (SQL) for external management and information exchange, each one has subtle differences, SQL extensions, and competitive options to separate them from their marketplace competitors. While each engine provides power and promise to an application team, the application architects should have a singular objective: to wrap and hide the differences, so the application does not know they exist.

Review the discussion earlier in this chapter on "vSQL Configuration Management" and abstracting RDBMS extensions into a common, application-level syntax. The objective of vSQL is to provide a SQL-*like* syntax for abstracting database calls that can easily be formulated into an execution-ready SQL statement for the particular engine.

The source code examples contain some function calls to exercise the vDDM. You may have to change a few of the support files to connect them into your environment. The code assumes that a database model exists in the form shown at the first of this chapter, with an EMP, ADDR, SEC, SITE, CTRY, and CSZ tables and their associated columns. However, if you have any existing data source, you can easily point the vDDM to it and change some of the tag-based identifiers in the source code. (In the project listing Main() subroutine I have also included execution-ready "create" statements to manufacture the tables on your environment). Here is a list of highlights:

The file DBSPEC.txt contains a connection string. Modify the string to reflect your appropriate connection information. Options are shown earlier in this chapter in the section titled "Application Data Structures." Don't forget to set up an ODBC Data Source Name matching the connection string's DSN entry. You can find the ODBC setup under your Windows Control Panel/ODBC or if in Windows 2000, Control Panel/Administrative Services/ODBC. Without defining a DSN, you'll need to add more information to make it "DSN-less." Microsoft ADO just needs the information to find the database. Typically a DSN-less connection is more flexible, but some network and database administrators don't like allowing them.

I've also included a notation in the DBSPEC file for opening an *MS Access* database. All you'll have to do is provide a DSN name that you've pointed to a valid *Access* database.

The file PKGSPEC.txt contains a list of files for use in specifying component vSQL. You can replace these file names with other file names, and of course include vSQL statements in the new file names that reflect elements of your target data model. The file names in PKGSPEC (PkgEmp.Txt, PkgAddr.Txt) provide examples of breaking apart component vSQL as explained in the section called "vSQL Configuration Management" earlier in this chapter.

The file Snip4Input.txt contains the following script input, and I have highlighted the spots you will need to modify in order to point the script to your own data model:

```
Define Simple Wrk1
Define Complex cntWork
Set $cntWork.Layout=@EmpID|@EmpName          'define the layout
Set $CntWork.LoadPrep=$STR("Source=ODBC")    'and the source type
####
Define Routine BrowseDemo
  Set $cntWork.Load=$STR("SQL:Select * from @EMP")     'go get the data
  set $cntWork.Browse=BrowseExample                             'now browse it
End Routine
####
Define Routine BrowseExample
  Set $Wrk1=$cntWork.Item(@EmpID)        'on the current row, get the column's info
  Set $Wrk1=$cntWork.Item(@EmpName)
  Set $Wrk1=$cntWork.GetRow                       'now just get the whole row
End Routine
```

To use the above script "as is" (strongly suggested) use/modify the following Oracle-ready "create" scripts to build your own versions of these tables:

```
create table emp( emp_id  number(10), emp_name varchar2(50),
  addr_id number(10), site_id number(10), emp_str_dte date);
create table site( site_id number(10), site_name varchar(50),
  csz_id number(10), sec_id number(10));
create table addr( addr_id number(10), addr_field1 varchar(50),
  csz_id number(10));
create table sec( sec_id number(10), sec_code varchar2(50));
create table ctry( ctry_id number(10), ctry_name varchar2(50));
create table csz( csz_id number(10), csz_city_st_zip varchar2(50),
  ctry_id number(10));
```

Let's walk through some simple functions to exercise vDDM capabilities. We'll assume the name of our dbEngine instance is *dbPer.* Visual Basic code follows:

```
dbPer = New dbEngine()    ' get a new dbEngine from the VDDM
'#### Initialize the tool resource factory
FactoryInit
'### Build a new text interpreter and input the Snip4input.txt file
Dim oT As New txtTerp()
oT.Init Nothing, "File=Snip4Input.Txt"            'input the interpreted script
'##Execute the BrowseDemo Routine in the Snip4input script
oT.Action "Execute", "Routine=BrowseDemo"          ' now execute it
'## Now view the output in the Immediate/Output window, the text interpreter will
'# attempt to browse every row in the table/database you pointed to above and
'# display the results
```

This rather simple series of actions can be further reduced to script. After all, couldn't we enhance the structural properties of the complex type and attach it to either a container or a txtTerp? We could then expose the txtTerp's interface to the Interpreter and allow it to drive *itself.* How abstract can you get with all this? We've only actually scratched the surface, and you should let your own creativity run with it.

NOTE *Some users of the vMach[1] environment program its interpreter to build more metadata instructions on the fly, then execute them as new inputs. This creates a fractal instruction set, and the seeds for a self-programming, learning machine.*

Examining Synonym Behavior

The vDDM's synonym engine powers its virtual referential integrity, its vSQL engine, and every form of abstraction concerning the data model. Before jumping right into synonyms, I'll show some of the mechanics for surgically exchanging information with the vDDM's column-level references.

We need to populate some data. The local function call dbPer() returns a reference to the currently instantiated vDDM. We'll designate the alias for ADDR_ID and drop in some data. The dbPer.Item() call is the master interface to exchange information directly with columns or with their aliases. The examples shown in Table 6-6 assume you have created the given tables with the equivalent of the "create" scripts provided above, but if you are attaching to your own data model simply substitute table/column names where I have used them.

Table 6-6. Exercising Staging Values to the vDDM

ACTION	RESULT
dbPer.Item("@AddrID") = 121	All ADDR_ID set to 121
Debug.Print dbPer.Item("@AddrID") Debug.Print dbPer.Item("DBModelValue|EMP:ADDR_ID")	Display the overall value 121
Debug.Print dbPer.Item("DBModelValue|Addr:Addr_ID")	Display table-column values - 121
dbPer.Item("DBModelValue|Addr:Addr_ID") = 400	Change Addr table-column value to 400
Debug.Print dbPer.Item("DBModelValue|EMP:ADDR_ID")	Display Emp local value, still 121
Debug.Print dbPer.Item("DBModelValue|Addr:Addr_ID")	But Addr Local value is now 400

Note the use of the alias for the first calls, then direct table-column addressing thereafter. These statements demonstrate that the alias will affect all columns of the same name, but the direct addressing method won't have this effect. We can still use vSQL to perform direct addressing to keep values from propagating (if necessary) as follows:

```
dbPer.Item("DBModelValue|@Emp:@AddrID") = 500
```

Let's take a look at the following pseudonyms and created synonyms and surrogates. We'll create a pseudonym for EmpSSN. Recall that the pseudonym stands on its own with no initial synonyms attached. It behaves like any other column, just as if it had been found in the database schema.

```
dbPer.Action "dbPseudo", "Tag=EmpSSN|Type=n|Size=10|Key=EmpSSN"
dbPer.Item("@EmpSSN") = 841
Debug.Print dbPer.Item("@EmpSSN")
```

The surrogate alias will create another name for an existing column as a change-control measure (or any other reason you can think of!). Next, we'll use AcctID as a surrogate for EmpID, and HomeAddrID for AddrID. The surrogate alias requires that one of the column references in the call (e.g., AcctID and HomeAddrID) does not exist. Here's the example:

```
dbPer.Action "dbAlias", "EmpID=AcctID"
dbPer.Action "dbAlias", "AddrID=HomeAddrID"
dbPer.Item("@AcctID") = 891
dbPer.Item("@HomeAddrID") = 898
Debug.Print dbPer.Item("@EmpID")        'will yield 891
Debug.Print dbPer.Item("@AddrID")       'will yield 898
```

Now let's reverse the assignment to show they really do share the same information:

```
dbPer.Item("@EmpID") = 8910
dbPer.Item("@AddrID") = 8980
Debug.Print dbPer.Item("@AcctID")       'will yield 8910
Debug.Print dbPer.Item("@HomeAddrID")   'will yield 8980
```

What if both columns exist in the model already? Whether a pseudonym, surrogate, or schema-derived column, if both references exist, the vDDM creates a pure synonym—a reference to one will be as though it's a reference to the other. Here are some examples of aliasing with synonyms:

```
dbPer.Action "dbAlias", "EmpID=SiteID"                       'alias SiteID and EmpID
dbPer.Item("@EmpID") = 9000                                  'set the value once
Debug.Print dbPer.Item("DBModelValue|SITE:SITE_ID")         'yields 9000
Debug.Print dbPer.Item("DBModelValue|EMP:EMP_ID")           'yields 9000
dbPer.Item("@SiteID") = 9500                                 'set the other value
Debug.Print dbPer.Item("DBModelValue|SITE:SITE_ID")         'yields 9500
Debug.Print dbPer.Item("DBModelValue|EMP:EMP_ID")           'yields 9500
```

From this example, we see values interchanging automatically after creating the synonym.

Examining vSQL Behavior

The synonyms play an important role in manufacturing vSQL statements. The following example includes the SQL identifier as the first parameter, followed by the vSQL text. The construction of the vSQL text follows the same basic syntax as a regular SQL statement, but the elements have been abstracted for application-level portability.

```
dbPer.Item("@EmpID") = 5000
Debug.Print dbPer.Item("SQL|select @AcctID, @HomeAddrID from
                @Emp where @EmpID = @EmpID")
```

The preceding code will yield the following string:

```
select EMP_ID , ADDR_ID from EMP where EMP_ID = 5000
```

The SQL generator will perform parameter replacement of the synonyms with their data model equivalents. The "equivalent" in this case centers on the column's role in the vSQL statement. In standard SQL, the engine's parser will look for columns in some locations and staging data in others. The vDDM SQL generator simply applies the same rules. In the example above, @EmpID appears twice, but is replaced with EMP_ID in one location (column identifier role) and with the column's current value, 5000, in the second location (column value role). The next example shows the same effect using the pseudonym EmpSSN built in the prior section.

```
dbPer.Item("@EmpSSN") = 3000
Debug.Print dbPer.Item("SQL|select @AcctID, @HomeAddrID from
            @Emp where @EmpID = @EmpSSN")
```

Doing so yields the following string:

```
select EMP_ID , ADDR_ID from EMP where EMP_ID = 3000
```

With vSQL abstraction we can break apart vSQL statements to mix and match their contents like components.

Another embedded vSQL power is at the database table level, where we can build canned insert and update strings automatically. The model already knows the column formats, so in the following example we'll use the data pushed in from the prior examples and execute the SQL generator. The only parameter required for Insert is the vSQL table name, while for the Update we need the table and the key column for the "where" clause.

```
Debug.Print dbPer.Item("DBInsertString|@EMP")
Insert Into EMP ( EMP_ID, EMP_NAME, ADDR_ID, SITE_ID) Values (5000,' ',8980,5000)
Debug.Print dbPer.Item("DBInsertString|@ADDR")
Insert Into ADDR ( ADDR_ID, ADDR_FIELD1, CSZ_ID) Values (8980,' ',0)
Debug.Print dbPer.Item("DBUpdateString|@EMP|@EmpID")
Update EMP set  EMP_ID=5000, ADDR_ID=8980, SITE_ID=5000 Where  EMP_ID=5000
```

In the next case, only those fields that have been updated from the application are included in the statement:

```
dbPer.Item("@AddrField1") = "1880 Bay St"
Debug.Writeline (dbPer.Item("DBUpdateString|@ADDR|@AddrID"))
Update ADDR set  ADDR_ID=8980, ADDR_FIELD1='1880 Bay St' Where  ADDR_ID=8980
```

For more advanced SQL statements, we need a way to abstract complex SQL. The following discussion shows how to accomplish this task. First, find the packaged SQL components in PKGSPEC.txt. One of the files referenced there, PkgEmp.txt, contains the following SQL components:

```
'###Fully formed vSQL Statement
EmpSelect=select * from @Emp
'###Fully formed vSQL statement with Join
EmpAddr=Select * from @Emp, @Addr where
          @Emp.@AddrID = @Addr.@AddrID
'###Partial vSQL statement with Join component only
EmpAddrCtryWhere=where @Emp.@AddrID = @Addr.@AddrID and
          @Addr.@CszID =  @Csz.Csz_ID
EmpAddrCtryFromWhere= from @Emp a, @Addr b, @Csz c
                where a.@AddrID = b.@AddrID and b.@CszID =  c.Csz_ID
 '###Partial vSQL statement with "select" and Table identifiers
EmpAddrCtrySel=select * from @Emp, @Addr, @Csz
EmpAddrCtrySel2=select *
'### Synonyms to combine vSQL components
EmpAddrCtry=@EmpAddrCtrySel @EmpAddrCtryWhere
EmpAddrCtry2=@EmpAddrCtrySel2 @EmpAddrCtryFromWhere
```

These packages are loaded into memory at initialization time through the Startup.txt specifications. From the software, let's walk through what some of the return values will look like.

Each component has a tag name that behaves like a synonym. Table 6-7 examines the contents of each, and the SQL it will produce.

Table 6-7. Synonyms for SQL Snippets

ACTION WITH COMPONENT REFERENCE	vSQL/SQL RESULT
Debug.Print dbPer.Item("@EmpSelect")	select * from @Emp
Debug.Print dbPer.Item("SQL|@EmpSelect")	select * from EMP

The first call simply returns the component's value, no different from a column-level value. The second performs the SQL conversion on the component, resulting in an execution-ready statement.

The next two statements get the same result with different parameters. The first example combines two vSQL components. The second example is a single vSQL component but is defined to contain the first two components. This shows that any level of abstraction is possible.

```
Debug.Print dbPer.Item("SQL|@EmpAddrCtrySel @EmpAddrCtryWhere")
Debug.Print dbPer.Item("SQL|@EmpAddrCtry")
select * from EMP , ADDR , CSZ where EMP.ADDR_ID = ADDR.ADDR_ID
                      and ADDR.CSZ_ID = CSZ.CSZ_ID
```

vSQL components can be very extensive and complex, but if formed correctly any team can experience high reuse across all application queries while maintaining consistent behavior. For example, consider the following vSQL components:

```
EmpSel=select * from @Emp
EmpAddrCtryFromWhere=  a, @Addr b, @Csz c
                where a.@AddrID = b.@AddrID and b.@CszID =  c.Csz_ID
EmpAddrComb= @EmpSel @EmpAddrCtryFromWhere
```

Note how the first vSQL is standalone, but the second one is not. The third snaps together the first and second for a more powerful whole.

Use the vSQL generator against your own data model and play with vSQL components. The power of abstraction and reusable SQL as building blocks will provide enormous flexibility without sacrificing consistency.

Examining vDDM Run-Time Structural Contents

The time has come to take a peek inside the vDDM and view the information driving it. These three categories of information are in the vDDM:

- Actual data model

- History of all SQL statements

- History of all error events.

The following software will browse the information for all three, just change the BrowseContext switch to move between contexts. The next example will also deliver every SQL statement encountered by the engine since program startup as a Last-In-First-Out (LIFO) queue. The project listings include similar blocks to also derive Errors and the structural model itself:

```
Dim strW As String
dbPer.Item("BrowseContext") = "SQL"     'optionally "Model" or "Err"
strW = dbPer.Item("MoveFirst")          'go to the first SQL statement in the log
If strW <> vbNullString Then
Do
strW = dbPer.Item("Reference")          'return the SQL Statement history
Debug.Writeline (strW)
strW = dbPer.Item("MoveNext")           'get the next one until done.
Loop While strW = "More"
End If
```

Table 6-8 shows notations providing additional views into the metadata for sharing with other parts of the application.

Table 6-8. Typical Metadata Queries

ACTION	RESULT
Debug.Print dbPer.Item("dbOriginKey|Emp_ID")	'get the key, e.g., @EmpID
Debug.Print dbPer.Item("dbOrigin|EmpID")	'get the column id, e.g. EMP_ID
Debug.Print dbPer.Item("dbOrigin|@EmpID")	same, with vSQL notation @
Debug.Print dbPer.Item("DBTableName|@Emp")	get the fully qualified table name
Debug.Print dbPer.Item("DBType|EmpID")	get the column type 'n'

Table 6-8. Typical Metadata Queries (continued)

ACTION	RESULT
Debug.Print dbPer.Item("DBColumnString|EMP")	get a string of all columns for the table
Debug.Print dbPer.Item("DBSize|EmpID")	get the data size for the column 10

Note how we can derive column-level characteristics for shaping structure on a screen (e.g., type and size).

Generating Data

Data generation serves a significant role in validating an application's integrity. Of the three pillars of science discussed in Chapter 5—observability, repeatability, and falsifiability—data generation is one of the few activities serving all three. Ultimately, the objective is to shake out all data-driven processes in the application from end-to-end. We need a comprehensive test data set to do this.

Several regions (or zones, environments, etc.) exist for shaking out an application (see Table 6-9).

Table 6-9. Typical Application Development Regions

REGION/ENVIRONMENT	ACTIVITY
Development, Component/Unit Test	Code and data modification, only environment where software change is allowed
Quality Assurance	Functional testing of the application features
User Acceptance Testing	Performance and validation testing against subset of "real" information
Production	Frozen, operation version of the application

Typically a development team will shake out a portion of the product or application in the development region, then migrate the features to the quality assurance region for feature-level and integration testing. The product or application then migrates to a user acceptance environment for performance and use-case evaluation. Finally, the product or application migrates to a frozen production environment after passing through this functional and performance testing sifter.

Test Cases and Test Data

Concerning test cases and test data, the bane of application delivery is using legacy/existing data to perform unit testing of new features (at the development level), especially when using complex and data-sensitive processes. Customer and end users like to ship their existing data sets for validation. While this is a worthwhile exercise, it is only appropriate in quality-assurance or user-acceptance testing environments, not in the development and unit test environments.

Invariably, the user's pre-existing data will not have all combinations of data conditions and values, so when these combinations appear in production the application falters. Additionally, user data will have missing or null values—a subject for comprehensive back-end data cleansing. We should protect desktop application from faulty data, but not broker and accommodate them so they can continue unabated. While we need a way to recover from faulty data, the recovery framework should be strategic and not surgically applied. The development environment needs both comprehensive and relationally complete information sets. This means that all data must conform to the following criteria:

Manufacturing pure test data shakes out every corner of feature and capability. Error-proofing in software will avoid overcoding the entire framework.

- Exercise the application's features with all combinations and permutations. Customer-supplied information sets cannot do this.

- Provide "pure" referential integrity with no holes in the information sets. User-supplied information typically has missing or disconnected information.

- Recover from but don't otherwise accommodate disconnects or faulty data. If application developers build code to accommodate the disconnects, they are only addressing a symptom of a larger issue (dirty data). In many customer shops, data is disconnected because of errors in existing applications. We certainly don't want to build accommodations for those errors into a new product. The more direct route is to find the holes in the existing data and repair them, but the customer will not be able to perform this activity if our application accommodates them.

Rather than allow the application code to "break," we need a way to identify information disconnects and flag them for repair. The actual repair of old data is not a direct responsibility of a new application (fixing legacy data). Database cleansing tools are more appropriate. It could be perceived, however, that the application can help find disconnects by not accommodating them (reporting them as data errors).

Producing Pure Information

All philosophy and "expectation management" aside, we need a way to generate pure information. For some data points, random values will do. For others, we may need sequential numbers, dates, or random values between certain ranges, etc. The vDDM already understands the layout of the model, and, as demonstrated above, can automatically manufacture an execution-ready SQL Insert statement if only the data is available and correct. This means that if we can manufacture data at the column level, we can systematically insert it also.

The data generator will input a file of scripted instructions (*PkgDataGen.txt.*) that are somewhat more rarefied than the txtTerp application prototype interpreter. The generator's syntax drives directly toward building dependency relationships between tables, generating the tables in their appropriate order, and connecting tables with each other using the manufactured information. For example, if we generate a series of EMP rows, each with their own EMP_ID, we might want to share the existing EMP_ID values with another table, effectively connecting them on the fly. Let's look at the original model illustrated in Figure 6-8, then the script specification for generating it.

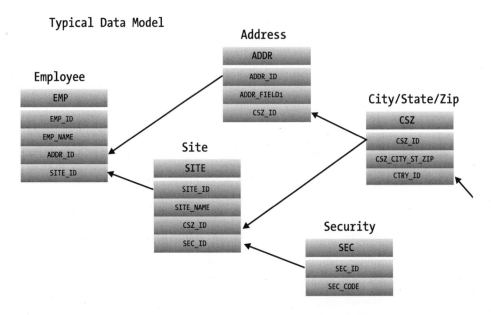

Figure 6-8. Example data model for generation

Now we'll define a routine for populating each table. The name of the routine will be the same as the vSQL name of the table, but will not require the @ symbol because of the context. Each routine definition will include parameters representing its dependencies.

Should we allow the database constraints to determine dependencies? This is certainly an option but note that many database definitions, especially those under development, are not fully populated with constraints. Additionally, most development databases are under the control of a developer, not an administrator, who would go absolutely crazy trying to keep up with the rapid-fire demands of the application developers. The bottom line: don't depend on the constraints being there. They might (should) be present in production mode, but we'll rarely use the generator in production, usually only in development. The following format of the generation routine resembles a txtTerp routine:

```
Define TableName(Dependency1, Dependency2, etc) as Routine
Statements to use in populating each column
End Routine
```

An example of the EMP table routine header follows, as it depends on the construction of the Addr and Site tables:

```
Define EMP(Addr, Site) as Routine
```

The generator will examine all routines in context and develop a dependency hierarchy. This will be its execution order for generating each table's information. In high-performance scenarios, we could multi-thread the generation commands to perform multiple table loads at once rather than a single-threaded, one-table-at-a-time operation.

Because multiple operations can occur at once, and some cannot continue until others are completed, we will add another checkpoint, or *phase*. Each phase level must complete before the next one can continue. If dependency threads create multiple parallel forks, we must simply verify that all dependencies are handled before initiating a table's load. The phases shown in the following table are static. However, true parallel and multi-threaded phases are context-driven and largely independent of other ones. The model illustrated in Figure 6-8 will generate the dependency path in Table 6-10.

Table 6-10. Referential Dependencies

PHASE	TABLE ROUTINE, IN ORDER	DEPENDENCY RULE
0	CTRY, SEC	In any order, or parallel
1	CSZ	Required to continue further
2	ADDR, SITE	In any order, or parallel
3	EMP	Final results

Within each routine, we can designate that the table's columns will accept one of the following values before insertion:

CommitCount: This value lists the total rows to insert before executing a commit (all tables). The default is "1," so initial runs of the data generator will have a performance drag. Raise it to a more appropriate value when reusing the script multiple times. Commit is automatic when the script completes processing for a given table or phase.

RowCount: This value gives the total count of records to generate for the table. Also, it provides for an additional parameter, the commit checkpoint count (e.g., RowCount 100,10 to commit at every 10 rows). The commit value overrides the general commit count for the given table. Commit is automatic when all records are written.

Increment: With a required From and By clause (Increment Column from *value* by *increment offset*), this value provides a way to insert integer surrogate keys into a column. The increment identifier can be used for populating other columns in the same context (see Suffix below). The increment applies to numbers or dates, for example "By 6" for an offset of six days (weekly offset).

Column ID: This value gives the string equivalent of the column's identifier (e.g., "EMP_ID"), the simplest form of information to display. This is handy for screen-based applications where a tester wants to verify that the proper column's data is being exposed to the user.

Suffix: The current increment value can be formatted and placed into the column as a suffix to the information already present. Thus, if a column has already been populated with its own column identifier, we can append the increment. (e.g., "EMP_ID" is now "EMP_ID 00000" for the 0th record). This provides uniqueness and visual integration to the information, especially when viewing large amounts of grid-based data or the results of a complex multi-way join operation.

Random: With a required low and high limit, the randomizer will execute the internal random number generator using the high and low values for a clamp and return the integer equivalent. This is especially handy for manufacturing random dollar amounts within specific ranges for a "retail transaction" effect. Additionally, we can designate any generated information as a random set. For example, if we want to populate the EMP table with random selections of ADDR_ID from the ADDR table, we can keep the ADDR_IDs in memory as they are created and use it as a selection pool when we later create the EMP table.

The default operation is to first truncate the table (delete all rows), then add one row at a time, increment all numeric values from zero by 1, including dates (from Today plus 1), and for string variables use the column identifier suffixed with the current increment. The PkgDataGen.txt file contains a number of commands to modify individual columns. I have given both examples of Random generation: one for random within a range and one for random within another table's columns. The following notation will load the file and execute the data generation process from the script.

```
dbPer.Action "dbGenerate", "File=PkgDataGen.Txt"
```

Listing 6-2 displays the contents of PkgDataGen.Txt.

Listing 6-2. PkgDataGen.Txt

```
Commit=10                                       'commit every ten rows
#
# spec for loading the EMP table - will require
#'that ADDR and SITE are done first
Define EMP(Addr, Site) as Routine
     RowCount 10                                'total rows to load
     Increment @EmpID From 100 by 10           'just increment this column
                                                ' from 100 by 10

#' take a random date in a 200 day
#'   window starting from 11/17/2001
     Random @EmpStrDt From 11/17/2001 to 200
# ' randomly take the ID from
# ' an existing ADDR row
Random @AddrID From @Addr.@AddrID by Lookup
#' randomly take the ID from an
#'   existing SITE row
  Random @SiteID From @Site.@SiteID by Lookup
 End Routine
#
Define CSZ(Ctry) as Routine
 RowCount 10
 Increment @CszID From 2000 by 10
End Routine
#
Define CTRY as Routine
 RowCount 10
 Increment @CtryID From 1000 by 10
End Routine
```

```
#
Define ADDR(Csz) as Routine
 RowCount 10
 Increment @AddrID From 3000 by 10
End Routine
#
Define Site(Sec, Csz) as Routine
 RowCount 10
#'let's randomize my row ID for this table
# Random @SiteID From 4000 to 5000
End Routine
#
Define SEC as Routine
 RowCount 10
 Increment @SecID From 5000 by 10
End Routine
```

Build your own version of PkgDataGen.Txt and submit it to the generator. Examine the contents of each table and verify that it loaded what you wanted. The process is easy enough to tweak and tune, including only the tables you want and disabling others. (You can disable a routine in the specification file using a "#" for comment.)

CHAPTER 7

Virtual Frameworks–
Screen Prototyping

In This Chapter:

- Leashing screen and report layouts

- Creating dynamic forms

- Summarizing application prototypes, vDDM, and uVIM

Screen and report layouts are the most user-visible and thus, the most volatile domain we have. Users constantly barrage us for enhancements, functionality extensions, tedious cosmetics, or completely new features. If these affect the look and feel of a screen, we're in for a software rebuild for sure. And users are so arbitrary about how the screens and reports should look—sometimes it's just the cosmetic fixes that kill us.

Since screens and their behavioral rules are traditionally embedded in the compiled software, the simplest functional or cosmetic fix will always require a software rebuild (and introduce risk). We need a way to manage this source of chaos before it starts, so we need to be prepared for it, and build its management into our framework from the beginning.

Application-centric user screen development requires rebuild for even the tiniest feature or cosmetic change.

 NOTE *This discussion will focus on development within the Microsoft Visual Studio (particularly .NET) environment, but the principles are easily applied elsewhere.*

Leashing Screen and Report Layouts

Nothing is that easy, so we shouldn't kid ourselves.

I've talked to application developers and web developers, and both draw the same conclusion: screen-level fixes (functional or cosmetic) introduce bugs. A significantly flawed assumption about "simple web development" is that the screens are easy to change and cosmetics don't affect behavior. While the cosmetics don't affect the behavior of the browser, they have a direct impact on the web application. In fact, web applications are more susceptible to cosmetic impact because of the perception, by the end user, of "easy changes."

Additionally, our reports, whether printed or screen-based, are susceptible to breakage in different ways than screens. Adding to the burden, users don't rip screens off the monitor on their way to a meeting. They base conversations or supporting materials from reports. Users ship reports to their customers and to the four corners of the business. They archive report contents for future analysis. In fact, reports are actually driving the business. Typically screens allow for the input and editing of information and for issuing requests for reports, but reports are often the drivers.

Don't design an application without reporting capability. Adding it later will be very difficult.

Once we generate the original reports, an endless chain of requests erupts for new reports, both in the sources and the output of information, and our software needs a built-in capability to manage it. Ideally, give the users a reporting tool they can self-configure (within certain boundaries). Whether we buy it or build it, make certain that the reporting environment can withstand high-speed iterations of user-driven change.

 NOTE *For reporting, give the user the capability of self-service, or you'll be chained to your creation forever. Many applications defer reporting to a dedicated tool such as Cognos©, Crystal©, or Microstrategy©. We can more easily support their raw requirements than embed special reporting in our applications.*

Driving Screens and Reports

Screens and reports can chain us to the end user because they are driven by subjective quantities. This is a perfect domain for our metadata brokers, leashing the various reporting capabilities and driving data. A metadata broker allows us to quickly shape and present exactly what the user wants, and deliver it as production functionality without changing binary software. The metadata describes the screen or report in abstract, user-centric terms, while the broker drives structure and behavior to meet the user's needs repeatedly and consistently. If we design them right, the screen and report brokers will service and wrap themselves around the user's needs on demand, and take us out of the chaos. Our software, not the user, is now in the driver's seat.

 NOTE *If we* must *have embedded reporting, tools such as VideoSoft vsPrint© can help bridge the gap, including building HTML-ready reports. Many grid components, such as Apex TrueDBGrid© can burst reports from their screen-level grid formats.*

Additionally, I've been on dozens of projects where the end user made requests that were outside the primary functional specifications. Some of these were cosmetic and very simple, eroding our ability to control them, while others were significant functional changes. However, a "few" can quickly become a flood, so we need a way to control them at the outset. We can invoke change control, but remember this is just another way to put a wall between the user and the delivery. With a rapid delivery mechanism, we don't have walls—we have a highway.

We'll require some serious thought as to how to characterize the behavior of the screens and the output of the reports, to the extent that changes—even wholesale changes—don't impact our software.

Furthermore, change in the program is one thing, change in screen appearance is another. By default, every screen-level control is intimately tied to application-specific logic directly beneath the veneer. Our first false assumption is that we can't separate these controls from the application because the development environment won't let us. But we can separate them, and we will. Using metadata, we can invoke an automatic, repeatable means to render a screen, and then activate it as a fully-integrated application resource.

Banging Out the Screens

In the common development model, developers specifically code each individual screen with carefully crafted application logic. Typical project execution includes installing a fleet of developers with a list of screens "to bang out." The predictable result is the infusion of many different styles of programming. Even with project guidelines, we'll see subtle inconsistencies everywhere. This also leads to behavioral inconsistency in look, feel, and navigation but more importantly, in error control and recovery.

CROSS-REFERENCE *See Chapter 1 for a discussion of the common development model.*

For clarity, I will use Microsoft Visual Studio terms to define a screen object (the Form*) and its content objects (the* Controls*).*

Once we finish configuring a Form's look, it's just an empty shell. It provides an end user with a strong visual representation of *a* possible screen layout. Typically, the first version is a sounding board, followed by collaborative iterations. We usually cannot apply software to the screen until its layout stabilizes. Unfortunately, this process is sometimes so protracted that we must start coding something or we'll never meet our deadlines.

When we add and position a Control on a Form (e.g., a TextBox, CheckBox, etc.), we are by default required to make it an application-centric entity. For example, we might define a text box for user login and call it *txtLogin,* and it's attendant event handler *txtLogin_Changed().* This creates a significant structural constraint. Since each physical Control will be application-centric by definition, the Form must accommodate the application-centric presence, position, and relationship of each one. Their behavioral management requires even more intimate API-specific software. We seem to become more deeply entrenched with every step. However, an architecture-centric model totally overcomes these constraints.

The following examples will use a simple ticket sales application as a springboard for discussion, accepting a purchaser's name, address, and displays a grid of purchased tickets.

The industry's "standard" Form development methods enslave a Form into an application-centric model de facto.

Figure 7-1 shows how a Form's internal implementation is tied to application-centric logic. Each Control has a custom, embedded, application-centric reference and individualized event handlers, each of which will perform specific duties for its own Control and no other.

A textbox *Change* event handling sequence will exist three times in the code, one for each text box (and each one with subtle coding differences to accommodate the application's requirements). If we require a new text box, it will receive its own visual location on the Form, and its own internal event handling. Thus, changes in the screen's appearance directly lead to software changes and program rebuild.

Another critical issue arises concerning *inter*-screen application logic. Varying developer-level skill and priorities—at the coding level—will ultimately define navigation quality and consistency. Each screen is often intimately dependent on other screens, and since individual developers rarely share complete application understanding, Form navigation and interaction become inconsistent as the rule. Senior architects usually spend lots of late hours retrofitting navigation to abate this condition.

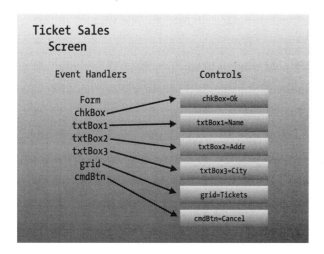

Figure 7-1. Application-centric Form structure

 NOTE *One user likes navigating to sub-screens with menu options while another likes command buttons. Still another likes double-clicking on tree or grid entries. Developers must accommodate. How do we build a user manual that's not completely confusing?*

The end user doesn't care why the screens are inconsistent or why they don't have the same look/feel/intuitive operation. They don't care if one or one hundred programmers have touched the functionality. Consistent, even intuitive behavior is expected by the user, and often the slightest deviation is a source of irritation. Coding application-centric software to such a stringent, subjective user constraint is extremely difficult.

Application-centric screen development is labor intensive and tedious. Small projects can produce dozens of screens, and a large application project can produce hundreds of screens, most of them very dense with feature points. Apart from the initial development effort, problems with maintenance and configuration management are of mind-numbing proportion. Like any application-centric model, it is doomed to eventual redesign and rewrite, if for no other reason than to simplify it.

If behavior is bad, it's just bad. And it's our problem to fix.

Finally, user interface behavior is a combination of individual Controls, the Forms, and the software to handle their events and exchange information. The event-driven nature of the Form and its Controls introduce alarming complexity and chaos that must be put on a leash.

Let's take a look at a framework that automatically manages the user's chaos, supports rapid-fire screen changes, and satisfies the most demanding users—all without rebuilding software.

Creating Dynamic Forms

While reviewing screen-level structural and behavioral inconsistencies, I understood them as symptoms of a deeper issue, the lack of control, or rather the unleashed nature of the Form and the Controls inside it. I sought a way to control the Form's behavior, but more importantly, a consistent way to manufacture Forms (and their content) so they could not go astray.

During this investigation I was subjected to the unfortunate duty of extracting some viral text from several Visual Basic 6.0 FRM files. In Visual Basic 5 and 6, the FRM file is the "master source" file used by the Visual Basic development environment to store Form rendering instructions and application code for a screen (the Form object). Similar constructs exist for Visual C++ and J++ for Java. Pop open Visual Basic and it will allow you to design a Form in fully-rendered visual format. Once saved to disk, it will appear on the hard drive as a text FRM file and a companion binary FRX file.

However, pop open an FRM file in Notepad or other textual editor and you'll see *structured text*. It seems that the published interface of the FRM file is simply text. The Visual Basic FRM file lists every control and its properties, size, position, whether they are inside another control (such as a frame), and much more. It's the total blueprint for the structural layout of the screen. The following are notations in the VB 6.0 FRM file for a TextBox and ComboBox control (note the consistency in the descriptions):

```
Begin VB.ComboBox Combo1
      Height      =    315
      Left        =    900
      TabIndex    =    1
      Text        =    "Combo1"
      Top         =    1020
      Width       =    1440
   End
```

```
    Begin VB.TextBox Text1
        Height       =    390
        Left         =    975
        TabIndex     =    0
        Text         =    "Text1"
        Top          =    420
        Width        =    1320
    End
End
```

In VB .NET, the situation is even simpler because the Form file is now just another source code file (*.vb). We can easily extract a Form's structural definition from either a .FRM or .VB file and use it for metadata. The following sample shows the same constructs as the FRM, only in the VB file (again note the consistency in the descriptions):

And, the beautiful thing, FRM content is metadata ripe for the picking.

```
Me.TextBox1 = New System.Windows.Forms.TextBox()
Me.ComboBox1 = New System.Windows.Forms.ComboBox()
Me.SuspendLayout()
Me.TextBox1.Location = New System.Drawing.Point(56, 40)
Me.TextBox1.Name = "TextBox1"
Me.TextBox1.Size = New System.Drawing.Size(96, 20)
Me.TextBox1.TabIndex = 0
Me.TextBox1.Text = "TextBox1"
Me.ComboBox1.Location = New System.Drawing.Point(48, 80)
Me.ComboBox1.Name = "ComboBox1"
Me.ComboBox1.Size = New System.Drawing.Size(112, 21)
Me.ComboBox1.TabIndex = 1
Me.ComboBox1.Text = "ComboBox1"
```

This is actual VB .NET code, but we don't want to execute it; we just want to interpret it for structural reproduction on a boilerplate.

This approach solves all the problems of consistent layout definition and visual management. The Visual Basic development environment can visually manage the screen layouts offline. We can always rely on VB's Form designer to faithfully render the screen and to save it in textual form according to a standard set of rules.

The plan was (at run time) to create an input stream for textual input and point it to the FRM/VB file as a text file. Then import the file as raw text, interpret the information in the file, and use it to paint a virtual screen onto a physical boilerplate prototype Form. What could be simpler?

The embedded prototype Form would be the only "binary" Form defined in the compiled program. Each time the Interpreter was directed to build a new Form from an FRM file, it would create a base copy of the prototype and paint it using the instructions in the FRM metadata.

Whenever I produce Figure 7-2 in customer meetings, I am met with either incredulity, gasps, shock, or laughter, but never derision. Would you believe that the two screens depicted below are exactly the same physical Form?

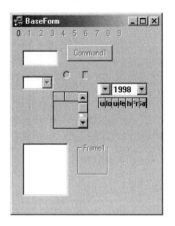 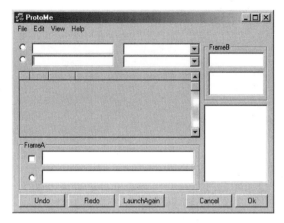

Figure 7-2. Prototype and run-time Forms

CROSS-REFERENCE *See "Project 4—Interpreters" to view the vUIMDemo.exe in action.*

In Figure 7-2, the Form on the left is the *prototype (BaseForm)*, prepared and bound into the physical program. The Form on the right is the re-rendered version of the Form on the left. Its layout exists only offline as metadata (FRM Text). An Interpreter reads this metadata and renders the appearance of the right-hand Form using the left-hand BaseForm prototype.

In .NET, the BaseForm is actually an empty shell. The Microsoft architects have allowed .NET developers to manufacture abstract instances of controls in memory and dynamically attach them to a Form's control list. This obviates the need to define base controls on the prototype.

Think of the BaseForm as the easel and paint (raw resources), the Interpreter as the artist, and the screen (right) as the completed rendering.

This is a very different approach than building application logic directly into a Form. We now have a single, integrated Form as the creational seed for all Forms, and we now render them all from external structural metadata (FRM/VB text).

The primary benefits are clear: the BaseForm prototype is pre-integrated and burned into the framework. Any run-time errors associated with BaseForm will rear their heads only once. All Form-level errors, fixes, and capability enhancements will have a common home.

Now can you see how we can change the layout of the screen without changing (or even restarting) the binary program?

Because we access metadata at run time (and at various places during run time), we would expect that the metadata files for Form generation would only be accessed on-demand, input, interpreted, and rendered as necessary. Thus, we can modify the offline Form metadata at any time before, during, or after a run-time session. We can deploy new applications, whole screens with their navigational rules installed, simply by copying new metadata files (FRM/VB files) into a repository for application-level use.

Regarding the FRM/FRX combination in Visual Basic, every FRM file has a companion FRX file containing binary information about the various Form-level controls. Typically, that file consists of default properties and configuration switches. In an application-centric model, each Form could have different base-level configurations. We might see consistency at first, but slow degradation over time as we tweak each one separately for various reasons.

Deploy whole applications with a text file copy, not a program rebuild.

With a BaseForm, we can define all base-level configurations in the BaseForm's binary (FRX) once. We won't be chasing these in hundreds of screens to verify consistency. Painting all Forms on the same boilerplate guarantees consistency of both visible and embedded behavior.

The program does not know what the application is until run time.

CROSS-REFERENCE *See Chapter 1 for a discussion of the differences between applications and programs.*

With this strategy, we have another powerful means to *program* the *program*, literally providing user screen layouts at run time that the binary program itself was completely unaware of when it was compiled and constructed. Indeed, when selling this particular aspect of the framework, I note to end users that the same executable program can run financial applications, marketing applications, HR applications, etc. (or jump between and across any of them). The list is endless, because the executable is unaware of the screen look, feel, or navigation. It simply renders according to what it finds in the FRM.

> **NOTE** *When we combine the Dynamic Form with an Application Metadata Interpreter, we have a completely metamorphic presentation. The structure and behavior (both visible and embedded) are dynamically woven.*

Of course, it's one thing to "paint a picture," but quite another to bind the picture into application behavior, connect it to a computing environment, and interact with the user. So, not only must we "fuel the factory" with metadata, we must configure the factory to exploit it and manufacture Controls that are pre-integrated to the computing environment, and enable external consumers to access the Controls consistently.

Now, let's look at the details of configuring Forms and Controls so we can manufacture them on-the-fly with structural metadata.

Controlling Forms

The first objective is to get the Form object on a leash. It must load, display, unload, and otherwise behave consistently in the navigation chain. When we allow Forms to float about unleashed in the run-time environment, we see the following "special effects:"

Forms have highly flexible, and thus completely unleashed, behaviors.

- We close a Form only to see it magically reappear in a partially initialized state. (Its "close" event stepped on and ignored another partially completed internal operation.)

- One Form launches another, but must share information or parameters with it, perhaps even returning results of the Form's activities. We must restore all prior Forms and faithfully return data or parameters.

- One Form must respond simultaneously to activities on another Form, even automatically displaying keystrokes or results.

- Forms must support Undo/Redo capability.

- Forms must enable edit-checks of information prior to exit, or allow the user to save its information. We must couple these with useful messages.

The FormAdapter Wrapper

These event and screen behaviors only scratch the surface, but each is highly complex and can cause screens to misbehave if not tightly and consistently managed. The solution is the FormAdapter, which wraps the Form object as shown in Figure 7-3. The FormAdapter expects the Form object to relay all of its event handlers into the FormAdapter object through a single function call *ctlEvent()*. This function call will accept parameters of any description from any Form event. Its first parameter is the event name, followed by the event's parameters. The FormAdapter wraps only one Form object, serving as the receptacle for all the Form's events.

The definition of the ctlEvent() interface pattern will be the same for every Form event, and we can use the same definition to broker events for all the Form's control's as well. Thus, the Form and its Controls appear structurally transparent for event management. The ctlEvent() definition is simple, as follows:

In .NET, we can define Forms and their event handlers dynamically, so everything can fit inside the FormAdapter from the outset.

```
Public Sub ctlEvent (strActionID as String, strActionData as String)
```

**Screen Framework
(Form Object)**

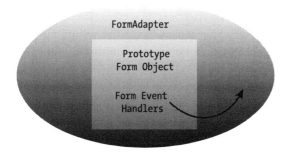

Figure 7-3. FormAdapter wraps the Form

The ctlEvent() interface call is similar in parameters to the pattern-based Action() reference. The ActionID carries the event name (e.g., Click, Change, Lost-Focus, etc.) while ActionData carries compound parameters associated with the event. The ctlEvent() serves in an event handler role, not a method role. While the Action() method can execute any internal function, great or small, regardless of duration or existing state, the ctlEvent() knows it's running inside an event-handling state and that it has to take care of business and get out quickly.

The ctlEvent() does not execute algorithms or large-scale processes. It's simply a gateway through which all events will pass, log their context, hand off to any triggers or observers, and leave.

Interacting with Forms

If an internal object must communicate with a Form, or the Form with the outside world, neither can talk directly with one another. The FormAdapter has complete control over the Form, its events, and also determines if allowing a particular event is safe. For example, if the Form invokes an event handler but the user attempts to close the Form while the event is underway, the FormAdapter can sense the danger and either prohibit closure or discontinue the running event. Either way, the user will see consistent behavior. FormAdapter also has direct access to the Form's Control information, and can expose it through an interface pattern for other FormAdapters to access. This allows each Form to receive parameters or return results with a consistent interchange protocol through the FormAdapter.

The FormAdapter enhances the basic capabilities of the Form, re-integrating it to a higher level of abstraction and control.

Managing a Form object, while critical to general screen behavior, does not directly address the detailed Form structure, but is the critical first step in stabilizing the Form object itself. As all Form-level Controls interact directly with the Form object, they must now interact directly with the FormAdapter. Since Form-resident Controls do not natively interface to this object, we'll have to wrap them as well.

Wrapping the Controls

Every Control (e.g., Text Box, Combo-Box, etc.) has a distinct interface. Each Control's original designer built its API with the assumption of end-use in an application-centric model. No industry standard exists for Control interface patterns. Thus, when our software wants to modify or retrieve a Control's properties, especially those in its display contents, we must carefully craft Control-centric software.

Each control has a unique API.

For example, the TextBox exposes its display value through its *Text* property. The CheckBox allows modification through its *Value* property. The ComboBox exposes the *Item* property and so forth. While these help them behave within the Form, their designers did not consider standardizing their interfaces, minimizing the software required to manipulate their run-time contents.

After all, we are all programmers aren't we?

The objective then is to wrap each Control with its own Adapter. In actuality, the largest part of the Adapter is an inherited template, allowing us to easily shape the remainder to the particular control's API. This will converge a Control's properties and methods into Item() and Action() respectively, plus a ctlEvent() to handle the Control's events in the same pattern as the Form/FormAdapter relationship. The simple steps to wrap and manage the Control are as follows:

1. Identify the Control by Type and Tag (using its *Tag* property, or in .NET by *Name*).

2. Identify primary API properties and methods, then abstract and expose them through Action() and Item().

3. At run time, create the Adapter and wrap it around the Control.

4. Record the Control Adapter's presence in the FormAdapter, keyed on its Tag/Name.

Note that in the configuration depicted in Figure 7-4, the Controls are wrapped but are not yet unhooked from their application-centric names (they are, however, symbolically detached from the Form's embedded event framework). Structurally wrapping and tagging all the controls is the most significant launch-point to high reuse.

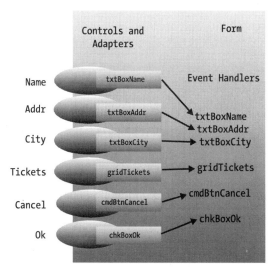

Figure 7-4. Default control infrastructure

The Adapters allow us to affect the Control's behavior and data through the interface pattern (Item, Action) not the Control's API. Now we can share information between Adapters (of any type) with simple assignment like so:

```
adp1.Item = adp2.Item
```

Structural conformity enables automatic behavior.

We're not quite done yet, but what we have here already has far-reaching implications. Recall the discussion of Observers in Chapter 3, and how they key on the Item property to relay information? We can now have automatic behavior at the screen level enforced by observation. If a given Checkbox should be checked/unchecked based on the value of a given Grid column, we can program the Checkbox, through a simple Observer connection, to respond as the Grid is browsed. If a Menu item should be enabled/disabled based on the value of another screen element, we can tie them together with an Observer so that the Menu item behaves automatically as the user engages the screen.

While we've wrapped the Form and the Controls, we still need a way to escape the embedded Form-level code to make them work for us. If we migrate their application-specific names and software out of the Form/Control and into the Adapters, we've accomplished nothing (apart from physically porting the real problem from one object to another).

The Form object is still bound to the application-centric plan because its Controls are still too individualized. So, the next objective is to define a means to dynamically manufacture Controls of any type, wrap them, tag them, and expose them to the FormAdapter. We need these three major resources to accomplish this goal:

- Prototype Form

- Factory for the Controls

- Fuel for the factory

Only revisit the Form object itself for rebuild when adding a new Control.

Providing the prototype Form is the easiest part, because we simply define a Form object and configure it. It's this second part—the configuration—that requires attention. At the end of creating the prototype, we want the Form-level software so stable that we'll never have to touch it again unless we need to enhance capability.

Now let's look at the configuration we'll need to automatically manufacture the Controls already on the Form.

Building New Controls

Two capabilities on every Control directly support dynamic Control manufacture, and streamline the required overhead for doing so. They are the *Load* method and the *Container* property.

 NOTE Container *is Microsoft's name for the actual property, not to be confused with the building-block container class discussed in Chapter 4.*

Each Control has a standard method called Load to dynamically manufacture new Controls of the same type. (To enable this capability in VB6, the Control must be defined as a *Control Array)*. In .NET they can be manufactured with a New() operator.

To build the required structures in the Form in VB 6, we must add one of each type of required Control (one textbox, one checkbox, one grid, etc.) and define each as a Control Array with index equal to zero (0). Thus a Grid Control might be actually defined as grid(0), likewise a TextBox control as txt(0). This allows us to later manufacture them dynamically.

We then open an FRM file for text input (the TextIO class will help us). Once in memory, we'll begin parsing and interpreting its contents for information on what controls to build and their various properties.

When the FRM Interpreter encounters a Control definition in the FRM text, it locates the associated control array on the prototype Form. The FRM Interpreter references a control's 0th array element on its first encounter and then uses a *Load* command each time thereafter to create a new one. What of the unused Control Arrays? They are invisible and disabled by default. Thus, each Control Array behaves as its own *seed*. Figure 7-5 represents the final structure.

Each Control is represented once as an array, and indexed multiple times for each Control of its type encountered in the FRM file. Each Control instance in turn is wrapped by its own Adapter, exposed to the outside world via the Control's original Tag name (in this example: "Name", "Addr", "City", etc.). The Tag appears like any other FRM property. Thus, using the Visual Basic designer, we can define how a Form looks, the position of all its Controls, and identify them with Tags, all embedded in the FRM metadata. The FormAdapter (not shown) wraps the entire picture.

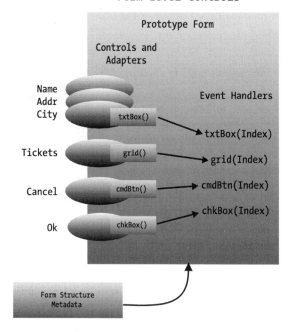

Figure 7-5. Final control infrastructure

In the .NET Framework, this approach is even simpler because we don't need predefined control arrays (we can manufacture a control at will with a simple *New* operator). Also, we can manufacture a control's Adapter, allow the Adapter to create a given control instance, and allow it to broker the control to the FormAdapter/Form combination behind the scenes.

In .NET, we don't really have to touch the control itself at the metadata Interpreter layer. In fact, we can now hide all API-specific objects inside their own Adapters such that the Interpreter is *only* aware of the Adapters, furthering our plug-and-play capability. For example, this allows us to present a TextBox Adapter to the Interpreter and it could be wrapping a plain TextBox, a RichTextBox, or some other proprietary or third-party TextBox-like control. We could also use a generic "container" wrapper to handle labels, frames, elastics, and other container-style controls.

We can now dynamically manufacture hundreds of Controls of any type and wrap them with Adapters internally customized (or generally fitted) for that type. However, this does not help us actually render them. Where do they reside on the screen, and do they sit inside another control such as a frame, elastic, or tab Control? These questions must be answered, or manufacturing and wrapping Controls is simply a novelty.

Containing the Controls

By default, we can use the FRM text properties to define and position any given Control. However, certain Controls contain others, including elastics, frames, and tabs. These Control types create a backdrop, or panel, upon which we can place and manage other controls. The Controls on the Container will behave in sync with the Container's primary Invisible/Visible and Enable/Disable properties, among others.

To this end, Microsoft included the *Container* property on each Control as a read/write value at run time. For Controls that physically sit on the main Form, the Container property will equal the Form object reference. For those controls inside (or nested in) other controls, such as those inside frames, elastics or grids, their Container property will accept the reference of the given containing control. If we examine the structure of the text FRM file, we'll see nesting rules supporting this activity, so we simply use the "most recently referenced" Control identifier as a container for its nested Control, as we browse and manufacture the structures on-the-fly.

In the .NET Framework, we only have to "include" a given control within a containing control's *Controls* list. This holds true for the Form itself plus any elastics, frames, etc. This again helps us organize the structure from the top-down rather than requiring a control to align with a specific parent or control tree.

Our FRM Interpreter will access an FRM file and use it to manufacture, position, nest, and configure Controls on the BaseForm prototype.

A significant side effect of contained Controls is in their *positioning* parameters. In the FRM file, a property will use an X/Y position relative to its container. We must use containers to get the proper screen-level nesting effects and the proper position, because the FRM/VB file only carries relative X/Y positions. This new completed construct is a *Virtual Form,* or vForm. We saw one as the ProtoMe Form in vUIMDemo, "Project 4—Interpreters."

Implications of vForm Rendering

Many developers first assume this metadata-based rendering approach takes a penalty in startup performance for an individual Form. In fact, the dynamic rendering method is faster than the traditional method of launching an embedded application-centric Form. Our only upper-limit on vForm startup performance is the same as an application-centric approach: the constraints of the language environment and supporting technologies.

Also, because we have a single prototype Form embedded in the compiled code, plus the surrounding Adapters to support manufacturing new ones, we radically reduce our binary file sizes. For example, the *vMach*[1] product embeds the *Virtual User Interface Manager* (vUIM) as a DLL. That's right, we manufacture every screen from a DLL-based boilerplate. Even with an application Interpreter,

Smaller, faster, and more flexible.

the vDDM, and the vUIM, combined with many other supporting frameworks, the binary executable requires a grand total of *2 megabytes* of file space (and it supports *every screen*, even the ones we haven't thought of yet!). Contrast this to an application-centric model, where the screens are embedded, bloating the binary program every time we change or add a screen.

 NOTE *The vUIMDemo is about 2 megabytes, yet can support an unlimited number of screens.*

The final product, the vForm, is comprised of a FormAdapter, the Form it wraps, the various Control Adapters, and the Controls they wrap (see Figure 7-6). Note a very special characteristic of this entity: The FormAdapter behaves like a database table, and the Control Adapters behave like database columns. We have effectively converted the Form and its disparate controls into a strongly leashed, building block information resource.

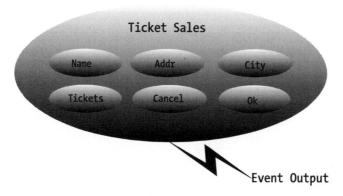

Figure 7-6. vForm structure

At run time, the vDDM and vUIM are structurally and functionally similar frameworks.

The vUIM now shares behavior and function with vDDM entities. We can now query, update, and otherwise manipulate every Form-level Control like a vDDM column reference. In fact, we can now set up Observers between vDDM columns and vForm Control Adapters to exchange information seamlessly, like a data-aware component, only with far more power and programmability.

Imagine now that we feed the Control Adapters and FormAdapter, by name and reference, to our Application Prototype Interpreter (Chapter 4). Each Adapter will automatically appear to the Interpreter (by Tag name) as a Complex variable type. We can now define Routines as event handlers, submit them to the Control Adapters, and create an interactive effect with the vForm and the Interpreter. Each time a Control-level event fires, it can transfer control to a metadata Routine in the Interpreter.

CROSS-REFERENCE *See "Project 4—Interpreters."*

In "Project 4—Interpreters," we used an interpreted syntax (called vScript) that we ultimately used to drive behavior (as metadata macros). Examine the following vScript syntax, using boldface to point out the FindEmpName Routine and the txtID/txtName controls as entities:

```
Define Trigger Routine=FindEmpName|Event=ReturnKey|Owner=txtID
Define FindEmpName as Routine
    Set vDDM.Item("EmpID") = $txtID.Item
    Set cntTest.Layout=@EmpID|@EmpName
    Set cntTest.Load=SQL: select * from @Emp where @EmpID = @EmpID
    Set $txtName.Item = cntTest.Item("EmpName")
End Routine
```

These vScript statements achieve the following results:

1. Set up all statements in Routine, then export the Routine Name (FindEmpName) as an Event Rule to the txtID text box Adapter. It will Trigger on the ReturnKey event, meaning when the user hits <Enter> or <Return>, the Trigger will fire.

2. When the ReturnKey Event occurs, the Trigger fires, then transfers control to the Interpreter and ultimately the FindEmpName Routine.

3. Once there, the Interpreter writes the vDDM's EmpID alias from the screen-level textbox called txtID.

4. Next, initializes a Container to receive two columns (EmpID and EmpName).

5. Makes the Container database call to retrieve the EMP information based on the EmpID value.

6. Retrieve the Container's EmpName information and put it in the screen-level textbox called txtName.

The final effect: When the user enters an Emp_ID value and hits <Enter>, the corresponding text box for Emp_Name will fill with information.

The vUIM, vDDM, and Application Prototype comprise a fully metamorphic desktop/server model called vMach[1].

The vForm presents an interactive interface for all other objects (internal and external). It provides a means to identify each Control within its domain. Components external to the vUIM can also insert Observers into the FormAdapter and Control Adapters for the purpose of event-driven callback.

Let's take a look at bringing multiple screens together for a common multi-screen application effect.

Managing Multiple Screens

Apart from manufacturing individual vForms, some lightweight infrastructure exists for their controlled startup, run-time management, and eventual shutdown. For this we use a UIManager class, an object holding references to active vForms and managing their navigation and state. For example, if we open a new vForm, we might want the current vForm to disappear (for now) but reappear later when we close the new vForm. Additionally, we might want to create several vForms in background and "hide' them (preloaded), only making them visible for certain activities. A UIManager can handle all these issues.

In combining all vForms, their interactions, and management into a cohesive whole, we create a dynamic, Virtual User Interface Manager (vUIM). The vUIM expands and contracts at run time, managing all vForms requested by the user, providing information and event interchange between vForms and vUIM consumers, and a single anchor point for consumers to identify the owner of the entire user interface domain. Figure 7-7 depicts a simple vForm configuration for a ticket sales application.

The vUIM serves a similar role to the user interface as the vDDM does to the database model. For example, an individual Control Adapter is functionally similar to a database column, and the FormAdapter is functionally similar to a database table, so the vUIM is functionally similar to the vDDM.

In many applications, a loose mapping exists between Tables and Forms, and Columns and Controls. The interplay between the vUIM and vDDM combines flexibility in handling specific screen-driven use cases with a consistent information access capability, both driven by metadata, and both ultimately executing their interchange with soft parameters, not hard-wired logic.

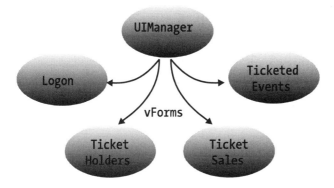

Figure 7-7. Ticket sales application

What is our ultimate goal? To build a program once, then service screen changes forever. We can enter Visual Basic design mode, modify screens, and save them to disk as text FRM files. The program will pull them in at run time as structural metadata. The final effect is the ability to make instant changes to screens—even build new ones—without changing software.

The vUIM and vDDM provide the ultimate combination in decoupling the compiled software from any kind of application dependency.

Screen Prototyping Summary

Some developers question all the effort to reproduce screen behavior to appear as a desktop application program—after all, shouldn't we just implement the screens using a browser? The answer is simple and has little to do with technology; it's about user perception.

Users *perceive* significant limitations in browser-based applications. Users have no such perception toward desktop programs. Users *perceive* desktop programs as having horsepower, able to use their desktop machine as a dedicated engine. Users *perceive* browsers as lightweight windows to a shared, overworked environment.

For high-dollar custom applications, many end users want a desktop program. Browser-based functionality is fine, they say, but the desktop-centric program means they have more local power. Not true, you'll argue—but they'll disagree. They have all those other high-productivity desktop programs, and their workstations are supercharged to perform all their accounting, spreadsheet manipulation, and other intense application-related operations. They don't want to share bandwidth with anyone unless it promises more power than they already have.

The vUIM allows us to change screen design without modifying software. Coupled with the vDDM and the Interpreter, we have a completely dynamic, metamorphic application.

Hence the phrase, World Wide Wait . . .

A subtle but significant truth about browser-based presentations is that most of the supporting software is performing functions totally outside of the screen interface. So even if we implement the screen itself in a web browser, there's still tons of behind-the-scenes code that must interface to it (we'll be writing all of that, too!). So why not use metadata to drive it as well? The result is to use interpretive logic to push HTML and JavaScript to a web browser (as we've done with the Form prototype introduced earlier in this chapter).

After all, isn't the browser itself just another desktop application? Users desire a desktop-centric application because of a perception of local ownership. Considering the potential power available on the average desktop these days, this is not an unreasonable desire.

Palmtop computers now have more power than desktop power-towers of two years ago.

The vUIM gives the users what they want. Since it's their primary window to the application functionality and all our high-tech capabilities, we owe it to them and to ourselves to make it the most powerful experience on their desktops—in run-time functionality, performance, and rapid development turnaround on their requests.

We'll have an engine performing metadata interpretation and blasting dynamic renderings into the display mechanism. Build the presentation in metadata and let our Interpreter engine push it out to the Web in HTML form, or directly to the monitor in application-screen form. Both methods provide a consistent, repeatable user experience and in themselves become wafer-thin utilities for user interfacing, not application-centric repositories for business rules and edit checks.

We realize the true power of the vUIM the first time we modify, extend, or add screens to an application without recompiling software—embracing accelerated reuse.

The vUIM framework operates seamlessly in Visual Basic, J#/J++, Java/JavaScript, and C++. With multiple languages we get more power and portability, plus enabled *multi-presence*, the ability to run the same product on disparate platforms simultaneously, behaving as inter-platform integration brokers. These options are only available once we begin thinking in terms of frameworks, patterns, metadata, connectivity, and not about the nuts, bolts, bytes, or the application logic itself.

A program can now exist simultaneously in multiple places, because it knows how to talk to itself anywhere in the enterprise.

What does the end user experience? Apart from the consistent and reliable presentation mechanism, we also get rapid maintenance turnaround. We can modify or enhance the application features in textual metadata, publishing changes with textual file copy, not program rebuild and redeployment. In fact, if a user is running a version of the framework on their desktop and the metadata files are stored on a central network file server repository, we can publish an entire application *instantly* by copying text metadata files into the repository. From a remote maintenance perspective, imagine *emailing* your fixes (attached in a self-extracting ZIP file) to an administrator, who simply clicks on the attachment, extracts it into the repository, and installation is *done.*

Can we imagine emailing our screen changes to the end-user? Let's say a user requests large scale functional or cosmetic fixes one day and the next day we email the changes. Two primary outcomes are evident: the user gets whiplash from the speed of the turnaround and we are able to break the fast-delivery barrier. We are now flying at *virtual mach*.

Now that's Rapid Application Delivery.

The vMach framework is all this and more, so to those using it, what we might first relegate to sheer imagination is already a reality now. Let's summarize where we've been.

Summarizing Application Prototypes, vDDM, and vUIM

In Chapter 5, Figure 5-1 depicts a virtual framework, constructed at run time. It never exists all at once until it is instantiated *on demand*. Figure 7-8 repeats this view, showing where each role fits.

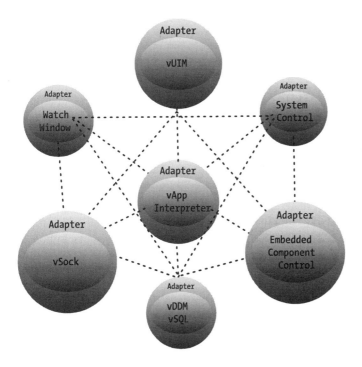

Figure 7-8. Multidimensional matrix

Each node represents a framework, with the vDDM and vUIM indirectly activated by the interpreted logic inside the Application Prototype. All the other frameworks support processing, control behavior, and provide run-time context. Some liken this schematic to a hub-and-spoke model, but when each one of the sub-frameworks can cross-communicate, it's really a multidimensional matrix. The model is not bound to single-flow connections between frameworks, since multiple Application Prototype Interpreters may instantiate multiple vForms, each with access and control to a common (or dedicated) vDDM. Multiple vDDM connections can exist if multiple database engines are involved.

vMach is a chameleon.

A metamorphic model is fluid, responding to application logic like a chameleon, behaving in any role, for any purpose. The software's capability level increases in strength over time. The application features it can support become wide, varied, and flexible, because at any time a feature is always just a dynamic assembly of capabilities.

We can now support multiple applications, roles, connectivity scenarios, and configurations dynamically without changing software.

Each time one of our brightest architects or programmers touches the software to build or strengthen its capabilities, the model absorbs that programmer's skill like a sponge. To the application developer, the framework is like a genie in a bottle, ready to explode with all that acquired strength to solve complex problems with repeatable success and accelerated reuse. To a novice, this is a rich mentoring foundation for understanding and applying concepts, leveraging the genius of those that came before them.

Each time we touch the genie's lamp, the magic begins again...

Like the genie's bottle, the framework has the capability to focus phenomenal power with simple efforts. Rather than unleash the genie by rubbing his lamp (and settling for three wishes), we harness and focus the genie's power whether he likes it or not.

Now that we have an architecture-centric platform for high-speed delivery, we still must deliver. Even if we deliver capabilities with architectural excellence, at some point we must deliver features, and this requires an application-centric project model. Our objective is to avoid having the project model impose itself on the architecture. The architecture should support and propel the project model.

Feature delivery still requires an application-centric deployment model, even if our delivery platform is architecture-centric.

The application-centric deployment model requires assigning features to specific people, who will build out a particular feature from end-to-end and be responsible for integrating it. We'll still need functional roles, but with metadata-driven architectures the features (even complex ones) fall out by the hour, not the week or month. Assembling a feature-based *team* is irrelevant, even useless. Assign the sum of feature-based work to a handful of crack application developers and cut them loose on a metamorphic architecture.

Watch the sparks fly.

The architecture-centric model enables a core set of capability experts who mentor the application deployment process. This fact has nothing to do with tier, language environment, computing systems, or technical issues. The core team deploys capabilities and maintains a *capability inventory*. The application developers map, assemble, and weave capabilities into features.

The architecture-centric model uses product delivery to support its various applications. It will by definition support a rapid-application delivery model or it will require re-architecture to meet this requirement. Any product that does not directly support rapid application delivery will not survive.

In the architecture-centric model, application teams of one are common.

Finally, the architecture-centric model is perfect to meet a technologist's career goals. The more experienced technologist acquires greater responsibility within the core product, and this goal should be treated as a prize. Novice or newbie technologists learn at the product's periphery and gain strength and understanding as they migrate toward the center. It's a mentoring and growth platform, and gives structure and predictability to our management model. Our feature delivery estimation processes will become more deterministic, meaning we can deliver a lot of products, on time, without overworking our most precious resources—the developers.

To summarize with a few final notes, see the sidebar.

....

A Few Final Rules to Live By

The construction of your binary executables should include the interface pattern (Action() and Item()) as their primary insertion points. This virtually eliminates spurious system-level errors associated with connectivity, COM, CORBA etc. It also eliminates the necessity to "rebuild everything" even though only a few things in one component actually change. This strategy allows rapid delivery on application features, focusing our efforts on building and delivering solutions and maintenance fixes, not explosions and mayhem in the depths of the binary components.

The application rules and implementation should migrate toward metadata-based interpretation, not hard-wired business application logic. This further migrates volatile business equations into fast-delivery form, textual rules, not embedded in the binary executable. Interpret all application structures—from metadata variables to the screen layouts. We can then deliver features with a simple file copy.

The database access layer should "sense" the schema at startup and configure itself accordingly. Ideally it should access the active database catalog to derive the actual schema. It should not have hard-wired access plans or scripts embedded in the binary executable. Otherwise, should the business or schema change in the slightest, it would initiate a rebuild of the binary components. We can stabilize delivery in the midst of information-system chaos.

Error control and recovery should reference predefined error identifiers and their messages from a repository in a database, or optionally in textual files, for access/input at run time. The entire application model, from database to user interface and everything in between, should obey a strict set of binary buckets for error reporting and should drive error detail toward internal time-sequenced error logging rather than try to bubble them to the end user's screen. We can effectively troubleshoot and re-deliver fixes faster than the user can complain.

....

Project 7–Fun with XML

This project shows how XML plays into the metamorphic model. We'll use the TurboCollection for these exercises, found in ProjectSeven in the /Project7—Frameworks—Screen Prototype/ directory.

The focus of this project is Extensible Markup Language (XML) for building transferable structures and interprocess communication. For an excellent resource on XML see *The XML Handbook*[2].

By way of introduction, XML comes in these two primary forms:

- *Presentation-Oriented Publishing (POP)* as we see in Adobe Illustrator or advanced WYSIWYG presentation forums. POP is very powerful for rendering detailed visual presentations.

- *Messaging-Oriented Middleware (MOM)* as we see in the information-transfer specifications between enterprises, applications, and RDBMS engines, to name a few. MOM is light and nimble for blasting transactions around and between components.

This discussion will focus on MOM XML, which can be described very simply. Each defined unit of information has its own tag, used as "book-ends" to the data itself. The tag serving as an identifier does not have to be unique. For example, Tag=Author, Value=David has a tag/value pair equivalent of:

```
"Author=David"
```

but the XML equivalent is:

```
<Author>David</Author>
```

This simple notation can describe breathtaking complexity and is naturally supported by the TurboCollection's structure. In the next example, each ParmNode *(pn)* can represent a tag/value, and the TurboCollection *(tc)* itself represents a "value" inside a "master tag" as follows:

```
<tc><p1>val1</p1><p2>val2</p2></tc>
```

The tags/values from <p1> through </p2> all represent the "value" for the <tc> tags. We can snap together smaller parts into larger parts (building blocks) to represent structural complexity. We can nest incredible depths and complexities, multiple dimensions, and reduce them to XML text (serialization), transfer them between components or across the Internet, then faithfully reconstruct the original structure from the XML.

Not only can we describe structure, but behavior as well. Because our interpreted behavior is also metadata text, we can wrap it all in XML and tell our target what the structure is, *and* what to do with it.

Let's start with some simple examples. The following code will define and load a TurboCollection with key/value pairs:

```
Dim strD As String
Dim tcP As New TurboCollection()
Dim tcA As New TurboCollection()
tcP.AddItem("David", "Author")
tcP.AddItem("Carla", "Spouse")
tcP.AddItem("Valerie", "Editor")
tcP.AddItem("Karen", "PowerBroker")
tcP.AddItem("Jacob", "Son")
tcP.AddItem("Callie", "Daughter")
strD = tcP.Item                          'now let's get a compound value
Debug.WriteLine(strD)
'Output should be:
Author=David|Spouse=Carla|Editor=Valerie
        |PowerBroker=Karen|Son=Jacob|Daughter=Callie
strD = tcP.Item(strdelim:="<>")          'now let's get it in XML form
Debug.WriteLine(strD)
Output should be:
<TCDATA><Author>David</Author><Spouse>Carla</Spouse>
        <Editor>Valerie</Editor>
        <PowerBroker>Karen</PowerBroker><Son>Jacob</Son>
   <Daughter>Callie</Daughter></TCDATA>
```

If we wanted to transmit the data delineated by the tags <TCDATA> and </TCDATA> we would use as the "value" everything between these tags. An important rule of XML, is that everything must exist within a pair of tags or it's not valid. While each of the internal values (e.g., <Author>David</Author>) represent valid notations themselves, when strung together side-by-side they are invalid and need the additional <TCDATA> tags to make them a complete XML message.

Now let's nest a structure to show how XML and the TurboCollection play together. We'll use the following code:

```
tcP.Clear()
tcP.AddItem("David", "Author")
tcP.Ref.tc = New TurboCollection()            'sub-list - nest one level down
tcP.Ref.tc.AddItem("Carla", "Spouse")         'add entry
tcP.Ref.tc.Ref.tc = New TurboCollection()     'nest another level down
tcP.Ref.tc.Ref.tc.AddItem("Jacob", "Son")     'add more
tcP.Ref.tc.Ref.tc.AddItem("Callie", "Daughter")
```

This time we'll display the information with the extended Form of the Turbo-Collection's *Dump*:

```
tcP.Dump("<>")                                'show structured nesting
Output should be as follows:
ID[] S[] K[Author] I[David] T[] Stat=[] Row[]
>>ID[] S[] K[Spouse] I[Carla] T[] Stat=[] Row[]
>>>>ID[] S[] K[Son] I[Jacob] T[] Stat=[] Row[]
>>>>ID[] S[] K[Daughter] I[Callie] T[] Stat=[] Row[]
```

Note how the ">>>" notation on the left shows us the level of nesting found by the *Dump* method. As a refresher, the tags for each [] combination are as follows:

- ID: optional Unique ID

- S: SortKey value

- K: ItemKey value

- I: Item value

- T: ItemType value

- Stat: Status value

- Row: row-level columns, if any

Now let's take a look at the XML string this will generate:

```
strD = tcP.Item(strdelim:="<>")               'show XML nesting
Debug.WriteLine(strD)
Output should be:
<TCDATA>
    <Author>
      <Author>David</Author>
      <Spouse>
        <Spouse>Carla</Spouse>
        <Son>Jacob</Son>
        <Daughter>Callie</Daughter>
      </Spouse>
    </Author>
</TCDATA>
```

Note how "Author" has two levels, one for the elemental information and one to depict everything under its hierarchy. We could define another ParmNode at the top of the structure to wrap everything, but the TurboCollection is only using the topmost key as a default.

Will this confuse the TurboCollection upon trying to reproduce the original structure from XML? Actually, no—the TurboCollection can faithfully reconstruct itself from this XML string. Next, let's use another TurboCollection and call the reconstruction function *UnstringXML*.

```
Dim tcA As New TurboCollection()
tcA.UnStringXML(strD)                        'reproduce struct from XML
tcA.Dump("<>")
```

This final tca.*Dump* above will reproduce the identical information as the tcp.*Dump*. We have successfully reproduced the nested structure.

But what if we've nested lots of levels and reproduced the original structure? How do we actually navigate it to find the details? Let's go hunting for some data using the TurboCollection's *FindXML* function, which will browse multiple nested layers in search of a key match:

```
Dim pWrk As ParmNode                     'some workspace
'
'find the Spouse Node and display it
pWrk = tcP.FindXML("Spouse")
Debug.WriteLine("Item=" & pWrk.Item & "  ItemKey=" & pWrk.ItemKey)    'found it
'
'now find the "Son" node and display it
pWrk = tcP.FindXML("Son")
Debug.WriteLine("Item=" & pWrk.Item & "  ItemKey=" & pWrk.ItemKey)    'found it
```

What if we have a much more complex problem, where non-unique keys appear in various levels of the structure? Let's add some "Friend" nodes to the various levels. We'll add some nodes tagged only as "Friend" to each level of the structure.

```
pWrk = tcP.FindXML("Author")
pWrk.tc.AddItem("Bryan", "Friend")          'Add to David's Friends
pWrk = tcP.FindXML("Spouse")
pWrk.tc.AddItem("Fran", "Friend")           'Add to Carla's Friends
pWrk = tcP.FindXML("Son")                   'find the "Son"
pWrk.tc = New TurboCollection()             'need a new nesting list here
pWrk.tc.AddItem("Chris", "Friend")          'add to Jacob's
```

```
pWrk.tc.AddItem("Zach", "Friend")            'add to Jacob's
pWrk.tc.AddItem("David", "Friend")           'add to Jacob's
pWrk = tcP.FindXML("Daughter")               'now find the "Daughter"
pWrk.tc = New TurboCollection()              'also need a new nesting here
pWrk.tc.AddItem("Abby", "Friend")            'add to Callie's
pWrk.tc.AddItem("Blaire", "Friend")          'add to Callie's
pWrk.tc.AddItem("Sara", "Friend")            'add to Callie's
```

Now if we do a *Dump* we'll get the following output:

```
tcP.Dump("<>")
ID[] S[] K[Author] I[David] T[] Stat=[] Row[]
>>ID[] S[] K[Spouse] I[Carla] T[] Stat=[] Row[]
>>>>ID[] S[] K[Son] I[Jacob] T[] Stat=[] Row[]
>>>>>>ID[] S[] K[Friend] I[Chris] T[] Stat=[] Row[]
>>>>>>ID[] S[] K[Friend] I[Zach] T[] Stat=[] Row[]
>>>>>>ID[] S[] K[Friend] I[David] T[] Stat=[] Row[]
>>>>ID[] S[] K[Daughter] I[Callie] T[] Stat=[] Row[]
>>>>>>ID[] S[] K[Friend] I[Abby] T[] Stat=[] Row[]
>>>>>>ID[] S[] K[Friend] I[Blaire] T[] Stat=[] Row[]
>>>>>>ID[] S[] K[Friend] I[Sara] T[] Stat=[] Row[]
>>>>ID[] S[] K[Friend] I[Fran] T[] Stat=[] Row[]
>>ID[] S[] K[Friend] I[Bryan] T[] Stat=[] Row[]
```

Note again the nesting levels for the individual entries, corresponding to the level where they were added. Now let's hunt down a level of the structure:

```
pWrk = tcP.FindXML("Son")          'find the first occurrence of the "son" level
pWrk = pWrk.tc.FindXML("Friend")   'find the first instance of "Friend" tag
Debug.WriteLine("Item=" & pWrk.Item & "  ItemKey=" & pWrk.ItemKey)
                               'show it (Chris)
```

With structured power, we can define records any way we choose. For example, we could have defined a single extra node at the "Son" level called "Friends" and then place all Friends underneath it. This would give us room to add "Cousins" or "Teachers" at the same "Son" level.

Let's now look at a much more complex version of the ParmNode's information. We can effectively extract and serialize every element of the ParmNode, reduce it to XML, then reproduce it elsewhere. For example, recall how the cntAdapter for containers in "Project 4—Interpreters," "Project 5—Error Control," and "Project 6—Data Integration" uses the TurboCollection to hold database rows of information. Let's set up the following row-based version of the TurboCollection as used in a prior project and reduce it to XML:

```
tcP.Clear()
'Add the first element for David
tcP.AddItem("David", "Author")
tcP.Ref.RowInit = 5                        'init for five columns
tcP.Ref.Row(0) = "01234"
tcP.Ref.Row(1) = "David"
tcP.Ref.Row(2) = "Southwest"
tcP.Ref.Row(3) = "Author"
tcP.Ref.Row(4) = "01/01/2000"
'Add the second element for Valerie
tcP.AddItem("Valerie", "Editor")
tcP.Ref.RowInit = 5
tcP.Ref.Row(0) = "43210"
tcP.Ref.Row(1) = "Valerie"
tcP.Ref.Row(2) = "West Coast"
tcP.Ref.Row(3) = "Editor"
tcP.Ref.Row(4) = "08/01/2000"
```

Next, let's take a look at the actual information:

```
tcP.Dump("<>")
Output should be:
ID[] S[] K[Author] I[David] T[] Stat=[] Row[01234|David|
    Southwest|Author|01/01/2000|]
ID[] S[] K[Editor] I[Valerie] T[] Stat=[] Row[43210|Valerie|
    West Coast|Editor|08/01/2000|]
```

Now let's look at the XML equivalent. I've broken it apart for visibility. The best part about XML is that white space and line delimiters are ignored between tags.

```
strD = tcP.Item(strdelim:="<*>")
Debug.WriteLine(strD)
Output should be:
<TCDATA>
```

```
<Author>
   <ParmNode>
     <S></S><K>Author</K><I>David</I><F></F><T></T><ID></ID>
       <Row>01234|David|Southwest|Author|01/01/2000|</Row>
   </ParmNode>
</Author>
<Editor>
   <ParmNode>
     <S></S><K>Editor</K><I>Valerie</I><F></F><T></T><ID></ID>
       <Row>43210|Valerie|West Coast|Editor|08/01/2000|</Row>
   </ParmNode>
</Editor>
</TCDATA>
```

Let's once again reconstruct a TurboCollection from this XML text:

```
tcA.Clear()
tcA.UnStringXML(strD)                      'reproduce struct from XML
tcA.Dump("<>")
Output should be:
ID[] S[] K[Author] I[David] T[] Stat=[] Row[01234|David|
     Southwest|Author|01/01/2000|]
ID[] S[] K[Editor] I[Valerie] T[] Stat=[] Row[43210|Valerie|
     West Coast|Editor|08/01/2000|]
```

Next, let's put our XML string to the test. I've placed the above XML string into a flat text file (XMLTester.xml) with the default XML header at the top:

```
<?xml version="1.0"?>
```

Find the file XMLTester.xml and double-click on it to view it in Internet Explorer. It will appear as a TreeView, so click on the +/- symbols to open or close levels.

The Virtual Dynamic Data Model (vDDM) discussed in Chapter 6 and the vUIM covered in Chapter 4 and in this chapter depend heavily on the TurboCollection. These models also rely on XML notations to transmit data around inside their frameworks. The interface pattern directly supports it. The Microsoft .NET Framework also rests on an XML highway for data and instruction interchange, as do a vast majority of web sites and internet information publishers. Run, don't walk toward XML to gain the greatest flexibility and extensibility in your information exchange and application reuse.

NOTE *Bonus Project: In the vUIMDemo directory is a file called Bonus-Projects.txt. Open this file in Notepad and follow the instructions for a deeper dive into the vUIMDemo's power.*

Epilogue

Here we are at the end, or like many things, the beginning of a new experience. I certainly hope that you now have the big picture of software development from the architecture-centric perspective versus the application-centric approach, and the possible acceleration of your productivity. What the teachers may not tell you and what your boss with the deadline may not care about, or even place a priority on, are often the things you need to make a part of your deliberate focus.

What's that, you don't have time to focus on all these flighty concepts, frameworks, and reuse models? Do you have time to spend 12 to 14-hour days (or longer), bustin' out the code? It's true that business leaders, end users, and project managers get frustrated and impatient when they can't see anything happening. Many of them feel that our lot in life is to spend long hours at the terminal. It's our chosen profession after all. Someday, it is assumed, we'll be a technical leader of this hapless lot and not worry ourselves about this object or that, we'll be in management, will have paid our dues, and will be above it all.

No time to do it right, but plenty of time to do it otherwise?

It is because technology moves so fast that we need to get the framework and architectural understanding fully grasped and under control. One day we'll be behind the curve on the technology, but if we're ahead of the game on architecture then learning the technology is no different than mastering a tool to meet an end.

The true *solutions architect* moves forward with building solutions regardless of the technology. We don't see architects putting finishing touches on a building's paint, wallpaper, or electrical work (that's the job of the implementers). Architects design and seed the solutions, often multiple solutions, and then mentor their implementers into using the frameworks, and into taking the frameworks to the next level.

Requirements Drive It All

Building cool frameworks with no potential user is a complete waste of time. I've seen developers get downright giddy over discovering some really cool gadget or gizmo, and they can't wait to share the joy. Not to dampen their excitement, but if we have no delivery point for it, it's just another toy. Delivering value is about delivering what someone has asked for, meeting their requirements. If we don't know what the requirements are, how can we possibly measure success or failure?

Can it do that? Was it supposed to?

Some products help us perform functionality tracking and requirements management. Apart from loading up a Microsoft Excel© with elaborate pivot tables and cross-references, or using Primavera© or MS Project© to track feature closure, we don't really have access to anything that lets us track a requirement from the user's fingers all the way down to a base *building-block* component, because all third-party requirements management tools assume an application-centric design.

Features supported by application-centric components cannot be easily removed and reapplied elsewhere.

While some software vendors may tout such a feature set, an application-centric design will nullify its usefulness for a high-reuse model. For example, if we trace a requirement from the user and weave our way into the various features supporting it, we will always ultimately drill down to an application-centric component that can have no other home other than where it is right now. If we approach a new problem, we will always find similarities in our feature-level inventory—but nothing to support it. All the required underlying technology and implementations are carefully crafted for its original problem domain, not our new one.

In an architecture-centric model, all features ultimately drill down to a reusable building block. Approaching a new problem, we can immediately map a feature-level inventory into our existing capability inventory. The difference, or *capability delta*, is where we then focus our effort.

The capability delta is our application starting point for all subsequent efforts—the essence of accelerated reuse.

Can we imagine arriving at a place in software development where every new problem is approachable by only addressing its differences from a previous problem? Can we further imagine that any new capabilities acquired in a subsequent effort are immediately available to prior efforts—increasing their value with little additional work? The vUIM and vDDM are examples of wrapping frameworks around what users ask for at a minimum on every upcoming project.

However, building a solution based only on what a single end user requires can leak fatal architectural flaws into our software. Strong, resilient architectures cannot be the result of simple "capability maturity" of application features alone. We must take several steps back and view the architecture itself as a general-purpose solution, and our end-user's requirements as a potential "feature set" riding on our capability foundation. If we build on a shaky foundation, then attempt to bolt on new capabilities without an integrated architectural framework, the sum of the whole will be worse than its individual parts.

I want to drive home the importance of requirements gathering, because many project managers and many more developers attach little or no value to it. This is highly unfortunate because as a developer, a lack of skill in this area will only inhibit our career path. We must focus our efforts, at a minimum, to what users are asking for, and build basic capabilities for what they consistently request.

Most of the technologists I meet don't place a lot of value in requirements gathering as an activity, usually because of its tedium or a bad prior experience. They were either held hostage by a project manager who took them through endless hours of word-smithing without any end user interaction, or they spent long meetings with the end user honing the fine details of the functional pieces. The first method is useless, the end user *must* be involved. The second method is tedious and boring to someone who just stepped onto the tarmac from flying at Virtual Mach all day.

<Yawn> Can we go now?

How to balance the needs of the end user and the means to implement those needs without falling asleep or flashing into a cinder? The key is to deliberately unhook ourselves from the nuts and bolts of technology. Oh, *that* again!

Yes, unhook ourselves deliberately. Did we achieve Virtual Mach—whiplash from the slingshot effect of our derring-do in the coding wars of the last project? Excellent, now we get our heads down out of the clouds and remember that the technology actually constrains our thinking. The end user will blurt out a feature and our mind will race down the implementation path to the natural conclusion. That's okay, it allows us to verify in our head what's "doable" and what the scope of an effort will really be. Just remember that the user wants feature delivery and is not (generally) interested in HOW we pull it off.

So why deliberately constrain ourselves to it, put our thinking in a box, as it were? Set the constraints of the technology aside and let the end user dream (and dream with them). Even if their dreams are not remotely achievable in this lifetime, they will give us a picture of their goals and ultimate objectives—a vision. What if their dream is only 50 percent achievable today? What if they agree to 40 percent of it? What if we're able to deliver an additional ten percent, and by the close of the project some new wonderful technology has arisen that allows us to deliver another ten percent (or more)? We're heroes.

Our next option is to take the user into the aircraft with us, let them cruise along at Virtual Mach for awhile. It's what dreams are made of.

But if we make decisions on what the technology "can do" today, we'll miss the mark. Because technology moves so far, so fast, every working day, the likelihood that we "can do" what they want in the not-too-distant future is a perfectly reasonable assumption. While we can't promise it today, only a framework will allow us to exploit it in the future. Only a framework will allow us to unplug a component and replace it with another one without affecting application behavior. Only a framework will allow us to expand the feature set from a distance, and will make us appear to be a master illusionist, the type of individual who waves a wand and makes features appear. Only a framework buffers us from the high-speed changes of the marketplace and the intense demands of the end user.

See You at Virtual Mach!

Technology changes. Requirements change and even morph into another form. We cannot possibly keep up with keyboard speed alone.

The difference between the marginally successful application-centric delivery model and the wildly successful and repeatable architecture-centric model creates a barrier not unlike the sound barrier an aircraft encounters when it reaches the speed of sound, *Mach One*. At this boundary, pilots say they feel a light tug on the back of the aircraft, just before they are propelled forward like a slingshot.

Mentally speaking, the light tug you might be feeling now is from years of experience trying to keep you bound in the application-centric model. Unlike the X-1 that took Chuck Yeager across Mach One, you cannot rely on the technology alone to take you there. Technology is simply a raw power source. Only in harnessing it—leashing it—do we get the power under control to propel us over the barrier.

Not easy, but worth it.

As depicted in Figure 7-9, if we use the application-centric model for everything, we'll start at the 80 percent mark and race to conclusion. We might iteratively experiment to gather some steam, but crossing the Virtual Mach barrier is a deliberate act of *will* requiring focus, effort, and creativity. On the other side of the barrier, we'll experience mind-bending productivity, or we can remain where we are, and still try to make it all happen—with keyboard speed alone.

Many have read this book and did not make it to this paragraph. They're either too busy implementing the things I've talked about or they've decided it's not for them. Others are skeptical, while still others are wondering how it will ever apply. I know this: the concepts, frameworks, and software I've discussed in this book actually exist and they reach the heights that I've proposed. It's been a very difficult journey for me to sit on the tarmac long enough to write down what it's like to fly at virtual mach. One of my colleagues, after experiencing the effect, said this:

How fitting that he chose a meta-morphic model (in nature) to describe the experience.

As a child I recall witnessing a Viceroy butterfly emerge from hibernation. It fought its way out of its prison, emerged victorious and beautiful, then fluttered off. I still remembered when it was a caterpillar, and my curious mind asked, 'Could the butterfly ever explain to the caterpillar what life is like now?'

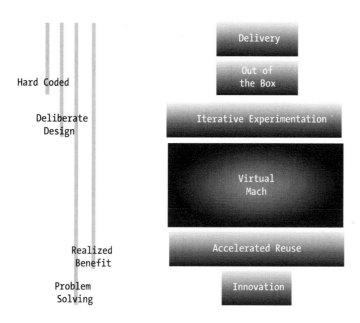

Figure 7-9. Virtual Mach Barrier depicted

Implementing the frameworks I've discussed will radically change our delivery methodology, our thought processes in solving a problem, and diminish the overall workload required to achieve our delivery goals. Let that negative mental tug continue for long enough, and it might win. You should run, not walk, toward the architecture-centric model and metamorphic frameworks. The acceleration you'll experience will be like nothing you've ever encountered.

When will you cross the virtual mach barrier? Can't tell for sure, but you won't find me on the tarmac. As I close this adventure, another flight plan awaits, the ground crew has fueled my vehicle, and my brow is beading sweat from the anticipation. See you in the air.

Soon the application-centric model will be a tiny dot on a distant, diminishing horizon.

Notes

Chapter 1:
The Starting Point

1. Gamma, Helm, Johnson, and Vlissides identified the most powerful and pervasive object-based reusable patterns (creational, structural, and behavioral) and gave them standardized terms and context in Design Patterns, Elements of Reusable Object-Oriented Software (Addison-Wesley, 1995).
2. Einstein, Albert. Remarks on Russell's theory of knowledge in P. A. Schlipp (ed.), The Philosophy of Bertrand Russell (New York: Tudor, 1944).

Chapter 2:
Building Blocks

1. Gamma, Helm, Johnson, and Vlissides identified the most powerful and pervasive object-based reusable patterns (creational, structural, and behavioral) and gave them standardized terms and context in Design Patterns, Elements of Reusable Object-Oriented Software (Addison-Wesley, 1995).
2. DataKernel Copyright © 1985–2002 Executive Design Consultants, All Rights Reserved.
3. vMach Copyright © 1997–2002 Virtual Machine Intelligence, Inc. All Rights Reserved. Patents Pending. The Virtual Metamorphic Adaptive Component Harness (vMach) is a reusable, distributed metamorphic architecture for Visual Basic 6.0 and .NET.

Chapter 3:
Best Behavior

1. Stephenson, Jack, *Standard VB: An Enterprise Developer's Reference for VB6 and VB.NET* (Apress, 2002, ISBN: 1-893115-43-7).
2. Sweeney, Mary Romero, *Visual Basic for Testers* (Apress, 2001, ISBN: 1-893115-53-4).
3. Resource Duty Framework proposal submitted to DARPA by Virtual Machine Intelligence Inc. (August 1992).

Chapter 4:
Power Tools

1. Many thanks to Dr. Richard Reese, School of Computer Science at Stephen F. Austin State University, Nacogdoches, Texas.

Chapter 5:
Virtual Frameworks—Error Control

1. vMach Copyright © 1997–2002 Virtual Machine Intelligence, Inc. All Rights Reserved.

Chapter 6:
Virtual Frameworks—Modeling Data Dynamically

1. Oracle, Teradata, DB2, and SQLServer/ActiveX Data Objects are trademarks respectively of Oracle, NCR, IBM and Microsoft. All Rights Reserved.
2. vMach Copyright © 1997–2002 Virtual Machine Intelligence, Inc. All Rights Reserved.

Chapter 7:
Virtual Frameworks—Screen Prototyping

1. vMach Copyright © 1997–2002 Virtual Machine Intelligence, Inc. All Rights Reserved.
2. *The XML Handbook*, by C.F. Goldfarb and P. Prescod (Prentice-Hall, 1998, ISBN 0-13-081152-1).

Index

Apress Titles

ISBN	PRICE	AUTHOR	TITLE
1-893115-73-9	$34.95	Abbott	Voice Enabling Web Applications: VoiceXML and Beyond
1-893115-01-1	$39.95	Appleman	Dan Appleman's Win32 API Puzzle Book and Tutorial for Visual Basic Programmers
1-893115-23-2	$29.95	Appleman	How Computer Programming Works
1-893115-97-6	$39.95	Appleman	Moving to VB. NET: Strategies, Concepts, and Code
1-893115-09-7	$29.95	Baum	Dave Baum's Definitive Guide to LEGO MINDSTORMS
1-893115-84-4	$29.95	Baum, Gasperi, Hempel, and Villa	Extreme MINDSTORMS: An Advanced Guide to LEGO MINDSTORMS
1-893115-82-8	$59.95	Ben-Gan/Moreau	Advanced Transact-SQL for SQL Server 2000
1-893115-91-7	$39.95	Birmingham/Perry	Software Development on a Leash
1-893115-48-8	$29.95	Bischof	The .NET Languages: A Quick Translation Guide
1-893115-67-4	$49.95	Borge	Managing Enterprise Systems with the Windows Script Host
1-893115-28-3	$44.95	Challa/Laksberg	Essential Guide to Managed Extensions for C++
1-893115-44-5	$29.95	Cook	Robot Building for Beginners
1-893115-99-2	$39.95	Cornell/Morrison	Programming VB .NET: A Guide for Experienced Programmers
1-893115-72-0	$39.95	Curtin	Developing Trust: Online Privacy and Security
1-59059-008-2	$29.95	Duncan	The Career Programmer: Guerilla Tactics for an Imperfect World
1-893115-71-2	$39.95	Ferguson	Mobile .NET
1-893115-90-9	$49.95	Finsel	The Handbook for Reluctant Database Administrators
1-893115-42-9	$44.95	Foo/Lee	XML Programming Using the Microsoft XML Parser
1-893115-55-0	$34.95	Frenz	Visual Basic and Visual Basic .NET for Scientists and Engineers
1-893115-85-2	$34.95	Gilmore	A Programmer's Introduction to PHP 4.0
1-893115-36-4	$34.95	Goodwill	Apache Jakarta-Tomcat
1-893115-17-8	$59.95	Gross	A Programmer's Introduction to Windows DNA
1-893115-62-3	$39.95	Gunnerson	A Programmer's Introduction to C#, Second Edition
1-893115-30-5	$49.95	Harkins/Reid	SQL: Access to SQL Server
1-893115-10-0	$34.95	Holub	Taming Java Threads
1-893115-04-6	$34.95	Hyman/Vaddadi	Mike and Phani's Essential C++ Techniques
1-893115-96-8	$59.95	Jorelid	J2EE FrontEnd Technologies: A Programmer's Guide to Servlets, JavaServer Pages, and Enterprise JavaBeans
1-893115-49-6	$39.95	Kilburn	Palm Programming in Basic
1-893115-50-X	$34.95	Knudsen	Wireless Java: Developing with Java 2, Micro Edition
1-893115-79-8	$49.95	Kofler	Definitive Guide to Excel VBA

ISBN	PRICE	AUTHOR	TITLE
1-893115-57-7	$39.95	Kofler	MySQL
1-893115-87-9	$39.95	Kurata	Doing Web Development: Client-Side Techniques
1-893115-75-5	$44.95	Kurniawan	Internet Programming with VB
1-893115-46-1	$36.95	Lathrop	Linux in Small Business: A Practical User's Guide
1-893115-19-4	$49.95	Macdonald	Serious ADO: Universal Data Access with Visual Basic
1-893115-06-2	$39.95	Marquis/Smith	A Visual Basic 6.0 Programmer's Toolkit
1-893115-22-4	$27.95	McCarter	David McCarter's VB Tips and Techniques
1-893115-76-3	$49.95	Morrison	C++ For VB Programmers
1-893115-80-1	$39.95	Newmarch	A Programmer's Guide to Jini Technology
1-893115-58-5	$49.95	Oellermann	Architecting Web Services
1-893115-81-X	$39.95	Pike	SQL Server: Common Problems, Tested Solutions
1-59059-017-1	$34.95	Rainwater	Herding Cats: A Primer for Programmers Who Lead Programmers
1-893115-20-8	$34.95	Rischpater	Wireless Web Development
1-893115-93-3	$34.95	Rischpater	Wireless Web Development with PHP and WAP
1-893115-89-5	$59.95	Shemitz	Kylix: The Professional Developer's Guide and Reference
1-893115-40-2	$39.95	Sill	The qmail Handbook
1-893115-24-0	$49.95	Sinclair	From Access to SQL Server
1-893115-94-1	$29.95	Spolsky	User Interface Design for Programmers
1-893115-53-4	$44.95	Sweeney	Visual Basic for Testers
1-59059-002-3	$44.95	Symmonds	Internationalization and Localization Using Microsoft .NET
1-893115-29-1	$44.95	Thomsen	Database Programming with Visual Basic .NET
1-893115-65-8	$39.95	Tiffany	Pocket PC Database Development with eMbedded Visual Basic
1-893115-59-3	$59.95	Troelsen	C# and the .NET Platform
1-893115-26-7	$59.95	Troelsen	Visual Basic .NET and the .NET Platform
1-893115-54-2	$49.95	Trueblood/Lovett	Data Mining and Statistical Analysis Using SQL
1-893115-16-X	$49.95	Vaughn	ADO Examples and Best Practices
1-893115-68-2	$49.95	Vaughn	ADO.NET and ADO Examples and Best Practices for VB Programmers, Second Edition
1-893115-83-6	$44.95	Wells	Code Centric: T-SQL Programming with Stored Procedures and Triggers
1-893115-95-X	$49.95	Welschenbach	Cryptography in C and C++
1-893115-05-4	$39.95	Williamson	Writing Cross-Browser Dynamic HTML
1-893115-78-X	$49.95	Zukowski	Definitive Guide to Swing for Java 2, Second Edition
1-893115-92-5	$49.95	Zukowski	Java Collections
1-893115-98-4	$54.95	Zukowski	Learn Java with JBuilder 6

Available at bookstores nationwide or from Springer Verlag New York, Inc. at 1-800-777-4643;
fax 1-212-533-3503. Contact us for more information at sales@apress.com.

Apress Titles Publishing SOON!

ISBN	AUTHOR	TITLE
1-59059-023-6	Baker	Acrobat 5: A User Guide for Professionals
1-893115-39-9	Chand	A Programmer's Guide to ADO.NET in C#
1-59059-000-7	Cornell	Programming C#
1-59059-024-4	Fraser	Real World ASP.NET: Building a Content Management System
1-59059-009-0	Harris/Macdonald	Moving to ASP.NET
1-59059-016-3	Hubbard	Windows Forms in C#
1-893115-38-0	Lafler	Power AOL: A Survival Guide
1-59059-003-1	Nakhimovsky/Meyers	XML Programming: Web Applications and Web Services with JSP and ASP
1-893115-27-5	Morrill	Tuning and Customizing a Linux System
1-59059-020-1	Patzer	JavaServer Pages: Examples and Best Practices
1-59059-025-2	Rammer	Advanced .NET Remoting
1-893115-43-7	Stephenson	Standard VB: An Enterprise Developer's Reference for VB 6 and VB .NET
1-59059-007-4	Thomsen	Building Web Services with VB .NET
1-59059-010-4	Thomsen	Database Programming with C#
1-59059-011-2	Troelsen	COM and .NET Interoperability
1-59059-004-X	Valiaveedu	SQL Server 2000 and Business Intelligence in an XML/.NET World
1-59059-012-0	Vaughn/Blackburn	ADO.NET Examples and Best Practices for C# Programmers

Available at bookstores nationwide or from Springer Verlag New York, Inc. at 1-800-777-4643; fax 1-212-533-3503. Contact us for more information at sales@apress.com.

apress™

books for professionals by professionals™

About Apress

Apress, located in Berkeley, CA, is a fast-growing, innovative publishing company devoted to meeting the needs of existing and potential programming professionals. Simply put, the "A" in Apress stands for *"The Author's Press™"* and its books have *"The Expert's Voice™."* Apress' unique approach to publishing grew out of conversations between its founders Gary Cornell and Dan Appleman, authors of numerous best-selling, highly regarded books for programming professionals. In 1998 they set out to create a publishing company that emphasized quality above all else. Gary and Dan's vision has resulted in the publication of over 50 titles by leading software professionals, all of which have *The Expert's Voice™.*

Do You Have What It Takes to Write for Apress?

Apress is rapidly expanding its publishing program. If you can write and refuse to compromise on the quality of your work, if you believe in doing more than rehashing existing documentation, and if you're looking for opportunities and rewards that go far beyond those offered by traditional publishing houses, we want to hear from you!

Consider these innovations that we offer all of our authors:

- **Top royalties with *no* hidden switch statements**
  Authors typically only receive half of their normal royalty rate on foreign sales. In contrast, Apress' royalty rate remains the same for both foreign and domestic sales.

- **A mechanism for authors to obtain equity in Apress**
  Unlike the software industry, where stock options are essential to motivate and retain software professionals, the publishing industry has adhered to an outdated compensation model based on royalties alone. In the spirit of most software companies, Apress reserves a significant portion of its equity for authors.

- **Serious treatment of the technical review process**
  Each Apress book has a technical reviewing team whose remuneration depends in part on the success of the book since they too receive royalties.

Moreover, through a partnership with Springer-Verlag, New York, Inc., one of the world's major publishing houses, Apress has significant venture capital behind it. Thus, we have the resources to produce the highest quality books *and* market them aggressively.

If you fit the model of the Apress author who can write a book that gives the "professional what he or she needs to know™," then please contact one of our Editorial Directors, Gary Cornell (gary_cornell@apress.com), Dan Appleman (dan_appleman@apress.com), Peter Blackburn (peter_blackburn@apress.com), Jason Gilmore (jason_gilmore@apress.com), Karen Watterson (karen_watterson@apress.com), or John Zukowski (john_zukowski@apress.com) for more information.